MR. TAMBOURINE MAN

The Life and Legacy of the Byrds'
GENE CLARK

John Einarson

Backbeat
Books
San Francisco

Published by Backbeat Books
600 Harrison Street, San Francisco, CA 94107
www.backbeatbooks.com
email: books@musicplayer.com

CMP
United Business Media

An imprint of CMP Information
Publishers of *Guitar Player*, *Bass Player*, *Keyboard*, and *EQ* magazines

Distributed to the book trade in the US and Canada by
Publishers Group West, 1700 Fourth Street, Berkeley, CA 94710

Distributed to the music trade in the US and Canada by
Hal Leonard Publishing, P.O. Box 13819, Milwaukee, WI 53213

Composition by Michael Cutter
Cover Design by Shawn Kaneko/Noel Eckert
Front Cover Photo by Michael Ochs Archives.com

Library of Congress Cataloging-in-Publication Data

Einarson, John, 1952–
Mr. tambourine man : the life and legacy of the Byrds' Gene Clark.
    p. cm.
  Includes bibliographical references (p.) and index.
  ISBN 0-87930-793-5 (alk. paper)
1. Clark, Gene, 1941–2. Rock musicians—United States—Biography. I. Byrds
(Musical group) II. Title.

  ML420.C536E56 2005
  782.42166'092—dc22   2005001012

Printed in the United States of America

05 06 07 08 09 5 4 3 2 1

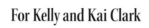

For Kelly and Kai Clark

Contents

     Gene's final days

     Epitaph: Here Without You...317
     The personal and musical aftermath of Gene's passing

     Tipton's Vein of Silver by Pam Richardson 325

     Acknowledgments..327

     About the Author...329

     Photo Credits 330

     Index..331

Introduction

Mr. Tambourine Man

Hey Mr. Tambourine Man play a song for me.
I'm not sleepy and there is no place I'm going to.
Hey Mr. Tambourine Man play a song for me
In the jingle jangle morning I'll come following you.
Take me for a trip upon your magic swirling ship.
All my senses have been stripped,
And my hands can't feel to grip
And my toes too numb to step,
Wait only for my boot heels to be wandering.

—Bob Dylan

Gene Clark was the tambourine man: the one standing center stage among the Byrds, between Roger McGuinn, with his ubiquitous, rectangular granny glasses and jingle-jangle Rickenbacker guitar, and David Crosby, with his impish grin and suede cape. Gene was the ruggedly handsome young man in the Prince Valiant haircut with an athlete's physique—exuding a cool confidence none of the other Byrds could ever match—nonchalantly bashing a tambourine on his thigh. He was the personification of Bob Dylan's "Mr. Tambourine Man," taking us all on his very own trip. That it ended far too soon is the tragedy, not the tambourine man himself.

Gene has been variously described as a hillbilly Shakespeare, psychedelic Johnny Cash, cocaine-fueled visionary, and tragic figure. He was none of these. Gene was a man of simple virtues, hard work, and integrity—deeply soulful and sincere. He was born with a gift for poetry in lyric and he dedicated his short life to that gift. "People who knew him say it was a gift that he never understood," surmises Gene's eldest son, Kelly Clark. And it cost him dearly.

Gene Clark was also a study in contradictions: the archetypal genteel Southern gentleman on the one hand, and belligerent drunk on the other. A complex individual, he was born with a genetic predisposition for the maladies that plagued him throughout much of his life. He never understood the mental disorder, the chemical imbalance, which at times tore him apart. He came to recognize later in life the family curse, alcoholism, yet succumbed too often.

"To think of Gene as a brooding hillbilly is so unfair to who he really was," protests Jim Dickson, the man who virtually created the Byrds and remained a mentor to Gene throughout his life. "In the first place, he was no hillbilly. Whoever said that doesn't know shit." While Gene's upbringing has often been painted in the sepia tones of an Ozark backwoods farmyard, he lived most of his early life in urban surroundings and attended a parochial school before public high school. His family, 13 children plus his parents, was hardly flush with money but neither were they hayseeds or country hicks.

Despite several personal obstacles, Gene managed to create a body of work that remains timeless, vital, and relevant—even though the "ex-Byrd" tag hung around his neck throughout his career. "Very few musicians had as much influence in creating new styles of music as Gene Clark," declares the *All Music Guide,* a popular music reference. Folk-rock, psychedelic acid rock, country-rock, alt.country—Gene helped give birth to each of these genres. He was an innovator ahead of his time more often than not. Gene recognized the power of the Byrds in a 1985 conversation with music historian Domenic Priore: "The Byrds probably are credited with more different areas of what's come out of the group, as the granddaddy group of all these other influences. And those influences have never stopped. You still hear it all the time. You turn on the radio and there is 'Turn! Turn! Turn!' or 'Tambourine Man.' It still surprises me, but it is an example of something that stands up." And it's still evident today.

For Gene, it was all about the lyrics. He was the incarnation of the medieval troubadour, the romantic balladeer, and the abstract philosopher. "I found him quite a good poet and I prefer to use that word more than 'songwriter' in describing him," offers former Dillard & Clark band mate David Jackson. "I always felt that that was the thing he was trying to be with his stage persona. These were pieces of poetry in a setting of music that made a wonderful marriage, a very rare marriage, in my view. It remains evocative to a large group of people even today. So it wasn't just of the times. He got to a place and the ability where he could describe a place deep within our humanity. I'm still struck with his ability to do that. And it was because of his words."

"A lot of people write songs but Gene wrote poetry and put that poetry to music," maintains singer-songwriter and Gene Clark collaborator Carla Olson. "People, especially in the 1960s, if you were writing pop songs there wasn't a lot of poetry going on. But Gene was a real poet. Sometimes you would look at his lyrics and wonder, 'Why'd he choose that word?' Then you would realize there couldn't have been another word other than what he chose. He really had a unique way of expressing himself. His songs were the songs with the most beautiful melodies in the Byrds. People like Gene are so driven by something inside them that none of us mediocre people can ever understand."

"When I was in school and I studied English literature, there was Byron, Keats, and Shelley and all those other writers of that time," muses ex-wife Carlie Clark. "I think of Gene and Dylan and other writers like Joni Mitchell, two or three hundred years from now they will be the poets of our time. The writings of these musicians will be the writings that will describe the times. There is not a single piece of music Gene ever wrote that anyone could be ashamed of or anyone could ever say, 'Oh, he must have been in a bad mood that day.' Even the frivolous stuff still holds its own today."

Fame came early for Gene—too early for him to digest it and come to terms with all the accoutrements that it brought him. At age 21 the world rested at his feet. He never fully recovered

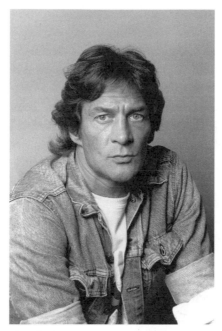

Gene in 1987.

from that instant adulation and it shook his confidence the rest of his life. "I think a lot of it for my father was the fear of success and the pressure," notes Kelly. "That contributed to his career failure, the self-trip up thing. He would shy away from it. But everything with the Byrds happened so fast that he didn't have any actual time to think about any of it. It wasn't his decision at that point. Afterwards it was all his decision and he wasn't very savvy with the business end. He just wanted to do the music. I think it really freaked him out. The huge shows, the flying, the tours, the screaming chicks all just freaked him out." Offers Gene's next youngest brother, David Clark, "Why was Gene the way he was? For one thing, Gene never understood himself. He did not feel like he deserved the adulation and the elevation he got in the Byrds."

"I'll tell you what my take on my father's life is," Kelly offers. "My father really just wanted to be a normal guy in a lot of ways. He wanted to chop wood and he wanted to have a family. He had this gift and there were people who wanted him to do it and I think he felt obligated to do it, and it also felt good for him to do it, but he couldn't handle all the stuff that was going on. A lot of people didn't. It's amazing he even lived through the 1960s and 1970s because a lot of those people didn't. So I think what really happened to my father is that he got sucked into this whole Hollywood Babylon thing and he really just wanted to be a good husband and father, but the whole lifestyle of Hollywood kept calling him."

Despite predictions to the contrary, Gene never quite emerged from the long shadow the Byrds cast on popular culture and music. They were America's answer to the Beatles, with all the hope and exaltation that title entailed. When Gene left the group abruptly in early 1966 all expectations were for a career that would transcend his former group. After all, he had been their principal songwriter, spiritual guru, and visual focus. In 1965 Gene Clark *was* the Byrds. "You could see McGuinn. You could talk to Hillman, but you could *feel* Gene Clark," describes fellow musician Taj Mahal. "There's a guy who was underrated in the Byrds. My god, the songs he wrote! He was a very deep man. I thought when this guy came around to do a song, he could draw you in like nothing I've ever seen. He was wonderful."

"Gene was the guy who wanted to get out of Kansas, come to California, and do the Oz thing," claims close friend Tom Slocum, "and suddenly Oz happened. He made all the money and did stuff by the time he was 21 that American pop music people could only dream of achieving and everybody projected their dreams onto him, thinking that he had all this knowledge or special powers of insight. All this psychobabble stuff. He was just trying to write songs."

All the acclaim left him restless and spiritually wanting, and he quickly moved on. "Gene was always the same way about everything," states brother David. "If he had an interest in something he was very particular about how it got done. And if it didn't get done that way he was not very pleasant to be around because he got very unhappy about it. The same thing as if he was done with it, he was done with it. It was behind him and he wanted to move on to something and he wasn't very happy with people who wanted to stay in the same place. And his professional career was very much full of that all along. Once he had achieved his goals he was ready to move on to something new and challenging. He had little patience for those who couldn't keep up." This would play out time and again throughout Gene's career.

"I think he longed to be accepted as just Gene Clark," offers frequent band mate and latterday Byrd John York. "I think he was tired of everybody thinking of him as 'ex-Byrd.' It's not that he wanted out of the role, it's that he wanted the public's perception of him to change. He wanted some acceptance for the value of his music. And that's completely understandable that he would want that."

"Once he got a taste of the Byrds' success, Gene never quite got over it or the fact that he left them," muses drummer Greg Thomas, who worked with Gene in the 1970s and 1980s. "Whatever the reasons, he made the wrong decision and he never quite got over that. Gene actually saw himself or considered himself a superstar. He believed what he had been told when he left the Byrds—that he would be as big as the Byrds." Offers Roger McGuinn, "The Byrds did cast a big shadow. Only David Crosby has escaped it, and maybe Chris Hillman with the Desert Rose Band, I guess. My solo career hasn't been able to escape the shadow of the Byrds, and Gene and Michael didn't either."

"That's part and parcel of the fact that the Byrds became so big," states former Dillard & Clark band mate and founding member of the Eagles Bernie Leadon. "The same thing is true for me. I'll never escape being an ex-Eagle. But that doesn't mean that has to define who I am. It was tough for Gene, sure. But the only way to escape it is to have a larger point of view. If fame itself is your summit, then becoming an 'ex-Byrd' must be the most important thing you've done. What I think is the tragic thing is that if Gene had believed in himself a little more, and had faith and a quiet confidence that it was all going to be all right, it all would have been. People did respect him, but he was so afraid that he resisted anyone loving him or embracing him and saying, 'Gene, you're great.' He didn't go out into the world and avail himself of hearing people say, 'Your music meant the world to me.'"

Gene's youngest son, Kai, himself a singer-songwriter, has his own thoughts on the price his father paid for his music. "He was scared of fame. Personally, I think he was scared to be famous, to be the one out front. He had it when he was younger, maybe because he was pushed there so quickly he didn't have time to really think about it. I don't know. But he definitely was scared of it and he needed things to get over that fear when he walked onstage sometimes. He would drink or whatever. I think he liked more the songwriting aspect of it. He wasn't a great performer who could move the crowd with him. Some people are born performers. The Byrds had that. He may have grown into that, he may not have, I don't know. I think he envied those who could do that. He wanted to be that guy out there, but he couldn't. I don't think people realize he battled those problems his whole life."

Gene's solo career was erratic, marked by peaks of sheer brilliance and lows of profound frustration. He never quite fulfilled the promise posited to him on leaving the Byrds, yet few lost faith in him or his abilities. "I'm not going to say that his whole experience in the music field was a tragedy," muses former A&M publicist Jim Bickhart, "but it was definitely one of not fully exercised potential, given his talent burdened with his own ill-conceived decisions and whatever demons plagued him. Every time he did something, I and a lot of other people were eagerly awaiting it and all too rarely did it live up to what we were hoping for. But that notwithstanding, we never gave up on him because we always knew how good he could be. You always wanted to root for him. But with the exception of a few things, it just never quite panned out for him. Some of it was his own doing and some of it was because of him being a person out of time. He was too eclectic even for *his* own genres. In the abstract that was great, but for making yourself successful in a pretty brutal hit-making business, it just didn't work."

Gene's life and career is often compared to another ill-fated figure related to the Byrds, Gram Parsons. Yet the two couldn't be any more dissimilar. Parsons was the Tennessee Williams story: born of old Southern money, he was a trust-fund baby and a student of prep schools and Harvard who squandered his talent and bowed out in a blaze of glory—live fast, die young. Gene's upbringing was Southern but poor, and he remained true to his muse throughout his life. Both were plagued by substance abuse, but Gene struggled to overcome it throughout his life; Gram embraced it as a career move and succumbed to it. "Putting the two of them together as songwriters," surmises Chris Hillman, who worked directly with both, "Gene was the better songwriter. Gram could have been a great songwriter, but he lacked discipline. Everybody's going on about Gram, but you should listen to Gene. Here was a guy who was not well read, but he could write lyrics that would make your hair stand on end."

Tom Slocum remembers, "Years ago Gene said something to the effect that he would know when he died if he was in hell because if Gram Parsons was there he would know where he was.

Gene said, 'Sloc, he's got a spike in one arm and a spike in the other.' What Parsons had going on had nothing to do with music. He got involved with some heavy people.'"

While the media has chosen to regard Gene Clark among the handful of rock music's tortured and tragic visionaries, those who knew him do not regard his life as tragic. "I don't think Gene was the tragic figure people made him out to be near the end," asserts Tom. "What he was trying to do, to be quite frank, was that he wanted to be normal, for lack of a better term. One could focus on his chemical issues, but if they focus more on why he was self-medicating I think you'll find out more about him.

"When Gene was focused he had a power. It's a legitimate power, like a white light. That's what he's talking about in that song. But with someone like Gene it could confuse him. He had these little battles, the dark side fighting with the light side. The dark side didn't win out. It didn't." His later years were marked by frustration that the music industry simply did not understand him. It contributed to his bouts of depression and substance abuse.

"I think that Gene never had any concept of how to achieve a successful level," suggests former Silverados band mate Duke Bardwell. "He was swept up in something that was happening with his abilities and that's the way it was. He never knew how to take his abilities and turn them into a successful business venture. That's the way it goes with most really truly poetic artists. If you make them compromise their poetry by being totally concerned with the business, they fuck their poetry up. It just does. Someone like Gene, he was just floating through this ethereal thing, talking and dreaming about it and writing it down, and there was no way he could connect personally to the business part of it. The Byrds all went off and spun off into all these other things and there was Gene, by himself."

Much of Gene's life was an emotional roller coaster that he never could quite gain control of. "He was one of the sweetest people," reflects Carla Olson, who to this day finds it difficult to listen to Gene's music without breaking down. "He would remember things about you and tell you. He had a fine-tuned memory about certain things. And then at other times you would go over there and it would be hopeless, like the lost weekend."

In the end, though, what Gene Clark left us with, and what he would most want to be remembered for, is his music. "He was definitely an old soul," Tom insists. "I was there when he wrote some songs, and he would write and write and he was focused like a laser. You could say to him, 'Gene, you want a cup of coffee?' or 'Gene, it's three o'clock in the morning,' and he'd still be writing, completely focused, oblivious to everything. I've known a lot of artists and worked with a lot of interesting people, but if you and I were here with Gene Clark right now, he would have filled this pad full of lyrics. That's how he approached a song, with a singular focus."

For Carla, Gene's legacy remains sadly unfulfilled. "It'll be the songs he never got to write that we can only imagine."

—*John Einarson*
Winnipeg

1

Kansas City Southern

It's about a 90-minute drive southeast from Kansas City, Missouri, down Highway 50 through rolling countryside past numerous pastoral farming communities with odd names like Lone Jack, Pittsville, Knob Noster, and Sedalia to the bustling town of Tipton: population 3,200, give or take a few. The highway passes directly through town, with a traffic light at the junction of Highways 50 and 5 South to slow your progress. The Break Time truck stop at the stoplight is as good a place as any to inquire if anyone knows where Gene Clark once resided.

While certainly the most famous Tiptonite, Gene's name nonetheless draws a blank stare and a shrug from the teenager behind the counter. Even the Byrds' name fails to elicit a response. On hearing a reference to "Mr. Tambourine Man," a middle-aged woman emerges from the back office, but she, too, fails to register the Clark name. How about Faherty or Sommerhauser? "Faherty?" The woman brightens. "Oh, yes. Everybody here knows the Fahertys, and the Sommerhausers, one way or 'nother. They either worked for them or are related. If that singer Gene Clark was a Faherty then I'm probably related to him, maybe a distant cousin."

"When I was in Tipton, Missouri, the year my grandfather died, in 1954," notes Bonnie Clark Laible, the eldest of Gene's 12 siblings and the one who raised him when his mother Jeanne was up to her elbows in diapers and dishes, "I found out I was related to almost everyone in the community. Everyone had married people they knew through the various families like Faherty and Sommerhauser. I couldn't throw a stone without hitting a family member!"

A phone call to resident historian Iola Potts leads to the stately pre-Civil War era two-story wood-sided manor with ample front porch on a corner lot at 304 Morgan, where Gene spent his first two years. There are no historical markers denoting the birthplace of the artist who would go on to help found folk-rock, psychedelic rock, and country-rock. In fact, there is nothing—save for a reprinted article from the *Kansas City Star* on the official Tipton Web site and a gravestone in St. Andrew's cemetery on the western edge of town—that recognizes Gene's birth or final resting place in the Sommerhauser family plot. Much like his career, Gene Clark's milestones go unheralded.

Tipton was founded in the 1830s by William Tipton Seely, who first visited the central plains of Missouri during the War of 1812. Returning years later to acquire some land and open a general store, he named the community that soon grew up around him Round Hill. When the Pacific Railroad Company began its move westward from St. Louis in the 1850s, Seely saw the potential of a rail link and lobbied hard to have the line pass through his property—even going so far as to offer incentives to the rail company in the form of free land, following the dictum that where the railroad goes, so goes progress. In the end, he succeeded and the line passed just a few miles north of Round Hill on Seely's land. This is where Tipton began. The Butterfield Overland Mail route to San Francisco was opened in September 1858 and it, too, passed through Tipton, further securing the community's prosperity and status.

A decade before the railroad arrived, though, German immigrants had come to settle in and around the farming community. Among them were Nieuffers, Lutzs, Kammerichs, Schmidts, Hoehns, Schrecks, and Sommerhausers. "My grandmother, Rosemary Sommerhauser, was the first American-born member of her family. Her father, Joseph, was an immigrant straight across from Germany," states Bonnie, the keeper of the Clark family history. "The Sommerhausers married into the Schmidt family; their families intermarried quite a bit."

Much is often made of Gene's Irish heritage, even though he was, in fact, only one-quarter Irish. That portion is the Faherty family, who trace their roots back to eighteenth-century Ireland. Arriving in America with four other Irish families just before 1800, the five groups worked as indentured servants in Baltimore and then traveled the river system westward, disembarking at Kaskasia, near the Missouri River. These Irish families, lead by Edmund Faherty, then ventured northward to farm around Ruma in southwestern Illinois. "They built a whole community there," notes Bonnie. "They built churches, a sawmill. The Whelans, O'Haras, O'Neills, and Fahertys formed a little community." Gene's great-grandfather, James Faherty, married Helena O'Hara, while another Faherty married into the O'Neills.

Disagreements between the staunch Irish Catholic families ultimately resulted in some members leaving. "Part of them went up north and part of them stayed in Ruma while another part of them went across the state line and settled in Missouri at a place called Perryville," Bonnie explains. (An historical marker in Perryville commemorates the Faherty home today.) "There were slave owners on the Missouri side and non-slave owners on the Illinois side. It all depends on which branch of the family you came from whether or not you came from a slave-owning branch of the family. We came from the Illinois side, the non-slave owning family."

At the recommendation of a priest who feared too much inbreeding among the families ("The Faherty and Sommerhauser families had double cousins going on, too," Bonnie confirms), James and Helena Faherty moved to Cole Camp, southwest of Tipton, where they farmed. It was here that Oscar Faherty, Gene Clark's grandfather, was born and raised. And it was here that Oscar met and married Rosemary Sommerhauser, an imposing, outspoken, no-nonsense 19-year-old. She was ten years Oscar's junior, but no less equal in stature. "My grandmother Rosemary was five-foot-ten in her stocking feet and she could look my grandfather dead in the eye," laughs Bonnie. "Most of my family on the Faherty side, including my grandmother, were close to six feet. They were big."

On June 21, 1920, at either Versailles or Cole Camp—no one is quite sure anymore—Gene's mother, Mary Jeanne Faherty (known to everyone as Jeanne), was born. In all, the Fahertys would raise six children. Oscar continued to farm in the vicinity until the Great Depression, when foreclosure forced him off the family farm. "The banks loaned the farmers too much money for what they were capable of paying and eventually the people lost their farms," laments Bonnie. "Grandpa was trying to modernize and bought new farm equipment, but couldn't repay his loan. So they moved into Tipton and my grandfather went to work in the feed mill." The uprooting would leave an indelible imprint on Jeanne. "Her parents losing everything they had always made Mom extremely frugal," Bonnie confirms. "It colored her whole life and it colored my dad's whole life because he grew up in the Depression as well. She saved everything. Every scrap of paper, every plastic bag."

Jeanne left Tipton in her teens, after completing only the eighth grade, to take a job as a domestic servant for a wealthy family that golfed out at Milburn Golf and Country Club in the Overland Park district of south Kansas City, Kansas. "Milburn was kind of *the* country club for all of the Kansas City area," offers Bonnie. "It was where the wealth was. So she was here working in Kansas City and met my dad on a blind date. My dad once said that he just fell crazy in love with her the first time he saw her."

Unlike Jeanne Faherty Clark's well-documented family history, the lineage of Gene's father, Kelly George Clark, is far more murky and mysterious—possibly for good reason, at the time. "Rumor has it that we are Native American on my dad's side," Bonnie reveals. "We suspect it was Osage, but we don't know for certain. The records were so poorly kept. We just came up against roadblocks. The name Clark is English, but it could have been an adopted name when settlers came through and renamed or Anglicized some of the Natives' names. That's what I think."

While open about her mother's family tree, Bonnie is cautious in discussing her father's roots and chooses her words carefully. "I'm going to say something that could be offensive to some people today, but was a fact of life in my father's time. I asked my dad once why he never tried to find out about his Native American background and he said to me, 'Because when I was growing up, Indians were just another form of nigger.'"

What *is* known about Kelly Clark is that he was born in Lenexa, Kansas, on November 11, 1918—the day World War I ended. His parents hailed from Rolla, Missouri, and he had a sister and three brothers. Gene is named after one of those brothers.

Gene's younger brother David offers further insights into the Clark side of the family. "There were two brothers named Clarke [sic] who came from England way back when, and went out west and settled around Adel, Iowa," David explains. "This has been documented. They had the English 'e' on the Clark name. One of them fell in love with and married an Indian girl, and this was totally unacceptable to the rest of the family. So they had this big falling out. The younger brother, who married the Indian girl, went even further west into the wilderness around Bolivar, Missouri, where he started a whole Clark chain without the 'e' on the Clark name. This is my dad's ancestral side of the family. He was my dad's great-grandfather and the Indian woman was my dad's great-grandmother. So there is Native American blood in our family and there may have been more that we don't know about. When we were younger and were running around we all looked like Indians. We turned a bronze color in the sun. We were conscious of our Native American blood as children. When Dad got out in the sun he would turn a flaming dark color and he had the very high, prominent cheekbones." David believes the Native American bloodline to be Cree from Minnesota.

The family grew up respectful of its Native blood despite the social stigma attached to it at that time. Gene would explore those roots later in life. "Gene was very much in tune with his Native American roots," suggests David, highlighting Gene's later friendships with guitarist Jesse Ed Davis and actor David Carradine. "Jesse Ed and him were very close. Jesse Ed, of course, was Native American. Jesse Ed's wife came to Gene's service in Los Angeles and she brought a talisman and asked me if it would be all right to place it in Gene's casket. And I told her of course she could and I walked up there with her. Gene was very close to that kind of thing, and anybody who had a Native American background, who was a little different than other people, he had a kind of camaraderie with. David Carradine claimed to have Native American blood and he and Gene were running buddies for a long time." Adds Gene's youngest son, Kai, "He was very into it, the whole spiritual beliefs of the earth, the land, the water, the trees, the sun and moon, and it inspired his writing."

Bonnie believes that her mother tried to hide the Native American heritage in her children. "There are also a lot of Spanish names in my family and my dad had olive skin and tanned very, very dark. So my mother named me Bonita and one of my sisters Dolores. If someone ever questioned our olive skin it could always be explained away as possibly Spanish. It was almost a ruse. But the rest of them didn't have those names. She might have been thinking, 'Well, these kids are kind of dark skinned. Maybe I should give them some reason to be like that.' But the Native American part is so obvious in pictures of my dad as a young man." Indeed, early photographs of Kelly and his father, Joel, reveal prominent cheekbones, squared jaw, and copper skin characteristic of Native Americans.

Kelly Clark was an unassuming man with the strength of ten and a heart to match. "My dad was only five-foot-six and weighed about 138 pounds, but he was one of the strongest human beings pound for pound that I ever knew," asserts David. "He worked with me until he was 77 years old in a machine repair shop, handling equipment. He kept his garden and house up and won beautification certificates for his flowers in Bonner Springs. He had a green thumb and could make anything grow." Adds brother Rick, "My dad had a nickname. They called him the Little Ox because he was five-foot-six and built like Hercules. I remember my dad liked to stop sometimes on the way home from work at a favorite bar of his called the Rose Room and the bartender was really tight friends with Dad. We were with Dad one day after working at the golf course and we stopped in to the bar. We were playing pool and Dad was having a drink. These other guys started making fun of my dad for no reason. They were pushing at him because he was a little guy, but these guys didn't realize that my dad was nothing but hard steel, all muscle. He knew really well how to take care of himself. These five guys started ganging up on my dad. The bartender yells out, 'Kelly!' and throws Dad an axe handle. Within a few seconds all five of them were laying on the floor bleeding and moaning. They just picked on the wrong guy. All the males in our family were like that."

Adds Bonnie, "Dad was a petite man, but was always in fantastic physical shape. One time when he was in one of his drunken rages it took three big policemen to nail him down. Even in his last year of life he was still strong and muscular."

Quitting school in his sophomore year to support his parents, Kelly found employment as a greenskeeper with the parks department for the municipal government of Kansas City, Kansas, at Milburn Golf and Country Club, where he met Jeanne Faherty. "Dad was instantly in love, but Mom wasn't too sure about him because he was a wild guy," laughs Bonnie. "He was working at the golf course, but he only had a menial job then." Despite her reservations, the two fell in love and married in a Catholic ceremony on May 29, 1941. They took up residence on Santa Fe near the country club. Bonita Elizabeth was born March 13, 1942, followed by Kelly Katherine on March 21, 1943. Tragically, however, Kelly Katherine was stillborn and is buried in St. Andrew's Cemetery in Tipton. (While Gene's grave is in the Sommerhauser plot, Kelly Katherine's is a solitary stone at the far south end of the cemetery.)

Drafted following the Japanese attack on Pearl Harbor in December 1941, Kelly Clark was declared 4F because he wore glasses. However, by the fall of 1943 the American military had loosened its requirements and in October he was recalled and assigned to radio and gunnery school. "Dad was home in early 1944," states David. "He was home on furlough when Gene was conceived. Then he went overseas and spent part of the time, the early part of his tour of duty, in England. A childhood disease kept him out of the Normandy invasion. That likely kept him alive. But he landed in Le Havre, France, in January 1945 and the Battle of the Bulge was raging. He was in the corps that supported Patton and they were kind of the mop-up crew. He went from Le Havre all the way to Berlin and he was in Berlin in May of 1945 when the war ended. So he basically saw the tail end of the war."

Kelly's younger brother, Harold Eugene, was not as fortunate. The story has often been told that Harold Eugene Clark died on the beaches of Normandy during the D-Day invasion. But the truth is he died during the ill-fated Operation Market-Garden, a British-led paratroop assault behind German lines near Arnhem, Netherlands, in September 1944 (which became the basis

Kelly Clark, 1944.

for Cornelius Ryan's book and subsequent movie *A Bridge Too Far*). "He was killed in Europe paratrooping into Remagen," Bonnie emphasizes. "Everybody thought it was at D-Day, but I found out it was at Remagen. It was a slaughter." The family learned of Harold Eugene's death shortly before Gene was born.

With Kelly off at boot camp and about to be shipped overseas, and with one toddler under foot and another on the way, Jeanne Clark moved into her grandmother's house in Tipton. It was here that Harold Eugene Clark, named for his fallen uncle, was born on Friday, November 17, 1944 (not 1941, as has often been reported). The large home offered comfort and the presence of family provided security. Bonnie recalls that the house was across the street from a funeral home and that they lived in the upstairs—just Jeanne, Bonnie, and baby Gene (family members recall Gene was never called Harold unless he was in trouble, when his mother would summon him: "Harold Eugene Clark, you get in here right now!"). The three remained in Tipton until Kelly's return from overseas in the fall of 1945.

"Dad was a sergeant before he was busted down to a private," smiles Bonnie, recalling her father's stubborn streak. "He left the army as a private. It had something to do with a French wine cellar." David picks up the story. "After they left Berlin they had to go back to England. He was basically a sergeant major at that point. They had confiscated some Cognac and they were having a little celebration while they were waiting for transport back to England. They already had their orders to go home and they were in their barracks. This is the story I got from a man who was there with them. The new lieutenant, fresh out of West Point, came in and here are a bunch of battle-hardy soldiers and he starts ranking them out for drinking on duty. But they weren't on duty. They were mustered out. The other guys in his unit always called Dad 'Pappy' because he was married and older than the rest of them and had kids. Pappy was the ranking officer and this lieutenant started picking on him. Dad told him they weren't on duty, but he kept on, so Dad finally stood up and knocked him right on his back. So he became a PFC, private first class. His muster papers have him as PFC."

His tour of duty complete, Kelly returned to work at Milburn Golf and Country Club in Overland Park. With another child on the way, the family moved to a small home at 4427 Mission Road in Kansas City, Kansas. It was there that Nancy Patricia was born on July 19, 1946. "Mom was a baby factory, year after year," Bonnie comments.

Soon after, Kelly took a job at the municipal golf course located in Swope Park in the Kansas City, Missouri, neighborhood of Raytown. The family was on the move once again, this time across the river to the Missouri side and an equally tiny house on the eastern side of the park, at the end of a secluded road at Seventy-ninth Street and Oldham Road. (The house no longer stands today, demolished in the 1960s to make way for Highway 435.) This would remain the Clark home until 1960, when they would move back across the river to Bonner Springs, Kansas. "Our family has been kind of migratory, but not like every two years," offers Bonnie. "More like every ten years there would be a big change in the venue."

Located on nearly 1,800 acres, roughly seven square miles along the Blue River in central Kansas City, Missouri, Swope Park boasts two golf courses: Swope Park Memorial Golf Course and Blue River Golf Course. Swope Park is also home to the Kansas City Zoo, Starlight Theatre (where, in August 1963, Gene would make a guest appearance with the New Christy Minstrels), a nature center, swimming pool, picnic grounds, rock climbing, and athletic fields. Its forested areas feature abundant oak and hickory trees, a lagoon, and plenty of hills and limestone outcrops to explore. The site was donated by land developer Thomas Hunton Swope in 1896 and remains one of the city's most popular attractions and among the largest urban parks in the United States. When the Clarks moved to Swope Park in 1949, much of the area remained open wilderness. Running through one end of the park was the Kansas City Southern railroad line and bridge. For the ever-expanding Clark brood, Swope Park became a private playground and inspiration for Gene's young imagination.

Like much of Gene's life, myth has blurred into reality. It has often been stated that he grew up on a farm. While not a farm per se, and certainly not a farm family, the Clarks did, in fact, grow up in a farm-like environment on the edge of Swope Park, a rural oasis in the middle of a metropolis. "It was pretty rural where we lived," explains David. "The site was on about 40 acres that was a mix of pasture, hills, and little creeks, fairly well out of the city at that time, which it isn't any more. Dad took care of both golf courses for the city at that time. And along with his salary came this little house on this property that we lived on." The house was, in fact, a converted trolley barn with no running water when the family moved in.

"Spartan" would be an understated description of the Swope Park residence. Initially it lacked even the basics of a simple family dwelling. "It was really just small, four rooms," David continues. "It officially had two bedrooms that were, as we got older, divided up into a boys' room and a girls' room. By the time I was in first grade we finally got running water. Before that we used outside facilities and for wash water and stuff like that there was a cistern. There was an old orchard area that was uncultivated for many years that did have some apple trees, pear trees, blackberry bushes, things like that that we harvested; hickory nuts, walnuts. That's how we made our living, basically, from the very beginning as far back as I can remember. We lived off of a small farmette, had milk cows for milk and butter, separated our own cream, churned our own butter, we cut our own wood for a woodstove in the house. Everybody had chores, from the time I can remember. By the time I was in grade school there were ten children in a little four-room house and everybody had chores.

"We kept as many as two calves and usually raised them up to butcher them. Dad tried butchering them a few times, but after a couple of failed attempts we took them to a slaughterhouse. We did raise about a hundred chickens a year. We would get them as chicks in little crates and raise them. Then in the fall we would prepare them."

"We lived really primitively for the first few years we were in there because we had to truck in water and my mother had to do the laundry outside in a boiler over an open fire," Bonnie confirms, recalling the family's rather rustic existence. "I remember that vividly."

Kelly converted the back porch into a kitchen and later added a narrow six feet by ten feet bathroom off one side of the kitchen, just big enough to accommodate a tub, toilet, and sink. The living room was ten feet by ten feet, with an adjacent dining room roughly the same size. The two bedrooms were also ten feet by ten feet "When we were growing up we basically lived in each other's pockets," recalls Bonnie. "By the time I left there were ten individuals basically living in a four-room house. There was the living room where Mom and Dad had the hide-a-bed, there was the girls' room at the front and all six of us were in there. There were two bunk beds and the littlest ones doubled up. The boys had a similar situation in the other room at the back. Just two bedrooms. It was quite a houseful. Then we had the dining room, which was the main feature of the house, with a huge 12-foot oak table. This was our family gathering place, the focus of the family. Family meals were important. We were all expected to be there."

"Gene wasn't a farm boy but he *was* a country boy," emphasizes Rick, debunking the long-held farm boy assumption. "We did have a working farm, though, because we had chickens and pigs and cattle and we had two ten-acre truck farms where we grew corn and green beans. With a 13-kid family you've got to raise your own food. Every day we all had our chores. I remember as a very young child before I went to school I had to feed the chickens or milk the cows and it would still be dark. Everybody had their own chores to take care of. When we came home from school we'd all have to go out and weed at least two rows of beans or corn before we could pursue our other interests or whatever we wanted to do playing out in the woods. But it wasn't the sole source of income for us; it was a subsidy kind of thing for the family because Dad still worked at the golf course. We had all of our own fresh eggs and drank fresh, un-homogenized milk straight from the cow. My mother churned her own butter."

Jeanne Clark was the dynamo of the family, raising an ever-expanding brood of kids, cooking, washing, canning, churning, and running the household. With her husband out working, she was the matriarch—a force to be reckoned with. The children still marvel at her ability to pull everything together. "Sunday dinner was always a special time," Rick continues. "My mother was amazing. I don't know how she did it, but in the morning she would go out and chop the heads off of three chickens, dunk them into boiling water, pluck all their feathers out, gut them, and fry them up. She would sit on the porch churning butter with this crank, cranking and cranking over and over before turning it over to someone else. We'd be cutting up beans. It was like a little assembly line. We would have three huge platters of fried chicken for Sunday dinner. And she would do all this before we all got dressed to go to mass. Then after mass she would prepare the Sunday dinner. It was wonderful."

David remains circumspect about those early years when the family went without more often than not. "I like to look at our life like that of the Waltons, but the Waltons had it really good compared to us. Sometimes we had it pretty tough. We lived pretty sparsely. There were good things. We learned to make do with what we had."

There is no doubt that Gene grew up without many of the comforts and conveniences others took for granted, often enduring ridicule for wearing hand-me-downs. Childhood friend and classmate Jack Godden, who lived not far from Gene in an old farmhouse on Seventy-seventh Street and Terrace Ridge in Raytown, remembers his astonishment on first visiting the Clark household. "You had to take a dirt road up and it was the only house back in the woods, way up high. I couldn't believe the first time Gene took me there. 'You live way back here?' It was kind of spooky in a way. They were a great family and I adored them, but they were very poor. I think he was kind of embarrassed about his family, ashamed of it. The house was pretty small, 13 kids and it was pretty cramped. But he had a great life, so I don't know why he would be ashamed of it." Jack's younger brother, David, visited the Clarks on one occasion. "Swope Park was pretty much an isolated area at the time, a real rural area, an underdeveloped area. The suburbs hadn't really gotten that far out. I saw the inside of their house one time and I thought, 'Oh, my goodness. This is what I've heard.' My mom and dad would say that Gene's family wasn't very wealthy, a poor family. My mother would always try and do whatever she could to help them with food or clothing. Gene came up from the bottom, no doubt about that." Comments Bonnie, ruefully, "It sounds like the Beverly Hillbillies and it was pretty close."

In later years, once Gene found fame, he rarely spoke of his childhood in Swope Park or Raytown, choosing instead to state he was from the more acceptable Bonner Springs, where the family moved in 1960. He never spoke of the hardships the family suffered during those early years. "We were known as a very strange family in the community because of the number of us," Bonnie concedes. "I'm not a bit surprised that he was embarrassed by his family. The whole family was supported by Dad's single income. So we were poor, simply because of the massive amount of people supported by one income."

Growing up with 15 people in a four-room converted garage on municipal land with no plumbing for the first few years was not something Gene wanted the world to know about. "When he was first with the New Christy Minstrels and then the Byrds especially, with their prominence," recalls David, "he was embarrassed about his past. He even gave interviews that said that he was a California boy. Some of the teen magazines at the time quoted him as saying he was from the San Fernando Valley. He created a whole new identity for himself to keep people from saying he was a hillbilly or a hick. In his early L.A. life he disavowed his family past." Confirms fellow Byrd Chris Hillman, "I never knew of Gene's family or their history. He never talked about it."

Jeanne Clark with Bonnie and Harold Eugene (Gene), 1945.

With Kelly at work from before sunup until sundown and Jeanne busy with babies (Mary Dolores and David had already arrived, and Daniel Oscar was on the way), the job of raising Gene and the other young siblings fell to the eldest, Bonnie. "I was the whip," she boasts. "I was the child discipliner. Mom was too busy having babies and cooking the meals. I raised Gene. I raised all of the kids, down to Dan, I would say. The first six of us were a unit. And nobody asked me if I could do it, it was just, 'This is your job.' My mom told me after I had left to join the service in 1960 and then come back that she never realized until I wasn't there what I did. It fell on my younger sisters when I left and they didn't have a clue because I had raised them. I didn't start pinning diapers on the others until I was five." Bonnie maintains that despite 13 children, Gene remained his mother's center of attention. "Oh, he was Mom's favorite child, absolutely," she laughs. "Mom fawned over Gene from the time he was an infant. I was the oldest child, the only child until I was three years old. Then this male usurper arrives."

Gene's character, the kind of person he would go on to become, was shaped by events and environment at Swope Park. His affinity for the land and nature was a direct result of those 11 years. And many of his traumas were first played out there as well. "My first recollection of Gene," muses Bonnie, "and I'm going to give you a snapshot here, was there was a severe storm going on. If you've never experienced a midwestern storm, it's something else. The lightning was severe, the sky was copper colored, and my mother was just terrified of storms because she was in a tornado as a young girl. And so Gene was feeling this terror all around him. I was probably in kindergarten at the time so he was probably three or four years old. My mom's cowering, Gene's cowering, so my dad picks Gene up and walks to the back door window, it's a fairly large window, and he's talking to Gene and telling him that it's just a part of nature and there's really nothing to be scared of, trying to buck him up and be a man, and he's terrified and wanting his mom."

What the children lacked in material possessions they more than made up for in imagination. With a whole park at their disposal, the Clark children's amusements were limited only by their imaginations. "We were so poor that we had to rely on what materials—hay bales, hickory branches, Sumac patches—were available to us to entertain ourselves," reflects David, wistfully recalling those unfettered days. "It built some pretty tremendous imaginations."

Gene's fertile mind was given free reign as he and his siblings explored, climbed, ran, jumped, and played out all their fantasies in their own private playground. Later Gene recalled his carefree, idyllic boyhood days in Swope Park in the haunting song "Something's Wrong," recorded on the 1968 album *The Fantastic Expedition of Dillard & Clark*: "Hours of joy when I was just a boy and never wrong I knew. Kites of red would fly above my head, the birds would sing their song." It was a time and place Gene would often long for in later years, knowing full well that he could never recapture the magic of simpler times.

"The orchard was a great place for all sorts of activity," David continues. "The woods were even better. These were our Magic Kingdom and everything around us our props for our adventures. There was a wood adjacent to our place that was seven miles long and three miles deep of park property. It supported a lot of activity for us. Our entertainments were basically self-constructed. In the early years we acted out *Sinbad the Sailor,* all kinds of Indian stories, mostly coming from books we read like *Drums Along the Mohawk. The Adventures of Robin Hood* was a real big one for us to act out. We did have a great area to live out our adventures. Gene's song 'Something's Wrong' very much depicts what it was like for us playing and then growing up. It was away from the mainstream of life, it was innocent, there was no knowledge of some of the things that were going on in the great world. It was like being on an island. We were isolated. We didn't have a lot of interaction with the outside world. Our school life was about the only thing and that was pretty much sanitized, too, in those days, because we went to a Catholic school, and a very old order Catholic school, which was very much based on the catechism—Latin and fire and brimstone where all bad little boys are going to go to hell if they don't straighten out. Being isolated like that, we had time to really enjoy life. We had our work, but on a normal June day, for instance, we would be up pretty early, there was no school, and if we could we would take off for the woods or the orchard or anywhere else where we could get out of reach or out of sight until we were detected and brought back to our chores. If we didn't get up early enough we went right to the garden to weed or hoe the corn, pick any vegetables that were ready, maybe even get involved in the canning of vegetables, stuff like that."

Although eight years younger, Rick attempted to keep up with his older brothers. "My memories of that time are of running around in the woods and exploring. We had some wonderful woods with a creek that ran through and some great rock formations. We would all fall down and either break something or cut something. Mom and Dad spent a lot of time rushing one of us to the emergency room when we were kids. I don't know how many trips they made. I can't say I regret anything at all about my early childhood except for the fact that Gene didn't like his little brothers hanging around when he was with his buddies."

"Gene had a very vivid imagination when he was young," avers David, who cites this as inspiring his brother's later songwriting abilities. "He didn't read much but what most people don't know is that in our younger years our entertainment was reading. There wasn't a television. It may have been stories like *Sinbad the Sailor* or Zane Grey stories. Those in particular were among Gene's favorites and fired his imagination. And when we went to act out these things we didn't just go outside and say we're this, that or the other, we made the costumes. If we were Sinbad the Sailor we got the whole garb on with eye patches and had swords, the whole works. I remember one year a storm blew a big limb out of a tree and it came down in a swoop shape and it kind of resembled an old Persian boat. Boy, that was *Sinbad the Sailor* for us. We had a mast on it and when we would move right the whole thing would rock like you were on the water.

The Clark children circa 1951. Back row: Nancy, Bonnie and Gene; front row: David, Christine, Dan and Dolores.

Yeah, Gene had a very vivid imagination, always. He would think of things and some people would say, 'What are you talking about?' and then we would act them out.

"One year we were cleaning out the cellar where we stored our fruit and stuff and Gene decided we were going to have a Halloween party down there. We spooked that place up real good. We even had a bedsheet back in one corner with a little head on it and when you pulled a drawstring it would come across the room out of the dark at you. It scared the bejesus out of you! And Gene was always the ringleader and would get the rest of us involved and tell us what to do. To produce the reaction he wanted he would stage the dangdest things you ever did see."

"We had a babysitter that would come over once in awhile so the folks could get out," Bonnie recalls, chuckling at the memory. "We had this huge oak dining room table and we would stand it up and make it our stage. We even brought in branches from outside to make scenery with. We would take the lamps off the tables and remove the shades to make spotlights, sheets off the beds to make curtains that the little ones would hold. And this babysitter was encouraging all this. 'You kids should be on Ted Mack's *Amateur Hour!*' she would tell us. So we would perform and sing."

Bonnie acknowledges her parents for allowing their imaginations' and feelings' free rein. "We were allowed our imaginations and our emotions. And that I'll give my parents credit for. They never said you can't be sad or anything. Our parents let us be wild Indians, that's what our grandmother used to call us. Expressing emotions came naturally to us. Our mother was very emotional. She could not stand up at a family dinner and give a speech without getting choked up."

Bonnie reveals one of their mother's indirect influences on Gene's character. "Gene was a neat freak," offers Bonnie. Indeed, in later years friends consistently point to Gene's fixation with keeping everything in order and tidy in his house. "My mom wasn't a very good housekeeper. If the floors got mopped it was like a brigade thing where we all did it. I did most of the house-keeping for a long time. She did the cooking and the child rearing, and she worked in the garden sometimes. But her housekeeping wasn't very good. In fact, Dad would come home every once in a while very frustrated and he would pick up a broom and go through the house because she just wasn't that great a housekeeper."

Gene would draw inspiration from another childhood source. "The Kansas City Southern used to pass by Swope Park," recalls Bonnie. "We could go up in the orchard and stand up on the hill and there was this huge arched trestle that went over Gregory Boulevard and the Kansas City Southern would come across and the black smoke would roll across the landscape." Gene's song "Kansas City Southern" would become one of his most enduring.

One amusement, however, was not tolerated by Kelly or Jeanne, once they found out about it. "We would take empty Tide boxes because they had this target on them and do target prac-tice with the kitchen knives," laughs Bonnie. "Gene was very good at it, we both were. This was one of the things we did as a family function, throwing knives at Tide boxes. It came to a screeching halt when Mom or Dad found out what was going on." In later years Gene and Rick would terrify band mates and friends with their knife-wielding prowess.

But while Gene's outdoor hijinks and practical jokes revealed an outgoing personality, David and Bonnie recall another side to his personality—a shy, reticent, insecure, withdrawn young man few understood. "Gene had a very sensitive side to him," David notes, recalling a particular inci-dent. "Mom had an accident once and Gene blamed himself. He really took it to heart." With a heavy conscience driven by guilt and a sense of duty, Gene quietly took on additional outside chores that his mother couldn't do. "He was super sensitive about things and he would blame him-self if something went wrong. If an animal, one of the critters we depended on for our livelihood at that time, if the coyotes got in and killed a calf, he took it very hard. He would blame himself for not locking the door right. And nobody was blaming him; he condemned himself. He was like that his whole life, blaming himself for things that didn't go the way he thought they should."

Gene carried a burden of self-recrimination that weighed heavily on him throughout his life. Frustration with the music industry wore him down, leading to excessive behavior later in life. David feels that far too often his brother is judged not by who he was but by what he be-came. "What many people fail to understand when looking at Gene, is that they look at him as an adult with many troubles in his life," he muses. "Some people have described him as a mon-ster. I know what he was like; I dealt with him. But there was a Eugene Clark as well as a Gene Clark. Very few people ever knew the other Gene."

Despite growing up in a large family, from an early age Gene tended to be a loner. Although he did enjoy the company of close friends, notably Jack Godden, he was certainly not gregarious and his interactions with others were often limited as a result of his shy nature. "He didn't play well with other kids," Bonnie reveals. "I recall that he would get frustrated a lot. Things just seemed to bite him. He would have an idea of how things should go and if they didn't always go that way he would draw back. If he felt personally threatened he could be very assertive, but if it was something to do with an idea he had or something he was trying to get across, he would draw back and get his feelings hurt if somebody didn't appreciate something he was trying to do. Gene was emotional but he was more like Dad in the way he kept the lid on things. He was a loner. He kept things to himself. I don't think any of us knew Gene very well. He wouldn't let anybody get past a certain layer. There was this persona and the rest of Gene was somewhere in there. He was hard to get to know. That was the basic part of Gene. He was very self-contained. He could be very warm and loving, but that could change in a heartbeat."

It is often difficult for those who knew him—even family members—to reconcile the two Gene Clarks: the cheerful, engaging yet shy loner with the vibrant imagination, and the frustrated, moody recluse who was sometimes prone to violence. In later years, Gene increasingly turned to alcohol and drugs to mitigate these swings in temperament. It's entirely possible that even Gene himself was not fully aware of the many sides to his personality as he became an adolescent. In today's world, manic depression (or bipolar disorder) is a common enough term and its diagnosis is far more prevalent. It is treatable. Millions of people are able to lead normal, happy, fully functioning lives with early diagnosis, proper treatment, and prescribed medication. It is no longer stigmatized. But in the 1950s, behavior of this nature was most often simply dismissed as moodiness, hyperactivity, or a nervous condition, and went untreated.

The symptoms of a manic-depressive or bipolar personality are marked by very pronounced shifts in a person's energy level and resulting mood. The afflicted experience dramatic swings—from a restlessness characterized by inability to sit still or sleep, an aggressiveness or manic euphoria of thoughts racing from subject to subject, to the other extreme, where feelings of hopelessness, anxiety, pessimism, intense frustration, irritability, and decreased energy prevail. It is, as one Clark family member puts it, "the highest of highs to the lowest of lows." Bipolar disorder usually develops in late adolescence or early adulthood.

There is a history of mental illness in the Clark family. Several family members have suffered, and in some cases continue to experience, symptoms of manic depression. One sibling is diagnosed paranoid schizophrenic; another suffers from debilitating bouts of depression, while still another is indigent due to a psychological problem. Nancy Clark Marconette, the next youngest after Gene, was on medication for severe depression most of her life and her sudden death in 1987 may have been related to the psychiatric medication she was taking. "She was very bipolar and had a whole lot of problems," confirms Bonnie. A few suggest that it may be the result of inbreeding from generations before.

"My sister Nancy had a lot of trouble with severe depression," affirms Rick, openly discussing for the first time the problems that plagued him and his siblings. "Gene had the same thing. But nobody even knew about it. It wasn't being diagnosed properly or even diagnosed at all back then. Depression was often passed off as being moody and not treated seriously. I witnessed it in Gene. The highs are way up there and then the depths could be a second later and totally unexplained from one minute to the next. It's really a roller-coaster ride. It's a trait, a hereditary thing, in our family. I've got another brother who has a severe case of it as well. Some of my sisters and brothers suffered from it to different degrees, but it is in my family. My mother had it and my dad. Gene didn't know it because nobody ever diagnosed it and he never got any treatment for it. God knows what could have been had Gene gotten some treatment when he needed it.

"It was a part of us that we didn't understand. There's a family history of being real high-strung. For example, when I talk I've gotta have something to do with my hands and things like that. I'll smoke like a chimney. And Gene did, too. He was always fidgeting or his leg was going. I understand it better nowadays with me. That's why I'm 51 and I'm not dead. After witnessing it happen to family members of mine I didn't want to go the same route. Finally I sought out somebody to get some help. After tests they said that I definitely have a kind of a bipolar, manic-depressive personality. I know Gene was afflicted with that. Hence a really great, sensitive, intuitive, intelligent songwriter ended up dead at the age of 46 rather than living a longer, more productive life. He did go to AA for three years, but they never treated him for any of his psychological problems."

Does Bonnie believe Gene was a bipolar personality? "Oh, yes. All of us are prone to it. I have learned to balance things a little better, but sometimes it's a fight. It's kind of hard to describe the shy, wild man that Gene was. He could be so warm and loving and you could walk up to him, he'd smile at you, and you would just melt. Then on the other hand he could turn around and be an uproarious bastard in two minutes. It was just like whiplash. But this, I think, comes from that heredity thing I was talking about, the in-marrying. Dad was one of these very calm people outwardly. Life could hit him with just about anything and he would never even flinch. But let him get drunk and he was a raging maniac. It was hard to believe that he was the same person."

Kelly Clark's method of dealing with his mood swings was to self-medicate with alcohol. All the family witnessed this. "Dad was an alcoholic," admits Bonnie, revealing another family secret that had an impact on the Clark siblings. "He could drink a beer occasionally and not go off the deep end. He learned to control that. But hard liquor? He couldn't deal with it. Dad was a late alcoholic, too, like Gene. Mom once said that there was a 20-year nightmare when Dad was in the depths of his alcohol addiction. She said the first 20 years of their marriage was a romance. Then there was the next 20 years, which was a nightmare because of Dad's alcoholism. And then he got cleaned up and the rest of their life was pretty good, except that their health was failing."

Offers Rick, "The way my dad would try to deal with his depression was to try to numb it with alcohol. And that's the way Gene dealt with it to a great degree. It was kind of passed down in the family."

"My dad was alienated completely from his own father because of my grandfather's alcoholism," states Bonnie. "Dad had to go to work when he was 16 years old to help support the family because my grandfather was a severe alcoholic. It's just generation after generation. And on my mom's side there was alcoholism too, but it was disguised as social drinking.

"Gene would have seen all this. I came home on leave once in the early '60s and there was a scene involving alcohol and me and Gene and a few of his friends. I was giving Gene hell about how he was going to embarrass the family and all of that. And he just turned around and he looked at me and said, 'You don't know what the hell you're talking about.'

"Gene could be very destructive," Bonnie continues. "The night we were arguing about his drinking we had gone out drinking with some of his friends and I saw him literally destroy some property. And I had never seen that behavior before. He couldn't participate in most of the gym stuff and he thought that the gym teacher had it in for him. The night that all this drinking and property destruction was going on, Gene walked in and tried to pick a fight with the high school coach at a restaurant called Truckers out at the edge of Bonner Springs. I wouldn't come in because I didn't like what was happening. Some of Gene's friends came out to the car and said, 'Bonnie, you better come in and get your brother before he gets his butt kicked.' So I walked in and said, 'Get yourself out to the car before you get yourself in trouble.' He turned around and looked at me and said, 'Why don't you mind your own business.' He had a cup of hot coffee in his hand and I just slammed my hand down over his and said, 'We both know who the kid is here. Get yourself out to the car!' He did, but he was muttering all the way, 'Don't anyone say a word.' He had a macho side. He was very big. He was six-foot tall and he was solid."

Given these circumstances, Bonnie has no hesitation in describing the Clark family as dysfunctional. "Oh, yes. I came to terms with that when I went back to junior college after my children were grown. I was knocking down straight As and my husband was very supportive, but I felt like it wasn't good enough. It was the 'not good enough' syndrome. So I went to talk to some counselors about it and asked them, 'What am I not doing right here?' They got me into adult children of alcoholics counseling. I'm not an alcoholic, but my life has been severely affected by what happened in my family."

Into this already volatile mix was thrown a curve ball that altered the family dynamic even further. Ada Rebecca (Becky) Clark, born August 5, 1954, was diagnosed with severe mental retardation soon after birth. "This was part of the family mechanism that didn't work," sighs Bonnie. "We had a severely retarded child in the house that the rest of the family revolved around, including Gene, who was in junior high by then. He grew up around this. This was a family focus, too. She was a wild little animal. She had the mentality of about a six-month-old child, but she was growing into this huge, unmanageable person. So Mom and Dad had to put her into state care to get her the care she needed. And the state put my folks through the ringer about why can't they take care of this child in their home? She didn't show any signs when she was born. It was a disease, a tumor in her brain that progressed. The doctors didn't expect her to live to be 18 years old." Today Becky lives in a group home in Lawrence, Kansas. Her brother Dan is her conservator and according to Bonnie, "Becky lives a happy life."

How did Gene deal with Becky? "I think he was terribly disturbed by her affliction," Bonnie speculates. "All of us were. We used to think, 'Man, we came out of the same gene pool.'"

Jeanne Clark's method of coping with the situation was both unconventional and in keeping with her deep-rooted Catholic faith. "Mom was a great believer in miracles," cites Bonnie. "This is how the family dynamic operated. After Mom found out that Becky was probably going to be severely retarded for the rest of her life, we got into the miracle business. We prayed a rosary every night on our knees, the whole family, Gene included."

Another childhood event left a lasting imprint on Gene. For decades it has been suggested in the media that Gene's fear of flying was the root cause of his abrupt departure from the Byrds in early 1966. It was too perfect a headline to resist: the Byrd who couldn't fly. The story had been attributed at the time to a claim by Gene that he had witnessed a plane crash as a child and consequently harbored a pathological fear of flying. Like so much of Gene's life, the story has taken on enormous significance in Clark mythology. Gene himself denied the veracity of the tale for years. However, the truth is he did, indeed, see a plane crash firsthand, as Bonnie relates: "He was someplace he wasn't supposed to be. There is a place in Kansas City called Cliff Drive that overlooks the old Municipal Airport. They're both still there. Cliff Drive was a notorious hangout for bad boys and he was forbidden to be there, but for some reason he was there anyway. And there was an airplane crash and he witnessed it. He told me it was awful. He saw people coming out of that plane on fire. It had to be when we were still living in Raytown." Rick confirms: "I thought that plane crash story was nonsense all my life too, until my mom told me a couple of years ago that, yeah, Gene did actually witness a plane crash when he was young. She told me years later that Gene eventually told her about it. I was shocked and surprised when she told me that. She never knew about it, though, until years later."

Gene's schooling began in the fall of 1949 when he enrolled at Our Lady of Lourdes, a strict, Catholic parochial school in Raytown on the east side of Kansas City. Jeanne Clark was a devout Catholic who insisted her children receive a proper Catholic education. She often attended mass several times a week and Sunday church was mandatory for the whole family. "Mom believed in the strict authority of the Catholic Church," Bonnie asserts. "There was no doubt in her mind that the church and the pope were infallible and whatever their minions did was justified. Her life revolved around the church and children. That was her life. She didn't have employment outside of the home, besides one sales job that didn't work, until Sarah [born in April 1963] was in kindergarten, and then she went to work in the cafeteria at the school, Sacred Heart."

Perhaps if Gene had attended public school from the outset, his educational experience might have turned out better. As it was he found it difficult to reconcile all the rules and often ran afoul of the nuns. "I can remember Gene getting into trouble a lot at school because he defied authority," claims Bonnie. "My parents would have to deal with the administration at school. At some of those Catholic schools there were truly some abusive people. I can remember some of those nuns being real nightmares. So some of Gene's acting out may have been justified. One time Gene had gotten into trouble at school and the nun had made him lie prone on the tile floor that was dirty from kids walking all over it. So he comes home and he's got the whole front of him all filthy from being stretched out on the floor. Mom asked him and he told her. She was incensed that she was going to have to wash that uniform again." Gene's parochial school experiences would foster a lifelong contempt not for religion—he was a very spiritual man—but for the Roman Catholic Church.

Childhood friend Jack Godden remembers Gene's lack of motivation in school. "He wasn't interested in school too much. He hated homework and there were a couple of teachers he didn't like at times. He would talk about them and wanting to get out of their classes. But we really didn't talk much about school because nobody liked school much back then. The nuns were mean. I had a nun knock me out with a stack of books. Mom and Dad wanted to take me to the hospital. And we had welts on our arms from being beaten with rulers. The parents thought the nuns could do no wrong until they saw those welts on our arms."

David recalls, "If he was interested in a subject, he was motivated in it. He was very much interested in history and did well with it. But he sucked at government." There was one subject that Gene demonstrated an early affinity for and it would serve him well. "We all were pretty good at English class because my mom was a stickler for using the English language properly and we learned that from a very, very young age. If we didn't pronounce a word correctly or didn't know the meaning of it, there was a very big, tattered dictionary that you got a lesson out of right then and there. Gene's vocabulary and use of words was a combination of what he picked up from that. He liked drama, but he didn't do a lot in the dramatic arts as far as performance because he was too shy. In the public eye he would just freeze up. That ran through his whole career. It was very hard for him to get up and perform. If it was a little gathering of people he knew well, he could play Macbeth and be great."

"Gene had to be set back, even in grade school," Bonnie notes. "He failed one of his early grades, maybe grade three. He just wasn't interested academically. He liked sports and music." As Godden remembers, "He was always doing push-ups and sit-ups, lifting weights, always keeping in shape." A fit, muscular, healthy athlete and swift runner, Gene played a variety of school sports and could just as easily have enjoyed a career in sports rather than music, had not a physical condition cut short a promising athletic career. "Gene had Osgood-Schlatter's Disease in his knees," confirms Bonnie, "and it kept him from participating in most gymnastic things." (Osgood-Schlatter's Disease is an adolescent affliction that hits just below the knee when the growth plate becomes overused or irritated, causing damage to the plate. The discomfort usually disappears with maturity as the growth plate fuses.) "When he was young

*Gene's photo from the Raytown
High School Yearbook, 1959.*

he could run out across the yard and do backflips, but he had bad knees. He used to imagine he was an acrobat. He was very acrobatic and athletic, but when his knees were ruined, that was out."

It was early on at school that Eugene Clark became simply Gene. David recalls the transformation: "Gene adopted the shorter version of his name when he was in grade school because it was more common to be called Gene than Eugene. One of the things that helped prompt that was the character of Eugene the Jeep in the Popeye cartoons and he did not like being called Jeep or being associated with that characterization. Nobody ever called him Harold. I heckled him once in a while in later years, but it was only in very good nature, believe me. His temperament wouldn't handle much of it." Gene later adopted the nickname 'Jinx' for Jinx the Cat. His younger siblings often called him that.

When Gene moved over to Raytown High School for the ninth grade, he entered an entirely different world from the strict, cloistered, parochial school environment, and with it he gained a new set of peers. Raytown today is a comfortable, middle-class, suburban neighborhood of Kansas City, Missouri, where you can expect to find well kept but not too pricey ranch-style homes. But in the 1950s, it was a rough and tumble community, working-class with a rural flavor. Here Gene would be introduced to fast cars, ducktails, bobby soxers, and rock 'n' roll. "Raytown was a place you probably felt more embarrassed to say you came from," postulates Jack Godden's younger brother David, who grew up in the neighborhood. "It was always made fun of. It was a place where a lot of underachievers lived. These types would prefer to go and drink beer and chase girls than get an education. That's why some people made fun of people from Raytown. It was a place a lot of people weren't proud to say they were from. It was considered a hick place in the 1950s and early '60s. Raytown was Smalltown, USA. I'm sure Gene wasn't very proud of Raytown."

Gene's Raytown buddy continued to be Jack, who he had first met at Our Lady of Lourdes. "Once we met we clicked like brothers and we stayed together all the time," laughs Jack, recalling their days together. "Every place we went we were always side by side, great friends. There wasn't a day that we weren't together. Gene was mild-tempered and loved to laugh. He had a great sense of humor. He drove me crazy with some of his jokes. They were so stupid, some of them, you couldn't help but laugh. We hiked all through those Swope Park mountains, climbed the rocks and the big boulders. Gene liked the outdoors. We looked for snakes on railroad tracks, stuff like that." Jack was aware of the family secret. "I knew about Gene's Indian background, but back then being Indian was something you didn't want people to know about. He was always a bit dark and had trouble growing a beard."

While the indelible 1960s image of Gene Clark is that of the quintessential American Beatle—long hair combed forward, Cuban heeled boots, turtleneck, jean jacket—he was very much a product of the 1950s American teen culture, sporting a greasy ducktail pompadour and more interested in fast cars and drinking beer than protests or poetry. Elvis and James Dean were his first idols. Despite being only three or four years younger, David Godden saw a vast gulf between Gene and Jack's generation and his own in Raytown. "It was kind of like *American Graffiti*. The guys were like that guy in that movie with the cigarette pack rolled up in his sleeve in the hot rod. There was a completely different mentality. They were the first generation of the baby boom, the first born, so they just seemed like they wanted to kick up their heels a little more."

Bonnie reveals that, for a time at least, her older brother kept some rough company. "Some of Gene's high school friends were quite notorious and in fact a few of them ended up in jail. He ran with a pretty rough crowd. There was one guy who he ran with and the last I heard of him he was in jail. They never did enough to coming down to having a record, but they were a wild bunch."

"We did get rowdy a few times and got in a little bit of trouble, not serious trouble, but we did light up some lights," admits Jack, smiling broadly. "Just having teenage fun, not juvenile delinquency. There was never a dull moment when we were together. The trouble we got into was maybe teenage drinking. But everybody was doing it. I didn't see it as serious with Gene. We always went to the drive-in movie to pick up girls. One of us was driving and the other two were in the trunk. He did get into a few fights over here in Grandview, the Coke Bar, messing around with someone else's girl. But Gene wouldn't back down. He could take care of himself. He had good strong arms on him. But that didn't stop other people from picking a fight. The worst fight I think I saw him in was when a guy came up and swung at him and hit him. But Gene picked him up and threw him across the table after he hit him. He just grazed Gene. We were pretty wild, Gene and I. I taught him how to drive to get his license and he wrecked my car teaching him how to drive.

"I had an old Studebaker with the top chopped off. No windshield. That was the car Gene and I used to take our dates out in. It was my dad's. We used to take off the exhaust manifold to make it sound real loud. That way we rode around like we were real cool." David Clark recalls the two friends having a heated argument over who would be Moondoggie and who would be Kahuna after they had been to see the *Gidget* movie. Gene wanted to be Kahuna and would refer to people he didn't like as a Moondoggie.

But before Gene could go gallivanting with Jack there were always chores to complete at home. Gene rarely shirked his responsibilities. "Gene's dad was very strict, in a way, as far as doing chores. Gene would be grounded if he didn't do what his dad said. He obeyed his dad. He was a hard worker, Gene was," Jack states.

As he got older, Gene was enlisted to work at the golf course alongside Kelly. He would spend his summers working every day at the course. "The only work Gene did other than play music in his life," notes David, "was turf work, working at a golf course or building a golf course, physical labor. There was a lot more to do than just mowing the grass. There was trenchers, backhoes, bulldozer work, anything from running a little bitty weed trimmer to operating a D5 Cat, which was pretty heavy duty. Gene became an accomplished welder and was very good at it."

By his early teens Gene had developed a passion for music. His rich tenor voice had already been tapped while he was still in grade school by the local bishop for the Kansas City Diocesan Choir. David remembers, "He went to practices and they sang at ordinations or

Gene and Jack Godden in Jack's Studebaker, Raytown 1960.

grandiose church events. One time I had the privilege of being at one of these things and it was something else, it really was. The old bishop, being an Irishman, loved that tenor voice of Gene's. And at the time, age had not tempered it any. It was high and it was clear. You could hear Gene's voice carry over the top."

In the Clark household, besides chores, there was one other constant. "The radio was on almost all the time in the house," Bonnie recalls. "And when we got a hold of the radio, Gene, Nancy, or me, we turned it to WREN in Topeka, which was rock 'n' roll. I was the one who brought rock 'n' roll into the house, Jerry Lee Lewis and Little Richard records. Gene listened to all that."

Before he discovered rock 'n' roll, Gene's tastes were far more eclectic. "Gene's roots were more like Nashville and Elvis Presley than Flatt and Scruggs," stresses Bonnie, addressing the common misperception that Gene was weaned exclusively on bluegrass music. "Dad played all kinds of music. He even played Spanish music. Gene was exposed to a wide variety of music. Once a year he would go with the Diocesan Choir and see the Kansas City Philharmonic. At home we listened to the "Firestone Hour," which was mostly classical music. We listened to the Grand Ole Opry and the Mercury Theatre."

Music was often an integral component of family gatherings. When you do without many things, you have to make your own entertainment. "We were kind of isolated where we were out there in Swope Park," notes Bonnie. "Dad would play harmonica and guitar and we would sit out on the front porch on the weekend and sing songs, the whole family. We grew up with music in the house. Country music, all kinds of music. We had a radio and it was our entertainment. We didn't have a television until 1954." As Gene told Mike Griffiths in an unpublished 1983 interview, "I remember watching my dad play guitar, but my hands weren't big enough to play guitar so he had a mandolin and he showed me a couple of chords on that and I just started messing around with that."

In his younger years, Kelly Clark had often entertained at rural social functions. A self-taught guitarist, he also dabbled on the banjo and harmonica. "My dad was a picker and player," boasts David proudly. "Guitar and harmonica were his mainstays, but he played a little bit more than that. At one time he had been a one-man band at barn dances and social gatherings around Lenexa. He had a harness that he put the mouth harp on and a foot cymbal and he would play the guitar and work the foot cymbal. Never sang that much. I don't think his voice was that bad, but I think he was self-conscious about it. So when Gene was really young he kind of got interested in playing and Dad showed him a lot of things. I don't think he encouraged Gene to play as looking at a professional career, but Gene got interested so he showed him how to chord and how to strum the rhythm with his thumb and pick a lead with his finger at the same time. So Gene picked up the guitar and he dabbled with it."

"I found him his first guitar at a garage sale," Jack Godden claims with considerable pride. "He already knew how to play. I think his dad was a little bit musical, but Gene didn't have his own guitar. It wasn't a bad guitar. I think I only paid $5 for it."

Whenever he could, Gene would pick up the guitar and practice. He was soon picking out tunes, but there was one song he could never master, much to his chagrin. "For all of his talent there was a song he couldn't play the way Dad could," reveals David, "and that was 'Under the Double Eagle.' Dad could play it in double time and Gene never could and that used to make Gene just furious. He could play it in straight time, but he couldn't play it in double time. At dances when he was younger, Dad would start off playing it real slow and gradually pick it up until he had it going at double time, and fast double time, too. I heard him do that many times when I was young."

For the shy young man, music became a form of expression and he took to it like a duck to water. Friends and family both recall Gene having a gift for melody early on. "Gene was always singing," David recalls. "He would practice his parts for the choir at home. Then he would hear something off the radio and sing that. Basically most of it was country music—Hank Snow, Sons of the Pioneers, stuff like that. He even got to the point where he got inventive and he started making up his own songs. He was probably ten or 11 years old by then. We would have these campfire songs and he would strum along with his guitar and we would sing things he was familiar with. One of the first originals that I can recall of his was called 'Big Chief Hole in the Pants,' about a chief who danced too close to the campfire and burned a hole in his pants."

Inspired by his father and older brother, David, too, took up a musical instrument, though to less success than Gene. "I never did really play the guitar, but I had a cello at one time that I decided I was going to play. I did all right for being 11 or 12 years old, but Gene thought it would make an interesting guitar so he took the bridge out of it and he restrung the thing and set it up like a guitar and played it like a vertical guitar. He could make sounds out of it that I couldn't as a cello."

Once television arrived in the Clark home, a Christmas gift from Kelly and Jeanne to the whole family, one of the first images on the tiny black-and-white screen transfixed Gene and set the course for his life. "After Gene saw Elvis, all he wanted to be was a rock star," laughs Bonnie. "He admired Elvis Presley greatly. He even styled himself quite a bit after Elvis. He was in a competition at school and one of the critiques they had of him was that he had imitated Elvis too much."

Gene had already begun to compose his own songs, but Elvis became his template. "I remember him coming into my room and saying, 'I've got this song I want you to listen to,'" Bonnie recalls, "and he would sit on the bed and he'd play the guitar for me. This was a song he wrote. This was junior high for him, high school for me. But by then he was becoming more sure of himself in his world. We were more like equals by then."

One of Gene's early Elvis-inspired compositions was "Blue Ribbons." Bonnie clearly remembers, "'Blue Ribbons' was a deliberate imitation of Elvis." In his deepest melancholy tone, Gene laments a lost love over a basic 1950s ballad-style, four-chord pattern with a minor chord twist thrown in (a later trademark of his songwriting style), strummed on an acoustic guitar:

"Well, I'll always love you to eternity. There's a story that must be told, 'bout a girl with a heart of gold. Now she's gone away it seems, someone else will hold my dreams. Oh, blue ribbons that remind me of you. Well, I'll trade those ribbons for a love that is true."

Written and recorded when Gene was 14 years of age, "Blue Ribbons" was committed to tape in Jack and David Godden's living room. "My dad took over WHB radio and built a recording studio, Artist Recording Studios," states David. "Gene loved the fact that my dad had a tape recorder in his house. So he loved to come over and perform, to see what he sounded like on tape. He had a great voice. I have a tape of Gene in our living room. It's a terrible production, but it's Gene singing 'Shenandoah' in our house. It was fantastic." One of those sessions resulted in the tape of "Blue Ribbons." Originally given to Jeanne Clark, the tiny reel-to-reel tape has survived and is now in the possession of Gene's sons, Kelly and Kai. "We found it in a very old box among his things after he died," reveals Kai. "The tape is from the 1950s. It was probably done when he was in high school. He wrote it himself. He sounds a little like Elvis and a little like Hank Williams. As far as we know it's the first recording he ever did."

In his freshman year at Raytown High School, Gene formed his first band with fellow classmates Joe Meyers on lead guitar, Joe's brother, Mike, on bass, and Eddie Hitchcock on drums. Gene played guitar and sang. The shy boy soon found himself the center of attention and female admiration, while fronting Joe Meyers and the Sharks. "Joe Meyers and the Sharks were a typical, very young garage band," recalls David Clark. "They could make some noises that sounded reasonably like music some times." In short order, the group became a popular attraction at church basement Catholic Youth Organization (CYO) dances and sock hops at the Coke Bar in Grandview, south of Raytown. "It was almost like a converted chicken shack that someone had turned into a teenage hangout because there was no place for kids to go," Bonnie smiles.

"Joe Meyers was one of the greatest lead guitarists," insists Jack. "Oh my gosh, could he play that guitar. I couldn't believe that he didn't pursue a career. Eddie Hitchcock was one of the best drummers we ever heard. I don't know what happened to him. Before Eddie there was another drummer, but he didn't get along with Joe so we found Eddie. Everybody loved to come and hear them. You couldn't get into the Coke Bar, it was so packed. The music was outstanding and everybody would stand around the bandstand and watch. Gene's voice was outstanding and they went crazy over him. Gene and Joe were always out in front and Eddie and Mike behind them. Joe eventually got Gene hooked up with an electric guitar. I would always have to stand in the back and tell them if the bass or the guitars were too loud. They would plug Gene's mic into the guitar amp." Accounts of the Sharks appearing on local television and recording a single are exaggerated. "It was just about having fun," Jack smiles. "Nobody looked at it as a career."

The Sharks' repertoire was your typical late '50s rock 'n' roll fare, everything from Elvis, Buddy Holly, and Little Richard to guitar instrumentals and pop ballads. But Gene was always the focal point. "They played rock and mild music in between rock and wild music," Jack muses. "Gene was the lead singer and had a fabulous voice. Joe couldn't carry a tune. That's when Gene went from being shy to all those women who stood around and listened to him. After the gig was over there was no problem picking up any women, that's for sure. He was a performer and he would even sing to his dates." Bonnie agrees that being onstage transformed her brother. "Gene kind of came alive onstage then. He needed an audience, he really did. But as far as one-on-one communication, that wasn't very good. His method of communication was a lot like Dad through his music. Mom was really good with language and Dad was good with music so Gene kind of got a combination of the two of them."

Bonnie chuckles as she recalls one of Gene's adoring fans. "I can remember this CYO dance and there was this cute little girl in her little matching sweater and skirt outfit and her little Ox-fords on and a bow in her bouffant hair just staring cow-eyed, swooning at Gene as he's singing 'Blue Moon' and I'm feeding him the words from the side of the stage."

"He was always dating the same girls as I was," Jack grins. "At first he was shy, but not after he got into the band. We ran around with one girl all the time that both of us really adored, Jody Hogsett. Her dad was the head prosecutor for Kansas City. Joe also started going with Jody, but Gene and I really liked her, too. We ran around with all the Catholic girls, mainly."

"He had lots of girls interested in him," adds Bonnie. "He was very attractive, but he was also terribly shy. But that didn't matter because the girls would approach him. I can remember one crush he had on a girl named Nancy Desenaux, of French extraction. She was very pretty, very stunning, but she was kind of like Max-Factor pretty, painted-on pretty. He used to ask me questions about her and that's how I knew of his interest in her. He got mixed up with this little so-ciety chick whose mother didn't like him because she felt he would never amount to anything. After he performed at Carnegie Hall with the New Christy Minstrels he called me up and said, 'I wonder how her mother would like me now?! She thought I would never be anything.'"

An unlikely booster of Joe Meyers and the Sharks was a local priest who began to promote the four teenagers for CYO dances, going so far as to party with the boys on occasion. "Father John Giacopelli, he was the one who went with us to every CYO dance," Jack remembers. "The bookings all went through the church with Father John. We were very close to Father John. He enjoyed being with all of us. He was just like one of the kids. We had a big wreck on Eighty-seventh Street, he was driving too fast, Father John, around some curves and he flipped that car with six of us in it. Gene was in the backseat with me and Joe Meyers. The car flipped and rolled seven times. He was going about 80 miles an hour. The whole front top was caved in. The only person that got hurt was Joe and he only had a scratch on him. We said it's 'cause we were riding with a priest. But the car was demolished. It was in the paper, the *Kansas City Star,* about the wreck. Talk about a wild priest! He was drinking quite a bit. That's when we did have that wreck."

In August 1960 the Clarks uprooted and headed back across the Missouri River to the sedate, rural community of Bonner Springs, Kansas, just west of Kansas City along Highway 32 at Highway 7 in Wyandotte County. When the Clarks moved to their new home at 410 West Second Street, Bonner Springs was considered a suburb of Kansas City but still far enough away, about 35 miles at that time, to be considered rural.

Employed by Jug McSpadden at the Victory Hills Golf Course on the Kansas side of the city, Kelly soon teamed up with Jug to build Dubs Dread, a golf course north of Bonner Springs in what was once Piper, Kansas (now absorbed into Kansas City). While Jug arranged the financing, Kelly designed and built the course. "Dad was not so much the architect as the person who made the dream happen," suggests Bonnie, who did not make the move with the family, having recently enlisted in the military and become the first of the Clark siblings to leave the nest. "He was the guy who kept the machinery operating. They built that golf course with secondhand machinery."

"My dad had the greenest thumb of any guy I ever knew," boasts Rick. "He was an expert on agriculture, horticulture, and turf management. Later on, people from golf courses all over the United States would call him up for advice. He was quite an authority. He was really into horticulture and made a greenhouse out of the back porch where he grew all kinds of exotic plants."

Though still tiny for 14 people (with Bonnie now gone), the new house did provide more living space as well as acceptability and independence. They were no longer reliant on the generosity of the municipality for housing or the ridicule of the community for their lifestyle. In Bonner Springs, the Clarks were just another family, albeit an unusually large one. "It was a two-story," Bonnie describes, "and it was arranged so that there was a living room and a parlor across the front of the house. Then there was a kind of dining area behind, but those areas all shifted depending on what stage the family was in, what use was needed for it. When I came back and moved in with the folks in 1967 we used the parlor as our bedroom for about nine months. Later, as the family grew smaller, the dining area was moved over to where the living room used to be and the kitchen was remodeled. There used to be two stairways up and down, in the front and back. When the house was remodeled around 1970, the one in the back was closed off. Upstairs, the girls all had one bedroom and the boys all had one bedroom. Gene didn't have his own room." Adds Rick, "We were all kind of stacked up in bunk beds upstairs while Mom and Dad's bedroom was downstairs."

Despite a more comfortable residence, the move brought new stresses and strains to the already delicate family fabric. "When we lived in Swope Park that little house that we lived in was part of Dad's pay," emphasizes Bonnie. "Up until the time they moved out to Bonner Springs I don't think he had ever had to pay a mortgage. Now he had a lot of new financial responsibilities. He had an obviously retarded daughter who was raising havoc with the whole family, and he had the responsibility of helping Jug build a golf course out there."

The move to Bonner Springs had a profound impact on Gene's life, tearing him away from the security of Swope Park and his friendships in Raytown. "Gene as a teenager was almost a split story in itself," reflects his brother David. "Growing up in the Swope Park area was a whole different scene than the transition to Bonner Springs. When we first went to Bonner

Springs we had left that virgin paradise where we could do just about anything we wanted to. Now we were confined to a postage-stamp yard. The house was bigger, a lot more room and I got lost in it the first time I was in it, but town living was different. There was competition. Gene was a good-looking fellow and a lot of the other fellows didn't like the interest Gene generated with the girls around town. There were a lot of conflicts and Gene was a tough kid. He could probably out-Indian wrestle anyone, but he wasn't well schooled in fisticuffs. He could knock your daylights out if he got a shot at you, but some of these people were more schooled in that and he got an education in it pretty quickly. So did all of us, which was something we did not enjoy."

The children missed the freedom of Swope Park and their own exclusive playground. "The only outlet we had now to simulate what we had left behind was the riverbanks of the Kaw River," David continues. "We spent time running up and down the banks of the river whenever we could. There weren't the same chores because we didn't have the acreage, but it shifted to more of a work life: school and work. As soon as Gene could drive and he would be out of school for the day or for the summer, he went to the golf course to put in a few hours in the evening. Unlike most teenagers, Gene never worked any other jobs like at a service station."

School was different now as well, and Gene's interests were channeled in a more practical direction. "He made very good grades in industrial arts in school and was very well liked by the industrial arts teachers," notes David. "One of the things that catapulted me toward industrial arts was Gene's success in it. I followed much the same pattern of school life he did. We dodged all the curriculum we could and spent most of our time in the school shop or somewhere else." David believes that if Gene had not pursued a career in music he might have made an excellent machinist or welder, as he enjoyed working with machines. His interest in music, however, drew him to join the Bonner Springs High School boys glee club, where he managed to overcome his shyness long enough to sing a solo for the girls glee club. He also developed a friendship with John Saunders, or J.D. as he was known, and the two would often go cruising in Gene's red and white 1958 Pontiac Chieftan. J.D. lived in Tonganoxie, west of Bonner Springs, and was a bit of a rabble-rouser with a mouth to match. Jeanne Clark was not fond of her son's new acquaintance and barred him from the Clark house.

The Sharks had already folded by the time Gene left Raytown. His rock 'n' roll aspirations were on hold as the family settled into their new surroundings, and Gene set about establishing himself in the community. While Jack Godden continued to make the trip out to Bonner Springs two or three times a week to hang out with Gene, the two would soon drift apart. Jack recalls that Gene was in another rock 'n' roll group in Raytown called the Royals, but has no recollection of who the members were or if they ever performed.

Gene's next musical endeavor following graduation from Bonner Springs High School in June of 1962 was a folk group known as the Rum Runners. Like the Royals, little is known of this aggregation. "The Rum Runners was a prelude to the Surf Riders," suggests David, who vaguely remembers this short-lived combo. "They were a 'Michael Row the Boat Ashore' coffeehouse folk group, Kingston Trio, Limeliters kind of stuff; really folkie kind of stuff. Gene got into that for a while and he did it for a while. What people don't realize is that Gene tried a myriad of things, which is obvious in his later music. But once he got where he wanted to go with this particular type of music, whether it was 'Michael Row the Boat Ashore,' the folk thing, then he was ready to move on and some of the people he would be with weren't ready to move on."

The folk boom had hit America by the late '50s after the Kingston Trio popularized traditional folk ballads like "Tom Dooley," bringing what had been the preserve of college campus hootenannies and Greenwich Village coffeehouses to the pop charts and mass appeal. Once the commercial possibilities were evident, the floodgates opened and innumerable folk ensembles with generic names like the Ramblin' Four and Rovin' Five (parodied superbly in Christopher Guest's film *A Mighty Wind*) surfaced, as former Elvis acolytes traded in their electric guitars and Scotty Moore licks for acoustic instruments and "hummin' and a-strummin'." Joan Baez became the role model for the poker-straight haired female folk followers and Bob Dylan soon emerged as the template for all the blue-jeaned, fleece-lined jacketed Woody Guthrie clones. Like many other teens across America, Gene found himself drawn to the simple virtues of folk music where more often the message transcended the beat. Singing of the verdant fields of colonial America, Appalachian mining disasters, or Civil War glories had far more appeal for an imaginative young man than "Peggy Sue." The folk movement had yet to morph into the topical song/protest idiom.

A chance encounter with an existing folk trio brought Gene his next musical move. Gene was working full-time at Dubs Dread with no particular plans for his immediate future. With J.D. in tow, Gene briefly moved out of his parents' house, staying with various friends until later returning home. Armed with a fake ID, doctored by a girlfriend to get him into the nightclubs of Kansas City where the drinking age was still 21 (she transformed the last 4 in 1944 into a 1— hence the lifelong, erroneous reference to his 1941 birthday), Gene was in the Castaways Lounge at 4334 Main Street when he heard the Surf Riders.

In an unpublished 1987 interview with Jon Butcher, Gene described how he came to be a Surf Rider. "Around 1962 I started getting into folk music because of the huge success of the Kingston Trio and Peter, Paul & Mary. I loved the harmony. I also was a big Limeliters fan. There was a group in town called the Surf Riders and I went to see them a couple of times. I had another group called the Rum Runners, we picked the name because it sounded folkie, and we were playing in a club on opposite nights to the Surf Riders. The Surf Riders were the big deal for the college crowd in town. This was about my last couple of years in high school. Two of the guys were graduating, one guy was going off to be a doctor and the other guy was going off to do something else so there was one guy left that wanted a musical career. And he asked me if I wanted to join and I said 'Sure.' So that was me and two other guys."

Jimmy Glover was a member of the Surf Riders and, while not disputing Gene's version, clarifies how the underage Bonner Springs resident came to join the group. "There were three of us, Mike Crum, who was professionally known as Mike Crowley, myself, and Gene Clark. That wasn't the original lineup. The actual start up of the band had to do with Mike Crum and three other guys, not including me. As those guys went into college, they dropped out. Then Mike took me and we were a duo for a very short period of time. And then Gene came in. Gene was driving a tractor on a golf course when we met him. We had heard of him, so obviously we must have known about the Rum Runners. So we took him in and he became a part of the group pretty fast. I think we introduced him as 'straight off the tractor, Gene Clark.'" Jimmy believes the Rum Runners was strictly an amateur outfit. For Gene, elevation to the Surf Riders was his first professional experience. "The Surf Riders pretty much had that particular market, the folk music thing, sewed up in Kansas City at that time. We played every night at the Castaways. We were a good group and we lined them up every night and were a phenomenon in Kansas City." Adds David Clark, "They got very good reviews and they went to places like some resorts on Lake of the Ozarks and a club in Oklahoma City. They got kind of regional and went to places like Wichita and Topeka all the time, while Gene was still working as much as he could at the golf course."

Often mistaken by music writers as a surfing music combo, the Surf Riders derived their name not from the surfboard craze popularized at the time by the Beach Boys but from the décor of the Castaways Lounge, which was in pretty much a *Pirates of the Caribbean* motif. *Kansas City Star* writer Brian Burnes notes that "papier-mâché palm trees decorated the interior, and beach sand was spread here and there." As Mike Crowley recalled shortly before his death, "We dressed up in three-quarter-length cutoff pants and Hawaiian shirts, just to go with the décor."

Gene became the attraction in the Surf Riders, both for his commanding voice and ruggedly handsome athletic appearance. As Mike told Burnes, "Gene had a big, booming voice, a very nice polished sound for such a young kid." Jimmy Glover concurs. "Gene had a very good voice at that particular time. We had three-part harmony but Gene was pretty much the lead singer. He didn't have great guitar skills, but he had an outstanding voice and a huge ability to write a song, even just on a whim. He could put together a song in no time at all. He wowed all the girls, that's for sure. Gene had a ton of girl appeal. He'd sit down and write a song about them and they would go crazy." Although already an experienced songwriter, Jimmy does not recall Gene putting any of his own compositions forward for the group. "We mainly did Kingston Trio stuff, Chad Mitchell Trio, and other folk things. We didn't do any original stuff at all." In terms of stage presence however, Gene took a back seat to the others. "Gene didn't talk much the audience. He pretty much just sang. Mike talked to the audience. Mike and I engaged the audience with comedy and Gene was the entertainer. He was the good-looking one, I was the 'jerk around,' and Mike was the good musician. Those were kind of our roles. Gene was the straight man."

And how did Gene get along with Mike and Jimmy? "He was kind of reserved then, shy and not a party guy," Jimmy recalls. "The way I remember him was when everyone was partying he was in the other room writing those songs."

Gene's talent and focus was *not* about to go unnoticed.

O n the evening of August 12, 1963, Gene Clark's life changed forever with an offer he hardly needed to think about twice. It was the golden opportunity the 18-year-old had always dreamed of. Plus it was a lifeline out of a dead-end future like his father's, and an escape from an increasingly strained situation at home, where 11 siblings ranged in age from four months to 17 years.

Singer Barry McGuire relates the event that brought Gene into the folk act at the top of the US pop charts. "The New Christy Minstrels were in Kansas City playing the Starlight Theatre, a big outdoor theatre, and one evening one of our members, Nick Woods, was out running around Kansas City. He went into a club or bar and there was a group in there singing and he was knocked out. He came right back and got the rest of us. 'You've got to come with me and hear this.' So about four or five of us went over to the bar to see this guy, and it was Gene Clark. He was part of this folk group. Gene had intensity, a charisma and focus, a look that was absolutely captivating. He had that little quirky kind of smile and a brooding intensity. You couldn't take your eyes off him. He would just stand there and put his chin down a little bit and kind of look up under his eyebrows at you and nail you. We needed another member in the group at that time, we had a member who was leaving, Dolan Ellis, and we all agreed that Gene was the guy because he sang great and his stage presence was phenomenal."

"It was a Lana Turner story," beams Bonnie. "Opportunity knocked and he stepped right into it. He had finished high school by then but he was still just 18 and living at home." As Gene himself recalled years later, "That was right when 'Green Green' was a hit and they [the New Christy Minstrels] were really on top at the time. Of course, I wasn't going to turn down something like that—it was right out of the movies. 'Kid, do you want to go to Hollywood and be a star?' So I said, 'Sure, I'd love to.' So I hopped on a plane and was gone."

It was literally that fast. New Christy Minstrels Svengali Randy Sparks had been impressed enough with Gene, and in desperate need of a quick replacement, that he offered the Kansas teenager a position in the ten-member ensemble that very same night. The next evening, Gene made a guest appearance with the Christies at the Starlight Theatre.

Gene bid farewell at a family gathering the following afternoon and boarded a plane for California later that day. "We were having a family reunion out at Wyandotte County Lake and it was all in preparation. Mom was busy getting all the foodstuffs together. We had these reunions about once a year. And Gene said goodbye to all of us at that family reunion and he was gone." As Jeanne told the *Kansas City Star*'s Brian Burnes, "We knew if we put our foot down and said no, that he would do it anyhow. So he joined the world."

"If Gene hadn't taken that opportunity when it came up," David Godden postulates, "he would probably have stayed in Kansas City and worked at a golf course like his dad." No one knew that better than Gene. "If Gene would have said no, they would have simply gone on to the next town and found somebody else," asserts Jimmy, who, along with Mike, was later recruited by Sparks for two of his other outfits, the Green Grass Group (Jimmy) and the Back Porch Majority (Mike).

Gala Chambers, Gene's girlfriend from the east side of Kansas towards Independence, encouraged Gene to take the plunge. "She was a little older than Gene and a knockout," recalls David Clark. "She was the catalyst for him going into the Christies. She saw it as a great opportunity for him."

The recollection some 40 years later of his brother's departure still moves David to tears. "Mom, of course, was disturbed very much about it. She feared a lot of things. Dad had had enough interaction with people back in his early years through his own music thing that he knew what the possibilities were, both negative and positive, and he wasn't exactly happy. But he was more than willing to see Gene go his own way. He was like that with every one of us: 'It's your life, go live it. You do what you want with it.'"

2

Set You Free This Time

Throughout his life, Gene Clark tended to compartmentalize his situations and circumstances, isolating one facet of his career, family, or circle of friends from another, as if one might somehow contaminate the other. When he moved to Bonner Springs in 1960 he virtually disavowed his earlier life in Swope Park and Raytown, rarely speaking of it and severing the relationships he enjoyed as a boy, with the exception of Jack Godden, though that, too, soon waned. When he joined the Surf Riders, whose popularity was centered round a Kansas City nightclub, few of his Bonner Springs acquaintances knew he was in the group nor did much of his family see him perform at the Castaways Lounge. Members of the Surf Riders knew little of his family situation and background. Those were two compartments that did not meet.

When he boarded that plane bound for California in August of 1963 Gene left behind him not only Kansas but his life in Kansas, and he seldom looked back. He closed that door as he stepped through a new one—a new locale, new career, new life, new persona—unencumbered by his past. Phone calls and letters home were infrequent. Although from time to time he would revisit memories of that past for inspiration, recalling in his mind simpler times, he rarely physically returned. Those occasions were few, yet no less memorable. For all intents and purposes Gene left his past behind. His sights were firmly affixed straight ahead. "If he was done with something it was behind him and he wanted to move on to something else," acknowledges David Clark. The events that would unfold in Gene's young life over the next two years, changes that would ultimately shape and define his entire career, went largely unseen by his family back home.

Gene joined the New Christy Minstrels in 1963—at the peak of their career. Among the myriad of rooftop, new colony, travelin,' ramblin,' and rovin' multi-voiced, hootenanny-folk aggregations that found fleeting fame and fortune in the brief heyday of the folk music boom, the Christies were the undisputed kingpins. Named for the Christy Minstrels, an organization in the 1840s that popularized African-American spirituals (often in blackface) and ballads of the day, the group was founded by Los Angeles-based folksinger Randy Sparks. He revived the name and concept in 1960, and employed his wife, Jackie Miller, and friend Nick Woods, along with a revolving door of personnel. Dolan Ellis and Art Podel became mainstays early on, but the group didn't really break out until singer Barry McGuire signed on and lent his gravelly vocal style to folk era classics like "Green Green," propelled by Nick's strident 12-string guitar picking on "Green Back Dollar" and "Saturday Night" (on which Gene would make his debut). The group became mainstays on the thriving college circuit as well as on national television including *The Andy Williams Show* and an extended engagement on ABC-TV's *Hootenanny*, all the while operating under the iron fist of Sparks. Besides Gene and Barry McGuire, who would find even greater acclaim as the voice of social conscience on "Eve of Destruction," other illustrious Christies who passed through the ranks at one time or another include Jerry Yester of the Lovin' Spoonful, Larry Ramos of the Association, Kenny Rogers (and several other members of his group The First Edition), and Kim Carnes. Overtly anti-political, the Christies went out of their way to offer wholesome family entertainment by homogenizing folk standards and Broadway show tunes for mass pop appeal. "We sang to everyone, from eight to 80," boasts Larry Ramos. "The Christy Minstrels were showbiz. Everybody understood what we were singing. The Christies brought people who might not have been folk music fans to that music." It was a winning formula and the youthful enthusiasm and fresh faces of the group members embodied the optimistic Camelot spirit of the Kennedy years. (The Beatles put the nail in the collective coffin for 'folk-lite' acts like the Christies in 1964, though they lurched on for a few more years.)

Gene's first recording session with the group was for the title track to the film *The Wheeler-Dealers*. Although his face graces the cover of their *Merry Christmas* album, his voice does not appear on any of the tracks, as it was cut a few weeks prior to his joining. With the Christies, recording sessions were sandwiched between tours and it seemed the group was constantly out on the road. "It was a grueling experience," Larry attests. "We averaged over 300 dates a year for three years running. I knew when my wife was going to have the babies because she was going to have a C-section. So I was home, I was there for the birth, saw the babies, kissed my wife goodbye, and went back on the road—not missing one show. Next time I saw my children was six months later." For Gene, an 18-year-old who had never been on an airplane before, the travel regimen was daunting though quite exhilarating initially. As Jeanne Clark reminisced to *Kansas City Star* reporter Brian Burnes about Gene's call to the family from Hawaii, "He was a kid in a candy store. He just kept saying, 'I can't believe this.'"

Rick Clark recalls with pride the time Gene came to nearby Lawrence, Kansas, for a gig with the Christies. "We all got dressed up and there are photographs of us all in my mom and dad's den getting ready to go see them in ties and jackets. That was a big deal at that time in Kansas City. All the local papers ran stories about the local boy who made good."

The assassination of President Kennedy on November 22 forced several cancelled bookings and Gene took the opportunity to come home for a visit, his first since leaving in August. "I was looking forward to seeing him because we were close in age and we had been comrades build-

The New Christy Minstrels in the fall of 1963 with Gene in the middle row, center, Larry Ramos above him on banjo, and Barry McGuire in the front row, center.

ing forts together," recalls David, who noted a change in his brother. "But when he came home he kind of had an air about him. He had been places and seen things. He had money in his pocket and he was a different person. He was dressed real snazzy, preppy hair cut, his Chicago trench coat, and he comes into a house that doesn't even have enough lampshades to cover all the bare bulbs. He kind of came off to me like he had an attitude about him. We were going to go some place so I went and put on the best clothes I had, which wasn't that much, and came downstairs to go with him. He says to me, 'Is that what you're wearing?' And I said, 'Yeah, why?' And he told me, 'Well, I just as soon you wouldn't go if that's what you're wearing.' So I said, 'That's all I've got to wear. What's the matter with you?' And he wadded up a twenty-dollar bill and chucked it at me and said, 'Go uptown and buy yourself some clothes and then we'll go.' I just thought, 'Where the hell do you come off with this shit?' Everybody noticed the difference in him. I threw the twenty-dollar bill back at him and at that point I think it kind of brought him back to reality and he apologized. We were glad he was successful, but he had no right to come home and act like God Almighty. I had shared a bed with him, ate out of the same plate, drank out of the same glass, and froze in the same room at night with him. We all shared rooms. At one time there were seven of us boys sharing two rooms, bunk beds, of course. None of us had any privacy until we left home and that's one of the catalysts for Gene leaving when he got that offer."

In early December the group was in New York to perform at Carnegie Hall and record *Land of Giants,* Sparks's ambitious pet project incorporating America's best-loved folk tales like John Henry, Johnny Appleseed, and Casey Jones into popular song (released in mid-1964 after Gene had left the group). Before Christmas the Christies were special guests on wacky comedian Jonathan Winters's television special. "We all gathered around the TV to watch," enthuses Rick Clark. "It was a Christmas special and Gene was the one who brought a bicycle out for Jonathan Winters for a Christmas present. Talk about proud." Boasts Bonnie, "I realized that he was a big star when they came through Tallahassee. I was completely blown away. Here was my little brother who had been trying to be a star ever since he was 12 years old and he's up there with the New Christy Minstrels who were the biggest thing at the time. This was before the Beatles."

On January 14, 1964, the New Christy Minstrels were special guests of President Lyndon Johnson at the White House for a state dinner honoring the President of Italy. "It was a wintry, snowy season," Barry recounts. "They flew us in from Denver and we were the only plane to land in Washington that night because the airport had shut down. We landed by presidential order because we were the entertainment at the White House. 'Get that plane down!' We drove in a blizzard to our hotel. We walked into the White House and nobody even looked in our guitar cases! Kennedy had just been shot two months before. We were the first group in the White House after that. We could have had anything in those guitar cases. It's funny when you consider the security nowadays."

After the concert, the band members were joined out on the town by some illustrious company. "We partied around Washington and Linda Bird Johnson and Lucy Baines Johnson, the president's two daughters, came out with us," chuckles Larry. "Those poor gals had Secret Service guys with them all the time. They could never do anything. When one of them would get kind of out there, one of the Secret Service guys would tell her, 'At ease,' and they would straighten up. These two girls were real Texan girls."

Despite the acclaim and attention—not to mention steady paycheck—that accrued from being in a successful group, nothing could dispel the reality that Gene was little more than one voice among nine others, a faceless chorus member, and not likely to enjoy center stage or record his own compositions. As ensemble member Gayle Caldwell told Christies historian Tom Pickles, "I quite well remember Gene Clark's initiation into the Christy craze; he was not nourished, supported, encouraged, or appreciated. With Dolan's exit, perhaps the guys felt that they needed no one else and considered Gene superfluous."

Randy Sparks soon recognized that Gene was no replacement for Dolan Ellis. "Dolan was a phenomenon himself," notes Barry. "No one was like Dolan. That's the problem when people try to compare people. Gene was a whole different kind of fruit than Dolan Ellis." As Randy told reporter Burnes, "Dolan was such a performer, with so much energy. Gene Clark was not that kind of personality. He was a very good singer who played the guitar adequately, but there was no flash. The idea was that their testosterone level would rise to the occasion. I came from old-fashioned show business, where you walked out and killed them." To Randy, Gene just couldn't rise to that same level. "He didn't evolve like I expected him to."

Inherent in the Christies' performance dynamic was a healthy competition. Each member sought to step forward and be featured in a song or two and the jostling for positions could become fierce. In addition, each member had a particular role or personality that they brought to the performance. "It was all very well orchestrated and choreographed," notes Larry. "Everyone had a role to play in the group and when somebody left we had to find someone to fill that role besides having the same vocal range, like replacing a tenor with a tenor. So there was a reason for pigeonholing people in the group." Ensemble members do not recall Gene being assertive enough to out-maneuver the more outspoken members. And when he did step forward, Gene's shyness and low-key stage manner, relying on the strength of the song and his voice rather than any contrived showbiz routine, paled against the more overt personalities in the group. "Randy remembers that Gene tended to withdraw into the ranks onstage rather than respond to the challenge to bring a dimension to the show, in sharp contrast to Dolan, who was a very flashy personality onstage," maintains Pickles. "Also, his style was not very different from that of Nick Woods, a key opinion leader in the group and, frankly, a much stronger vocalist. The result was that Nick had far more step outs in the arrangements than Gene did. Furthermore, whenever Gene did have a step out, he didn't really bring anything new to the arrangement, more or less a mild echo of Nick."

"Gene didn't have much schtick," the late Mike Crowley suggested, "and the New Christy Minstrels were all seasoned performers. They were looking for something from Gene that he couldn't give them."

For the other members of the ensemble, Gene remained an enigma. "I don't remember Gene socializing much with the other people in the Christies," offers Barry. "We performed together, traveled together, ate together, and then we lived across the street from each other, but I never really knew Gene. We were like casual acquaintances even though we worked together. We had a common bond in our music and I loved him and felt he loved me, but we never spent any real time getting to know each other. Gene was always a mystery." Gayle Caldwell recalls Gene as "a shy, sly, sensitive, closed, but rich-voiced man with great musical instincts." Adds Larry, "He was quiet and a loner. Very withdrawn within himself."

"I didn't think of Gene as a country boy," muses Barry. "He did a song about 'We'll run the ridges of our green land Tennessee,' and I used to love it when he sang that song. It felt like a real authentic moonshiner's song and he just nailed it. But I thought of him as a city guy because I met him in Kansas City. He dressed really stylishly and clean. I never knew about his background."

In addition to the competition within the group, the rigors of the road and the pace of the group began to take a toll on Gene. "Traveling with the Christies was a nightmare," sighs Barry. "Everyday you were up at five or six in the morning, get to the airport at seven, get on the plane at eight, fly to the next city, go to the hotel, then go to the auditorium, do the show, back to the hotel, get up the next morning, and do the same thing, day after day after day. Someone in New York introduced me to marijuana and that became my salvation from the Christy Minstrels because I would get loaded and just sit there in my cloudy dream world. It was just me and one other person who were doing marijuana in the group, not Gene." For Gene, the constant flying became a concern. "He was a white-knuckle flyer," Larry states, "definitely. If anything caused him to leave the group, it was all the traveling and flying. I was lucky; I loved flying. It never bothered me."

"Gene had a phobia of flying and, of course, that's what we did in the Christy Minstrels," continues Barry. "We flew every day. So he didn't stay in the group very long because he just couldn't handle getting on airplanes every day. He just wouldn't be there when the plane would be taking off. 'Where's Gene?' It frustrated our road manager, but the ensemble was so big that we could do it without one person, it didn't hurt. Gene never said he was leaving. Just one day he was gone. One day he was with us, and the next day he wasn't. The word was he wasn't working out and missing airplanes so we had to get rid of him."

On a tour across Canada in early February 1964, Gene heard the Beatles for the first time. Soon after, in Norfolk, Virginia, he found a jukebox that featured the Beatles and spent an evening pumping nickels into the machine, drinking in the vibrant new sound. "I couldn't really tell, but I knew they sounded different," Gene told Jon Butcher in a 1987 unpublished interview. "I had to investigate because there was so much talk of the Beatles all over the place. So when 'She Loves You' and 'I Want to Hold Your Hand' came out I played them all night long in this little coffee shop. I flipped out. 'She Loves You' had to be the greatest rock 'n' roll song I had *ever* heard. And I quit the Christies the next day and went back to L.A. to find a way to start a group like that because I thought that was it. I felt a vibration at the time that this wasn't just a fad. These guys were into something, something really powerful spiritually."

"It's a true story that he did hear the Beatles, that he did drop a lot of nickels into a jukebox and listen to that song over and over again," confirms David Clark. "And it wasn't that he was so enthralled with the Beatles, but he was trying to figure out how they were doing it. That's why he spent so much time listening to it. He told me he couldn't hear it on the radio so when he found a jukebox with it he played it over and over to figure out how to make that sound. That's what was really the catalyst."

The Beatles may have saved Gene from the humiliation of being fired. According to Tom Pickles, "Randy had concluded that Gene was not working out and had every intention of firing him. Most telling, Paul Potash from the Back Porch Majority had been hired to be his replacement as early as January of 1964. I suspect his much-quoted accounting of his decision to leave the Christies was a somewhat defensive whitewashing of the true dynamics at the time. If he did indeed quit, it was because he saw the writing on the wall and opted to beat Randy to the punch, by a very narrow margin of time."

"There was really no future for people to work with Randy," insists songwriter Daniel Moore, who befriended Gene in Los Angeles when Daniel was a member of the Fairmount Singers, a rival folk ensemble. "There was no piece of the pie. He paid good salaries to people, but that was it. Randy was a real good guy as long as you were working for him. But there was no future and I think Gene realized that."

The Christies' home base was Los Angeles and during their limited off time the group would return there. Randy owned a five-bedroom ranch house in Encino in the San Fernando Valley. Equipped with bunk beds, it was dubbed the Folk House as members of his various ensembles stayed there while off the road. Daniel also resided at the Folk House when not touring. "Gene was pretty young, so was I, and he was kind of a jock, swarthy, very healthy, and a real sweet guy. He looked like he could have been a running back in football. He was really in good shape, and with a real nice singing voice. He was just a happy-go-lucky guy, good sense of humor. He was kind of a country boy, he didn't seem like a big city guy. He and I got together one weekend when we were both in town and wrote a couple of songs. Then a few months later he was out of the Christies and he ended up staying at our house."

With little more than his 12-string guitar, a wardrobe of stylish clothes, an old 1955 Ford convertible, and a dream to play Beatle-style music, Gene set out in search of kindred spirits. "He thought the Christy Minstrels music was kind of square, which it was," recalls Daniel. "The Beatles knocked the pins out of it right around that time. That transformation from 1963 to 1964 was pretty fast. Boom! The folk scene was gone. I got back to L.A. in November and went to the Troubadour and the folk scene was over."

Judy Moll worked at the Troubadour—the best-known folk club in Los Angeles—and recalls the night the universe changed. "One night in early 1964 all these Capitol Records people were going around with these badges saying 'The Beatles are coming!' with four little moptop haircuts on the badges and everybody was saying, 'What's a Beatle?' We didn't know it at the time but that was the end of the folk world that night."

"Gene had already done the folkie thing with the Surf Riders and New Christy Minstrels and he was already looking for something else," notes David Clark. "The New Christy Minstrels were good for him. It gave him that professionalism and became his ticket to ride. It unlocked some doors for him that might not have otherwise been unlocked. But nonetheless, that's not where he was at or what he was interested in at the time. He told me that." What Gene was interested in was British Invasion rock 'n' roll.

The impact of the Beatles on the culture of North America cannot be overstated. Quite simply, they altered the very fabric of society. No one under the age of 25 was immune to their pervasive influence, whether in music, fashion, or hairstyle. Those few Luddites who resisted would find themselves swept under a rushing tide. But the revolution in music the Beatles created was, in fact, all too familiar to those who heard the Liverpool quartet's influences: Chuck Berry, Little Richard, Carl Perkins, the Shirelles, and Marvelettes, to name a few. What the Beatles did so well was to take American rock 'n' roll and R&B, filter it through English do-it-yourself folk skiffle and Hamburg Reeperbahn grit, add an accent, and throw it back at American teens eager for the next new thing. The folk music of the previous few years was cerebral; the Beatles were a jolt of electricity aimed a bit lower. Yet among their influences could be heard the strains of folk music. "I might have been one of the first people to dig what the Beatles were into musically," claims ex-folksinger turned Beatle acolyte Roger McGuinn. "In their chord changes I could see degrees of complexity that folk music had gotten to by that time, and it struck me as being a groovy thing. So I started singing their songs in coffeehouses."

A native of Chicago, James Joseph (later Roger) McGuinn III (born July 13, 1942) had discovered folk music in the late '50s after a brief fling with rock 'n' roll. An accomplished guitarist and banjo player, he had worked as an itinerant guitarist accompanying a variety of folk artists including Judy Collins, the Limeliters, the Chad Mitchell Trio, and even lounge lizard Bobby Darin during his brief folk fling. Somewhat of a fixture in folk music circles, he had rubbed shoulders with Bob Dylan in Greenwich Village and even auditioned for the New Christy Minstrels. "Jimmy McGuinn, that's what he was called back then," Larry laughs. "He took my place in the Christy Minstrels for *one day.* That was on a Sunday and on Monday I got a frantic call from Randy asking, 'Hey Larry, can you fill in?' And I asked, 'Why? What's wrong with Jimmy?' and Randy replied, 'Jimmy got picked up by Bobby Darin to go on tour.' I think he's in one publicity shot, but he never performed with the Christies at all. I found out later on that he was putting in his bio that he had been a member of the New Christy Minstrels for a couple of years. I just thought, 'What a liar.' "

Once the Beatles finally landed on America's shores, Roger was working as a songwriter in New York's fabled Brill Building, grinding out surfin' songs. Hearing the clarion call, he began integrating Beatles songs into his Greenwich Village baskethouse sets. "I was hanging out with the Holy Modal Rounders' Pete Stampfel and Steve Weber," Roger recalls. "Pete, Steve, and I were working at the same coffeehouse passing the hat around. I had been working with Bobby Darin as a guitar player and then he asked me to write songs with him in the Brill Building. My instructions were to listen to the radio and write songs like what we heard on the radio. At that point the Beatles came out and I was really enamored with the sound of the Beatles. They were mixing elements of folk and rock because they had been a skiffle band, but they were kind of doing it kind of subconsciously. They were shooting for a 1950s rock style, but they were blending a lot of things together, sort of under the hood. I don't think they really knew what they were doing. Anyway, I picked up on it and Pete, Steve, and

I would take these songs apart in the coffeehouses and say, 'Listen to this. They're doing fourth and fifth harmonies like bluegrass modal or Appalachian modal songs. This is really a cross between folk and rock. So that's the origins of folk-rock really. It started in Greenwich Village."

As Roger explained in Richie Unterberger's *Turn! Turn! Turn!: The '60s Folk-Rock Revolution*, the first book to explore in detail the evolution of the genre, "It was tremendously appealing to someone who had been in folk music and heard all these chord changes in folk music, and then heard them put into a different beat. They made it into, like, a heavy 4/4 beat."

In the spring of 1964, Troubadour owner Doug Weston hired McGuinn to open for Roger "King of the Road" Miller and Hoyt Axton. "I don't remember what month it was, but think it was the early spring. It was cold in New York when I left because I was wearing a black raincoat when I got off the plane in L.A." Roger brought his New York set list with him. "Here I was doing something that was rubbing people the wrong way, running contrary to the folk movement. I was in a folk music club playing Beatles songs, mixing up the Beatle beat with folk songs that I already knew. This was something that I started doing back in New York at the coffeehouses in Greenwich Village and then I brought it out to the Troubadour. I was really getting a terrible audience reaction, the total cold shoulder or 'The Freeze,' as Jack Kerouac used to put it. The folk purists absolutely hated what I was doing. It was blasphemy. They wanted to stone me or burn me at the stake. I remember Roger Miller taking me aside and saying, 'I see what you're doing up there and it's good but you'd get a lot further if you didn't get angry with the audience.'"

"McGuinn was the first guy who was like a total Beatles fan," acknowledges Judy Moll. "The minute he heard the Beatles he started playing Beatle tunes, regardless of the fact that everyone was making fun of him. He may have thought he was a visionary, but everyone thought he was goofy doing that. He would perform folk songs like 'Delia's Gone,' but to Beatle tunes. But there wasn't much of a crowd when he performed there. He would be in there periodically filling up time between acts. Most people thought he was a joke."

Gene Clark didn't think so.

With little happening in his own career, Gene was cooling his heels in the Troubadour one night when he chanced upon Roger. As Gene recalled the moment, "I met McGuinn there in the Folk Den and he was sitting in a corner strumming his 12-string guitar and singing a Beatle song and I thought, 'Man, this guy's got the right idea.' I went up to him and said, 'Look, do you mind if I play with you?' And he said, 'No. Have a seat.' I had a 12-string, too. And we went on for about three weeks like that, playing as a duet. We decided we'd become like a Peter and Gordon or something like that and be a duet, doing the English style. So we started writing songs immediately."

Roger was instantly taken with the young man from Kansas. "Gene struck me as a lumbering country boy who had an awful lot of talent," muses Roger. "I was 21, so I was a couple of years older than Gene, but he seemed more mature than 19. I didn't know he was 19. He seemed more like he was in his twenties. He seemed to have a more worldly attitude because he had just come off the road with the New Christy Minstrels. He'd been on the road with them and I guess he had run into a bit of difficulty, but he didn't really elaborate. My first impression was that he was a sympathetic soul. 'Wow, here's somebody who is really ahead of the curve here.' He was keen on the Beatles and for a member of the folk community that was a rare thing at the time. We had a common dream of doing something like Chad and Jeremy, maybe forming a pop duo. That was our goal. If it hadn't been for Gene discovering what I was doing at the Troubadour, the Byrds may never have happened."

Despite their mutual respect for the Beatles and a shared folk music experience, it's important to make some distinctions between Roger and Gene from the outset. While Gene may have appeared worldly to Roger, he was, in fact, much less so. Of the two, Roger was far more the savvy, experienced city boy. "We didn't talk about our pasts or our families," allows Roger. "We were more living in the now. He didn't tell me a lot of his background. I think he told me where he was from and it was obvious he was kind of a country boy. That was totally alien to me, having been brought up in Chicago and having just one brother." Also, in spite of—or perhaps as a result of—his New Christy Minstrels stint, Gene had hardly been a die-hard folkie steeped in Appalachian ballads and Celtic madrigals. Roger had the folk pedigree; Gene had the commercial pop folk experience. He would hardly be the one to suggest "The Bells of Rhymney" or "Turn! Turn! Turn!" Gene wanted to write and sing Beatles-inspired pop songs and had a knack for a turn of phrase in the boy-meets-girl genre. Roger sought to marry folk-influenced themes to a Beatles beat. He was far less likely to be able to write "I Knew I'd Want You" or "Here Without You." Their strength was that each brought their own unique sensibilities, experience, and perspective to the mix. "Gene wasn't really a folkie, you know," Roger clarifies, "so that's probably why he liked what I was doing, because it wasn't pure folk."

In subsequent years, the two have often been portrayed as having little in common other than music, and socializing rarely. In fact, despite their differing personalities, Gene and Roger developed both a mutual respect and friendship in their earliest days together. "We were both guitar playing, singing, writing people and we wanted to get a thing going," says Roger. "We were playing around in coffeehouses and running around trying to find places to play, and there weren't many. So we'd end up at somebody's house." Gene recalled, "I remember Hoyt Axton liked us and thought we had something going, as did a couple of other people. Everybody else was snobby toward us because they didn't like this Beatles stuff, the die-hard folkies."

What the duo lacked was a high harmony voice on top of theirs. While Gene's voice was rich and full, Roger's voice tended to be thin. The two blended well in unison and often doubled each other later in the Byrds, but they needed something more, and found it, again, at the Troubadour.

"We never got to the stage of performing as a duo," reveals Roger, detailing how David Crosby came onboard. "Actually Crosby came along quite quickly. The visual picture I have as I remember it—David tells it differently—is Gene and I were sitting out in the Folk Den, which was the front room of the Troubadour, at a table with our guitars and writing songs. And David walked in and started singing a harmony spontaneously and it sounded good." Despite the obvious musical attraction, Roger was wary of this interloper. "I had met David previously, in 1960, back when I was working with the Limeliters at the Ash Grove and David was an actor in, I believe, an Edward Albee play. He wasn't a singer yet, although he had a guitar and I was actually teaching him some chords and stuff. I showed him some Bob Gibson songs. And then he said, 'I'm going up to Santa Barbara to see my mom. Do you want to come along?' He had a convertible and so we went up to Santa Barbara together and I stayed at his house for a few days. I went to some parties with him and that's when I realized what kind of guy he was. People would be taking me aside and saying, 'What are you hanging out with a guy like that for?' So I kind of got the impression that he had some problems. I didn't hang out with him after that. So when David showed up at the Troubadour, yeah, he sounded good, but I didn't want to be in a group with him. I tried to tell Gene my experience with David, but it didn't matter to him. But the kicker was that David had access to Jim Dickson in the World Pacific Studios for free. That was enough to sway me over to saying, 'Well, David's got some problems, but with a free studio we can probably overlook his problems.'"

David Van Cortlandt Crosby's privileged upbringing was the antithesis of Gene Clark's meager Swope Park and Bonner Springs experience. Born on August 14, 1941, in Los Angeles to Academy Award-winning cinematographer Floyd Crosby and his wife, Aliph, young David grew up in the exclusive, well-heeled community of Santa Barbara. He attended private schools (where he was frequently expelled for misconduct) and debutante balls before enrolling in the Pasadena Playhouse acting school. Fleeing soon after to pursue a career as a folksinger, David followed the Woody Guthrie template, making his way to New York's Greenwich Village and Florida's Coconut Grove to ply his wares on the folk club circuit. Later arriving in San Francisco, he joined the Bay Area's emerging early '60s folk scene in the company of Dino Valenti, Paul Kantner, and David Freiberg. Returning to Los Angeles in 1963, a brief spell with commercial folk ensemble Les Baxter's Balladeers brought David his first notoriety.

Prowling the city's coffeehouses, he next encountered music business gadfly Jim Dickson. As talent scout-cum-producer-cum-manager and anything else in between, Dickson had earned a reputation on the L.A. folk scene for his work with the likes of Odetta, Hamilton Camp, and the Dillards, not to mention discovering the enigmatic Lord Buckley. Jim's additional credential was his access to World Pacific recording studios at 8713 West Third Street in Hollywood. Studio owner and friend Dick Bock allowed Jim free reign after hours to record whoever he managed to nab in the clubs and coffeehouses. "The way that I worked with all of those guys, Dino Valenti and David and others I was working with, was that I would tape them and if I could get them a deal we'd make a deal, and if I couldn't, I'd give them the tape," confirms Jim. David cut some demos for Jim in early 1964, but no record labels showed any interest. "I had told David that I thought he ought to be in a group," he continues. "I didn't tell him that I didn't think his voice had enough authority to be a lead singer, but that's what I had heard from Warner Brothers and others.

"David came to me saying he had met these two guys and would like to get a group going and he would sing harmony with them. If I got involved, David thought he could pull it off. So he brought them in to the studio where I first met them. I liked the way the three of them sounded together with acoustic guitars and it seemed like it would be worth working with them." With Jim Dickson and World Pacific studios to sweeten the deal, David threw his hat in the ring with Gene and Roger. The trio was christened the Jet Set after Roger's fixation with airplanes.

David recalls his initial impressions of Gene. "He was a pretty interesting guy, Gene. He was completely different from the rest of us. We were all different, but Gene was more different. He was from Missouri, a family of 12 or 13 kids. So he came from a place not only that we were unfamiliar with but that we didn't understand at all, and he was a very odd duck to us. He was a country boy in the big city and there was a sense of naïveté about him, but he was a deep country boy, a guy with very deep feelings. A very different kind of guy. And Gene was good looking, and athletic. If he took his shirt off anybody within a hundred yards would be looking at him. Athletic is a very polite way of putting it. He was a good-looking boy."

"The idea that they were two city slickers and a country hick would never have occurred to me," Jim counters. "Gene was easily as cosmopolitan as they were. McGuinn was a little older and even a little bit more pseudo-hip. But David was about as hip as a piano bar singer at the time."

Jim would play a significant role in Gene's career, both during and long after the Byrds. Some have described him as almost a father figure to Gene, offering advice and support at critical junctures—even opening his home to Gene when he had nowhere else to turn—whenever the singer was in need of guidance or direction. More than the other Byrds, Gene and Jim developed a close bond. "Gene was always very, sort of what they call, 'wired'," Jim offers, "without benefit of anything. Most people, to get like Gene, would have to take two big Benzedrines a day. Gene just was naturally that way, very intense, very high-strung, very antsy. It turned into many more complex problems as time went by, but he came that way. But it didn't seem to be irrational to me in any way. Gene wasn't so much a dope smoker like the others at that time. He was pretty clean and he had a lot of energy.

"He was one of the most powerful kids I had ever seen," Jim continues, "incredibly muscular. I watched him pull the outer husk of a coconut apart with his bare hands that you and I couldn't have taken apart with a tire iron. He just stuck his thumb in and ripped it apart saying, 'It's just like a zipper,' and pulled off a piece and started tearing it apart. He was incredibly strong. He could have kicked all of our asses at once. Gene could eat half a box of corn flakes, half a dozen eggs, and a pound of bacon for breakfast, and drink all your orange juice and milk at the same time. He had this enormous appetite. That was in the early days when he was healthy and young and very high-strung."

The trio continued to rehearse and write songs throughout the summer, though Gene was far and away the most productive of the three. With an eye toward song publishing and recognizing that Gene was accumulating an impressive backlog of songs, Jim took Gene alone into the studio in the early summer to record seven of Gene's own compositions, accompanying himself on acoustic 12-string guitar. "One of the things a publisher does is tape the new songs," acknowledges Jim, who, with Eddie Tickner, administered Gene's catalog under Tickson Music. "Gene was virtually writing so many songs we could hardly keep up with it all. He would sometimes write ten a week, looking for the right one. Some would be modifications of other ideas he already had. Gene was just a high-energy guy." What these seven tracks represent is Gene's songwriting before the folk-rock of the Byrds, and they support the claim that he was the least folk-oriented of the three. Whereas David had recorded Dino Valenti's later folk chestnut "Get Together" and the traditional "Jack of Diamonds" for Jim, and Roger had arranged "Turn! Turn! Turn!" and "The Bells of Rhymney" for Judy Collins's third album, Gene's early demos reveal an obvious leaning toward the pre-Beatles pop charts. There is little evidence in songs like "All for Him," "It Never Would Come to an End," "I Can Miss You," "The Way I Am," and "Why Can't I Have Her Back" to suggest that Gene had absorbed the folk idiom. These are pop ballads sung in a voice reminiscent of Elvis Presley's crooning ballad style. The voice is strong and the use of the odd minor chord in the arrangements would become a hallmark of Gene's later style. Astonishingly, none of these songs would even be attempted by the embryonic Byrds, nor would they have suited the group. He would produce a whole new slate of songs for the group.

While Gene's strengths were his lyrics and melody, his musical arrangements tended toward the simple. Friend Daniel Moore recognized Gene's early limitations. "Gene wasn't much of a player. He was more of a singer and he was a better singer than most people at that time. So he wasn't very proficient on the guitar. He couldn't get into any complex chords as a player or writer and I think that held back his writing skills a bit. But he had a great-sounding voice. Gene was better at lyrics and melody."

Gene brought his new Jet Set friends over to the Folk House to meet Daniel. He outlined the group's game plan, though it was met with some disdain. "When I met them in early 1964, they told us they were going to use drums," Daniel remembers, smiling at the recollection of folk artists turning to rock 'n' roll. "None of the folkies used drums or electric guitars. That term folk-rock hadn't been invented yet, but that's where they were going." During this period the trio recorded a McGuinn-Crosby composition at World Pacific replete with Beatlesque harmonies and "yeah yeah's"—the three even go so far as to affect British accents. Accompanied solely by their 12-string acoustic guitars, "The Only Girl I Adore" is more representative of Gene and Roger's initial Peter and Gordon approach than anything folkie or remotely Byrds-related.

The vacant drum position was filled by the recruited Michael James Dick (born June 3, 1946, in Spokane, Washington), who manned cardboard boxes until the Jet Set could afford to purchase a proper drum kit for him. The story goes that he was spotted on a street by Roger and Gene and solicited as their drummer based solely on his long, Beatlish hair. The fact was that Michael had experience as a drummer and conga player prior to becoming a member of the Jet Set. (The easygoing Michael would later exchange his Dick surname for Clarke.)

The four saw their future unfold before their eyes in early August when they took in the Beatles' first movie, *A Hard Day's Night*.

"We saw that movie together and we all got that same feeling," enthuses Crosby. "Beatle music was very close to folk music. The essential elements of the synthesis that took place with Beatle music are folk music changes, much more complex chord changes, put to a rock 'n' roll backbeat with bass added. You add bass and drums and take those kind of changes, then you get to where Beatle music started to happen. And, of course, once they found that place, then they were off and running. They created a whole new genre. But more than just the music, it was the insouciance, the complete lack of proper respect for authority, that was very appealing to us. Gene as well. All of us, but Gene and I probably more than Roger, were

Early publicity photo of the Byrds, late 1964, featuring (left to right) Chris Hillman, Gene Clark, Roger McGuinn, Michael Clarke, and David Crosby.

entranced with the idea of having girls getting totally excited about us. That was very appealing. Hell, we didn't really know what was possible. None of our friends had ever made it. I don't know if we really believed we were going to make it. We all had a dream of being Beatles."

From the get-go Gene was positioned as the lead singer in the group. He had the strongest voice, penned the most songs, and was by far the better looking of the three singers. "Oh, yeah. He was the obvious choice as lead singer," insists Roger. "He had a good, strong, solid vocal range and style that was very full bodied, whereas my singing was thinner and not quite as developed. I wasn't the obvious choice for the lead singer." Confirms Jim, "Gene was the focal point. I didn't plan it that way, he just was the lead singer. During all our early rehearsals until I brought in 'Tambourine Man,' he was our lead singer. McGuinn used to sing with him, the same melody just to fill it, and Crosby sang the harmony. That was the way it was constructed. He was always thought of—not just by me, but by the whole group—as the lead singer. He stood in the middle, he was the energy in the group, he wrote the songs and sang them and they sang with him, except for a couple of songs that he had written with McGuinn and one that McGuinn had written with Harvey Gerst before he met Gene."

Roger was, however, the best guitar player of the three, so the lead guitar role fell unquestionably to him. Gene would man the rhythm guitar slot, with David and Michael underpinning it all as the rhythm section: a quartet, just like the Beatles. The problem was that David proved unable to play bass and sing. "You just have to have the right knack," David admits. "I don't know how someone can play a bassline and sing something else at the same time. It's like dialing two telephones with both hands. I could do it playing rhythm guitar, but I could not do it playing bass."

"David was going to be the Paul McCartney of the group," Jim smirks. "David first told me when I met them, 'I'm not going to play guitar because these guys both are better than me.' But he found he couldn't sing and play bass and couldn't play bass anyway. He didn't know what to play and how to play." When it became evident that the group needed David more for his voice than his bass playing, Jim suggested relegating David to vocals only and expanding the group to a quintet by bringing in another protégé of his on bass.

Chris Hillman (born December 4, 1944) was raised in San Diego county, south of Los Angeles. After a fleeting interest in rock 'n' roll, Chris found his calling as a bluegrass mandolin prodigy, performing alongside veteran players at the tender age of 16. Stints with the legendary Scottsville Squirrel Barkers and the Hillmen (working with Vern and Rex Gosdin) brought him to the attention of Jim Dickson, who produced sessions for the latter group in 1963. By the following year, Chris was in Los Angeles as a member of another of Randy Sparks's folk troupes, the Green Grass Group (ironically sharing the stage with ex-Surf Rider Jimmy Glover). A talented player and decent harmony singer, Chris was on the lookout for greener pastures when Jim contacted him. The only problem was that Chris wasn't a bass player. He had never picked up the instrument before. Nonetheless, he was a player and Jim felt confident that he could make the transition to bass. After all, he couldn't possibly be any worse than David. Chris gamely accepted the challenge and joined the others. "I sort of just fell into it," he smiles. "I don't know why they even hired me. I didn't look the part; I didn't have the cool hair like they did. I had to put stuff in my hair to straighten it. But I feel it was all predestined."

Chris and Gene connected instantly, discovering they had much in common. It would be a bond of brotherhood that would outlast the Byrds. "My first sense of Gene was that he was more of a centered person than the other two," muses Chris. "He was just a regular guy, he looked you in the eye, and he was someone I could instantly relate to. He was certainly more accessible and approachable than the other two. McGuinn was a little standoffish, Crosby was in another stratosphere, whereas Gene was just a straightup guy. Out of central casting, yes, you would have put him in *Oklahoma* alongside Gordon MacRae, he was that straightahead and focused. He was maybe 19 or 20 years old, the same age as I was, maybe a month older than me. He was just a great guy and we could relate, right off the bat. He had a 1955 Ford convertible and it was a really neat car. He was the only guy in the group that had a car, having just been in the Christy Minstrels.

"Gene was a country boy in the city," Chris continues. "He had the same thing I had, but he had a little more confidence obviously because he was a good singer and already proven songwriter, whereas I, being a bluegrass mandolin player, was the shiest kid on the block. But we did relate on that one level of both coming out of that rural background. His family, though, was 13 kids, mine was three other siblings; he had a Catholic background, I had no strong religious background. But those weren't issues for us. What we did relate on were a lot of other similar areas. So obviously Mike, Gene, and I got along great. We lived together, the three of us."

"Gene, Michael, and Chris shared an apartment down on Melrose," states Roger. "David and I were living at the Padre Hotel over on Cahuenga, a little bit north of the Hollywood Freeway. It was an old wino's flophouse hotel, but it was like $3 a night or $15 a week or something. John Phillips turned me on to it. David and I would take the bus down to Melrose to rehearse with them every day at the house until the cops came and then we had to throw marijuana down the toilet." Roger recalls that happening frequently. "Then David got a car and I think he moved out of the Padre. He must have gotten some money from his mom or something like that. We didn't divulge our financial holdings at that time. But I was still living at the Padre and David would pick me up in the morning and share some chocolate milk and a joint. He'd say, 'Here, want some breakfast?' We would drive over to the house on Melrose and rehearse. David and I were actually pretty friendly at that point."

"We were all in the same boat," affirms Chris. "We were starving, we had no money. Gene and I would write some bum checks. But we always made up for them. By the grace of God we weren't arrested on check fraud. We were starving and we were buying groceries down the street and it got so bad we had to buy them with a bad check for ten dollars, which was a lot of money in those days. The funny thing was that Roger was getting money from his grandparents. So the starving musician was not starving and certainly wasn't sharing with us. We were literally hustling to get by or had girlfriends with money. I remember meeting an old friend of mine, Eric Hord, who was a musician from San Diego who ended up backing the Mamas & the Papas. And I'll never forget him saying, 'Hey, man, you need some money?' I told him, 'Man, I have no money.' He gave me ten dollars. That was like getting a hundred dollars today. And I've never forgotten that when I still see him today. It was the nicest thing. Gene, Mike, and I got by on our wits. We survived it all.

"I'll give you an example of the kind of guy Gene was then," Chris stresses. "We were behind maybe two months on the rent, but the minute the Byrds started making some money, Gene took it upon himself, not me, to pay that landlady back. He went up to her door, knocked on her door, and said, 'Here's the back rent.'"

Chris recalls a humorous moment between the three struggling roommates. "Mike was a goofball, but a lovable goofball nonetheless. He disappeared one night saying, 'I gotta get outta here. I'm going to get some cigarettes.' So he leaves the house. The next night we're walking down La Cienega and this guy drives up in a blue Cadillac convertible and says sweetly, 'Oh, Mike?' Michael turns his head and says, 'I don't know who the hell that guy is,' and Gene and I are just howling with laughter. And Gene says to Mike, 'Gee, Mike, that must be the gentleman you got your cigarettes from last night.'"

Gene, Michael, and Chris spent many evenings hanging out at the Troubadour. That's where three-time national fiddle champion Byron Berline, in Los Angeles to record with the Dillards on their third album, *Pickin' and Fiddlin',* first met up with Gene. (Gene had already befriended banjo player extraordinaire Douglas Dillard, and Chris was a fan of the Dillards' mandolinist, Dean Webb.) "Gene didn't have any money," chuckles the affable Oklahoman, recalling his first encounter with Gene and the start of a lengthy professional relationship, "and had to borrow thirty-five cents from me for a pack of cigarettes. He came back to the table and said to me, 'You know, by this time next year I think I'm going to be making a lot of money, Byron. Yeah, we're forming this group. It's not bluegrass or anything,' and I said, 'I didn't imagine it would be.' And that was the Byrds. And, god, I heard him on the radio the next year and he was sure right. Every time I saw him after that I'd tell him he didn't have to pay me that thirty-five cents, I'd rather have him owe me."

Despite the camaraderie between the three, at World Pacific studios Gene would fall in with the other two singers. "Gene would get back in with Roger and David because he was one of the main guys in the front, and Mike and I were holding down the rhythm section," acknowledges Chris.

With a loan from influential art collector Naomi Hirshorn (in return for a percentage of the group's profits in perpetuity), the Jet Set acquired the necessary equipment they needed. Watching *A Hard Day's Night,* Roger zeroed in on guitarist George Harrison's Rickenbacker electric 12-string guitar and decided that was the ticket for the Jet Set's sound. Gene acquired a Gretsch

Tennessean model electric guitar, Michael a set of Ludwig drums (like Ringo Starr), and a Fender electric Bass guitar (replacing the $50 Japanese model Chris had been using). "Having good instruments was important," David suggests earnestly. "When we first got real guitars, that was just about as good as attracting girls."

Still not flying under the Byrds banner yet, the Jet Set performed at Hoot Night at the Troubadour. "They wanted to see how the audience would respond to them," states Jim. "Up until then, David had been hiding from his buddies the fact that he had been doing anything that was rock 'n' roll. By that time, there were the five of them in their black suits with their instruments and Gene was on guitar. David had no instrument and he tried to wiggle like a rock 'n' roller and people laughed at him. He was very uncomfortable. He never went onstage without a guitar for a long time after that. So that's when he started getting on Gene's case to get him to stop playing guitar so *he* could. He claimed that McGuinn and Clark didn't blend well together on guitars."

David embarked on a campaign to erode Gene's confidence and get that shiny Gretsch Tennessean model guitar out of his hands. "After the Troubadour, he started telling him his timing was no good," allows Jim. "I've seen jazz players spook each other out of playing the same way when their time was excellent. You start telling someone they're dragging and you can talk them out of being able to play. So he did that to Gene and Gene, not to be negative, didn't resist it. He could stand in the middle, pick up a tambourine, or not. He tried maracas, but that didn't work very well. He just had the tambourine to have something in his hand because you couldn't hear it over an electric band onstage. It just gave him something to hang on to."

"That's absolutely true," confirms Roger. "David was manipulative and Gene was a little bit slower than him when it came to thinking. Although I don't think Gene was dumb, I think he played dumb sometimes, that's sort of a country boy trick, that Fess Parker kind of mentality where they're going 60 miles an hour under the hood but they look like they're going three miles an hour. Anyway, David shook Gene, he totally demoralized him, he shook his confidence on rhythm guitar so badly that he couldn't play any more. That was the whole basis behind it, so he had to get the rhythm guitar away from Gene. And it was a nice rhythm guitar, it was a Gretsch that we bought and David was kind of covetous of this guitar. He knew he wasn't going to get the Rickenbacker so he got the Gretsch."

Did Gene relinquish the rhythm guitar role willingly? "No, not willingly," David confesses, still insisting that Gene was not a competent enough guitar player at that point. "Eventually I'm sure that it bugged him. I'm sure it did. But he wasn't very good at it, he wasn't very accurate at it, and I was a better rhythm player than he was. That became evident as we went along. And he was a better front man. He was good looking! He was a handsome dude and when he was standing up front there it gave the girls something to admire."

As Chris recalls, "Gene was very naïve. I love David dearly, but he was just a mischievous guy and to keep his position secure he would lash out and weaken the other guys. He certainly managed to do that with everybody. But I'm sure he's grown out of that. He manipulated Gene out of the guitar. But really, in hindsight, they could both have played guitar. It would have been no big problem." In fact the Byrds did appear on television on at least three occasions with Gene playing a third guitar. In spite of these instances, though, Gene managed to turn the situation to his advantage. "To Gene's benefit, by giving up the guitar, he was even stronger onstage. He'd come through that curtain with that tambourine and every woman in the house would look at Gene Clark. The guy could have been the next John Wayne. He had that rugged Western look.

"Just to give you an example of what Gene had to go through, the only thing that kept Crosby at bay was Gene's physical size," Chris insists. "When Gene left and I started singing, I'll never forget Crosby turning to me, we were doing a vocal session, and saying to me, 'If you're going to sing with us, you have to sing in tune.' David had that thing about him. If anybody threatened him or he perceived it as a threat, he would lash out. And David Crosby was lucky that none of us popped him. He was really asking for it. It was the most different set of people with diverse backgrounds you could find, that was the five of us."

Byrds co-manager Eddie Tickner cites the surrendering of the guitar as the beginning of Gene's silent retreat from the Byrds. "Crosby made fun of Gene's guitar playing, so finally Gene became the tambourine man when they took the guitar out of his hands. He gave Gene a hard time. That was the cause of it. It made a nervous wreck out of him. He had a problem. He was a very nervous person."

Rehearsals continued nightly at World Pacific studios under Jim Dickson's tutelage. He would tape the group, then sit down with them and analyze their sound like a coach reviewing the post-game video with the team. It was sometimes painful to confront their own inadequacies night after night as the group struggled with their instruments and attempted to find a suitable vocal blend. Despite being relegated to slapping a tambourine, Gene remained the focal point of the group and continued to present songs for them to learn. His maturity as a writer was growing exponentially as songs like "You Won't Have to Cry," "I Knew I'd Want You," "Here Without You," and "She Has a Way," all light years from the songs represented on his seven-track demo a mere two months before, entered the group's expanding repertoire.

"He didn't know the rules about music so he ignored them blithely and that made for very good writing," David acknowledges. "He used chord formations and ways of doing things that other people just hadn't done because they were used to doing it by the common rules. He had no idea what they were so he just did what felt good. He had steeped himself in folk music and in Beatle music and he knew what he wanted and where he wanted to go. And he was prolific. He would show up every week with new songs and they were great songs. Roger being an incredibly smart guy and having a great song sense could see that there was something wonderful about Gene's writing. And there was. He dominated the songwriting at the beginning. I had only just begun writing songs when I encountered him. He was a much more accomplished songwriter than I was. He had the desire for it, he wanted to do it, and it felt good to him. He had a knack for it and he knew that that was what he was supposed to be doing."

These and other early rehearsal tracks have appeared several times on albums beginning with *Preflyte* (1969), *In the Beginning* (1988), and an elaborate two-CD box set titled *The Preflyte Sessions* released by Sundazed Records (2001). (Sundazed discovered the original tapes languishing in Capitol Records' vaults.) "On some of those cuts on the *Preflyte* album," Gene noted, "Michael Clarke is playing cardboard boxes and it's just the effects that were put on it later that make it sound like drums."

Prior to Chris coming onboard, Jim secured a one-off contract with his friend Jac Holzman, owner of Elektra Records for whom Jim served as talent scout, to record and release a single. The Jet Set (with all things British dominating the charts, Holzman preferred the name the Beefeaters), minus Michael, who wasn't quite accomplished yet, were augmented for the session by *Shindig* music director Ray Pohlman on bass and session drummer Earl Palmer. Jim produced the session with assistance from Paul Rothschild (who later produced the Doors). Two tracks were deemed suitable for the single's release: "Please Let Me Love You" composed by Gene, Roger, and friend Harvey Gerst, and "Don't Be Long" by Roger and Harvey (later reworked and re-recorded by the Byrds as "It Won't Be Wrong"). While the single received limited release in October before promptly disappearing, it did reveal the progress the group was making toward evolving a distinctive sound. With amplified 12-string guitar (it's likely that Roger did not have his Rickenbacker yet and merely added a pickup to his Gibson acoustic), there is a nod in the folk direction, more so than on the Peter and Gordon-like "The Only Girl I Adore." The Beatles influence remains strong on both tracks. While Gene takes the lead vocal on the former, the three voices are front and center on the latter track.

While all this activity was going on in Los Angeles, Gene's family was blissfully unaware of his new group, assuming he was still out on the road with the New Christy Minstrels. Long stretches without contact were the norm. Gene had established a new life for himself and severed himself from his past with minimal contact. Months would go by with no word whatsoever. "We didn't really know that he had left the New Christy Minstrels immediately," cites David Clark. "That was kind of a shock. He had been in Southern California for probably six months before anybody knew he wasn't with the New Christy Minstrels any more. He kind of let that string out as far as he could. Why didn't he come home or notify us? Because he wanted to come home the hero, on top of the heap, like his first return home with the New Christy Minstrels. He was almost like a god in some peoples' eyes and that was quite an ego feed for him. He wanted to get something going and return with something even bigger, but when he got to L.A., he couldn't. He had already built this un-crossable bridge for himself. That's why we didn't hear from him until the Byrds were already a hit."

Besides his new musical aggregation, Gene had other more compelling concerns that fall. He had received his draft notice. Roger and Michael had already dodged that bullet; now it was

Gene's turn. As brother David tells it, "Gene was drafted but he had an old football disease in his knees, Osgood-Schlatter's Disease, like water on the knee. That's what kept him out of the army. This happened between the Christy Minstrels and the Byrds. This caused him a lot of stress at that time. I heard conflicting stories about other things that he did to kind of enhance the situation, like going in looking like he had just crawled out of the gutter and putting on an act and wearing women's underwear. I wouldn't put it past him."

The Vietnam War was already looming large and would touch the Clark family directly. "Our brother Dan was drafted and went to Vietnam and served there for 18 months," reveals David. "He was awarded a Purple Heart and the Bronze Star. He went over in the middle of 1969 and came back in early 1971. It really bothered Gene to know that one of his family was over there. All of us knew people who didn't come back. Dan doesn't talk about it, but it's his story to tell. I've seen all sorts of ways that vets deal with the emotional stress of battle with drugs or alcohol and for others it was other things. Dan chose a religious solution. Some of these people, and I still see them, are still in 1968 when they came back."

Recognizing that rewriting Beatles songs was hardly the pathway to success, Jim Dickson began to exert more sway over the band's musical direction by urging them to draw more on their folk roots. "The Byrds' background was primarily in folk music," Jim points out, "and though they seemed to be prepared to abandon this background to follow the Beatles, it was, to me, their strength. As their manager, I felt it should be retained as an element in their music. McGuinn understood that the Beatles had been using some folk songs to write songs on top of. So he did that with 'It Won't Be Wrong.' McGuinn's taste in folk songs, to me, wasn't that great, but he did know how it worked and he was the better musician of all of them."

Jim was already well acquainted with Bob Dylan's songwriting and saw the potential in electrifying his lyrics. While the Byrds are credited with inaugurating folk-rock, a marriage of the two musical idioms, and Roger is credited with defining the musical structure and signature sound through his jingle jangle Rickenbacker electric 12-string, it was visionary Jim Dickson who initially saw that such a marriage was possible. He pushed his charges, often forcibly, to consider the possibilities (David put up the most resistance; as he admits, "I just didn't get Dylan at that point"). With Dylan as the poster boy for the protest movement and the enfant terrible of the folk scene, at least four of the five Byrds were well aware of him and his music (Michael's prior knowledge of Dylan is uncertain), while Dickson had already convinced Chris's earlier bluegrass outfit, the Hillmen, to record Dylan's "When My Ship Comes In." Whether or not they saw any redeeming value in electrifying his material however, was another matter.

Having produced Hamilton Camp's folk album *Paths to Victory*, Jim had connected with Dylan's publishing company and received an acetate of an unreleased Dylan song, "Mr. Tambourine Man," recorded in a shambling duet with Ramblin' Jack Elliot. Jim first attempted to get some of his bluegrass acts to cover the song, including the Kentucky Colonels featuring Clarence

White. When they balked he took the acetate to the Byrds. As Jim tells it, "I wanted to do 'Tambourine Man' from the beginning. The song was bigger than they were at the time."

"Jim suggested to us that we try something really out of left field and do a Bob Dylan song," Gene recalled. "Something a little more intellectual, something a little more poetic, and a little more together. And we thought, 'That's a pretty far out idea,' doing some real poetry to this kind of folk-rock music. We were looking for a song that hadn't been done yet and Bob sent us a demo of him and Ramblin' Jack Elliott playing 'Mr. Tambourine Man' and I went, 'Man, what a trippy song this is!' McGuinn decided to work up an arrangement of it and edited it down to what could be an AM single. Dylan came into town and came down to see us because Jim knew Bob, I guess, and he said, 'Come down and listen to what these guys did with one of your songs.' Dylan appeared one night with Bobby Neuwirth and Victor Maimudes at the studio. He had just gotten back from England, meeting the Beatles, and he was all jazzed because he had met John Lennon and he and John had become pals. He loved it immediately. He said, 'Man, this is great, an electrified version of 'Tambourine Man.' What a trip.'"

The *Preflyte* sessions reveal "Mr. Tambourine Man" to be very much a work in progress with quasi-military drum rolls throughout. It would take Roger's arranging experience, and a little help from the Dillards' Dean Webb, to come up with a credible arrangement. "They were rehearsing at World Pacific studios where we recorded," recalls Dean, who was a friend of the group members. "They were in there trying to work out 'Hey Mr. Tambourine Man.' They were all fighting and squabbling and couldn't seem to get the right kind of harmony on the thing. So they asked me, 'How would you do it?' So McGuinn stayed in the room and I sang a tenor part to him, a first harmony part above what he did. Then they ran the recording back and I put a baritone part on it. And they liked what I was doing, more or less a straight harmony on it. They were trying to be more folky and modal, which I didn't think fit. I just put a triad harmony on it. So then they learned the parts that I had put on tape and sang it."

Initially Gene was the lead singer on the song as they worked up their arrangement, but Roger's voice ultimately graces the *Preflyte* version and eventual hit single. "Gene was talked out of doing 'Tambourine Man' by David," maintains Jim. "He would tell me 'We can't do these Gene Clark songs, they're all just chinka chinka, nothing,' but he would tell Gene his songs were the greatest. He hated Dylan even more. He tried everything he could to stop 'Tambourine Man' including following Allen Stanton of CBS right into the men's room, telling him he didn't know what he was doing and that the song sucks. He was anti-Dylan until we had a hit, then he was an expert on Dylan. David was very changeable."

Working on "Mr. Tambourine Man" became the catalyst for the group's own individual sound, and rehearsals began to move in the direction of integrating folk music and rock to British Invasion-style arrangements. The Searchers, a Liverpool quartet and contemporaries of the Beatles, had already broken ground with a similar concept including the use of an electric 12-string, but it would be the Byrds who would take the concept further. McGuinn found his calling in being able to bring together his two loves: folk music and the Beatles. His position within the group was strengthened by his new prominence as arranger and this led to more lead vocals. "Roger's an intellectual, he's very smart, and he's a brilliant musician," concedes David. "He was smarter than any of us, smarter than me, smarter than Gene by a considerable amount, and he did understand what to do. And when we encountered the Dylan material he was a genius at translating it into something accessible to regular people. We were the first people to put good poetry on radio. That was the Byrds."

As Jim noted to author Unterberger in *Turn! Turn! Turn!: The '60s Folk-Rock Revolution*, "It was not folk-rock as a goal, but to bring a contemporary format to the best of the dying modern folk music. The Byrds used what skills they had, mostly from folk music, and given the instruments they chose, found a sound compatible with the Beatles." What would be tagged folk-rock in 1965, as spearheaded by the Byrds, represented a marriage of folk music's literary sense—its poetic form and lyrical message—with the uptempo, electric guitar-driven beat of rock music. It was an infusion of Merseybeat with a poetic, literate sensibility. Beat with brains. Under the aegis of folk-rock, pop music became relevant, meaningful, politically conscious, and a true art form.

"We weren't a garage rock band," Chris told writer Rob Hughes in an August 2003 *Uncut* interview. "The uniqueness of the Byrds came from having no idea what to do, except trying to copy the Beatles. We worked this out through trial and error every night. We were trying to come up with the sound, which we did eventually."

The trademark Byrds vocal sound evolved from adapting the traditional folk music triad to the Beatles sound. "They watched the Beatles and saw where John Lennon sometimes doubled the lead with George Harrison or Paul McCartney," notes Chris. Gene and Roger would often double the lead parts, with David's harmony weaving around the melody. "That would give me a fullness to my voice that it lacked," Roger acknowledges, "and would give him maybe a little sprightliness to his voice, a little more edge."

It was David's unique gift for harmonies that was the icing on the cake. "I'm a better harmony singer than Roger. That was my gift. I could complement Gene's songs very well. But that had a lot to do with the nature of Gene's songs. Gene wrote changes that lent themselves to my kind of nonparallel, contrapuntal kind of harmony. One of the reasons the Byrds did what they did, sounded the way they sounded, was that if you have three parts, all the places to move are taken up. So you can really only move the three parts basically parallel. It takes a lot of effort to get them not to be parallel. Crosby, Stills & Nash managed that, but almost nobody else. Other than that, when you hear three voices, they're mostly moving parallel. If you have three, then one's on the top and the other one can move around between the third, the fifth, the fourth, the sixth. The other one has all that room to move, to create that tension by the relationship between it and the melody. And because just about all the Byrds' harmony was two-part, I had room to move. So my harmony could become a second melody and that creates emotional tension. It just does. For example, I reversed the melody in 'Eight Miles High.' You can't do that in three-part, it's much more difficult."

Soon the group had worked up arrangements of other Dylan songs such as "Chimes of Freedom," "Spanish Harlem Incident," and "The Times They Are A-Changin'" and delved into Pete Seeger's extensive catalog for "The Bells of Rhymney." With the band evolving its own distinctive musical identity, a new name was the next order of business, something more hip than the Jet Set. "It was actually over Thanksgiving dinner," Gene explained, recounting the dinner at Eddie Tickner's house in November 1964. "We got the idea just from the turkey. It was sitting on the table and we were trying to think of a name. And I said, 'What about Birdses?' because Dino Valenti had written a song called 'Birdses' and it was actually a very clever song, very cute. And Roger turned around and said, 'No, how about just Birds? We spell it with a y like the Beatles spell the 'beat' in Beatles like the beat.' I said, 'Yeah, that sounds good to me.' So we took a vote on it, everybody said fine, and that was it."

Through the intervention of an unlikely third party, jazz great Miles Davis, Jim convinced Columbia Records to sign the group, after an audition for impresario Benny Shapiro in his living room prompted Benny's teenage daughter to run in believing she had heard the Beatles. Miles tipped off Allen Stanton at CBS and on November 10, Gene, Roger, and David (Michael and Chris would sign up later) had a contract with one of the biggest recording companies in the world. It was a bold move on the part of Columbia Records to sign the unknown group, who even had yet to perform in public. As Gene speculated, "When Columbia Records signed us, they signed us on a fluke. They said, 'Well, hey, Capitol has the Beatles, we need a group. This is a good vocal group. We need a group like this.' So to save time and money, because they had a limited budget, they just said, 'Let's hire the best guys, cut a track, give it that sound, let them do the vocals, and see what happens.'"

At 10:00 a.m. on January 20, 1965, a three-hour session convened at Columbia Records' studio at Sunset and El Centro in Hollywood to record the Byrds' debut CBS single, "Mr. Tambourine Man," backed by Gene's "I Knew I'd Want You." Terry Melcher, son of Doris Day, was assigned producer of the session. "When I told Terry who I wanted to record with, he was thrilled because they were his heroes," Jim recalls. Melcher hired the top session players including drummer Hal Blaine, Larry Knechtel on bass (who created that distinctive swooping bass slide in the intro), Leon Russell (whose electric piano would ultimately be mixed out of the final version), and Jerry Cole. "They did all the Beach Boys records as well, Hal Blaine and those guys. Hal worked out with me the drum part for 'Tambourine Man,' which was a combination of the original military drum and a basic rock 'n' roll drum. He recorded the rock 'n' roll drum part, then overdubbed the military drum thing afterwards. It was combining those two rhythm tracks that turned the military thing into something else that you can't recognize, and gave it its different energy and emphasis. It's swallowed by the basic rock beat, but it's there. Terry used it and was able to accent it with what Jerry Cole was playing and it all worked. He was sort of amazed. In my mind I had already planned for Hal Blaine, Larry Knechtel, and Leon Russell to do the session because Michael obviously wasn't ready, they all weren't ready to do the session. McGuinn was."

Roger would end up the only Byrd to play an instrument on the track. Gene and David contributed their voices (Gene doubling Roger, with David on high harmony), Gene taking the lead vocal on the B-side track. Chris watched the session, while Michael didn't even attend.

Adapting the rhythm from the Beach Boys' recent hit "Don't Worry Baby" and grafting to it Roger's own 12-string guitar figure drawn from Johann Sebastian Bach, Terry crafted a little bit of magic in that three-hour session. Columbia, on the other hand, wasn't quite sure what they had and sat on the record for several months. In the interim, the Byrds began to doubt themselves. "In the early days when they were ready to give up, a dozen times, Gene pulled it together," maintains Jim. "McGuinn was ready to leave and be Dino Valenti's guitar player and stuff like that. It was Gene's determination that kept it together. Gene never ever said to me, 'Ah, man, I don't feel like it,' in those early days. He was always ready to do it, always committed. He would rather be working than sitting around. He was more of a team player who wanted to keep it together, more committed to being positive and getting it right. He was the most positive member of the group by far in the beginning."

Having signed with Columbia Records, the group found themselves barred from World Pacific studios for rehearsals and moved over to a sculptor's studio run by Vito Paulekas and Carl Franzoni. Vito and Carl were legendary hipsters on the L.A. scene and were into LSD long before anyone else. It was at their studio that Gene believed the Byrds truly found their magic as a group. "These people were artists and they had an art studio. We set up in there and McGuinn came in with his 12-string and started playing 'The Bells of Rhymney.' He was already a Pete Seeger fan. I was into Pete Seeger, but not as much as he was. He could hear through the kind of very straightahead, simple vocals into what Pete was playing. He was really into his approach to songs. Roger started playing this riff and everybody just got right into it. It was an art studio and everybody got into dancing and we played it about three or four times. That was the first night that we really realized we could play, that there was some kind of magic that we didn't even know what it was. It just happened. Crosby was singing beautiful high harmony and everything came together."

The sculpture studio also witnessed one of the group's most embarrassing moments. As Roger tells it, "I remember one time Jim Dickson hired this guy named 'Jimmy something' from Las Vegas. He was a choreographer and his job was to teach us to do dance steps like the Jackson 5 or something. He worked with us for a week after which he threw his hands up and stormed out of the studio saying, 'You guys don't have what it takes to make it in show business! I quit.'"

In order to keep the Byrds going, Jim and Eddie arranged for them to perform in public. Their first attempts—at a high school, a bowling alley, and a private party—were less than stellar. But the management team struck gold when they secured an extended engagement at a down-on-its-luck Sunset Strip supper club seeking to redefine itself as a hip spot.

Ciro's Le Disc, located at 8433 Sunset Boulevard, just down the street from the more hip Whisky-A-Go Go, had been one of the grand nightclub/supper clubs in the heyday of the Sunset Strip. Headliners like Xavier Cugat, Abby Lane, and Sammy Davis, Jr. had entertained such patrons as Errol Flynn and Mae West, all decked out in tuxedos and gowns. Legendary mobster Mickey Cohen had held court at Ciro's in the 1950s. But the club had recently been sold to another restaurateur, who decided to make it a rock music venue. One of the first groups hired was the Byrds. They debuted on Monday, March 26, 1965. That date marks the beginning of the youth revolution in Los Angeles, with Ciro's as ground zero. "Nightclubs began booking long-haired, countercultural-type bands," emphasizes Domenic Priore, author of *Riot on Sunset Strip: Rock 'n' Roll's Last Stand in Hollywood 1965/66*. "Slicker, more predictable house bands in the mode of Johnny Rivers took a back seat."

"In a word, the Byrds were different, arguably unique, at least for Los Angeles," asserts Billy James, a publicist for Columbia Records at the time. "The booking at Ciro's was, for the Los Angeles music and art scene, transforming. It was the Ciro's engagement that transformed us all. The Byrds' impact was truly extraordinary. It became a magnet for people from different parts of the city. It became an inspiration for Sonny & Cher, the Leaves, the Turtles, the Seeds, and Love, all these folk-rock groups. And then there were the freaks, Carl Franzoni and Vito Paulekas and all those folks. The Byrds didn't create those people, but they encouraged them to be as outrageous as they were. And, of course, the young Hollywood crowd, like Peter Fonda, were all there."

Someone else who witnessed the Byrds' debut at Ciro's and subsequent shows was Morgan Cavett. Son of Academy Award-winning screenwriter Frank Cavett, Morgan was managing the New Balladeer coffeehouse in West Los Angeles and knew David Crosby from the times he performed at the coffeehouse. David invited Morgan to Ciro's. According to Morgan, there was already a buzz about the group among other musicians. "I knew they had a deal with Columbia and that was a big deal. Anyone who had even a hint of a real record deal was a big thing at that point."

Morgan describes the mind-blowing scene at Ciro's that March. "You would walk in and there was a level around where there were tables, cocktail tables, then it would drop down and there was a dance floor and more tables with a stage at one end of the dance floor. There was a fellow named Vito Paulekas, who was a sculptor, and his wife, Sue [Suzy Creamcheese of Frank Zappa fame], who went to Hollywood High where I went. They had this group of hippies before that term came into use. Somehow they had hooked up with the Byrds. There was all these kind of leftovers from the Beatnik generation but not yet hippies. Rock 'n' roll wasn't respectable yet, so it was kind of a weird, eclectic combination of berets, beads, and bellbottoms. The Byrds played and there was a groove happening and Vito, Carl, and their group—which ranged from little kids to teenagers to older women, old people, gay people, black, white—all dancing and just flailing away with wild abandon. They weren't doing any kind of normal dance you'd ever seen before. They were just being totally moved by the music. You didn't have to be a cool dancer. They made it all right where you could just kind of go out there and groove and just bounce around and you were accepted. Even self-conscious guys like me, who couldn't dance unless they were shit-faced, could be cool. The Byrds broke down all those barriers."

"Onstage the Byrds were very much trying to be like the early Beatles," Morgan continues. "I remember them in suits and ties and their hair was, for the time, very long. They had that groomed look. Their music was so fresh and new. You never heard anything like that, all that was good so far from electric rock 'n' roll. They had wonderful harmonies and songs that weren't the Frankie Avalon-Fabian teenybopper songs. They were bringing poetry and musicianship that had not been seen before. It was like, 'Wow!'"

For those outside of Los Angeles who bought the group's records in the 1960s, Byrds music was generally regarded as the kind you listened to carefully. Theirs was a music with a message, an intelligence and literary sense, cerebral, unlike most pop music at the time. But for the patrons of Ciro's, the Byrds were first and foremost a dance band. One such dancer was Judy Moll. "Everyone was dancing, dancing, dancing to the Byrds at Ciro's. By then it was no longer the beautiful supper club. It was a great, big place with a lot of room for dancing. Throughout the whole Byrds set you would stay on the dance floor. They were just everything when they were playing Ciro's. We were down there every night dancing, everybody was. Everybody in the music industry went there every night." Adds Cynthia Webb, soon to become Chris Hillman's girlfriend, "We would just let the music go through us and dance. They played very loud, but it was powerful."

Roger recalls some sage advice from their manager before their Ciro's debut. "Jim Dickson said to us, 'You have a big responsibility as a dance band because if you don't get the beat right, people are going to trip and fall down.' So we took that seriously and really worked on our rhythm to try and get it solid. Jim was always full of lots of good wisdom and pieces of advice. He was the real reason why we pulled together and became a good band."

"The Byrds played five sets a night," notes Jim, who recalls that the group performed a number of cover songs from British artists (including an early influence, the Searchers' "When You Walk in the Room"), "and by about the second set they would be warmed up and by the end of the night the music was so magical! They were doing a Beatles song, 'Things We Said Today,' and David would get to the line 'Me, I'm just the lucky kind' and it would always make him smile and pick the band up. David was the emotional heart of the band by then. If he was in a down mood, the band couldn't play; if he was up and happy, he's very infectious and he infects everyone with his feeling. It's hard to be happy when he's down in the room and it's hard to be unhappy if he's having a great time. Something about that moment in that song would turn the whole thing on and it would be just magical for the rest of the night.

"Hundreds of important people in Hollywood came out because we put lines in front of Ciro's. There hadn't been a line in front of the club since Peggy Lee right after World War II. Ciro's had been dark for a long time, but it opened up with a little bit of rock 'n' roll. We took that old club and brought it to life, stacked people up outside of it, which caught everybody's attention. Because if you went to Beverly Hills, you had to drive through Sunset Strip in those days, for sure. You go by and all of a sudden here's old Ciro's alive and happening. We had people like Sal Mineo, Lenny Bruce, and Steve McQueen, not part of the crowd we were in, but the Byrds had everybody dancing who wouldn't have danced in public. It was the greatest time in all of our lives. The band never played better live. They came close at the Trip under pressure, but nothing like Ciro's. It brought them together in a way they hadn't been. If you could have heard how 'The Bells of Rhymney' sounded at Ciro's with Michael on the cymbals playing perfect time, it was just so great. They never sounded like that on a record or anywhere else. CBS wanted to record them live at Ciro's, but we had one problem. I told them, 'If you will let me take out anything that I don't think is up to standard, then I will agree to it.' At that time I still had control over everything. They said they couldn't do that and so we didn't record them live. I've been sorry about that decision ever since. But I didn't want anything bad to get out and they did a couple of things that weren't that good."

Gene's former New Christy Minstrel mate Barry McGuire witnessed the excitement at Ciro's. "The next time I saw Gene was opening night at Ciro's with the Byrds and he was center stage singing the leads. Man, they just blew everybody away. It was one of those instant explosions of 'Yes!' A huge yes. Phenomenal power, fun, ripping harmonies, great arrangements, killer musicians, and Gene was right in the middle of it. I wasn't surprised to see him there, just happy for him. I had just left the Christies and I couldn't get a job at the time, so now I was in the streets broke and here was Gene in a group exploding on the scene. I thought, 'Oh, man, I wish I had left last year; I could've been a part of this group.'"

Bob Dylan himself joined the group onstage on one memorable evening. Roger recalls the moment: "He came by Ciro's and listened to a set of ours and he said, 'Ooh, I didn't even recognize some of my own songs,' because we had changed the beat to them. I think it was our influence that got him to go electric, which got him booed off the Newport Folk Festival stage in 1965. But eventually it caught on. We turned him on to the fact that his music could be done electric. He instantly got together with his outfit for 'Like a Rolling Stone' and that kind of stuff."

Like the individual Beatles, distinct personalities began to emerge among the five Byrds. "David Crosby was the most extroverted, as I recall," notes Cynthia, "because he had this very aggressive personality and he was kind of a punk. He needed more limelight. He was definitely cocky, a bit obnoxious. I remember Gene in the front with the tambourine and the beautiful voice, beautifully blending with Jim McGuinn's voice. I thought Gene was very introverted. I suppose you could call it brooding, but a very introverted kind of personality. He appeared intense. Jim McGuinn seemed more serious to me somehow. Michael Clarke was this surfer-looking guy, on the drums at the back. Everybody brought something wonderful to the group. There was this great balance. Chris Hillman sometimes looked like he wished he weren't there. He wasn't the same as the others. He didn't want to be a frontman and loved traditional music. Each one of them was different, but that's what made bands great, all the different kinds of people together."

"Women loved Gene's demeanor," notes Denny Bruce, who was drumming at the time with a band that would become Spirit, before joining Frank Zappa's Mothers of Invention. "There was something about his coolness. Girls liked him a lot more than they did McGuinn. I would say it was between Gene and Michael Clarke who all the girls thought were cool. Crosby was a little too chubby and Chris was a nice guy. But in pure sex appeal, Gene and Michael were kind of the Brian Joneses of the group."

Sensing that something very unique and exciting was happening, almost a cultural explosion right under their noses, Columbia Records finally released "Mr. Tambourine Man" on April 12, 1965. "Goddard Lieberson at CBS knew what was going on and appreciated it for what it was," suggests Billy James about the label's leap into rock 'n' roll. "Individuals in sales and promotion knew what was going on. It's been well chronicled that the major record labels were way behind vis-à-vis rock 'n' roll, and Columbia has to be tarred with that same brush. It took time for what was happening in Columbia's West Coast office to be fully appreciated and embraced by headquarters in New York. But someone made the decision to work the record and it became a hit. Columbia's previous number one single was a tune called 'Go Away Little Girl' by Steve Lawrence and Eddie Gormé, so that encapsulates where the company stood regarding rock 'n' roll."

As Richie Unterberger declares in *Turn! Turn! Turn!: The '60s Folk-Rock Revolution,* " 'Mr. Tambourine Man' was different from what was on the radio. This was music with meaning, music to feed the body and the mind. The result was that elusive treasure: a new sound. Quite apart from the innovative brilliance of the music, never had lyrics of such literary quality and ambiguous meaning been used on a rock record." Adds Billy James, " 'Mr. Tambourine Man' was poetry, it wasn't 'She's So Fine.' I remember a promotion guy asking me for the lyrics to the tune so he could give it to a disc jockey in San Francisco. That was poetry."

By June "Mr. Tambourine Man" was No. 1 across North America and on its way to the same around the world. Actor Jason Ronard, a close friend of Gene's and Dylan's buddy Bobby Neuwirth, remembers: "I asked Dylan once, 'Did you make Gene Clark famous?' and he said, 'No, Gene Clark made me famous,' and he meant the Byrds doing 'Tambourine Man.' They really put Dylan on the map."

By the summer of 1965, folk-rock was a part of the lexicon of not only the music business but of the wider culture itself. Respected magazines like *Time* and *Life* devoted major coverage to this new phenomenon. Folksingers fell over themselves in a rush to either trade in their acoustic Martins and Gibsons for electric Rickenbackers and Fenders, or, if they were too poor,

Bob Dylan joins the Byrds at Ciro's, April 1965.

simply added a pickup and plugged in. Bob Dylan's catalog was plundered from all sides by hundreds of artists desperate to cover anything the man penned. By late summer the pop charts were overrun with folk-rock wannabes, including the Turtles, Sonny & Cher, the Grass Roots, and We Five (even Frankie Valli and the Four Seasons, under the guise the Wonder Who, released a version of Dylan's "Don't Think Twice, It's All Right"), as well as those with more legitimate folk pedigree, like the Lovin' Spoonful, Simon & Garfunkel, Donovan, and the Mamas & the Papas. Session guitarists were required to have a Rickenbacker 12-string at the ready and tambourines were now de rigueur. Barry McGuire weighed in with his own bit of folk-rock bombast, composer Phil Sloan's "Eve of Destruction." Dylan himself struck a folk-rock nerve with "Subterranean Homesick Blues" before owning the pop charts for the remainder of the summer with the monumental "Like a Rolling Stone."

By turning a Dylan acoustic folk song into an electric pop hit, the Byrds defined the sound and substance of folk-rock. Although there would be a surfeit of imitators extending right up to today with groups like REM, the Byrds are the true originals. "Just about the only thing that everyone who listens to early folk-rock can agree upon," muses Unterberger, "is that the Byrds and Bob Dylan were folk-rock."

The Modern Folk Quartet had emerged during the folk boom only to now discover the landscape had suddenly altered and it was either get onboard the folk-rock gravy train or get out of the road. As MFQ lead singer Cyrus Faryar suggests, it all started with the Byrds. "There was something about the Byrds that was quite a phenomenon. The Byrds whet our appetites for folk-rock. Whatever sweet music the Byrds came up with, they legitimized this transition from folk to folk-rock and made folk-rock a genre, an existing genre, which was acceptable. It was a necessary transition to go from folk to folk-rock. We did our transition in New York and we came back [to Los Angeles] and we had a booking at the Troubadour, three shows a night. We had wearied of the folk thing and went through this big change when we were in Manhattan. We had developed a rock set when we played with the Lovin' Spoonful at the Cafe Wha? in the Village. We polished our chops as a rock band there. So we did the first two shows at the Troubadour in our folk stuff, we came out in our folk outfits and sang our folk songs. But before the third show we went backstage and changed into our rock outfits and came out for the third set on this unwary public. People reeled aghast and some fled as I brought out my Rickenbacker and we were all suddenly electric and cranking out electric tunes. The folkies were largely horrified. There were a lot of purists there, into the whole Appalachian thing. So it took a little bit of time, but we gradually won people over. Like the musicians who got tired of playing just folk music and banjos and wanted it wired up, their audience had the same hunger. The Byrds came along and satisfied that. Timing is everything. A month earlier or a month later, who knows?"

While the five young men in the Byrds, all barely in their twenties, may not have changed, the world immediately surrounding them certainly did. They were now bona fide stars. A month earlier they might have been wondering where their next meal was coming from; now they had everything and anything their hearts' desired, virtually at their beck and call. Each day was filled from dawn to dusk with an endless round of television appearances, photo sessions, magazine interviews, recording sessions, management meetings, business meetings, autograph sessions, personal appearances, promotions, concerts, tours—an exhausting regimen. Girls of every size, shape, and color were at their individual or collective disposal. Drugs were proffered free of charge. Their company was sought at social functions. Any public pronouncement was given weight. Privacy was a thing of the past. It was the Beatle dream come true.

Even as their debut single was still climbing the charts, Columbia Records summoned the group to the studios to produce an album's worth of tracks to capitalize on the group's rising popularity. This time the quintet would eschew session men and instead play their own instruments on all the tracks. Many of the *Preflyte* songs were recorded for the album sessions. Besides the obligatory Dylan covers ("All I Really Want to Do," "Chimes of Freedom," "Spanish Harlem Incident") and Pete Seeger tribute ("The Bells of Rhymney"), the band was pressured by Jim Dickson to cover a Jackie DeShannon composition, "Don't Doubt Yourself, Babe" (with a Bo Diddley 'shave and a haircut, two bits' beat), as a nod to her for her early public support of the group (Gene and Jackie briefly attempted to write together). The novel decision to rock up Vera Lynn's World War II anthem "We'll Meet Again" belonged to Roger. Of the remaining tracks, five were either written exclusively by Gene or in collaboration with Roger. Clearly Gene was far ahead of the others in the songwriting sweepstakes.

"I think Gene and I started writing together," acknowledges Roger, "and then he took off and thought, 'Hey, I can just do this myself.' He was very prolific. He was writing songs every day and really working at it, whereas I was kind of not as interested in doing that. I think Gene probably discovered that he didn't need to collaborate any more and just started doing it by himself. But it really paid off for him on that first album." Jim claims that Gene could write as many as 20 songs a week, but only one would be worth recording. "That's normal for any songwriter," suggests Roger. "Volume really makes a difference. If you sit down and write a hundred songs you might get five or ten that are good. That's the way it works, and gradually you get better at the process and write better songs in your shotgun approach. But the shotgun approach really does work."

"I was the only one who was really writing a lot in those days," Gene conceded. "I'd come into the group with a whole album's worth of songs ready and it quickly became clear that I was a lot more comfortable than the others and a lot more prolific at songwriting. I didn't feel slighted that my songs were on the B-sides. Of course, I made a lot of money. The Byrds had so much character: you had McGuinn with the 12-string and the glasses and Crosby with the unique hippie thing—people weren't into that yet. A lot of these things overshadowed a lot of the songwriting and things like that. So maybe, in a way, being in the background kind of created a mystique that, in the end, might even be beneficial. I certainly didn't suffer that much."

Terry Melcher again steered the sessions, with input from Jim. "Terry got along fine with Gene," Jim recalls, countering a long-held myth that the producer had little regard for the group's principal songwriter. "They did 'I'll Feel a Whole Lot Better' together and Terry liked it. Terry wasn't that fond of David. If you didn't think David was the most marvelous thing in the world, then David was not happy with you. When McGuinn finally started to sing 'Tambourine Man,' Terry really got enchanted with McGuinn. But he never slighted Gene at all because he recognized Gene had the power in his voice. He had the songs, sure, but until he wrote 'Feel a Whole Lot Better,' Terry and I didn't think any of them had hit potential. It wasn't that they were great songs, but it was good to have self-written songs, which we mixed with the other stuff. If you listen to *Preflyte* there is only one outside song and that's 'Tambourine Man.' That's the way we came to CBS. Once we did 'Tambourine Man,' the idea of doing several more Dylan songs on the first album nobody disagreed with, except maybe for David for a while."

Gene's characteristic minor key ballads revealed a sophisticated ability far beyond his young years and offered a distinctive left turn from the usual three-chord pop. Songs like "Here Without you" and "I Knew I'd Want You" established the young songwriter as the master of melancholy. Notes Chris, "Gene had this same sort of odd melodic pattern that would always include a couple of minor chords and he would always fit right into that place." While still working within the boy-girl context (he had yet to absorb the Dylan school of abstract lyricism), Gene was far better equipped to express his emotions openly in lyrics than were the others in the group. "Gene was fairly mature in an emotional, romantic kind of male way that I wasn't," offers Roger, acknowledging Gene's gift for penning emotionally charged love songs. "I was like a pre-teen when it came to that. My interests were science fiction and gadgets and things like that. I really wasn't there with the male/female love song thing. I couldn't sincerely even sing a song like that, much less write one. And Gene was like a Latin lover compared to me. He was a handsome guy, very suave and cool with that. He was popular with the ladies." While Gene enjoyed the company of women, few remember seeing him with anyone on a regular basis. "I think he kept his girlfriends very quiet," recalls Cynthia. "I don't remember seeing any of them. I think he was very private, from what I remember. There were so many parties back then, but I don't remember Gene with anybody." Jim chuckles, "Every time Gene broke up with a girl he'd get a good song out of it and every time he'd get a new girlfriend there would be a good song."

In an era when albums were generally regarded by record labels as an attempt to cash in on a hit single (with the prerequisite hit followed by substandard album filler), *Mr. Tambourine Man* is an anomaly, a consistent recording from start to finish. There are no filler tracks among the 12 songs. Widely regarded as the first folk-rock album, it is instead a bit of a schizophrenic affair—with Dylan and Seeger covers awash in 12-strings and lush folk harmonies alongside straightforward pop-rock songs with a strong British Invasion flavor. The latter were largely from Gene, who had not fully integrated the folk-rock template quite the same way Roger had. But to his credit, it's Gene's songs that shine through the brightest, and none more so than "I'll Feel a Whole Lot Better," which became the flip side of the group's next single, Dylan's "All I Really Want to Do."

Gene explained the genesis of one of his best-known songs: "There was a girlfriend I had known at that time, when we were playing Ciro's. It was a weird time in my life because everything was changing so fast and I knew we were becoming popular. I could feel this thing happening. I didn't know how far it was going to go, but I believed in the 'Tambourine Man' thing and all that. This girl was a funny girl, she was kind of a strange little girl and she started bothering me a lot. And I just wrote this song, 'I'm gonna feel a whole lot better when you're gone,' and that's all it was, but I wrote the whole song within a few minutes."

Based around a pounding rock chord pattern and intro riff that Gene later admitted was copped from the Searchers' "Needles and Pins," the inclusion of one simple word elevated the song beyond the usual rock fare. "I had to love that song where Gene sings, 'I'll *probably* feel a whole lot better when you're gone,'" Jim laughs. "Not 'I'll feel,' but 'I'll *probably* feel a whole lot better.' He tried to drop that out on a later take but I told him, 'No, that makes the song, Gene!' There's that little hesitation in it." Underscores Chris, "If Gene had never written anything but 'I'll Feel a Whole Lot Better' it would still be considered a classic. And the key word is 'probably.' What a great idea. That was way ahead of everybody."

On June 28, "Mr. Tambourine Man" reached No. 1 on *Billboard*'s pop charts. Released the week before, the group's debut album, *Mr. Tambourine Man,* would eventually rise to No. 6 on the album charts. Back in Bonner Springs, the Clarks were about to learn what their eldest son had been up to for the last year.

"The Byrds kind of blew in on us back home here, just like it did on the rest of the world," marvels David Clark. "When 'Mr. Tambourine Man' came out, that's when we found out about him. He phoned home. Not only that—a crate of magazines arrived at home with all these pictures of the Byrds, handbills, advertisements, and we all thought, 'Where did this come from?' We were very much in the dark about how it all came about, how he came to be in the Byrds. Gene did not come home when he was in the Byrds. They did not play in Kansas City and I never met any of the original Byrds until I came out there in 1969.

"When the Byrds hit, it was so big, but the Midwest wasn't in tune with that kind of music. We didn't hear it much here or know much about it, so it was kind of a surprise to everyone. Even though the Byrds were known, they weren't magnificently popular in this part of the country. Being insulated by all that I really didn't get the full grasp of what was going on. Then I would be in a Ben Franklin store walking by the music stand and there would be my brother's picture on the cover of a magazine or on the record stands.

"There was a point when I was between my freshman and sophomore years in high school when more and more information was coming out about the Byrds and I realized, 'Wow, this is really big.' But I had no connection with it. I was completely left out of it by him, so was the whole family and his friends in high school. Everybody felt the same neglect in that. 'At least you could have let us know what was going on.' But to build this persona he couldn't let anyone know about his past. In his glory days with the Byrds he did not elaborate on family or anything like that. Pretty soon he had built these impossible puzzles for himself, wondering how the hell he would get out.

"When Gene hit it big in 1965 he was only two years out of Bonner Springs," David stresses. "Five years away from Swope Park. He was only 20."

3

Eight Miles High

While they may have appeared on our television sets as cool, calm, and collected, the five members of the Byrds were, in reality, still mere boys coming to terms with a level of success, adulation, adoration, and reward none of them could ever have envisioned even six months earlier. Imagine being 20 years old with the world literally laid out at your feet—people fawning over your every word or need, sycophants trumpeting your achievements at every turn. For Gene and his fellow Byrd mates, life became the stuff of dreams. Few adults had breathed in that rarified air yet here were five young men instantly elevated to the dizzying heights of stardom and acclaim—anointed as America's own Beatles—and expected to act accordingly. Some Byrds adapted better than others.

"In the early days of the Byrds, we had only been together about eight months before we had our first monster No. 1, a worldwide No. 1 record," Gene marveled in a 1984 interview, ruminating on the almost overnight success the Byrds enjoyed and all the trappings that came with it. "So immediately we were thrown into the category with the Beatles and the Rolling Stones. But they'd already been together for several years and had paid their dues and come all the way up. They had gone through all the ropes, which we hadn't experienced yet. We started out as kids; I was 19. You're a bunch of kids on the street and you're looking for your next donut money. You go in and cut a record for Columbia Records and all of a sudden you've got a No. 1 record. Then here you are in limousines in London, England, hanging out and meeting John Lennon. Then flying back to California and hanging out in Beverly Hills with the Beatles again, exchanging thoughts and ideas. Nobody was prepared for that kind of dimension. We dreamed about it and thought it would be a lot of fun, but then all at once it became a reality. We kind of halfway wanted it to happen, but didn't really expect it and weren't really ready for it when it did happen. The shock of being put in that position, I'll be real honest about it, I couldn't handle it."

Throughout the early months when the Byrds first came together, Gene's disposition remained optimistic. He was, as his band mates and associates confirm, driven to make the band a success—writing, performing, and compromising for the good of the group. He was the energizer, the motivator, especially when their fortunes looked bleak. Few recall any of the dramatic mood swings that characterized his adolescence. But the scope of the group's success in the summer of 1965 and the pressures attendant with that level of acclaim began to weigh heavily on Gene's young shoulders. As Chris Hillman observed, "I didn't see the mood swings in the early years. I don't recall seeing them. I don't recall having a problem with Gene." The clashing of egos, money, godlike adulation, and the presence of various stimulants all conspired to exacerbate an increasingly fragile situation.

One week following the release of the group's debut album (and two days after "Mr. Tambourine Man" hit No. 1 on the *Billboard* charts), the Byrds were back in Columbia's recording facilities to tackle another Dylan cover, the topical "The Times They Are A-Changin'," intended to follow on the heels of "All I Really Want to Do." Several attempts at laying down a satisfactory track failed to create the magic that producer Terry Melcher sought and, in the end, they all agreed to revisit the song at sessions slated for later in August.

The other song laid down at that same session, however, was startling in its lyrical complexity and instrumental virtuosity. "She Don't Care about Time" remains among the finest of compositions in Gene's extensive canon. What is so astonishing is the growth in Gene's writing; that he could produce such a deeply inspired abstract poetic vision only a matter of months after the more simplistic boy/girl themes found in his *Preflyte* and *Mr. Tambourine Man* contributions. In that short period of time, Gene had managed to assimilate the Dylan aesthetic and was capable of spinning his own image-laden poetry.

"Bob Dylan probably did more to make McGuinn and the others believe in Gene as a songwriter," suggests Jim Dickson, "because he recognized, even before I did, the quality that Gene had as a songwriter. As Gene moved along and wrote more songs later, I was just stunned at what he could do. Some of his early songs were so trivial there sometimes wasn't a word you could find to call the song in it. You wouldn't know what to call the song. But later on he wrote some remarkable songs."

Chris noticed the growing sophistication in his friend's songwriting and wondered where it came from. "It wasn't that he decided to go out and read novels or anything every day. He never read a thing. He just grew as a writer. He was so prolific. It just came to him. He would just write and write and write. And he would show Mike and I the songs first. Gene took criticism well. There were some we were very candid with him about and he actually laughed. He'd have written five songs in a week and three of them would be great. That's pretty good odds. Is that the idiot savant syndrome? No, not necessarily. But he would come out with these most poetic of phrases. I don't think there was any epiphany when he suddenly changed into this deep substance. I think it was from just doing it. He was listening to Dylan, too, and started searching for better ways to express some things."

For Roger, the transformation in Gene's songwriting caught him by surprise. "He went from 'I Want to Hold Your Hand' to 'Positively 4th Street.' The Dylan thing was obvious in his songwriting and I don't think we appreciated it because we thought it was kind of a knock-off of Dylan and we were going, 'Well, Dylan is Dylan and Gene Clark isn't.' But listening back to his stuff it really was good quality. He did have the poetic touch. Over the years I've come to appreciate it. We knew he was inspired by Dylan's songwriting."

Bob Dylan himself took note of Gene's maturity as a songwriter. "We saw some value in Gene's stuff, Dylan saw more," Jim insists. "Dylan was most interested in Gene Clark. Gene was the songwriter and Dylan understood the value of Gene Clark as a songwriter more profoundly than any of us. That, in itself, created an attitude, some of it positive, some of it negative and jealous."

For someone whose childhood poverty necessitated that his games be the product of a vivid imagination, loved wordplay, and was often more comfortable expressing his emotions in lyrics than simple conversation, the move to embrace Dylanesque poetry seemed obvious. "He had a way of putting things down with all kinds of images to follow," noted Gene, regarding Dylan's unique gift. "Instead of just saying something in a plain and simple way he gave you things like, 'Ancient empty streets too dead for dreaming,' places to go in your imagination that weren't real common for musical writers in those days. Some people had good imagery, but not the kind of high-rolling poetry that he had." While still dwelling on relationships, with lyrics like "Hallways and staircases, everyday to climb; to go up to my white-walled room, out on the edge of time," Gene was framing them in a much more elaborate context.

Besides Gene's complex lyrical exposition, "She Don't Care about Time" also boasted an innovative contribution from Roger, an adaptation of Johann Sebastian Bach's "Jesu Joy of Man's Desiring" in the guitar break. As Roger revealed to *Record Collector* writer Peter Doggett, "That was subconscious. I didn't think in advance 'Oh, I'm going to put this on there.' I'd been playing the tune a lot and some of those notes just filtered through." He remembers an admirer of that particular solo. "George Harrison loved that guitar break on that song." Clearly the track represented the Byrds' ability to step beyond Dylan cover tunes and craft their own folk-rock masterpieces.

Like "The Times They Are A-Changin'," however, the group would set "She Don't Care about Time" aside until later. A more immediate order of business was the group's first national tour, organized for July. The spartan travel arrangements on those early tours were a far cry from the luxuries afforded touring rock artists today. The Byrds' trek across America was in a regular Continental Trailways excursion bus replete with standard bus seats. No bunks, bedrooms, bars, or kitchen like today's touring buses; just your normal 60-passenger bus pulling a trailer with the group's gear (including new Fender Dual Showman amplifiers boasting 100 watts— the loudest on the market at the time—courtesy of CBS, who had recently acquired the renowned instrument maker). Along for the trip were L.A. scene-makers Vito and Carl and their entourage of crazed hippie dancers whose uninhibited gyrations caused quite a stir in the heartlands of America.

"You can imagine touring the American Midwest in 1965 with these freaky people and the kind of reaction we got," Chris recalled to Rob Hughes in *Uncut* (August 2003). Kim Fowley, a member of Vito's entourage, describes Vito as "like a Timothy Leary version of Fred Astaire." As dancer Lizzie Donohue remembers, "They thought we were something from outer space. In Paris, Illinois, they actually threw us off the dance floor."

The Byrds' reputation for copious drug use was not about to be curtailed out on the road. David Crosby admits to bringing a substantial quantity of marijuana on the bus with him. The problem was that their driver was a middle-aged Continental Trailways employee not inclined to condone illegal drug use. "We wanted to smoke pot on the bus but we didn't want the driver to know," chuckles Roger, recalling their devious plan to deceive the driver. "He was a square guy who we figured would turn us in or something. So I devised a little method of putting a joint into a Dixie cup and you could smoke it inside the Dixie cup and the smoke wouldn't escape. You could then open a window a little bit and blow it out. I remember that but don't remember a lot more, except that David almost got us busted because the bus got pulled over for something. David had a pound of pot on him. He almost got us put in jail, but that didn't happen." In Duluth, Minnesota, an earnest police officer searched the bus only to come up empty-handed after David tossed his stash out the window. At another stop, he defiantly barred an officer from boarding the bus.

The five members of the Byrds got their first taste of Beatle-style mania on that tour and while it was satisfying on an ego level, it was equally frustrating for musicians who took their craft seriously. As Gene recalled in a 1984 radio interview, "We could have played out of tune all day. Nobody ever heard us anyway; they were just screaming their brains out. No one even heard the notes we were playing, but the excitement level was incredible."

The endless highway miles, with stops in towns and cities not yet used to long-haired musicians in capes and granny glasses let alone a mixed race and gender troupe of dancing freaks, provided the opportunity for a few hijinks. "I remember one time when Gene pretty much saved our butts," laughs David. "We had these little things called crackerballs, little things with fulminate of mercury that you throw against something and they go 'Blam!' Roger and I had those with slingshots. We were in Virginia Beach on the balcony of our hotel and we were flicking them around. We shot one and it blew up against a wall right next to some guys who were out on their balcony, some drunken fishermen rednecks. And they came right across the balconies towards us and pushed the door in that I was trying to hold closed and were beating on me and Roger, beating on me anyways. And Gene showed up and they took one look at Gene, he didn't have his shirt on, and they decided they were going to stop immediately."

"Gene made me laugh," Chris remembers on that summer trip, "because he would do this fabulous old Southern black man accent. It wouldn't be politically correct nowadays, but he could do this accent and he would read these labels on the fireworks that we would throw out the windows. Gene would read in this accent, 'Light fuse and retire quickly,' and he would go 'Retire quickly?' and fall asleep snoring. He would do the whole scenario and I would be falling on the floor. He kept me laughing. We were all having fun. He was funny and he didn't take it quite as seriously as the other two."

The late Michael Clarke reminisced about the sense of camaraderie fostered on that first tour in an unpublished 1984 interview with Holger Peterson in Edmonton, Canada. "We had to stick together because we were about the only thing that looked like us around the country. We would go out on tour and we would get some serious crap out there. Immediately after the record came out we went down South and if you know anything about the South in 1965, it was like Australia with the aborigines. They wouldn't serve us in restaurants. 'Hey, did your barber die?' 'Are you a boy or a girl?' So we had to pretty much stick together."

Between firecracker antics and dope smoking, the group whiled away the off-hours sleeping or playing guitars. Roger discloses that they were pretty much stoned all the time, though others recall Gene not partaking to the same extent. "Yeah, Gene smoked pot," attests David, "but not as much as I did. I smoked it like a chimney. I don't remember if Gene did it much, but we all did it. I'm not sure if he did LSD. I know the rest of us did. I remember Roger and I doing it and walking around Hollywood, wandering down Sunset Boulevard and winding up on the roof of a building that we had no right being on. Going into Will Wright's ice cream store and frightening the people in there with the intensity we were projecting. Roger and I were both very comfortable with it. We didn't do it very often, but we did do it."

"Gene was the least involved with drugs in the Byrds," Jim insists, "and I never saw him drink in the Byrds days. Crosby and McGuinn were smoking dope, but Gene didn't do much. He would get really paranoid if he did. They would get him into it and I remember one day he said, 'The place is surrounded by police!' There was a motorcycle cop parked on Melrose giving somebody a ticket and Gene came in with the announcement that the place was surrounded. McGuinn poured his grass into the toilet and then it didn't flush down so he rescued it."

On their return to Los Angeles the Byrds re-entered Columbia studios to complete a third single. "All I Really Want to Do" was, in hindsight, a poor choice as a follow-up to the phenomenon that "Mr. Tambourine Man" had become. Weaker, lyrically pedestrian, and lacking the innovation or sparkle of the latter, the single was beaten out of the Top Ten by a note-for-note cover of the same song by Cher (of folk-rock bandwagon jumpers Sonny & Cher), who had witnessed the Byrds firsthand at Ciro's. Suitably chastened, the Byrds intended to return to the Dylan cupboard for the more politically conscious "The Times They Are A-Changin'," only to abandon that idea (even though Columbia had already pressed several hundred advance copies in picture sleeves) in favor of another Dylan opus, the more morose "It's All Over Now, Baby Blue." The Byrds were so sure of the proposed single's hit potential that they boldly brought an acetate to a local radio DJ to spin on the air, only to receive tepid response from listeners and, more ominously, Columbia Records.

While the Byrds' reputation had been built on the back of Bob Dylan, they obviously needed to step away for their next single. But before they could do that, Britain beckoned.

s "Mr. Tambourine Man" ascended the charts, the management team of Jim Dickson and Eddie Tickner had scored a major coup by hiring the Beatles' former press agent, Derek Taylor, to serve in a similar capacity with the new group. Derek had left the Beatles' employ after a falling out with manager Brian Epstein and had come out to California in search of new challenges. He found them—and more—with the Byrds.

"Derek Taylor was absolutely essential to the Byrds' success," insists Eddie. "It's unimaginable. He just knew what rock 'n' roll was really all about. And he had the experience. He was the first rock 'n' roll publicist. He had been in it long before anyone else even thought of it." Besides his innate media savvy, Taylor offered an all-important entry into the British music scene. Noted Gene, "He had the connections at that time with Radio Caroline, which was a broadcasting pirate ship outside of England that broke [introduced] the Beatles and the Byrds and the Rolling Stones and played all the things they wouldn't play on the BBC." By late July, with Taylor working his UK contacts, "Mr. Tambourine Man" was No. 1 in Britain. For him, it was time for America to conquer Britain. Unfortunately, despite the allure of experiencing "Swinging London" at its pop culture apex, it was not the right time for the Byrds.

"In hindsight, our mistake was we shouldn't have come over then," acknowledges Chris in the August 2003 *Uncut* interview with Rob Hughes about the ill-fated decision to cross the Atlantic on the heels of their first cross-continental trek. Exhausted and racked with colds and flu, their British debut was an unmitigated disaster. "We should have waited. But Derek convinced us to go, partly because he could triumphantly march back to London and show Brian Epstein his band. It wasn't a successful tour because we were too tired. We had been on the road for a long time prior to that." The British press was merciless in castigating the group, who were set up for a fall by being touted as America's answer to the Beatles—a tag they knew full well they could never live up to. "That was nonsense," admitted David. "The Beatles knew it and we knew it." Plagued by poor sound (their Fender Showmans were left behind in favor of English gear), small venues, illness, fatigue, and vastly overhyped expectations, coupled with a notoriously lackluster stage presence that created more tuning up time than audience repartee, there was no way the group could triumph. Headlines like *Melody Maker*'s "Fans Go Cool Over the Too-Cool Byrds" dogged them at every turn. *New Musical Express* reviewer Keith Altham was particularly scathing in his rebuke of the American pop sensations: "Stage presentation is nonexistent, and so is any communication with the audience. The audience don't like it. Neither do I." Chris conceded that fact in a media statement soon after the tour. "We don't have any choreography or unified stage movements. We don't laugh and joke with the audience and maybe we were a little cool. But it wasn't intended to be an affront to the audience. It was simply that we expected our music to do the communicating for us. So we learned something in that respect." In the wake of this adverse publicity, a concert in Portsmouth was canceled due to poor ticket sales and plans for a return trip before Christmas were shelved. It was the Byrds' first public humiliation. Regardless, the Beatles attended several of the group's concerts and, dismissing the media barbs, invited the group to socialize within their inner circle.

In an insightful 1979 interview for BBC radio, Gene recalled the rush he felt on arriving in London and of later meeting his heroes. "This is one of the things I will never forget. It's the highlight of my life. It's one of those memories that's so incredible you can never forget it. Flying into England for the first time and landing at the airport and thousands of people waiting at the airport. They parked the airplane at the end of the runway and brought out police guards to get us. Whereas eight months before that we were figuring out where we would get the next donut, having this kind of thing happen to us—'Tambourine Man' was No. 1 in England at that time, 'Help' was No. 2, and 'Satisfaction' was No. 3.

"We played a club on the tour schedule called Blazes and I remember while I was onstage I looked out and saw these two guys sitting with their shades on and I realized it was John and George. I got a rush of excitement and thought, 'Oh, oh, here they are!' So that night we all got together and went over to Brian Jones's flat. I remember sitting on the floor talking to John. There were some guys from the movie biz, some guys from the Stones, the Beatles, and Byrds

The Byrds perform on American International Picture's "The Big T.N.T Show" in 1965 along with other musical stars Joan Baez, Ray Charles, Petula Clark, Donovan, Bo Diddley, and the Lovin' Spoonful.

all in this house. We were looking for a record to play and there wasn't anything but Bob Dylan, Byrds, Beatles, and the Rolling Stones to play. So there was nobody but Dylan to play because he was the only guy not in the room.

"We were staying at the Grosvenor House Hotel [actually the Europa Hotel in Grosvenor Square] and we kept suites on both ends of the floor," Gene continued. "We literally had the whole floor of the hotel and we kept music going day and night. I mean, you would find Donovan, Marianne Faithfull, some of the Stones and some of the Beatles, all these different people playing all day and all night. It was a great vibe going on, people getting together and exchanging ideas and playing songs. You'd walk in and there would be Crosby and George Harrison sitting and playing guitars together. That went on for a couple of weeks."

Gene felt a spiritual empathy with John Lennon, who he regarded as one of the finest songwriters of all time. As he told Jon Butcher in a 1987 unpublished interview, "I consider John Lennon and Bob Dylan two of the best minds that we probably had or have in the twentieth-century mainly because, in my opinion, they were able to transcend just good, common logic and knowledge and get into the fact that the world is in trouble. And they were getting something out that was making a statement about it and, in a way, point some kind of direction." In a 1985 conversation with music archivist Domenic Priore Gene allowed, "John Lennon in particular liked our group and, of course, he liked Dylan, too. So he thought there was something in all this that was a little more than just another rock group. He liked the fact that we used the Dylan songs and he liked our own material."

The Beatles connection continued as the Byrds returned to Los Angeles. On the evening of August 25, with the Fab Four safely ensconced in comfortable digs in the exclusive Beverly Hills enclave of Benedict Canyon, the Byrds were summoned for a social visit. On a break while touring America (just ten days earlier the Beatles had crushed all attendance records with their Shea Stadium appearance before 56,000 screaming fans), the Beatles were cooling out and sought the company of L.A.'s hippest musicians. "When the Beatles came and we went to visit them, it was like McGuinn and Crosby couldn't wait to get into that door," smirks Chris, "like a couple of pups scratching at the door. But Gene was a little more reserved and came in later." Stoned on acid, a summit meeting of sorts was convened in a colossal bathtub in what had once been the home of Zsa Zsa Gabor. Actor Peter Fonda was also in attendance that night. (John Lennon later revealed that the line "I know what it's like to be dead," from his song "She Said She Said" was inspired by a statement made that night by a suitably stoned Fonda.)

Three days later George Harrison and Paul McCartney attended recording sessions at Columbia Studios, where once again the Byrds worked on "The Times They Are A-Changin' " and Gene's "She Don't Care about Time." While the former continued to prove problematic in achieving the right feel and tempo, Gene's song stunned the two Beatles, especially George, who asked for an acetate from the session to take back to Britain. The two stayed long enough to watch drummer Michael Clarke add a harmonica part to "She Don't Care about Time" before disappearing into the night.

Hobnobbing with rock 'n' roll royalty, attending the most exclusive clubs and parties, and partaking in the latest recreational drugs were all de rigueur for the five Byrds by the fall of 1965. They were the pop flavor of the month, the group de jour for the teenyboppers, and their faces were plastered across every teen magazine. In addition, record royalties were starting to flow in and for some Byrds the checks were much larger than for others. In the record business, he who writes the songs makes the money. Songwriter royalties are generally paid out before artist royalties (though that is not necessarily the case nowadays). Having written the flip side to a million-selling single, Gene stood to reap in excess of $20,000 (in 1965 that was significant; you could buy a trendy Laurel Canyon pad for $20,000 then. Today that house would sell for a cool $2 million). Gene had also penned five tracks on the group's debut album and the flip side of their second single. "We were all so busy that we really didn't notice how many songs Gene had written until the first album came out and he bought a sports car," grouses Roger. "He was into Ferraris and we were still starving." While clearly an exaggeration, there was no doubting that Gene's wallet was significantly fatter than the others. And his lifestyle would adjust accordingly as well.

"Success changes everyone, I don't care who you are," insists Chris, musing on life as a Byrd. "Everybody's paying attention to you. All of a sudden you become this immortal being. Everyone is listening to your every word. And in your mind it's never going to end. Looking back on it now I'm not bitter about it, but I have complete disdain for it, the whole celebrity culture we have created. Celebrity worship. The entertainment industry is not conducive to a normal lifestyle. The ones who survived it, the older actors like Gregory Peck, the Bridges family, or the Nelson family, knew when to come into that doorway and separate fantasy from reality. But the music industry is the younger cousin of the movie business and the behavior is unbelievable. It is rife with temptation and Gene got successful, we all did, but he started making money first."

Flush with money, Gene's first acquisition was an MGB sports car before trading up to a Ferrari, the ultimate 1960s dream machine. He and Michael resided together on Stanley Hills Drive for a brief time until Gene went off on his own, renting a modest home at 2014 Rosilla Place on a quiet cul de sac in Laurel Canyon, just up a hill off of winding Lookout Mountain Avenue. At the top of a steep incline, the white stucco dwelling was set above a garage with a balcony that overlooked the street. There was only mountainside facing the front of the house, which was bordered on two sides by tall trees. Judy Moll lived in the house next to Gene's and Barry McGuire was across the street. "It was quite a street!" smiles Barry. "Judy Henske lived on that street and Jackie Miller Davidson [ex-New Christy Minstrel]. I think Spanky McFarlane lived there. A lot of parties up on that street." Despite the close proximity to fellow players and performers, over the next few months this would increasingly become Gene's retreat from the maelstrom that was, for him, the Byrds.

Gene's life accelerated at a rapid pace. He suddenly found himself among the elite of Hollywood, socializing with music and movie cognoscenti, racing cars down Mulholland Drive with Steve McQueen, attending parties at exclusive Bel Air homes or at Hugh Hefner's Playboy Mansion, and dating starlets, dancers, and models. There was always a table for him at the Whisky-A-Go Go and the Troubadour. Beautiful women were freely available. More than Roger or David, Gene was the focus of female adulation—his dark, brooding visage appealing to women—and he and Michael played the field. "Gene had that James Dean thing going for him, that smoldering, broody intensity and charisma," Barry notes. "But Gene wasn't a bad boy like James Dean, who had bad-boy charisma." It is no surprise that Gene would fall into this lifestyle given his humble roots and yearning for the finer things in life, if for nothing but show.

"Gene was definitely a country boy at heart who suddenly had all this stuff going on around him," offers Chip Douglas (Douglas Farthing Hatlelid), who met Gene while a member of the Modern Folk Quartet when the Jet Set was trying to take off. "On a couple of occasions I took a ride with him in his Ferrari but, boy, he would just tear around those turns on Sunset Plaza as fast as he could, like it was a Le Mans racecourse. I was scared to death getting into that thing with him. He never hit anything, which was amazing because he would just scream around those corners and you couldn't see anyone coming."

"He was all of a sudden getting way more of a social life," Jim Dickson explains. "He had this Ferrari and was starting to really love Hollywood. He was dressing like Sonny Bono. He ingested that whole lifestyle. The others were still scuffling around the street, so to speak. That was because he got the first real money beyond session money, from the backside of 'Tambourine Man.' That was the first cash that came their way, the first money in thousands rather than a hundred here and a hundred there."

Money drove a wedge between Gene and the other two front line Byrds, Roger and David. The money was in songwriting and with the release of their debut album Gene had that Byrds market cornered. The other two were determined to get in on the action and Gene soon found himself having to jockey for position against obviously inferior songs by his two band mates. "I guess we were real jealous that he'd had so many songs on the albums that we all wanted his air time," admits Roger. "He made enough to buy a sports car and we didn't. That did create a lot of dissension." Jim notes, "They were jealous of the money he was making, but failed to write as well."

To his family back in Kansas, Gene's newfound wealth and status as teen idol and Hollywood icon was unknown. "Gene was very secretive about his affluence at that time," recalls brother David. "Did we reap any benefits from it in any way, shape, or form? No. The only thing that Gene ever bought my mom and dad was when he came home in November 1963 he bought them a new TV so they could watch the New Christy Minstrels Christmas program. That's the only thing I knew of that he did. Did he help support my mom and dad financially? If he did, I never knew about it. And if he did, our lives did not change. We plugged along very much in this very economically sluggish life that we had. Early on I started working at any-

Roger McGuinn: "Gene was into Ferraris and we were still starving."

thing and everything I could find just so I could have clothes that fit. So did some of my other brothers and sisters. I think that caused some misunderstanding and alienated him more from the family. I remember one time Dad went to a superintendents' meeting in Stillwater, Oklahoma, and he was pretty well noted among the golf course superintendents. But all of a sudden he became 'Gene Clark's Dad' and that was tough. He was at a meeting on grounds care at that conference and someone hollered out to him, 'Hey, Kelly, is that boy of yours sending any of that big money home?' Dad just looked at him and said, 'That's none of your goddamn business.' And it wasn't their business."

While some family members embraced their newfound notoriety, others resented it. "Having a famous brother definitely influenced me," allows younger brother Rick, who basked in the refracted glow of a famous sibling. "And it got me a lot of girlfriends at the time. I was in the eighth grade when my brother had such great success in the Byrds and so all the girls in the school wanted to be my girlfriend at the time. I felt like the king. It was only because my brother was famous, but it enhanced my social life." David, on the other hand, found the attention less appealing. "The repercussions went a lot further than even Gene realized. My life changed after that. I was a brother of a famous musician. I wasn't David Clark; I was Gene Clark's little brother. In a way that offended me. That was him; he does what he does and I do what I do. We would get letters in the mail, pen pals, and all of my friends who wanted to meet or impress a particular girl would drag me over and say, 'This is Gene Clark's brother.' It was constant. We lost our own identities. In school we were Gene Clark's brothers and sisters because of the popularity of the group at that time. I was glad for him. I just didn't like being known as Gene Clark's brother."

On September 10 the Byrds returned to the recording studio. The dithering over a suitable third single had resulted in pressure from Columbia Records to come up with a strong release. Despite the completion of Gene's "She Don't Care about Time," the label and producer Terry Melcher believed that Roger was the voice of the Byrds. His was the consistently identifiable voice on "Mr. Tambourine Man" and "All I Really Want to Do" as well as the bulk of the tracks on the first album. In the music business you stick with a proven formula, and for the Byrds that was Roger McGuinn. Roger's genius in crafting the essence of the folk-rock sound was also not lost on the label executives and producer who looked to him to construct the group's next hit. He did not disappoint them. Taking a traditional folk song that Pete Seeger had derived from a Biblical passage in the *Book of Ecclesiastes* in the Old Testament, Roger conceived an arrangement for "Turn! Turn! Turn!" that was breathtaking. Two years before he had arranged the song in a folk context for Judy Collins's third album. But this time around he adapted it to his chiming Rickenbacker 12-string and the Byrds' patented harmonies.

"I was a Pete Seeger fan and a Beatles fan and mixing the two," acknowledges Roger, who reduced the number of verses, added minor chords to offset the melody, and altered the time signature and overall feel of the song. "Actually Pete liked what we did back when we recorded it and sent me a long letter saying that he really enjoyed the arrangement of it. He said, 'Dear Byrds, I liked your rendition of "Turn! Turn! Turn!" very much. I thought it retained its artistic integrity. My only musical query was why you didn't repeat the first verse again?' and obviously the answer to that is because of time. We wanted it playable on the air. As the years have gone by he's been sending me letters telling me that he's really gotten into it. It's totally different from his arrangement, but he loved it." Gene recalled that Roger came up with the arrangement on the group's tour bus and played it for the others. "We all said, 'Hey, let's cut it.'"

Not everyone in the Byrds organization, however, was in favor of the song becoming the group's next single. Jim thought the lyric and message, quoting Biblical scripture, was inappropriate for a pop group and the message too simplistic, offering only black-and-white alternatives to an increasingly more complex universe. He was overruled by Roger and Terry. "The only problem we had with it," Gene recalled years later, expressing the reservation that some of them held, "was that it was a bit absolute. 'There is a time for this and for that.' It left no doors open. So when McGuinn brought the thing to our attention we all bucked a little bit at first. But by the time we had an arrangement for it in the studio there was no doubting that record and it was almost an instantaneous No. 1."

The massive success of "Turn! Turn! Turn!," a gamble at 3 minutes, 49 seconds—more than a minute longer than the standard pop single of the day—vindicated Roger and Terry's determined stance and marked the point where Jim's influence over the group began to wane. The timing of the single was fortuitous and furthered its success, coming as it did just as the Vietnam War was beginning to dominate the nightly news, student protests and civil unrest were on the rise, the dark specter of the Kennedy assassination remained a fresh wound on the collective American psyche, and the impending Christmas season affirmed the 'peace on earth' homily of the song's message. It was an unmistakable statement of optimism in troubled times, simple enough in its theme and tone for any teenybopper to digest, yet sophisticated enough to pull in the folkies and intelligentsia. As noted folk-rock chronicler Richie Unterberger underscored in his book *Turn! Turn! Turn!: The '60s Folk-Rock Revolution*, "The Byrds were still unequaled at striking the ideal balance between folk and rock, realism and wishful thinking, passion and intellect. With 'Turn! Turn! Turn!' they had concluded the year of folk-rock's triumph on its highest possible grace note." With "Mr. Tambourine Man," and then with "Turn! Turn! Turn!," the Byrds had set the folk-rock bar and raised it beyond anyone's reach. Having taken folk-rock to its apex, it was now time to move on to new frontiers, leaving their folk-rock contemporaries in the dust.

For Chris, "Turn! Turn! Turn!" articulates a profound statement that continues to resonate today. The song remains an enduring voice of a time, place, and era. He credits the Byrds' mentor, Jim Dickson, with inculcating that sense of relevance in their music. "The thing that Dickson drilled into our heads was, 'Go for substance. Go for depth in your material.' And he was absolutely right. He used to tell us, 'Do something you're going to be proud of in ten years.' That's a very important concept to instill in a 19- or 20-year-old kid."

Released on October 1, 1965, the single "Turn! Turn! Turn!," with "She Don't Care about Time" on the flip side, rocketed to No. 1 by early December. As the song was ascending the charts, the Byrds were packaged off on a Dick Clark Caravan of Stars tour along the eastern seaboard in the company of folk-rock one-hit wonders We Five, fellow Columbia Records stable mates Paul Revere and the Raiders, and the inimitable Bo Diddley. On this trip the Byrds were allowed their own exclusive mode of transportation: a Winnebago camper van equipped with bunks.

Prior to the tour, though, the group returned to the studio in an effort to lay down tracks for a second album. This time Gene would find his dominance as the group's principal songwriter challenged by Roger and David. "McGuinn and Crosby just messed with him, constantly," admits Chris on the power struggle emerging from within the group and the divisions within the ranks pitting Byrd against Byrd. "Especially knowing them this long, Roger to this day is just one of the strangest human beings I've ever met. Gene in his normal days was someone I would trust far more than Roger. The only thing I regret in my life is that I didn't have the confidence from the get-go because I would have put a lot more stability in that band and offered a lot more, but I was no match for McGuinn and Crosby mentally at that point. And neither was

Gene, but he dealt with it better than I did. I was so shy at that point." Jim, too, would discover a coup d'état underway to diminish his influence within the Byrds, who accused their Svengali of manipulating and bullying the group members into towing his line.

"Jim was a force in all of it, and not necessarily for the good," avers David on the growing rift between manager and artist. "He was a bully and very manipulative. He loved fucking with our heads and he was very good at it because he knew way more than we did about everything. So he was very good at working us against each other. Part of the friction that developed between us was Dickson's fault on purpose, it wasn't even by accident, playing one off the other." Chris concurs with David's assessment of Jim's controversial relationship with the group. "Dickson was controlling. He was a brilliant guy, but he played people off each other. But he did have a vision and he was good at it." Chris points to another bone of contention as well. "In hindsight, those guys, Dickson and Tickner, were taking 25 percent as managers back then. That was an outrageous amount of money for 1965. And they had the song publishing, too, Eddie and Jim. Sonny & Cher were making twice the amount of money we were. Who knew back then?"

Album sessions that September were marked by frequent conflict, mostly verbal, occasionally fisticuffs. With Terry as ally, Roger exerted far more control over the direction of the album than their debut release. What would become the *Turn! Turn! Turn!* album lacked the consistency of the debut and was marred by several weak tracks. Songs such as Roger and David's "Wait and See" and Roger's rearrangement of Stephen Foster's "Oh, Susannah" (which faced a threatened mutiny by Michael Clarke) were chosen over superior material from Gene, who was far too passive to assert his position and was steamrolled by the other stronger voices. "He was living as the third singer under the shadow of McGuinn and Crosby, who were older and probably somewhat manipulative of him at the time," observed Chris.

In one of the most bewilderingly implausible decisions the group would make, Gene's magnificent "She Don't Care about Time" was omitted from the album, a move that would adversely affect its quality and strength. An additional Clark composition, "The Day Walk" (incorrectly titled "Never Before" on a later Byrds compilation), one of Gene's most overtly Dylanesque creations and far superior to at least half the tracks on the album, was inexplicably left to languish in the tape vaults for more than two decades. "One of the problems we had by the release of the second album," Gene conceded, "was the animosity growing amongst the group. Especially about me, because I was making a lot more money than anybody else from the royalties."

The two obligatory Dylan covers, "Lay Down Your Weary Tune" and "The Times They Are A-Changin'," lacked the drive and sparkle of the Dylan covers on the first album, as if the band were somehow meeting obligations rather than selecting the best material. Undeniably the Byrds seemed tired; even the album cover photo captured that weariness.

Gene's three tracks, "Set You Free This Time," "The World Turns All Around Her," and "If You're Gone," were all indicative of his expanding poetic vision and gave the album its highlights. "Set You Free This Time" was conceived during the group's ill-fated trip to London following an evening on the town with Paul McCartney and is indicative of the kind of dark, pensive, haunting, melancholy mood piece Gene had an uncanny gift for spinning. "There was a lot of that in Gene," suggests David. "He was a little Macbethian, a little Shakespearean. He wasn't good enough to be called a Shakespeare, but he did have some of that dark, brooding Macbeth thing. And he could get off the deep end into being in a dark place pretty easily." Notes Roger, "He had a brooding quality. There was a lot of deep sorrow under the hood. He wasn't a happy, bouncy kind of guy." Chris admits that he had some difficulty relating to Gene's songs at that time. "'Set You Free This Time' I couldn't figure out until years later how good a song it was. I was honing in on the melody and the groove instead of the lyrics at the time. It was very Dylanesque." (A measure of the growing lack of regard for Gene's creative input came during sessions for "Set You Free This Time"—the other Byrds failed to stay behind in the studio while Gene finished his vocal overdub.)

"Gene was one of those people who couldn't sit down and discuss what he felt inside with most people," muses Rick Clark, who found his older brother able to articulate his emotions best through song. "Somebody interviewed Gene once and asked him, 'How come a lot of your songs are so sad and about so much pain and heartbreak?' and Gene told him, 'Well, when you're happy, you don't sit down and write songs. You're too busy enjoying being happy. It's when you are alone and in that deepest darkest place—all that has to be released in some way.' Gene was painfully shy in a lot of ways." For "If You're Gone" Roger and Terry created a droning harmony, a Gregorian chant-like sound that almost became an additional instrument, on top of which Gene sang a solo lead. The drone served to enhance the melancholy in Gene's lyrics and vocal delivery.

With the release of *Turn! Turn! Turn!* at the beginning of December, just as the single of the same name was topping the charts, it was clear that Gene's position within the Byrds had eroded. With a diminished role, just what his future participation in the group would be was uncertain. Was he being pushed or was he retreating from the group he had founded with Roger and David? David supports the latter. "Yes, but it wasn't really a fight for supremacy. It was an organic thing that happened as each one of us fell into the role that we were best able to cope with. I was obviously the harmony singer, that was my gift, and the rhythm guitar player fell into that because I was better at it. Whether Gene liked it or whatever, Roger, who was unquestionably the leader of the band, could hear it and wanted it that way. I don't think there was a whole lot of duking it out. That's just how it worked. I don't know how Gene took it. He was very inward and like Roger, but in a completely different way. He was not a warm and fuzzy, out front kind of guy. So I don't really know exactly how he felt about it."

Back in May, as "Mr. Tambourine Man" was charging up the charts, the Byrds had opened for the Rolling Stones on several dates in Southern California. At the San Diego Convention Hall, the British bad boys of rock had been delayed and the Byrds were forced to extend their set until the headliners arrived. "By the time we got there," recalled Mick Jagger, "they had run out of their own numbers and were playing ours," in reference to the Byrds' early repertoire that featured covers of many British Invasion hits, like the Stones' raucous version of Buddy Holly's "Not Fade Away."

During the Stones' swing through California, Gene had struck up a friendship with the equally moody and charismatic Brian Jones. Later, on the Byrds' British tour, Gene spent several evenings with Brian, either at his flat or on the town. The two had much in common: both were Dylan disciples who had been driving forces in launching their groups, only to be shunted aside as fame drove a wedge between them and their band mates.

Now on the road through November with the Dick Clark Caravan of Stars tour, the Byrds were booked to appear as one of the featured acts for the Rolling Stones on November 24 at Pittsburgh's Civic Arena. Over dinner prior to the concert, Gene and Brian discussed various notions for songs. Unable to leave their hotel due to the throng of fans surrounding the place, the two enjoyed steaks in Gene's room with Roger joining them briefly. Gene shared with Brian the seed of a song he had been mulling over since the Byrds' trip to London, inspired by the plane ride itself. Brian was encouraging and the two bandied ideas back and forth. "I had an idea for some lyrics," Gene recalled in a later interview, "and wrote them on a piece of paper during the conversation with Brian. Later on I found them in my jacket pocket on the tour bus. I took my guitar and started making up a melody for it. The initial idea was discussed on the plane over the Atlantic on our trip to England, but the actual writing of it started on a tour with the Stones when we were back in the States." The song in question would be Gene's crowning achievement as a Byrd, yet also his swan song.

B ack in the Winnebago, the thread of the song that would become "Eight Miles High" began to gel with input from the others—plus the constant presence of a surprising influence. As David recalls, "I had discovered John Coltrane and I was playing *Africa Brass* over and over again. We had a reel-to-reel tape machine hooked up to a Fender amp in the Winnebago that we were in. So we were cruising down the road stoned out of our fricking gourds listening to Coltrane. We were very much steeped in this whole Coltrane thing. And we pulled up to this railroad crossing and got the cosmic giggles because it was a train full of coal, a coal train, and we were listening to Coltrane. I remember us laughing like fools."

Roger remembers, "We had stopped at David's friend's house who had the latest Coltrane release and some Ravi Shankar and we made the tape on my new Phillips tape recorder. That was our music on the trip."

In a 1978 interview with CHUM radio in Toronto, Gene shared the story of how "Eight Miles High" emerged as a collaboration between the three Byrds songwriters. "I started writing a poem that didn't have any music to it. And the poem had words to it like "Eight miles high, and when you touch down, you find that it's stranger than known.' I was into it because I was writing about a trip we had just done to England and the culture shock going over there and being very famous and having to live up to that. So I just came up with a couple of chords to play the poem to Roger and David Crosby with. We had been listening to these tapes of Indian music, Ravi Shankar, and John Coltrane all this time because we enjoyed listening to that kind of music, it was good traveling music. And Roger, I remember, suggested, 'Well, why don't we take that poem and put it to this kind of a jazz rhythm and do the kind of Coltrane licks in it' because it was so into our heads. So then David came in and said, 'Yeah, that sounds good. Let's arrange this,' and it ended up the three of us collaborating on the song and that became 'Eight Miles High,' which was the influence that we got from Coltrane's *Africa Brass* and *India*."

Gene never failed to acknowledge "Eight Miles High" as his favorite Byrds number because of the collaborative nature of its genesis. He was more than willing to share the writing credit for the composition. "I wrote all the words except for one line that David wrote, 'Rain gray town, known for its sound,' and then Roger arranged it, basically, so I had to part something with those guys. There were a lot of images I got from thinking and remembering things we'd done on the English tour. I decided that I wasn't going to get a single out of this deal, because I'd already written so many songs with this group that they're gonna grab up the singles for their own stuff, you know, so I split it with them so I could get a single. That and they really did help me write it, too."

In later years Gene would perform "Eight Miles High" as a solo acoustic number, asserting that was the way he originally conceived it before Roger's arrangement. Stripped down, the song does retain Gene's characteristic haunting, minor key ambience.

Originally credited to G. Clark, R. McGuinn, and D. Crosby, the song has undergone a revision in recent years, to the point that Byrds reissues now credit the songwriting to McGuinn, Crosby, and Clark, with Gene instead pulling up the rear. Despite the song being a collaborative effort, while Gene was alive the credits reflected the reality that it was he who wrote the bulk of the track. Since Gene's death, however, Roger has turned about-face. "I think I wrote some of the words, too," he states today. "Gene didn't have it all done. First of all, it was my idea to write it about the airplane, the 'eight miles high and when you touch down,' was my idea. It wasn't a done song. We kind of said, 'What'll we write about?' because Gene had the chords, the changes, the *Em, G, D,* and *C*. I think I might have come up with the *C* down to *Am* thing because that was like a Bob Gibson riff that I used to do. So it was a collaborative effort. In hindsight, I think Gene kind of gave himself more credit for it. He was upset at one point about a song we did later in McGuinn, Clark & Hillman and said, 'I'm not going to let this happen again where you guys get credit for a song I wrote.' But it's not really true. We really did collaborate on it. I can't give you specifically who wrote what lines but I know I was involved in the writing process as well." David would level a similar accusation at Roger and Chris for tracks he insists he composed but was denied appropriate credit for, on the group's 1968 *Notorious Byrd Brothers* album.

While no one challenges Roger's assertion that he did contribute to the song, there is little doubt that the bulk of the composition originated with Gene. "In royalties, it's a three-way split," contests Jim Dickson. "But in the writing, Gene wrote all but one line in the song. McGuinn took a third for what he played on the record, the sort of Coltrane-esque style, the way he played it. Gene would give away a part or a half of a song to get it used. He never resisted doing that. David wrote one line. The rest of the song is Gene's song." The question remains: would Roger have altered the credits if Gene were still alive?

Before the group could commit their collaborative effort to tape, they were scheduled to appear on the most prestigious of 1960s television variety programs, watched each Sunday evening by tens of millions across the continent. On December 12, the Byrds were special guests on *The Ed Sullivan Show,* performing "Mr. Tambourine Man" and "Turn! Turn! Turn!" The event was momentous, placing the group before an audience of millions of young fans who, despite the group's appearance on several regional television shows, had yet to see them in person. They were the epitome of cool: David sporting his green suede cape (not that anyone could tell the color, with black-and-white TVs), Roger in his granny glasses, and Gene front and center, slapping his thigh with a tambourine. It was also not without its acrimony. "That's the one moment when I regret that nobody had taken Crosby outside and shaken him right up," grouses Chris. "Gene? He was great. McGuinn was fine. But David Crosby got into an argument with the producer of the show, Ed Sullivan's son-in-law. That's why we only ever did the show once and the sound was so horrible. Crosby was so nervous, so scared, that at the rundown, because it was a live show, he starts yelling at the director and producer, 'You guys don't know how to record this music. You don't know what you're doing.' On and on. So the producer's thinking, 'You punk little kid' and he says, 'Your rundown is over. We're going to tape at eight, then you're off the show.' Everybody in the booth started applauding. So, consequently, when we were on we got a bad sound. Gene was fine, he was a professional. I was the Bill Wyman in the back. David was the cause of 99 percent of the bad business moves in the Byrds, I hate to say it, but that's the reality of it all."

For the Clark family, Gene's appearance on the top-rated television show was further evidence of his stardom, even though he had yet to return home since leaving the New Christy Minstrels. "I remember my sister calling me and telling me, 'Get out of bed, your brother's on TV!'" laughs Bonnie Clark Laible. "My husband was a policeman and had weird hours so we went to bed early. But we caught the tail end of it."

Following a concert in Hawaii, where Gene, Chris, and Jim dropped acid and embarked on a trippy wilderness adventure, the Byrds were ready to commit their latest creation to tape. In the interim since the release of the *Turn! Turn! Turn!* album, Terry had been dismissed as producer following a power play by David, who managed to convince the others, as well as Columbia Records, that Terry was not serving their best interests. (When asked recently in *Vanity Fair* whether Charles Manson was the most dangerous person in Hollywood, Terry, who knew Manson briefly in the 1960s, replied, "No, David Crosby was.") With Jim temporarily producing and Dave Hassinger, best known for his work with the Rolling Stones on "Satisfaction," engineering, the Byrds entered RCA Studios in Hollywood on December 22 and laid down a raw, uninhibited take of "Eight Miles High," along with another Eastern-flavored composition, Roger and David's "Why." Despite being thrilled with the results, the band was forced to re-record both songs a month later at Columbia's own recording facility for the single release.

Although there are only slight differences, notably in Roger's guitar solo, Jim nonetheless insists that the first version, cut at RCA and released 22 years later on *Never Before,* is the superior version because it captures the spontaneity and energy the group poured into the session. "It's a better track. We didn't finish it, really, so it's not a better vocal, but it's a more organic track. Michael played better on it. The second one wasn't bad; it just didn't have the feel to it. But the one that I did at RCA was the demo I took to New York to talk to CBS about what their next plan was, the plan that got scrapped when Gene wouldn't fly. I just threw on some vocals because David [Crosby] wanted to get out of the studio. We had David Hassinger and that's why the group was happy to go to RCA because that's where he was. He cut those sides. The plan was to substitute our track, but CBS had a weird engineers union so we had to redo it. We were going to bring the track over and transfer it over to CBS's 8-track and then finish it, redo some of McGuinn's guitar parts where he had made a flub, plus do all new vocals. But that never got done so they had to do it from scratch."

Nothing in their previous body of work even hinted at the aural assault of "Eight Miles High." Byrds fans were hardly prepared for the extraordinarily innovative sounds the group was about to bestow upon them. Opening with a throbbing bass line, Roger unleashes a torrent of raga-like notes inspired by Coltrane's *India.* "We listened to it so many times over and over," confirms Roger, "that when we got back to the studio in L.A. it was steeped into us and we started playing that kind of music. The guitar break was obviously a tribute to John Coltrane. That's one of my favorite guitar things I've ever done." What follows is an account of the group's experiences landing in London and the cold reception they encountered, sung over an urgent, jazz-infused instrumental passage reminiscent of an airplane soaring to heights. Gene takes the lead vocal in unison with Roger while David's ethereal harmony weaves around their almost otherworldly melody. "I reversed the melody in 'Eight Miles High,'" David explains. "You can't do that in three-part, it's much more difficult." The choice of the title was intended as a double entendre given the tenor of the times. "High" would be a cue to those hip enough to catch the group's drift. Unfortunately the ploy backfired.

"It was about lots of things," Gene told writer Domenic Priore in 1985. "It was about the airplane trip to England, it was about drugs, it was about all of that. A piece of poetry of that nature is not limited to having it have to be just about airplanes or having it have to be just about drugs. It was inclusive because during those days the new experimenting with all the drugs was a very vogue thing to do, so people were doing all that at that time. All that was kind of in the poetry. But it has meanings of both. It's partially about the trip and partly about drugs."

Released in April 1966, the single was almost instantly tagged a drug song and subsequently banned by the influential programming service tip sheet *Bill Gavin's Record Report.* Consequently, the record was dropped in several key markets and only reached No. 14 on *Billboard*, a shattering defeat for such a dazzling single. "We could have called it 'forty-two thousand, two hundred and forty feet,' but somehow this didn't seem to be a very commercial song title," snipped Roger in a press release in response to the ban. In fact, originally the song went under the title "Six Miles High," the actual altitude of their plane, until Roger convinced Gene that the word "eight" had a much better ring to it than "six." Dickson and Tickner went as far as to retain lawyer Marshall McDaniel, who dispatched a letter of clarification to *Gavin*, to no avail. In spite of the *Gavin Report*'s damning indictment, the reality was pop radio was uncertain of what to make of this strange recording. As Roger notes, "I remember taking the demo of 'Eight Miles High' to New York and playing it for a lady radio DJ in New York, a big DJ, Allison Steele, and she said, 'Where's the single?' And I said, 'That was it.' And she went, 'Oh, no, I don't think so.'"

Regardless, "Eight Miles High" was a groundbreaking recording that inaugurated the psychedelic era a year before San Francisco bands like Jefferson Airplane and the Grateful Dead put their own stamp on that label. Initially termed raga-rock for its innovative synthesis of the extended improvisational East Indian raga form associated with sitar master Ravi Shankar, the music that the Byrds were unintentionally giving birth to was free-form acid rock. In *Eight Miles High: Folk-Rock's Flight from Haight-Ashbury to Woodstock,* the companion volume to *Turn! Turn! Turn!,* author Richie Unterberger cites "Eight Miles High" as a seminal step in the evolution of rock music: "The Byrds were so far ahead of the curve that they were playing music that had yet to be named." They had succeeded in transcending their earnest dependence on Dylan covers and folk standards to craft their own distinctive sound. Clearly Dylan could not have conceived a song as remarkably original and innovative as "Eight Miles High."

"It was my favorite moment," acknowledges David, concurring with Gene's sentiment that "Eight Miles High" embodied the Byrds at their creative peak. "It was when we actually started to come into our own."

In January 1966, when "Eight Miles High" was still several months away from release, Columbia made the surprise decision to follow up the No. 1 success of "Turn! Turn! Turn!" with Gene's melancholy folk lament "Set You Free This Time." As the group was in the midst of bidding farewell to folk-rock, the song was a stunning tour de force for Gene that embodied his Dylanesque poetry—hardly pop single material. Columbia realized their error in judgment and a week later moved "Set You Free This Time" from the A-side of the single to the B-side, replacing it with the rockier "It Won't Be Wrong," a rewrite of Roger and Harvey Gerst's Beefeaters song "Don't Be Long." (Roger has subsequently suggested "Set You Free This Time" was more of a Gene Clark solo single than a Byrds track, distancing himself from the song.) Reaching only No. 79 in the US, the single failed and Gene took it especially hard, feeling it as a personal blow.

Columbia did, however, commission a video of the group performing "Set You Free This Time" for promotion on British television, but the film was never completed. "The first time we were filming 'Set You Free This Time' on the beach, David didn't want to be there," recalls Chris.

"So David begins to needle Michael, who was gullible. 'Hey, let's leave. We don't want to be here.' Dickson, being volatile, jumps on Crosby, physically. And Gene saved Crosby. He grabbed Dickson and pulled him off. Gene looked like Arnold Schwarzenegger, from doing a lot of farm work or something. He was a strong kid." Adds Jim, "Gene, seeing that that was unfair, let me go. He didn't know David was gonna hit me. David ran like hell, yelling, 'Hold him again, I want to hit him again!' And Gene said, 'I'm not going to do that, David.' He was holding me to keep me from catching David and kicking the shit out of him. David saw me being held and turned around and hit me in the face. But that wasn't what Gene had in mind."

With an acetate of "Eight Miles High" in hand at the end of January, the Byrds were set to travel to New York for a concert hosted by influential DJ Murray the K and an important photo shoot. On the day in question, Gene arrived at the airport in a state of heightened anxiety that only worsened as he sat on the plane, awaiting take off. Technical problems delayed departure and Gene's unease deepened with each ticking minute. Shaking uncontrollably, he suddenly jumped up, loudly announced he wasn't going to fly, and promptly exited the plane. In so doing, he left not only the plane but—ultimately—the Byrds.

"I watched him get off the airplane and he was so scared," recalls Jim. "He had a premonition that something was wrong with the plane. When he got off he was white-knuckled. Michael almost left too because he was so impressed with how scared Gene was. But he looked at me and said, 'Well, if you're staying, I'm staying.'"

Roger clearly remembers the pivotal event. "I didn't notice his flying phobia at that point. I guess he hid it well. But the day he walked off the plane he was having a panic attack. He was in a cold sweat and just totally uptight. His hands were shaking and he was saying, 'I've got to get off this plane!' I tried to calm him but it wouldn't happen. Actually his panic was contagious. I started to pick up on it myself thinking, 'Wow, maybe he knows something.' A premonition. Because he was kind of a spiritual fellow even though he didn't practice any religion, he was kind of open to supernatural things. So it occurred to me, being into that kind of thing myself, that maybe he knows something. And then the captain came back after Gene left and he started giving us a pep talk, saying things like, 'I think I know how to do this,' and like air guitar he had an air steering wheel in his hands, showing us he could do it. 'I feel pretty confident I can fly this thing. It's gonna work out okay.'"

Roger's words to Gene as he walked off the plane would be prophetic. "I remember saying to him, 'If you can't fly, you can't be a Byrd.' That was on the plane. He did leave the plane and we all kind of figured that was it for him, although I guess he still was around. But I don't remember what he did after that."

The remaining group members flew on to New York, but the damage had been done. "The unfortunate part of that trip to New York," Jim reveals, "was that Avedon and Penn had both agreed with the senior art director at CBS to do pictures of them, and the art director who had done the Kennedy stuff had wanted to do a catalog, a book, on the Byrds like had been done with the Beatles. He wanted to top the Beatles one. With Barry Feinstein and Curt Guenther and myself, I was very careful what pictures of the group we let out. I had seen the Rolling Stones pictures and how classy they were. So we had all this lined up, but when Gene didn't go to New York, CBS's agreement to buy the first 200,000 books to cover our costs—we were going to sell the books at concerts—well, without Gene all of the pictures became obsolete, and the whole thing was canceled. CBS put the group on the back burner after that."

Although Gene did appear with the Byrds on a couple of occasions following their return, for all intents and purposes he was no longer a member of the group. Recording sessions in February did not include him. A press release in early March served official notification that Gene Clark had left the Byrds citing personal reasons and the pressures of fame. The media immediately seized upon the obvious tagline, "the Byrd who wouldn't fly," and ran with it, so much so that even on his death 25 years later they were using it in Gene's obituaries.

In leaving the Byrds, Gene became the first member of a top echelon pop group to quit at the height of success, stunning the music world. "How could he do such a thing?" It would become the defining moment in not only his career but in his life. He would forever be regarded as an ex-Byrd.

Precisely why Gene left the Byrds remains contentious four decades later. Certainly the flight to New York alone was not the single motivating factor. There were several issues at work. His exit from the plane that morning was only the final act in a drama that had been playing out for several months. Gene had already spiritually withdrawn from the Byrds by the time he stepped off that airplane. Increasingly isolated within the group, Gene saw his position and influence shrinking by the second album's sessions. In a bid to enhance their roles at Gene's expense, Roger and David had asserted their own agendas. With either Terry Melcher or Jim Dickson behind them, Gene found his position untenable, caught in a power play for control of the group without an ally (Chris and Michael were regarded as junior partners then—the power brokers were Roger and David). His role and contributions were being marginalized. As Jim recalls, "David was being more hostile to Gene onstage, putting donkey ears behind his head, stuff like that, breaking him down, treating him as trivial and as a square." The decision to cap Gene's songwriting contributions on the second album to three tracks and to exclude his exceptional "She Don't Care about Time" in favor of weaker tracks written or arranged by Roger and David only furthered Gene's isolation.

As Columbia Records publicist Billy James notes, "Gene was not considered one of the leaders. When we needed decisions or needed someone to present opportunities to, he was not one of the people we went to."

Los Angeles musician Denny Bruce remembers running into Gene the night before the airport scene. "I was with a friend, it was in early 1966, and he liked to smoke pot and didn't have any, so we went to a woman's pad, she was slightly older, and her name was Butchie. She was a folkie out of New York. She was like one of these good old souls that if you needed a joint or two you could go up to her place and it was always, 'Sure, here you go, no problem.' So my friend and

I go there and Gene Clark is sitting in the living room looking like a guy who hadn't slept in a week, dark circles under his eyes. They were in the middle of a conversation where he said, 'Look, I'm due at the L.A. airport tomorrow to go on this tour and I just can't see myself getting on that airplane. I just can't do it.' And she was saying, 'I know you're tired of all the arguing in the band, but you don't want to really walk out of a successful career.' In those days guys just didn't quit big groups like that. Gene was the first to walk away from a major band. But you could tell Gene mentally was exhausted. And the next day he didn't go on that airplane and left the band. He really looked like a guy who didn't want to be where he was at that time."

Years later Gene offered his own justification for quitting America's number one group: "I just had a nervous breakdown. It really wasn't a fear of flying or anything like that, even though I was starting to get nervous about flying because I had done so much of it. I had just done it every day for so long and I was starting to get crazy. Finally I just had had it. I couldn't go to New York that day. I just said, 'Look, I've got to rest. I've got to lay down. I'm falling apart.' And I told McGuinn, 'I've got to get off this airplane. I'm falling apart, man. I've just had it.' And that's really what happened. I literally went to bed for three months. I had just broken apart; the tension and the stress and the whole thing of it.

"It was the general craziness of it all, the accelerating rock group-fan magazine nuttiness. I wanted us to take a break for a while. The Byrds were such a unique group. You had such an incredible mix of personalities that when you put them all together, there was magic. You also had tremendous egos in that group, myself included, a tremendous amount of ego and conflict all of the time. It was the one group that could probably never get along, that's the way it was with the Byrds. Basically, the group had a nervous breakdown."

Gene's trepidation over flying had been evident two years earlier, with the New Christy Minstrels. The rigors of touring by plane with flights every day had contributed to his departure from that group. Faced with a similar situation in the Byrds, Gene chose to opt out. Rodney Dillard remembers a foreshadowing of Gene's flight anxiety months earlier. "We were on tour with the Byrds and Gene started freaking out as we were boarding our DC-3 plane. He started shrieking and just lost it. He had a premonition, a nightmare, that the plane was gonna crash and he couldn't get on it. He scared the rest of us so much that none of us would fly." Adds Roger, "Well, he definitely did have that problem. It was told to us, and then somebody said later that it was a myth, that he had experienced a DC-6 or something crash in Missouri or Kansas City. That's probably what scared him."

With money from his songwriting providing a comfortable living, Gene saw no reason to endure such anxiety. "Gene had a girlfriend he didn't want to leave," Jim discloses. "She danced on *Hollywood-A-Go Go* and was a real hot number. Gene was ready to sit back, write songs, make hit records, and not leave town."

"He didn't like flying because it made him feel uneasy," offers Gene's brother David. "And when you couple that with frustrated nervousness and the use and abuse of alcohol and drugs, it becomes a runaway schizophrenia. Even he didn't understand where it came from. One of the themes that you can see all the way through Gene's life was that he did not understand himself. He really didn't. He would come and ask me sometimes, 'Why do I do this shit?' I tried to tell him once, 'You would do well if you would take a break from the stimulants and stuff and try maybe through therapy or something to understand yourself better so you know what drives you to do these things.' But he was also a person that believed in his own strength, that he did not need anybody else. And he needed people more than he knew."

Cut off from his family and roots, estranged from his own band, surrounded by sycophants and hangers-on, Gene found himself with no one to turn to as the pressures of fame mounted. Increasingly he turned to alcohol and drugs to deal with those pressures. "The more this happened, the more all these pressures built up, the more he got into the drugs and alcohol," maintains David, "which had become a constant with him by the time I was down to visit him in 1969." Adds Rick Clark, "Gene did not understand the godlike worship that people were expressing towards them. Roger and David had different personalities and were more equipped to handle it and actually thrived on it. But it all made Gene so uncomfortable because he was basically shy. That led to a lot of the trying to kill the pain or trying to hide from the feelings of 'I don't deserve being treated like a god.' He was very uncomfortable with that stardom aspect."

As Gene Clark reflected to Holger Peterson in 1984, "All at once we were considered one of the big three and the element of your private life goes away. I really didn't know what to do or which way to turn. It was pure, simple, nervous frustration. You don't know how to deal with it all at once. You've got a lot of money, a lot of attention, and no privacy. It got big too fast. Even though I did have a lot of fun, I did want some privacy."

Michael Clarke told Peterson, "I understood why he left. We all wanted to kill him. We were all in it together and should have stuck together. But it got pretty bananas after a while. We couldn't agree on anything. It became a band against each other and that's when you start making mistakes. When you start letting other people make your decisions for you because you're too lazy to make them yourself, that's when you get screwed. And that's what happened. It was too bad that it had to be like that, but that's just what happened."

Years later, Michael went to Gene's rural retreat in Mendocino, California for a short visit. Like old war buddies, the two friends whiled away the hours in nostalgic reflection on their Byrds days. A friend recalls the two calling up and singing drunken renditions of Byrds songs over the phone. After Michael left, Gene came across a notebook in his house and, opening it, laughed at what he found. "It said, 'Fuck you for quitting' and it was signed 'Mike.'"

David Crosby insists that fear of flying was only one symptom of a larger crisis mounting for Gene. He agrees that Gene did suffer a nervous breakdown. "I can completely understand that. Think about it: country boy from Missouri, 12 siblings, then suddenly L.A. and stardom. Bam! So no, he wasn't ready for it. And he had, as we all had, little sycophants whispering in our ears saying, 'No, no, you're the one.' I think it was very tough for him. I think it was a complete culture shock coming to California in the first place, and showbiz. Real culture shock. And I think that when we started to get successful and make money and have legions of girls around, it got very complex for him. And Gene wasn't a complex guy." Does David believe that he contributed to Gene's departure? "I'm sure I was tough on Gene," he concedes. "I'm sure I was tough on everybody. I'm not patient with people and I tend to express myself. But I don't think it was the reason he left the band."

Chris Hillman witnessed the transformation in Gene in the ensuing months and worried about his friend. "If there was ever a classic Hollywood bad novel where the character gets eaten up and spit out, that's Gene," he notes. "He wasn't equipped to survive. Something happened to him. I don't know what clicked in him but something snapped in Gene. I can't pinpoint what, why, or where. Maybe it was an underlying something, maybe it was drug-induced, but something snapped. He started dating this dancer and some of these dancers were so high maintenance. Great-looking, but just mind-numbing. Here's this guy just out of Kansas and she got to him. I thought that they had done some acid or some god-awful thing and it just got to him. And if there was a history of alcoholism or anything genetic in that type of behavior in the family, who would know?"

Gene had become increasingly moody and reclusive, distant from the others. The manic depression—mood swings and erratic behavior that manifested in his adolescence—were again becoming pronounced. He was clearly suffering from severe depression, though no one recognized the symptoms at that time. Today, Roger assesses Gene's problems at that moment as the result of his undiagnosed condition. "There were psychologists who knew about things like that, but it wasn't as popular a belief then as it is now. He obviously was manic-depressive, I would say that. But drugs were involved in that. He had a bad acid trip. He went out with this dancer and she screwed him up. I don't know what happened, but he really suffered from that relationship."

"His frustration with the music industry was tremendous," insists David Clark, recalling later conversations with his brother. He remembers Gene telling him that he had gone as far as he wanted to go in the Byrds and, ever restless, it was time to move on. "For one thing, he had already accomplished what he wanted to and he was no longer interested in that. He didn't want to stand there and do the same old crap he'd been doing for two years. He wanted to move on. He was very creative. He would be thinking of something else and miss his cue. Then he would get self-conscious. The more this happened, the more all these pressures built up. But it was out of frustration and people not hearing what he had to say. He had gone as far as he could go with them and all this frustration made him very nervous. Once he had gotten to a certain place with something in his music, then he would decide if it was worth going on with and he would perfect it and then he was done with it and he was ready to move on. Or if it wasn't the direction he wanted to go, or he was being steered by other people in a direction he didn't want to go, he would leave the project and go do what was in his head. For him it was about the message of the songs. 'Mr. Spaceman' just was not his thing. He was moving beyond that. By the time the *Turn! Turn! Turn!* album was complete, he was done with the Byrds."

Cynthia Webb was Chris Hillman's girlfriend at the time and observed the stress the group members experienced in dealing with the machinations of stardom. "I think they were getting tired of each other by 1966. Chris was living off Kirkwood. He didn't see much of Gene, but he did see more of David for some reason. But Chris and I kind of hung by ourselves quite a lot. I just remember Chris being frustrated at playing the bass. I don't think he loved it. His first love was still the mandolin and he would play it all the time at home. Chris was more of a natural kind of guy and I think he got fed up with a lot of the showbiz image part of it. He didn't like their look, the straight, mop top hair. Chris's hair is naturally curly and he would have to wash his hair with this stuff and put this net on it to keep it down so it would be totally straight. They had to do a lot of traveling. I don't think it was easy for Gene to travel, as I recall. He started internalizing a lot of this stuff that was going on and it made him even more tense. I think Gene, as I remember him, preferred to be by himself, strumming his guitar and writing. It was hard for him, all the attention. Chris was okay with it, but sometimes I remember him not wanting to do it. It got wearisome and you get tired."

Attempts were made to dissuade Gene from leaving the group. Manager Eddie Tickner remembers trying to broker a solution. "Gene was not happy. He asked me to help him get out of the band. I went to the other guys because they didn't want to let him out. But Gene was not going to get on another airplane. Only Brian Wilson could stay home and remain in a band. But if you can't fly, you can't go anywhere. The other guys felt his leaving the band was not acceptable." (Beach Boy resident genius Brian Wilson had recently taken the unprecedented step of redefining his role in the group by choosing to remain off the road in order to write, arrange, and record tracks for the group to complete, allowing them to tour with a stand-in bass player. Given Brian's obvious dominance over the Beach Boys' songwriting and direction, the move was accepted by the others. But it was unlikely that Gene could have carved out such a role in the Byrds, given his diminishing stature and jostling for power within the group.)

"I tried talking him out of it," Jim laments. "He wouldn't listen; he wouldn't do anything. Nobody wanted him to leave."

While Roger and David remained mute on the subject, Chris endeavored to reason with Gene. "Actually, I did try to. I had bouts of a little wisdom at that age and I told him I thought he was making a mistake. Part of me thought that with Gene gone maybe it was an opportunity for me, but I did try to get him to think it over. But he wanted to go. 'I really want to do something else.' He had visions of grandeur as a solo artist. Which could have happened. I think that fire was stoked by Dickson and Tickner, who saw a double payday."

Roger also alleges that Gene's exodus was encouraged by Jim and Eddie because they recognized Gene's potential as a solo artist. Given Gene's appealing looks and proven singer-songwriter track record, there is some wisdom to that notion. "When Dickson was in the hospital about 25 years ago, Camilla [McGuinn] and I went to see him. At that point I think he thought he was going to die or something because he started telling me things he hadn't told me before. And one of them was that it wasn't Gene's fear of flying that was the reason for Gene's departure, but actually Dickson and Tickner were grooming him to become an Elvis Presley solo artist. Dickson told me that, but he denies it now. I'm not lying about this. Dickson did say it to me. Maybe it was a confessional mood because he thought he was going to die. But I stand by what I heard Dickson say. It did make sense to me. Looking at the individual talents in the group, it did make sense that Gene was the one most equipped for that sort of career." Jim counters Roger's contention indignantly: "The idea that Eddie and I wanted to turn him into another Elvis Presley is just McGuinn's imagination. I didn't even like Elvis Presley then."

Quite the contrary to Roger's assertion, Gene's departure from the group was not hastened by any designs on a solo career, nor was it, as David insinuates, precipitated by whisperings in his ear that he was the star. At that point, Gene had no future plans whatsoever. His solo career would, in fact, not even get off the ground for the better part of a year. His leaving the Byrds was the direct result of serious depression and imminent necessity to get out of the band and all the trappings that now surrounded it. His mental health and stability depended on that. Indeed, Gene admitted that he took the next three months off just to recuperate and find his inner focus again. He wanted nothing to do with the music business at that point.

Although the Byrds carried on without Gene, they never again enjoyed the same level of success. By the end of 1967, first David, then Michael, would be gone. Chris departed in late 1968, leaving Roger to mount an entirely reconstituted Byrds lineup into the early '70s.

What did the Byrds lose with Gene out of the lineup? "What the Byrds lost when Gene left was soul, honesty, a certain wonderful creative streak that was completely different," suggests David. "Gene was an absolute one-off. Nobody else wrote like that—nobody else wrote those songs. There was simplicity, a naïveté, to those songs that the rest of us couldn't create. I couldn't do it, Roger couldn't do it. Gene could. To me, I thought the five of us had a magic and I didn't want it to go. I liked him, and I liked his music. The Byrds were done when Gene left; we were never the same after that. I always said there were only ever five Byrds."

"The five guys, that's the Byrds, the original five," Chris concurs. "We did okay as four, but probably didn't attain as big a niche in the success train as the five. We survived without Gene, but on another level. We lost the songs, his songs, and maybe a little more resonance on the vocals. The original essence of the Byrds was those five guys. Gene was a part of that essence. Separate all of us and we weren't the greatest players, but together it worked. You take the Stones and you separate them and they're not the greatest players either, but together, you can't touch them. That's the magic. David is right. Gene was handsome, sang real well, and the girls were screaming for him more than any of us. With that Prince Valiant haircut, he'd smack that tambourine backstage with a 'Let's go, guys!' attitude and lead us out onstage.

"We lost a heck of a songwriter. To this day, and I'll be the first to admit it, I never realized how good a songwriter Gene was until after he was gone. He used these very interesting word groupings, which were far deeper and heavier than any of the rest of us could come up with. Listen to something like 'Set You Free This Time' and you'll see what I mean."

"Gene was kind of the rudder," muses Roger, "like a stabilizing force. In the studio, Gene and I would double the lead parts and that would give me a fullness to my voice that it lacked and would give him maybe a little sprightliness to his voice, a little more edge. We lost a great song-writer. We lost a romantic kind of grounding force. He was the attraction, he and Michael Clarke. Michael was a cute-looking boy, but Gene had that sort of mature, romantic lead kind of thing going and we lost that."

Often burdened with the lion's share of blame for Gene's departure as his tormentor, David remains circumspect about the way he treated Gene in the Byrds. "I didn't understand why he left, but I did like him. At that time I was very young and I didn't understand a whole lot of what was going on. I was just a blithe spirit breezing along, stoned out of my mind, happy as a clam doing what I did. And sometimes I would create wreckage and other times I would create beauty, but I really wasn't too aware or really understood what he was going through all that well. I was more concerned with myself."

Jim is far more cynical about the way Gene is remembered by David and Roger. "David's been kind to Gene in interviews ever since. But he didn't say that at the time. He was very pleased to be rid of Gene at the time. They've all mellowed a lot about Gene. No one wants to speak ill of the dead. And McGuinn finally said that he never realized how valuable Gene was as a songwriter. Perhaps to some degree that's true of everybody."

The next Byrds album, *Fifth Dimension*, found the group taking their jazz and raga experiments further, even exploring the metaphysical and science fiction, while still keeping a foot in folk-rock. Could Gene have adapted to that direction and been able to contribute? Roger has doubts. "He would have gone along with it, but he never was really into that stuff. He had one sort of main thing that he did and that was the romantic, poetic thing. That was Gene." Gene's predilection for pensive, melancholy ballads might have found few supporters among band members on the experimental album.

There is little remaining evidence of the songs Gene was composing at the time he quit the Byrds. He did not record any new material until late summer of 1966. Those songs, many released the following January on his debut solo album, *Gene Clark with the Gosdin Brothers*, found Gene still working within a folk-rock context. By then the Byrds had already flown that nest and were exploring far more daring musical territory. Perhaps the times had passed Gene by.

Some of Gene's solo material, arranged and recorded with Leon Russell, was lush with baroque-flavored orchestration, suggesting that Gene was looking to take folk-rock in a whole new direction. Songs like "Echoes" and later "Only Colombe," replete with strings, piccolos, and harp-sichords, and boasting evocative, image-laden poetry, are two examples of these explorations. But for the most part, the tracks on *Gene Clark with the Gosdin Brothers* would have found little favor with the other Byrds, nor earned a place on *Fifth Dimension* or its follow-up, *Younger Than Yesterday*, one of the finest examples of exploratory, mind-expanding, Summer of Love music. "I think we gained some mobility," suggests Roger, on the impact of losing Gene. "We were freer to explore different musical directions because the grounding and the steadiness and anchoring Gene gave us was sort of a drag on the whole thing. So we gained a dexterity and flexibility to go flying into doing these other crazy things we did."

Where Gene would prove to be a visionary was in his daring integration of traditional country music and bluegrass—two idioms shunned by the pop world and the hip rock cognoscenti of 1966—into folk-rock and pop. It was a path he first trod on *Gene Clark with the Gosdin Brothers* with tracks like "Tried So Hard" and "Keep on Pushin'," only to follow that route more directly soon after in the company of Douglas Dillard. In that sense he was pointing the way, not so much ahead, as the Byrds were, but rather back to an authentic roots music that would find acceptance several years later. Gene would become one of the pioneers of a return to American country-folk music, yet—like so much of his career—rarely garner due recognition for his efforts. Even the Byrds, post David and Michael, would become the avatars of what would be labeled country-rock, with 1968's *Sweetheart of the Rodeo*. By then, Chris was coming into his own as a gifted songwriter and singer.

Gene's exit from the Byrds was in many ways a double-edged sword. It removed their Dylanesque romantic poet, but allowed two more songwriters, first David and then Chris, to fill the breach. "Gene's leaving really brought Chris out," underscores Roger, "because Chris was a shy guy. He was like even scared to face the audience at first and gradually he emerged as a monster songwriter."

"We were lucky that it did still work without Gene," David surmises. "We were able to make at least one really good record without him and we were able to perform well without him. But we were better with him." On tour in Southern California that April the group was met with cries of "Where's Gene?"

"Chemistries are magical," concludes David. "They're like soap bubbles. They're very fragile. They pop into existence and you go, 'Ah, isn't that beautiful!' Then you try to touch it and, poof, it's gone. And the Byrds were a magical chemistry."

4

Out on the Side

Besieged by the Los Angeles media and heartbroken fans after the startling announcement of his departure from the Byrds, Gene sought refuge back home in Bonner Springs, Kansas. It was his first time home since the Byrds' success the year before and their fame dogged him on his homecoming. No one back home knew yet that Gene was returning not as a Byrd, but as a former Byrd.

"Gene came home for a couple of weeks and he was not in a good place mentally," remembers Rick, who, like all the family, had watched his brother's rise to fame from a distance with a great deal of pride. Now they would get to visit with a bona fide star and hear all his wondrous stories. Only Gene didn't want to talk. "It was a big deal around town. 'Gene Clark of the Byrds comes home.' But he didn't want that at all. There were people showing up at the house wanting his autograph, all this stuff. And he didn't want anything to do with that. Reporters would call the house and he would tell them, 'Don't you ever call me at my parents' house!' and hang up. He just wanted to get away from all that and not have it follow him to his mom and dad's house. He just wanted to hide from it for a while. My mom and dad knew that he was very disturbed and in turmoil. It was hard for them and for all my brothers and sisters because everyone knew he was very unhappy. He tried to hide it or make it out like it was no big deal, but when you're that devastated no matter how much you try to make somebody think that everything's okay, they know it's not. This was his mom and dad and brothers and sisters. They didn't realize how all that jealousy affected him, to have his own band mates turn on him like that, how deeply that affected him. Gene tried to brush it off like it was no big deal. 'I left the Christy Minstrels and it was cool; I don't need the Byrds.'"

Gene's mother told *Kansas City Star* writer Brian Burnes in a January 17, 1999, *Star Magazine* feature, "When he left here and got into all that, it was completely separate from our family here. He very seldom discussed anything about it when he was here. It was more like 'I'm home, so let's be a family right now.'" Comments Rick, "There can be a lot of downs in this business and he didn't want the family to know what he was going through."

"That was Gene compartmentalizing his life," insists sister Bonnie. "He wanted his family to be a private thing. He never wanted us to be used by either the Hollywood scene or locally. But eventually he would sit down with a guitar and start playing his music and that was how he communicated, through his music."

Rick recalls conversations with Gene where he expressed his disenchantment with the superficial nature of the music business and the Hollywood lifestyle. "Oh, man, he got chewed up and spit out. When you are kind of used to a genuine lifestyle where people smile at each other and say 'Hi,' 'Thank you,' and 'Please,' and when they give their word it's a bond, it's not a false manipulation, and then you find out that the people who are giving their word to you are the ones who are stabbing you in the back, the hurt and the scars were so deep. Gene was not able to grasp that people could be that cruel and hateful. He had never experienced that. Being thrown into the fray at a vulnerable age with a kind of naïveté—that wasn't a hillbilly thing, he wasn't a stupid country bumpkin, he was just a very sensitive person who believed in honesty and respect and peoples' words being their bond. To be thrown into a situation where a person's word is an ulterior motive to a certain extent, to find out that the person you placed your trust in and who, with your own moral upbringing and background, made you feel safe only to hurt you deeply by betraying you, that's what really fucked Gene up."

Nonetheless, David noticed a transformation in his brother since his previous visit. "He was really more genuine this time. He didn't have this big star thing, even though he was a much bigger star than he had been in the New Christy Minstrels. He was a little mellower. First time he and I saw each other we kind of wrestled around and it was more like it used to be."

But while some family members recall the visit extending over several weeks, David points out that, in fact, Gene's visit was in two stages. He arrived by train on the Super Chief from Los Angeles and spent a few days with the family. During that time, Gene and his mother, Jeanne, and youngest sister, Sarah, journeyed to Tipton to visit his grandmother, Rosemary Faherty. A day or two later Gene boarded the train again and headed east. No one in the family quite knows where Gene was headed, but David speculates it was New York. A week later Gene returned and spent a few more quiet days with family and friends.

Despite the secure sanctuary home afforded, Gene knew that his life was no longer in Kansas and he returned to Los Angeles in early March to review his options. Still flush with money (he would pocket a sizeable check for writing the flip side of the Byrds' recent No. 1 "Turn! Turn! Turn!" with another check on the way for co-writing "Eight Miles High"), Gene could afford to cool out indefinitely and take his time. "He was still earning money long after leaving the Byrds," emphasizes Jim Dickson, "because the money for the first two albums came in after he left and they still had to pay him. His estate is still getting money from the Byrds today." Although plans were announced for a solo career, Gene was hardly in a suitable headspace to jump back into the fray. He would later characterize this period as akin to being out in the wilderness, adrift without a rudder. "For at least a year I was spaced, I was confused, I tore my telephone off the wall," he recalled to Los Angeles DJ B. Mitchell Reed in a 1974 interview. "I wouldn't fly on an airplane anymore."

The period from early 1966 to 1968 marked a troubled two years for Gene, unbroken until he teamed up with Douglas Dillard in the spring of 1968. Although it was one of the most creative chapters in his life in terms of churning out songs, his public performances during that time barely made double digits. If Gene had been seeking success as a solo artist more aggressively, he would have been ushered into a recording studio within weeks of announcing his departure from the Byrds in order to capitalize on all the attendant publicity. The fact that the announcement came in March and his first solo single did not appear until December reveals not only Columbia Records' lack of confidence in Gene as a viable solo artist, but a lack of ambition on Gene's part plus the promotional weakness of the Dickson-Tickner management team.

The most formidable obstacle Gene faced in launching a solo career was earning acceptance from the record-buying public in general and Byrds fans in particular, who were less inclined to embrace an offshoot of the wildly popular group. This was still 1966 and loyalties tended to be toward groups, not individual artists, especially an artist who had fled such a beloved group as the Byrds. The fans' perceptions leaned more toward feelings of betrayal. "How could he leave the Byrds?" Overcoming that impediment would not be easy.

"Very few artists have succeeded on the same level as the bands from which they sprang," Modern Folk Quartet's Cyrus Faryar postulates on the fickle nature of solo success. "There is something about the dynamics of a group that broadens the base of its appeal and popularity. You've got three or four guys in a band and the fan base can love or admire one or the other or all of them. But if you've got a single person, the focus is reduced. It's like marketing. If you come to the counter and there is only one object to purchase, your choices are buy it or not. If there are two or more objects your choices are one or the other. It's the same with solo singers. They either like you or they don't. Whereas if you're part of a band they might not like you as much as one of the other guys, but you're all in the same group. Even the Beatles, look what happened to them. They had to struggle hard to achieve their solo success. And the record companies were still powerhouses at the time and promotional budgets were all-important. The record companies did have the power to make or break you."

Similarly, the music business in 1966 was still geared primarily to promoting and marketing pop bands, combinations of musicians with an identifiable collective image, more so than individual solo artists. The singer-songwriter era was still a few years off. The Top 40 singles chart remained king and groups were made or broken on the basis of their singles success or lack thereof. And the main avenue for promotion was the teen magazine, and the vehicle used to drive that avenue was the teenybopper appeal of the recording artist. Even as they were conceiving work that was more sophisticated lyrically, like "Norwegian Wood" and "The Word," the Beatles were still regarded as cute, mop-topped pinups. Certainly, despite their more cerebral approach to music and the stoned, cool hipness they exuded, the Byrds found themselves fodder for *Teen Screen, Sixteen, Tiger Beat,* and *Teen Set,* all aimed squarely at the female teenage fan who could be expected to buy a group's singles straight into the pop charts. Magazines like *Hit Parader* tended to draw in the male faction by emphasizing musicality over cuteness, though they, too, still proffered the occasional fluff piece (an analysis of Chicago blues legend Muddy Waters's influence might be sandwiched between an exposé on 'Fang' of Paul Revere's Raiders and a Hollies pictorial). Promotional photo shoots were as important as recording sessions for any mid-'60s band; a new pose was always needed to send out to the magazines.

Consider the plight of Buffalo Springfield, one of the era's most creative, innovative, and influential bands who spawned the later careers of Neil Young, Stephen Stills, Richie Furay, and Jim Messina. Collectively, Buffalo Springfield was packaged as cute and cuddly and peddled to all the fan mags as the pop flavor of the month. "Win a Dream Date with Buffalo Neil!" The image of Neil Young and Stephen Stills—two of the greatest songwriters in American rock as well as two of its most notoriously reclusive egomaniacs—splashed across the pages of *Teen Set,* kibitzing about playing croquet with Chad & Jeremy, hosting a kite flying contest or an ice skating party for fans, boggles the mind today.

That was the wisdom of the time, however. It's only later that groups or solo artists were promoted on the basis of their unique creativity and individual musical innovation. Few artists were afforded the luxury of being taken on their own terms. If Gene Clark wanted to launch a successful solo career, he would have to play the game using the template of the period. While folk-rock may have elevated the pop song toward something of greater artistic merit, the starmaker machinery remained tried-and-true in 1966.

M arketing a dark, brooding, romantic singer-songwriter like Gene, who sang deep, esoteric poetry would not be easy. Compounding all this was the reality that Gene was not a public personality, nor would he fly or tour—two requirements for a shot at success. If Gene was ill equipped to deal with being in the Byrds, he was even less able to mount a solo career. His confidence as a performer had been shattered by the adulation that followed the Byrds, as well as the sniping from his band mates, and his growing doubts over his own abilities plagued him throughout this period.

With a management contract from Dickson and Tickner in hand and still very much a celebrity, Gene set out to form his own backing band from an assortment of friends and associates on the L.A. music scene. After turning down an offer from ex-Dillards drummer Dewey Martin to join his new group, Buffalo Springfield, Gene assembled Gene Clark & the Group by early May. The band consisted of drummer Joel (known to everyone as Joe) Larson from the Grass Roots, guitarist Bill Rhinehart, formerly of the Leaves (who had scored a minor folk-rock hit with "Hey Joe"), and Chip Douglas, late of the Modern Folk Quartet, on bass. Gene would provide the rhythm guitar and lead vocals as well as the band's repertoire.

Still a teenager, Joe Larson had come down to Los Angeles from San Francisco in mid-1965 with his group, the Bedouins, at the behest of Elmer Valentine and Lou Adler. A song called "Where Were You When I Needed You" had already been recorded by Phil Sloan, under the name the Grass Roots, for Adler's Dunhill Records. With a hit on its hands, the label needed a Grass Roots group. Elmer had seen the Bedouins performing in San Francisco and so brought them down, putting them up at the Tropicana Motel on Santa Monica, a favorite oasis for musicians arriving in Los Angeles. Here Joe befriended Byrds drummer Michael Clarke, who frequently hung out at the Tropicana. (Joe claims that he was brought in on several occasions by Byrds producer Allen Stanton, who temporarily replaced the ousted Terry Melcher, to overdub drumming parts on Byrds recordings, unbeknownst to Michael.)

"I met Gene on Sunset Strip," Joe recalls. "We played in a place called the Trip across from Ben Franks. Everybody either went to Kantor's or Ben Franks after the clubs closed. We came down to record 'Mr. Jones' and 'Eve of Destruction' for Dunhill. We became the house band and one of the bands that played there was the Byrds. Michael and I hit it off and I started hanging out with him. Between sets we would be out on the stairway or in the abandoned club upstairs doing what boys did in those days, smoking joints or whatever. Gene was kind of a standoffish, sort of weird guy. He was a different kind of guy. I ended up living with Michael, and Gene would come over all the time, so I got friendly with Gene.

"Gene and I and Bill Rhinehart had a passion for cars. Gene had an MGB, Rhinehart had a 912 Porsche, and I had a Mini Cooper. We would go up to Mulholland Drive and race. So it was the car thing that first brought us together. He was like a maniac driver. He would get that MGB going sideways. Rhinehart actually got his airborne, but Gene managed to keep his on the road. When Gene got his Ferrari, that was a major deal. It was beyond belief. We would be down there high out of our heads going, 'Wow, man, a Ferrari!' Gene was becoming increasingly upset with the situation with the Byrds. By then I was living on Wonderland Avenue in Laurel Canyon with Chip Douglas. Around that time we started playing over at Gene's house, kind of coming up with new songs and working on stuff like Dino Valenti's 'I Don't Ever Want to Spoil Your Party.' That was a favorite we always loved playing. If Gene was at a party and there was an acoustic guitar around, he would play that song." (Ironically, the Valenti song was recorded and subsequently abandoned by the Byrds during a 1965 recording session. David Crosby handled the lead vocals.)

When Gene broached the idea of forming Gene Clark & the Group with Joe, the drummer recommended his friend Bill Rhinehart as well as his roommate Chip Douglas, who had recently left the Modern Folk Quartet. Chip and Gene already had a history. Chip, along with Cyrus and Henry Diltz, came from Hawaii in 1961 to Los Angeles where they hooked up with Jerry Yester to form the MFQ, whose brilliant harmonies and arrangements set them apart as one of the finest folk ensembles on the circuit. "I think our paths probably crossed first at the Troubadour in 1964," notes Chip. "He and Jim [Roger] McGuinn and David Crosby used to sit around in the Troubadour bar area in the front of the club on Monday nights, Hoot Night, practicing their stuff in the corner on acoustic guitars. Just about every Monday night they would be there, working out these three-part harmonies. I remember one song in particular they were playing back then that never made it onto a Byrds album, but I later recorded it with the Turtles, and that was 'You Showed Me.' I always remember that one for some reason."

Chip followed the success of the Byrds over the next two years and would often run into the various members of the group at the Troubadour. Taking their own cue from the Byrds, the Modern Folk Quartet traded in their Martin and Gibson acoustic guitars for Rickenbackers and an electric bass. "I knew Jim Dickson, who was managing the Byrds," Chip continues, "and he mentioned one night that David Crosby had made Gene crazy and that he had to get out of the Byrds to keep from going nuts. I think Gene was frustrated because he was a songwriter—and he wrote lots of songs—but lots of those songs did not end up being Byrds songs. That's what I think bugged him the most. He wanted more of his songs recorded by the group, but he had two other guys to deal with who had opinions on those songs and perhaps they didn't think they were right for the group. I knew he had a lot of tunes and was always writing."

The newly assembled Gene Clark & the Group began rehearsing Gene's recent batch of songs at his house on Rosilla in early May. Gene's vision for the group was, as he later articulated, along the lines of the Beatles' *Rubber Soul* album. "It was a folk-rock oriented group, I would say," confirms Chip, "but Gene really wanted to be like the Beatles. That was his biggest influence. He wanted us to be the next Beatles." Released in late 1965, *Rubber Soul* embodied the Beatles' first true integration of folk influences, notably Dylan and the Byrds, country music (something the Beatles had always had an affinity for), and rock. Gene found the album not only a revelation but a confirmation of the sound he wanted to pursue. He articulated the sound of Gene Clark & the Group to *Hit Parader:* "In the short time together, we've worked up a lot of material. It's kind of a strange sound. We're working on some things, which are a mixture of country, western, and blues combined. It's the kind of simplicity that the Beatles use: guitar riff-vocal-hard-hit kind of thing. Most of the material is original. As yet, we haven't got any real vocal thing going. I'm doing all the vocal, with some harmony mixed in."

To *The Beat*'s Thermon Fisk in a July 9 feature, Gene surprisingly hinted that the group might incorporate some vaudeville numbers into their set, though there is no indication of them having done so.

As Chip recalls, "It didn't sound like the Byrds or the Beatles. It sounded like some guys who were trying to do something, but it didn't come out right. I remember doing 'That's Alright By Me.' One of my favorites was 'Keep on Pushin'.' Another was 'Needing Someone,' which was one I liked a lot. 'Elevator Operator' was one I kind of contributed some lyrics to, along with Joe Larson. Joe kind of came up with the idea to begin with and Gene jumped on it after he heard Joe singing it. I added a couple of words to it when we were working on it. It was really Joe's song and he and I were working on it when Gene kind of took it over. I guess our names got lost in the credits."

Gene's insecurities—not only as a frontman but as a bandleader, a role he had never played, even as far back as his earliest Kansas City combos—hindered the group from the outset. Notes Joe, "Gene was a celebrity and did have enough oomph that he could have put together a winning combination. But he was starting to get pretty nuts by this time. He wasn't sure what he wanted. He had trouble getting his ideas across. We would rehearse every day and he would try the same song we had been doing for a week, only now we would redo it. He expected everything to happen as he had imagined it. He had sat down and imagined a whole new thing and he would say 'Here's how it's gonna sound' without really explaining what he wanted us to do. He had some idea in his mind of what he wanted it to sound like but he was terrible on showing it to us. I think McGuinn put together the musical sound of the Byrds, not Gene."

Six weeks after rehearsals began, Gene Clark & the Group debuted at the Whisky-A-Go Go on June 22 for a two-week stand, on the heels of a dazzling six-week stint by new group Buffalo Springfield. Ads for the engagement made particular note of Gene's Byrds pedigree. Expectations ran high among the Hollywood music set and Byrds fans for Gene's triumphant return to performing. It was not to be.

"There was all this pressure on Gene," Chip explains. "This was supposed to be *better* than the Byrds, but how could it be? We didn't have Crosby or McGuinn. People were expecting the Byrds and we were all nervous. They didn't come up raving about us afterwards. There were a few little groupie girls who said, 'Gosh, you guys are great,' but that was about it. I had some

Gene Clark & the Group outside the Whisky-A-Go Go, June, 1966: (left to right) Chip Douglas, Bill Rhinehart, Gene Clark, and Joel Larson.

friends come out, like Judy Henske and others, and they were hardly overwhelmed. They just kind of went, 'Hmmm.' That was it. No one was going, 'Hey! Wow!' It wasn't a joyful experience I remember, like playing with the Turtles, which was a big relief to me after being in that rather tense situation with Gene."

Joe agrees with Chip's grim assessment of the Whisky gig. "We never got the response we thought we would get. We had all these people from all these different bands, all these people we knew, and we would draw a big crowd, but nobody would respond. I think it was because Gene didn't sell the songs. He was up there, just singing them and hoping they would just come to *him*, maybe bring what the Byrds had done. I think he was expecting too much too soon. He had lived that Byrds crazy thing."

In a concession to his Byrds success, Gene included "I'll Feel a Whole Lot Better" and "She Don't Care about Time" in the Group's set list. The remainder of the material was new, which may have contributed to the indifferent response from the audience when presented with so much unfamiliar material. In an ironic twist, one of the opening acts during the group's Whisky engagement was the Doors, whose success would ultimately eclipse even that of the Byrds.

The failure of the Group to elicit an encouraging response, or even any kind of reaction beyond indifference, was borne heavily by Gene. "He was disheartened fastest and biggest of all of us," sighs Joe. "He was ready to be received and was expecting all the kudos. He was looking to take the step past the Byrds that he was hoping to take." During the two-week engagement Gene's behavior became increasingly more unpredictable, largely due to the muted response his debut garnered coupled with a severe case of nerves. The pressure of mounting a solo career in the shadow of the Byrds troubled Gene and the members of his group found his erratic behavior unsettling.

"When we started playing the Whisky, Gene started losing touch," observed Joe. "I didn't know what he was going to do. His mood swings were immense. He'd be cool, then he'd be out of his mind. One of the last days we played the Whisky, we were onstage doing a song and Gene turned around and looked at me and he had a look in his eyes. Then he started climbing up the side of the stage into the rafters. Literally just climbing up. I thought he was just goofing around, but he kept going, and he climbed all the way across the ceiling of the Whisky. At the time, before it burned, it had an open span and truss bowstring ceiling. He crawled up to where the dressing rooms were and we kept on vamping onstage hoping he would come back and he never did. So I just said, 'Thank you very much, everyone. We're Gene Clark & the Group. Good night and have a safe drive home.' That was how the set ended.

"Gene had that kind of nervous energy," Joe continues, "where he always seemed to be flexing or tensing, real physical stuff. He would scare me sometimes. He'd get that look in his eyes and I'd get out the door. He had a violent streak, more than the rest of us. If someone said something in a restaurant or somewhere he'd get right up in their face. He was emotional." Chip recalls some good times between the four musicians, but underneath the youthful bonhomie,

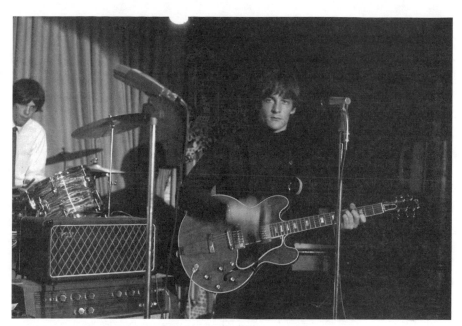

Gene onstage with the Group at the Whisky, June 1966.

Gene remained a more conflicted personality than the others. "We would practice for a while then go down to the Beef 'n' Beer and have a hamburger and some lunch. Gene would pick up the tab most of the time, but we never talked about money. We knew he was doing okay because he had that Ferrari. It was a used Ferrari, though. There was a picture of us standing around that Ferrari that was used in some teen magazine. Gene was kind of a quiet guy. He wasn't really talkative. But every once in awhile that laugh or smile would come out. He would have a couple of beers, but I don't recall him sitting around the house drinking. I don't remember us doing any pot either. It might have helped us relax a little more. He was quick to laugh with us guys, but he was a melancholy kind of guy. Gene had a serious look on his face, but then suddenly someone would say something funny and he would laugh. But he was a brooding guy who always seemed to have a lot on his mind."

Joe counters Chip's claims about Gene's use of drugs and alcohol. "We all smoked a lot of pot, but Gene was starting to drink a lot. He was a big vodka fan. We were going to all the hot spots. We were living large. We played every day and thought about music, but it started to get cloudy. The rest of us were living hand to mouth, living simply, and then all of a sudden Gene got a lot of Byrds money and went girl crazy and car crazy and started buying guns."

Besides the pressures of launching his own career, Gene had something else that unsettled him: a clandestine affair with Mamas & the Papas beauty Michelle Phillips. Recently estranged from husband and Mamas & the Papas guiding light John Phillips, Michelle was a Hollywood brat with a roving eye. Gene was a definite catch for her, though the affair remained a closely guarded secret among the Laurel Canyon elite until Michelle's tell-all biography, *California Dreaming,* was published in the 1980s. For Gene, knowledge of the affair could jeopardize his friendship with Papa John, a man known for his physical intimidation.

"Gene was having this big affair with Michelle Phillips during the time our group was practicing," acknowledges Chip. "We would show up to practice and Michelle would have to leave, then later on after we had been rehearsing for a while and had been to the Beef 'n' Beer, the phone would ring and Gene would say, 'Okay, practice is over,' and as we would be leaving Michelle would be coming in. That affair was going on the whole time the group was rehearsing. I'm sure it didn't add to the calmness of his demeanor. He didn't talk much about it, but if it came up he would just have a little smile on his face."

"We were living just a few blocks away from each other in Laurel Canyon," recalls Michelle fondly. "I started seeing Gene through Cyrus Faryar and his wife, who lived down the street from me. They were friends with Gene and I was friends with them. I believe that's where Gene and I started seeing each other. Cyrus's house was kind of halfway between my house and Gene's house. There was a lot of socializing going on back then. We just hit it off really well very quickly and started to have an affair. But we kept it very, very quiet. Gene and I never went out together, never had dinner at a restaurant, because I knew that it would just *enrage* John if he knew that I was seeing one of his peers. So that was just something we never did. I remember going to Catalina Island with him one weekend. We were on his manager Jim Dickson's boat, and I remember thinking that was risky because someone could have seen us. We got really good at keeping it a secret."

Despite the physical attraction, Michelle found Gene a troubled individual. "He was a very sultry, perplexed man. Very introspective. And he had this gloom around him. Although I must say that he had a very sweet and charming side to him. He was very sexy in that brooding kind of way. But you never knew whom you were dealing with. Gene was very torn about the relationship with me. He felt extremely guilty. As a matter of fact, not once but twice he woke me up in the middle of the night and told me that I had to go home, that it was all wrong. 'We shouldn't be doing this.' I don't think it was because he was afraid of John. I think he honestly felt that if the situation were reversed he would feel badly.

"I definitely think he was having a nervous breakdown," insists Michelle, "and the affair with me was not helping things any. He would have a lot of mood swings. He would be fine for a while then he would get deeply, deeply depressed. I think he felt very remorseful about the affair and knew it could go nowhere. There was just a lot of pressure. It could never have lasted, for many reasons, but also because we had very different temperaments. Gene was sweet and lovable and I'm sure that all the adulation and the fame really troubled him because it's not an easy thing to deal with. I don't remember him drinking a lot, but I think he was smoking a lot of pot. Gene was always writing songs. Like John, he always had his guitar in his hands. I was very attracted to the fact that he was a very creative, soulful kind of guy. He made me feel really good."

Mutual friend Cyrus describes the two as the ultimate 1960s Hollywood nouveau riche couple. "I remember one of my most vivid memories of that time was seeing Gene and Michelle in her XKE tooling out of the driveway and going somewhere. It was a very picturesque sight, I must say, because they were both lovely people—young, handsome, and beautiful, fine car, lovely day. It was perfect." Indeed, Gene confided to friends that he fantasized about he and Michelle becoming the king and queen of pop music.

The brief affair came to a shattering denouement on June 4 at a Mamas & the Papas concert at the Melodyland Theatre in Anaheim. "It was a theatre-in-the-round," Michelle recalls, describing the tumultuous events of that evening. "Gene happened to mention to me that he had never seen us perform. 'Well, I'll get you some tickets! You can go see us at Melodyland.' So I called the office and told Bobby Roberts's secretary, Carol, 'Can you get me a couple of tickets for Gene Clark?' assuming that would be it, Gene would go see us at Melodyland and no one would know and that would be the end of it. But when we came bounding onstage, Cass was the first one to see Gene. Cass knew what was going on between Gene and me. Well, we almost fainted dead away. There was Gene in the front row in a bright red shirt! You could not miss Gene Clark! He was the most obvious person in the entire room. And he was sitting there just grinning from ear to ear. Cass just gave me this quick glance and a look of terror came across my face. Since it was a theatre-in-the-round and we hadn't determined which mics we were going to take, Cass and I just grabbed the mics in front of Gene so that John and Denny would be forced to go to the other side of the stage. Everything was fine almost to the end of the concert, but by that time Cass and I had really loosened up. We were practically singing the entire show to Gene, and he was having a ball. John was there with his girlfriend, Ann Marshall. He was seriously dating at this time. But I still knew that if he knew I was dating Gene, it would really be bad news.

"We were in the middle of a song and I heard John scream into his mic, 'Get the *fuck* over here!' So Cass and I bounded to the other side of the stage and the Papas were now in front of Gene. I remember feeling this stark terror. Even though I could see Annie Marshall in her little green dress sitting right in the front row and I knew that John was having an affair with her, I also knew that this double standard existed and there was going to be this big scene. So we finished the concert and I ran off the stage, ran to the dressing room, grabbed my stuff, and I ran into the parking lot because I had driven myself there. I jumped into my little XKE and was about to put the key in the ignition when John jumped out, grabbed the door, and basically pulled me out of the car in front of people who were streaming out of Melodyland. He grabbed me by the arm and said, 'You're fired!' It was my birthday. Apparently word had gotten back to John that I was seeing Gene, but he didn't have any concrete proof until he saw him in the front row. I just looked him straight in the eye and I said, 'You know, John, I don't think you have the authority to fire me.' And he said, 'You wait and see. You're out of this group. You're never singing with this group again.' I got into my car and all the way home I was thinking, 'Naw, he can't fire me.'

"I went to my birthday party at Cyrus's and Gene was there. I said, 'Gene, how could you do that?!' 'What?' He seemed completely oblivious to what had gone down, although he knew that something had happened onstage but he wasn't sure what or why. I think he was sorry, but he didn't know that that was going to happen. Everything that Gene was afraid of he kind of brought on. He was afraid that John was going to find out we were having an affair. He was afraid of John's ire and he was afraid of hurting a contemporary of his, on a man-to-man thing. But inadvertently he brought it all on. And I, stupidly enough getting the tickets for him, never said, 'Oh, and by the way, seat him at the back.' It never occurred to me to say that. That was the end of the affair with Gene. There was so much pain associated with what had happened, so much drama, we never spent another night together."

As Papa Denny Doherty recollects, "I wasn't aware of the affair until we were playing Melodyland and Michelle started blowing kisses at Gene. John freaked out and was about to come off the stage after him with his guitar. The affair ended pretty quickly after that. I didn't want to have too much to do with Gene because he had had an affair with Michelle. Too much infighting; a little too close. After that Gene didn't want to be seen and we didn't want to see him. It was a little rock 'n' roll infighting."

Three weeks later Michelle received written notification via the group's lawyer that she was, indeed, no longer a member of the Mamas & the Papas and was prohibited from referring to herself as Mama Michelle. The letter was signed by John, Cass, and Denny. "I was fired because I was seeing Gene," she acknowledges. Nonetheless, her affection for Gene remained.

Within three months Michelle was back in the fold. "After I had been let back into the group, we were on our way to Miami for a concert," Michelle remembers. "Lou Adler had put on an extra roadie to travel with us in the cabin of the plane to keep us from fighting. There was a lot of tension between me and Cass, and me and Denny because we had had an affair, and John and I were trying to keep it all together for the sake of the group and presumably for the sake of the marriage. But on our way to Atlanta, John and I were drawing. And I took a pen and drew Gene's face on John's palm. How provocative was *that*?! And he saw it. We were on the ground in Atlanta and John turned to me and said, 'You're fired!' So I got up and started to get off the plane. And Terry Dean, the roadie who had been put on the plane to keep us from fighting, actually tackled me in the middle of the first class cabin. He said, 'You can't go! Get back in here!' I said, 'No, I've just been fired. And if I'm fired then they can do the fucking concert without me.' Terry sat me down in a back row and told me, 'Michelle, you can't do this.' He kept it all together and we headed to Miami. John had said when he saw the drawing on his hand, 'That's Gene Clark!' And I said, 'Oh, don't be silly.' I said to Terry, 'He tried to accuse me of drawing Gene Clark's face on his palm! Would I do something so provocative?' I was scrambling. I was so guilty. I don't know what I was thinking."

Michelle remains wistful about Gene. "He had this wonderful smile. He was a great guy, such a unique character. He was cute." As singer Carla Olson, who recorded with Gene in the 1980s, chuckles, "Gene gloated over that relationship until the day he died, that he had stolen Michelle Phillips from John."

In mid-July, following the unmitigated disaster of the Whisky engagement, Jim Dickson took Gene Clark & the Group into Criterion Studios in Los Angeles to record demos in anticipation of cutting first a single, then an album, for Columbia Records. Gene had officially resigned from his Byrds contract on May 2 and signed as a solo artist under his own name on July 10. The group laid down their entire live set list, but in the end the results were deemed unsatisfactory. "I remember it was a tense recording session," offers Chip, "and things didn't sound quite as good as they had sounded in rehearsal. Everybody was a little uptight; Gene was uptight and disappointed. I suppose we all were. All we played were Gene's songs. I don't know what ever happened to that tape." The whereabouts of the tape remain a mystery. Jim's recording archives were ultimately sold and many of the Byrds rehearsal tapes plus dozens of demo sessions cut by Gene, including the session with the Group, have since disappeared, rumored to have been thrown out inadvertently in the 1980s.

Chip feels that Gene's songs during that period were simply not commercial enough to have been successful or even worthy of release. Although he had been writing feverishly, Gene's continued fixation with Dylanesque wordplay and morose, minor key ballads made the songs less accessible. "Gene had a lot of great songs on those first two Byrds albums with the help of those guys. He just didn't have the right guys in us to do his songs with. I liked Gene's songs, a lot of them, but I also thought a lot of them were very complex, very deep. There were all these words he would put in his songs, the more complicated words the better. My impression was that they weren't commercial songs that people could like or get into. People liked simple songs then. It seemed like it got very tense, nervous, during that session and everyone was disappointed at what it sounded like. We could all suddenly hear it wasn't very good. It just didn't have it. Nothing was working right."

The fruitless sessions led to the breakup of the group. Chip laughs as he recalls the manner in which Gene presented the news to the other three. "It was right outside the garage on Wonderland Park at my house. We had this little meeting, we were all down on our haunches in front of the garage door, and Gene said, 'Here's the thing, fellows. I'm dissolving the group. I don't want to continue with this group. But if Joe and Bill want to play with me, that'll be okay.' In other words, 'Chip, I don't want you in my group.' He didn't give us a reason, just that it wasn't happening for him. That was within a few days after the recording session. Things just fell apart after that session."

Gene finally entered Columbia Studios on August 26 to lay down tracks for his debut solo album. Accompanying him for the sessions were Chris Hillman and Michael Clarke from the Byrds, Bill Rhinehart from Gene Clark & the Group, and studio stalwarts Glen Campbell and Jerry Cole, the latter a veteran of the "Mr. Tambourine Man" recording. Jim explains the choices: "Chris Hillman was a better bass player than Chip Douglas. Chip was probably a better musician, but he didn't work as hard. He was more of a kick back kind of guy from Hawaii and didn't have the aggression for rock 'n' roll. We went with who could make the best record." Also involved were keyboard player and future Beach Boys collaborator Van Dyke Parks. Producing the sessions was Columbia Records staff producer Larry Marks, who was assigned to do the album after Gene expressed reluctance to work with Terry Melcher. "Gene was really chasing the Beatles at that point," suggests Larry, on the direction Gene had in mind for his first solo release. "He was kind of thrilled to be doing his first solo album, but there was a lot of pressure on him. A great deal of it was self-imposed, as I recall." It was Larry who brought in Campbell as well as a young arranger and keyboard player making a name for himself in the industry, Leon Russell. On the first session the assembled players laid down tracks for two of Gene's recent compositions, "Couldn't Believe Her" and "Is Yours Is Mine." Gene returned to the studio August 29–31 to cut two countrified numbers, "Keep on Pushin'" (co-written with Bill Rhinehart) and "That's Why" (retitled "Tried So Hard"), along with "I'll Feel Better" (retitled "I Think I'm Gonna Feel Better")—no relation to Gene's "I'll Feel a Whole Lot Better"—and "Last Night" (retitled "I Found You").

The sessions were interrupted on September 2 when Gene made a startling decision to rejoin the Byrds, albeit temporarily, to assist them when David Crosby fell ill. The Byrds had found bookings drying up in the wake of Gene's departure. "Eight Miles High" had failed to achieve the chart success it rightly deserved, stalling at No. 14, while its follow-up, "5D" ("Fifth Dimension"), had fared even worse at No. 44—putting the Byrds in the doldrums. Beginning a 12-night stand at the Whisky-A-Go Go, David's voice failed on the opening night. Unable to cancel and with little time to rearrange the set to reduce David's vocal load (which had increased since Gene's exit), the others placed a panicked call to Gene to help bail them out. Gene dutifully obliged. After all, his career was somewhat in limbo, too, though he had no interest in rejoining with a solo recording already in the works.

The Kings of the Strip were back! Assumptions were incorrectly made that Gene had seen the folly of his decision to leave and had rejoined the fold. Hardly the case. Gene stuck around long enough to play a few more gigs with the group in Northern California.

"The very first time I ever saw the Byrds was at the Fillmore Auditorium around September 25, 1966," recalls writer and later A&M Records publicist Jim Bickhart, "and Gene played with them. I expected to see the quartet and there was Gene Clark with them so I thought that was cool. I just thought he was back with them. There was no reason to believe that he wasn't. But he was probably recording his own album at the same time. It was quite a treat because they had clearly reintegrated some of his lead vocals into their repertoire, like 'She Don't Care about Time.' It was also unique to see him perform on a few things from the *Fifth Dimension* album that he hadn't recorded." In retrospect, Bickhart feels that Gene's return was not all serendipitous. "One gets the feeling that the fact that he was doing Byrds gigs at the same time that he was recording his own album suggested that he may have had some misgivings about what he was up to."

Not so. Gene returned to Columbia studios for further sessions four days later and continued sporadically throughout October and into November. Besides the previous list of players, he was joined by guitarist Clarence White, session drummer Earl Palmer, and banjo player extraordinaire Douglas Dillard. "Clarence was just getting into electric guitar at the time," Larry recalls. "We were trying Clarence out on a couple of things. I think Jim Dickson brought Clarence by and introduced him one night." In subsequent years, Clarence's work on the album has been singled out for praise, yet the fact is his contributions were limited. "Glen Campbell did a lot of the guitar playing on that album," points out Larry, who also recalls Bill Rhinehart's Beatles-inspired guitar work on tracks like "Elevator Operator."

On September 29, Gene recorded what has often been termed his most esoteric composition, the deeply image-filled "Echoes." Originally titled "Regina Dance," the song represents the pinnacle of Gene's Dylan-influenced excursions and is a stunning exploration of his psyche at that point in his career. "When I first heard 'Echoes' it so overwhelmed me that he could write that," Jim marvels. "I really began to look at Gene in a whole other way after that song. He brought me a tape with a different song on it that he was enthused about. I listened to it and didn't think much of it, but there was a big blank space on the tape and then there was 'Echoes.' And I listened to that and I thought, 'Wow!' I took it to Leon Russell and he kind of overdid it and Gene never could really put a vocal on it with all that music overwhelming him. It lost its reality in the vocal. But just the poetry was amazing. I had all the lyrics printed in a full-page ad paid for by us in *Billboard* and *Cashbox*. I was just stunned that Gene had written that song. That whole song sort of takes place at the Whisky-A-Go Go. 'You can watch Regina dance in the crystal panes of glass'—that was the girl's name who danced in the glass cage at the Whisky. 'On the streets you look again at the places you have been' was so good. That was his introspection about leaving the Byrds and what happened after that. I said, 'Wow, Gene, that song is incredible.' It's really a poem, a great piece of poetry. It was exactly about that world he was in at that moment and it was so clear."

As a poetic vision, "Echoes" is a masterpiece of complex emotions and angst laid bare; as a recording it is a mini-opera of swirling strings and flutes, though Gene did suggest to friends that he was less than enamored with the overwrought arrangement. Gene's troubled soul-searching in the wake of his exit from the Byrds is revealed in such lines as:

Here the castles you can build,
out of dreams you have fulfilled,
won't keep out all of the ill will that is blowing;
and you'll look still for a trace of an opening in the place,
where you'll find the life that you were used to knowing.

Session logs reveal that the music score was composed by John Cole and arranged by Russell Bridges (aka Leon Russell) for the paltry sum of $400.

"Leon and David Gates [later with hit-makers Bread] were kind of both trying to get into orchestrating by doing arranging at that time," recalls Larry. "It was hard to get Leon to do things for anybody else because he mostly did things for himself. But he gave 'Echoes' a lot of thought and you've got to give him credit for much of the sonic style of that track. It was probably one of the most produced things we ever did with Gene. It was a one-of-a-kind track. We were looking at it as a single and we thought it might be the thing we might wrap the album around, but after that I was gone and Gary Usher took over."

Always reluctant to interpret his own lyrics, Gene nonetheless offered this explanation of "Echoes" to writer and music archivist Domenic Priore in a 1985 interview: "It's a generalization of a lot of feelings. I like the poetry in 'Echoes.' It's sort of like the poetry on the *No Other* album. It's just that I had a chance to get into doing a little deeper thinking. Sometimes I like to write basically just, you know, love songs that have some kind of meaning. I try to write songs almost always that have some kind of meaning, even if they're light. But with 'Echoes,' that was just things that appeared evident to me about the world. One of the things about good poetry or anybody who I consider a good poet is they leave it up to the listener's or reader's imagination to analyze it in their own situation, to kind of apply it to their own life however they want to do it, or to apply it to a general basis. And that's sort of how I feel about 'Echoes,' and a lot of the things I wrote."

By the beginning of November, after a falling out with Columbia executives that had nothing to do with Gene's album, Larry Marks quit and headed over to the recently launched A&M Records label. He was hastily replaced in the producer's chair by current Byrds producer Gary Usher, whose previous credits included working with the Beach Boys. Despite the switch, Jim Dickson maintains that *he* actually supervised the sessions. "I pretty much made that first solo album and Gary Usher just sort of stood there. He got kind of enthusiastic about one song, the one about the tar paper track ["So You Say You Lost Your Baby"] and wanted to get involved with that, but as far as the basic recordings, the stuff with Chris, Michael, and Clarence, those recordings, he just sort of sat there through all that." While several tracks on the album would ultimately bear Usher's producer credit, only two tracks ("Needing Someone" and "So You Say You Lost Your Baby") were cut from scratch with the new producer; the others were already laid down in one form or another.

Leon Russell returned on November 9 to arrange the strings for "So You Say You Lost Your Baby" (for $175 this time). Following that session the Gosdin Brothers came into the studio to overdub their backing vocal harmonies onto the tracks. It was Jim who suggested his client team up with the country music duo.

Vern and Rex Gosdin had started their musical career in their home state of Alabama in the early '50s before heading first to Atlanta and Chicago, then west to settle in California. Although more country music than bluegrass, the duo—Rex on upright bass and Vern on guitar— hooked up with the Golden State Boys, a popular bluegrass quintet based in Southern California and regulars on the country music television showcase *Cal's Corral*. In 1963 a young mandolin player from San Diego, Chris Hillman, joined the Golden State Boys, who soon morphed into the Hillmen, a quartet featuring Vern, Rex, Chris, and Don Parmley on banjo. The Hillmen recorded several sessions for Jim at World Pacific studios in 1963. After Chris left to join Randy Sparks's Green Grass Boys and eventually the Byrds, Vern and Rex worked as a duo, often backed by flat-picking guitar virtuoso Clarence White of the Kentucky Colonels. By 1965 Vern and Rex were working under the management aegis of Jim Dickson and Eddie Tickner, whose other clients included the Byrds and the Dillards. In September, Jim produced a recording session for the Gosdin Brothers and they cut a version of the then-unreleased Gene Clark song "The Reason Why" on an audition tape for Columbia Records.

Although Gene knew the Gosdin Brothers in passing, it was Jim's idea to put the three together on Gene's debut solo album. "I had them [the Gosdin Brothers] open for the Byrds off and on," Jim told rock historian Alec Palao (who spearheaded the recent re-release of the Gosdins' early recordings), "because I felt bad about leaving them behind." Alec believes that Vern and Rex were not particularly enamored of working with Gene or seeking any kind of long-term partnership with the ex-Byrd. "Dickson basically felt that he owed them for having concentrated so much on the Byrds. But Dickson didn't really know what to do with them."

Vern had already been given a tape of the tracks. "I did all the arrangements at my home and we went into the studio and put it down," he states. "I just had the demos. I was painting the inside of my landlord's house and I arranged the songs. I had a tape player in there and did the arrangements on every one of them. We sat down and worked through the arrangements at Gene's house and my house. We had a wonderful time doing the album. Gene was nervous about doing his first album. Gene was a good fella, but he was into drugs too much."

By November 18 the album was completed. One week later Columbia released "Echoes" backed by "I Found You" as Gene's first solo single, accompanied by a giant, two-page ad in the music weeklies that boasted, "Announcing the solo debut of a first-magnitude star," and reprinted the entire lyric sheet for the A-side. In fashionable striped T-shirt, leather jacket slung over his shoulder, photographed half in silhouette, Gene offers an affecting presence as a mysterious and brooding soul. Despite the ad and Gene's presence in all the teen magazines, the single failed to chart. Larry Marks laments, "We just couldn't get enough fire going for Gene. We never were able to pull off that radio-packaged single for him. It just never quite came together."

"You know what blows my mind?" asks Domenic Priore about Gene's lack of success with "Echoes." "Gene was plastered all over the teen magazines in those days and he was a teen idol. The girls really dug Gene, so it's really a shame that Columbia didn't know how to capitalize on all the free publicity these teenybopper magazines were giving him back then. They saw him as rugged, handsome, poetic, and romantic. I truly think that they should have been cranking out Gene Clark records, with all his good songs and obvious 1966 teen appeal. What a cool time for a guy like Gene Clark to have teen appeal. Columbia blew it."

Although Gene certainly had teen appeal, what he lacked was a hit single to cement that appeal. While "Echoes" was brilliant, it was simply a little too deep and cryptic for the pop crowd to latch onto. But, on the other hand, Gene had no desire for that sort of success. It bred the kind of fan adulation he feared, having suffered that in the Byrds. Gene no doubt desired to be a successful singer-songwriter, but he coveted acclaim as a creative artist in his own right and on his own merits—not as a teen magazine flavor of the month.

Jim Bickhart believes that "Echoes" failed not because of the fans' unwillingness to accept it, but because of missed opportunities in a misunderstood marketplace. "In that particular time period, it was quite common and not all that far-fetched for a song like 'Echoes' to be a hit. What made the pop charts was eclectic enough. If you look at the pop charts from that era, 1965 to 1967, there was everything from teenybopper to psychedelic to Motown to Memphis stuff. It was a very mixed bag, which was one of the reasons why it was such a great era for music. Somebody could conceivably be a pop star *and* a potential teen idol and *still* be doing something that wasn't perceived as bubblegum music—and Gene Clark obviously had no intention of doing anything like that. But having been the lead singer of a major band he could still be a teen idol, assuming he could somehow muster together something new that was still commercial.

"It was an interesting era for that kind of stuff, pre-*Rolling Stone* magazine," Bickhart continues. "The whole idea of treating this music seriously hadn't quite caught on yet. But if some kids will buy your record and somebody will play it on the radio, then it doesn't matter. They can promote you any way they want. If you think about it, given how the Byrds came to be known over time, looking back at their first album, it was not in step intellectually with a lot of what was around it, but it had a couple of hit singles—so who cared? In terms of the marketing machinery it was, 'Okay, we've got something to work with here. These guys are making music that doesn't necessarily sound like anything anybody else is doing but a couple of them are cute and they look kind of interesting in pictures so let's roll with it. Let's sell them as teen idols even if they wouldn't normally be.' That could have happened with Gene's solo career. If 'Echoes' had been a hit, it wouldn't have mattered. It would have been, 'He's still a pop star so we can do what we want with him.' He may be a deep, brooding pop star, but he's a pop star, and maybe *Tiger Beat* would have written about his complex, indecipherable lyrics, but he's still cute."

The gap between Gene's leaving the Byrds and the release of his first record may have further mired his chances for success. Teen memories are fleeting and the lifespan of a single is barely three months. There had been no Gene Clark product in almost a year. "Nobody really thought he was going to really leave the Byrds and it just takes time to get it together," Jim Dickson explains. "There wasn't that much pressure to get some Gene Clark product out from anybody and he was doing other stuff. He had that little group for a while. And he went through a lot of other changes and his time was pretty full. It all just seemed to flow naturally at the time. There was always something going on."

Was the long delay more the result of Gene's own insecurities or Columbia's uncertainty over his viability? "I would have to assume it was Gene," Bickhart postulates. "I'd be willing to bet that the guys at Columbia were saying, 'Yeah, absolutely. So when is he going to do a solo thing for us?' I wouldn't be surprised if Dickson and Tickner were of the same mind. They would have wanted Gene working." But as Dickson points out, "There were several factors, the flying was one, not going on the road at all was another. Gene would have liked to have stayed in Hollywood with his chick and just record. He had money and the road brought little after expenses."

"He didn't have it in him to do the grind that, in that era, was probably more necessary," avers Bickhart. "In those days it was much more of a whirlwind. Not only were you touring and promoting your product, but also you were expected to put out records much more regularly than people are now. That's one of the things I've always found remarkable when you compare that era with almost any time subsequently, where you have groups or soloists putting out two albums a year plus several singles and touring. And most of what they put out was better than what people take three years to put out now. But in order to have that kind of star-level career in that era you pretty much had to try to do that. Even if you were a one-hit wonder you had to be fairly prolific until they lost faith in you. If Gene's work ethic for whatever reasons wasn't up to doing that, then it was going to be harder for him to compete in that marketplace. Especially given that he was heading in a musical direction at that moment that turned out to be several years ahead of its time."

In an effort to promote his debut single, Gene reluctantly appeared solo for the first time ever in his career, just his voice and acoustic guitar, at the Santa Monica Civic Center, opening for the Count V, Standells, Seeds, Turtles, and Love. It was a bit of a reunion for Gene with the latter two groups, as Chip Douglas had since joined the Turtles and ex-Byrds roadie Bryan Maclean was a founding member of Love. For longtime Gene Clark aficionados, the thought of him performing "Echoes" alone on acoustic guitar is enough to elicit goosebumps.

In January 1967, Columbia released Gene's solo album under the odd billing of *Gene Clark with the Gosdin Brothers,* elevating Vern and Rex Gosdin to co-starring status on an album of Gene's songs. It was a bit of a surprise and the result of both Gene's own lack of confidence and Jim Dickson's largesse. While the Gosdin Brothers' harmonies certainly graced the tracks exquisitely, it's doubtful whether they deserved co-billing. "The Gosdin Brothers were not involved in that album at all when I was there," insists Larry Marks, who produced much of the album. "I knew them, but I was doing a Gene Clark solo album, that's all, and that's the way it would have finished if I had stuck around to the end. Even if they had done the singing on it, which was great, it wouldn't have been *Gene Clark with the Gosdin Brothers.* It was Gene's album. Dickson might have thought it was good marketing for both artists. Gene was fairly dependent on

Jim. Gene needed taking care of on a personal level and he needed someone like Jim to keep him on the straight and narrow. They were kind of co-dependent." Dickson disagrees: "Not giving the Gosdin Brothers credit would have been unthinkable," he asserts. David Clark recalls Gene telling him that he had wanted to title the album *Harold Eugene Clark,* but was overruled by the record label.

Gene Clark with the Gosdin Brothers is an anomaly. Folk-rock based, its songs are also much more pop-oriented than the Byrds' songs, with healthy doses of Beatles, baroque, and Buck Owens influences. By early 1967 folk-rock was on the wane, yet the album seems to capture Gene in a time warp. In many ways it accurately represents the sound of the Sunset Strip circa 1966. But by 1967 those sounds were definitely changing. All the songs are short and, with the exception of "Echoes," fairly lightweight pop fare for Gene. That's not to say it's a bad album. Quite the contrary, the songs on *Gene Clark with the Gosdin Brothers* are a very pleasant first solo effort. But they're a far cry from "Set You Free This Time" or "She Don't Care about Time," suggesting Gene was going for a more mainstream style. Clearly the high point is the lush "Echoes" and the low is the rather pedestrian "Elevator Operator." The Gosdin Brothers' harmonies are stellar throughout and contribute much to elevating some ordinary tracks.

Often mislabeled the first country-rock album, it is far less country-rock than pop, with "Tried So Hard" and "Keep on Pushin'" boasting Douglas Dillard's brand-new Rickenbacker electric banjo, dubbed the "bantar." "The *Gene Clark with the Gosdin Brothers* album along with *Younger Than Yesterday,* which I believe came out almost exactly at the same time, were the first times that, other than the Beatles doing 'Act Naturally,' I heard a rock 'n' roll band playing anything resembling country music," acknowledges Bickhart, "and Gene Clark's album was clearly more in that direction. It wasn't really until the Eagles came along that that stuff was viable."

Fans expecting to hear Byrds music on *Gene Clark with the Gosdin Brothers* were disappointed. Despite the presence of three of the five original Byrds, the distinctive elements of the Byrds' sound were conspicuous by their absence. "We couldn't have McGuinn play on that album because that would be the 12-string and it would be the Byrds again," confirms Dickson. As for David Crosby, "I don't think I was asked. I think there was a gulf between us. I think he wanted to establish himself as a solo artist and he would have liked it if he were a lot bigger than the Byrds. We were all very competitive and were all trying our best to be self-promoting."

In a bizarre marketing move, Columbia released the Byrds' latest effort, the stunning *Younger Than Yesterday,* two weeks after Gene's album, thereby dividing Byrds fans' loyalties and dooming Gene's chances to stand alone in the marketplace. Quite simply, his album was overwhelmed by the much better-known Byrds and Gene got lost in the shuffle. "When Gene put out his first solo record the same time the Byrds did, CBS didn't push it," asserts Dickson, who cites Gene's abrupt departure from the group as the cause of the label's loss of confidence in him. Gene became regarded as less reliable. "They had no faith in Gene staying there or doing anything. The

Byrds name sold the record, they had a name already, Gene didn't. CBS wanted to keep Gene so they made the record, but they didn't have much faith in him and didn't push it." Despite positive reviews and critical praise, Gene's effort sank without a trace.

Gene remained philosophical about the album's failure in his 1985 interview with Domenic Priore. "The album sort of never went anywhere at the time. Of course, now it's a collector's item. At the time it was on the same label the Byrds were on and I think that they sort of felt they had a conflict of interest with Gene Clark coming out on one side and the Byrds coming out on another. 'The Byrds were already a more saleable product, so we'll probably put the promotion behind them.' So that's where it went."

Upon the album's release, Gene performed at the Ash Grove in March accompanied by the Gosdin Brothers and Clarence White, who himself would become a Byrd a little more than a year later. The fact that Gene worked with Vern and Rex only at this gig and perhaps one other (Vern maintains they played the Hollywood Palladium) reveals the concocted nature of their relationship versus the organic growth of the Byrds or, later, Dillard & Clark.

Trying to move forward, Gene assembled a new backing band—this time dubbed the more sophisticated Gene Clark Group—and accepted another weeklong engagement at the Whisky. Joining Gene this time out were Clarence White and two veterans of the Mamas & the Papas' touring band, 'Fast' Eddie Hoh on drums and bass player John York.

Born in New York, John had migrated westward to California in the mid-'60s where he found work as an itinerant bass player with artists like Johnny Rivers, the Sir Douglas Quintet, and the Mamas & the Papas. John and Gene would work together several times over the next 23 years. This configuration of the Gene Clark Group played a weekend at the Whisky-A-Go Go in March 1967 before going their separate ways. It was, for Gene, another disappointment. "What I remember about the gig was that there were a lot of record people there," offers John, "and they are usually the worst audiences in the world. People who work at record companies usually get free passes to go to concerts. I remember Eddie, Clarence, and I thinking that Gene had so many great songs, that it was cool to be playing those songs and not just running through Byrds hits, that kind of thing. Gene was so prolific and we were playing a lot of really good songs. We played just a few songs and the audience was basically ignoring us. They were talking loudly and Gene got pissed off. He turned to us and he said, 'Let's just play a blues. Let's just jam.' We said, 'Are you serious?' And he said, 'Yeah.' So for the rest of the set, I don't know how long it might have been, we didn't do any of the songs that we had prepared to play. We just did an extended blues and he walked off the stage. He just didn't even want to present his music to these people. He turned his back on the audience and finished the entire show with his back to them. That was the end of the show. I think maybe at that point he wasn't emotionally prepared to win them over. Maybe he felt that just being there was enough. But that's not necessarily the case with an audience. He was surrounded by people who reinforced the idea that his music would be appreciated. And I think even now people who appreciate Gene's music are into it for the content, the dynamic, the soul of it, the strength that is in his music."

Chris Hillman feels part of the problem with Gene's solo career was a lack of direction from his management. "He had the look, but he needed the right song and needed to be made over or groomed as a solo guy. He needed to learn to engage the audience but still be Gene. It would have been ludicrous for him to be up there and be Bobby Darin, trying to dance and do mic tricks. But there were some things that could have been done, but he needed good management. Then it could have happened. That's what a manager's job is. To redefine it, reinvent it, and present it in an honest way. And they weren't doing that with Gene."

On April 24, Columbia summoned Gene back to the studio to take another stab at a hit single. "So You Say You Lost Your Baby" had been released earlier that month but, like "Echoes," had failed to dent the charts. Executive producer Gary Usher and wunderkind Curt Boettcher ran the sessions for the new single. (Boettcher, who had scored chart success with the Association and artistic plaudits with Millennium, went uncredited, as he had yet to sever his contract with Our Productions and officially join Columbia's staff.) Gene was given an old Ian & Sylvia folk song, "The French Girl," to record—a surprising move, given the sheer volume of his own material. The track was an extension of the "Echoes" experiments, with harpsichord and orchestration bathing Gene's sympathetic vocal delivery in a wash of classical, neo-baroque folk-rock—somewhat akin to the Left Banke's hits. The intended flip side, Gene's "Only Colombe," a far stronger composition than most of his debut album tracks, was given the same treatment with more positive results (the presence of backwards guitar adds a contemporary psychedelic edge absent from "The French Girl"). Gene affects his most fervent Dylan voice on "Only Colombe." He returned to the studio on May 10 and May 17 to finish up the tracks, while Boettcher added elaborate backing harmonies that did not sit well with Gene.

Coming on the cusp of the much-vaunted Summer of Love, "The French Girl" was a step backwards and hardly indicative of Gene's own creative muse. In the end, Columbia shelved the proposed single, much to Gene's relief. (A single of "The French Girl" released that spring by Daily Flash on UNI may have pre-empted Columbia's plans for Gene.) The two tracks were not unearthed until 1991's *Echoes* compilation album, which coupled the Gosdin Brothers tracks with a smattering of Gene's Byrd oeuvre and the aborted 1967 single. In mixing these two songs some 20 years later, Gene insisted the backing vocals be excised from the tracks.

It has been speculated for decades that Gene, Usher, and Boettcher actually recorded enough tracks for a second Columbia album, though the label's studio logs and Gene's contract card indicate that the sessions described were the only Columbia sessions following his debut solo album. The failure of his debut album was hardly justification for pursuing a follow-up. Columbia had all but washed its hands of Gene and let his contract lapse the following month without any intentions of renewal. As far as they were concerned, "Gene Clark the Solo Artist" simply wasn't viable.

Jim Bickhart wonders why the label was so quick to jettison Gene. "Subsequent events proved that Gene Clark may never have been a viable commercial commodity outside of the Byrds, but the fact that Columbia dropped him after one, somewhat eccentric album—you had no way of knowing that his next album wasn't going to be his own 'Mr. Tambourine Man' with perfectly appropriate commercial product for the time. I guess they just weren't thinking that far ahead. They were thinking in terms of the moment." As Jim Dickson surmises, "Gene made a lot of good tries at making it, he made a lot of good music. But there is a lot of luck in getting that break. If one good song on his own had been a hit he would have had a whole different career. Sometimes you just don't get a hit song because things don't come together."

While his former mates in the Byrds appeared at the first-ever Monterey Pop Festival in June 1967 (organized in part by Papa John Phillips, thereby ensuring Gene would not receive an invitation), Gene retreated to Laurel Canyon to plot his next move. He would not perform in public that summer, choosing instead to write relentlessly and record demos. "I hadn't realized at the time some of the human drama surrounding Gene," allows Cyrus Faryar. "None of that was visible with him at that time." Adds Barry McGuire, "Gene never really knew how loved he was or how good he was because of his lack of confidence and lack of self-esteem. It was already there, but he didn't know it. He was very introverted. I don't think anybody ever knew Gene. Even his friends didn't know him. He just never really shared his being with anyone. It was all closed up inside. I felt like he had secrets that only he knew and he never shared them with anybody. They were all kept inside. I knew ladies that just loved him. The girl I was with at the time just ached in her love for Gene. She was pained by his lack of self-appreciation. 'Oh, poor Gene,' she would just groan. She just loved him so much."

Cynthia Webb recounts a memorable encounter with Gene. "One night, on acid, I was having this canyon walk and I was really tired and had been out a long time. And I knocked on Gene's door in the middle of the night, woke him up, and he came to the door. And this was one thing about him, he was so nice and so good. He saw me, I was like this wild beast, and I said, 'I need to rest.' And he brought me in and gave me paper and pens and brought me some tea and he kept on getting up to check on me. I just sat in his little house and closed myself out until morning, then I said goodbye. This was somebody who could understand a little panicked moment. That was very sweet and very dear to me. Even though I didn't know him well, I felt I could go to him in that situation. It was something I will never forget."

Despite having left the Byrds under strained circumstances, Gene continued to remain sociable with several of his former band mates. "I do remember hanging out with him," states Roger. "We were friends. He was around Hollywood and we would get together. He would come over to my house or I would go to his house and we'd hang out. He had a Ferrari at the time and I remember being with him when he washed his car and he was stenciling in the Pirelli tires with white stuff, playing with his Ferrari. It makes sense now, knowing that he came from a poor background, because he was really into that car. It was kind of a badge of success, like he had really made it."

Gene could still be found on occasion at the Whisky where he kept a table off to the side, away from the glare of the general public. Michael Stuart-Ware was the drummer in the Sons of Adam before joining the group Love. He recalls seeing Gene at the Whisky one night. "The Sons of Adam had a gig at the Whisky, but after a couple of weeks Mario decided we had run our course and the crowd wasn't that enthusiastic about us playing there any more, so he gave us our notice. Jack Tanna, aka Joe Kooken, our rhythm guitarist—who once asked a chick at Gazzarri's for her number and she wrote down "Beechwood 45789" but he didn't get it— decided to start up a petition drive. 'We want the Sons of Adam to stay at the Whisky.' The last few days of our tenure there he was going around at all the breaks asking practically every single person in the club to sign this stupid petition. Really embarrassing, but there was no talking him out of it. He thought that if he got enough signatures Mario would be forced to change his mind and keep us on. So he sees Gene sitting by himself trying to have a drink in peace and, with the house PA blaring, he goes over and shoves the petition in front of Gene and makes him sign it. Jack's thinking, 'All right! I really scored! I got a member of the Byrds to sign our petition!' So he walks back over to the stage, where the rest of us were getting ready to play the next set, and he's looking down at the signature, then, real disgusted, he throws the petition down and says, 'Look what that asshole Gene Clark wrote!' Gene had signed it 'John Lennon.'"

On July 26, Gene cut several tracks at legendary Gold Star studios in Hollywood under the auspices of South African trumpeter Hugh Masekela (a friend of David Crosby's), who had been a surprise hit at the Monterey Pop Festival a month before. Hugh had guested on the Byrds' current single, "So You Want to Be a Rock 'n' Roll Star," which was their rather jaundiced take on the industry inspired musically by a Masekela recording session Chris Hillman had attended. The sessions with Gene, which also included Chris on bass, are a strange addition to Gene's growing canon of unreleased tracks. Three songs, "Without You," "Don't Let it Fall Through," and "Yesterday Am I Right," feature multiple horns including trombone, sax, and trumpet along with flute and harpsichord. The latter sounds like a cross between the Doors' "Touch Me" horns and the Mamas & the Papas, an odd combination indeed. Imagine Gene Clark—sensitive, Dylan-influenced folk-rock singer—backed by Blood, Sweat & Tears or Chicago and you get the picture. An acetate of this track was pressed up on the Chisa label, for which Hugh, actor Peter Fonda, and soon-to-be Byrds manager Larry Spector were principals (Gram Parsons's International Submarine Band, along with Fonda, cut tracks for Chisa that summer). Speculation is that Gene intended to use these session tracks to hustle a new recording contract.

While studio logs have long since disappeared and memories of those sessions are vague, there is some conjecture that Leon Russell may have provided the elaborate and bizarre musical arrangements for the three tracks. Jim Dickson recalls Leon being hired around this time to provide arrangements for some of Gene's songs. Gene himself alluded to further sessions with Leon after his participation on *Gene Clark with the Gosdin Brothers.*

"Gene abandoned many projects unfinished," Jim opines. "There are as many reasons." One of those tracks, "Back Street Mirror," ended up on an obscure album by British actor-turned-singer David Hemmings (recently reissued by Rev-Ola Records). According to Jim, "Eddie Tickner had already paid for the track from Leon Russell with Gene, so we just took off Gene's voice and put on David Hemmings's voice. It was an existing track that we had in the can, but no one wanted to put it out." (The Byrds also played on Hemmings's album.)

"Gene wrote so damn many songs we just couldn't even tape them all," he chuckles. "He would come with a notebook full of songs. And if you didn't tape them quickly he would forget what tune he wrote them to. We did try to promote Gene's songs to other artists any which way we could." Several acetates and reel-to-reel tapes from this period survive today in the hands of collectors, but others have long since gone missing. One surviving tape lists "Whatever," "One Way Road," "Bakersfield Train," "Got to Get You off My Mind," "Back Street Mirror," "Down on the Pier," and "Only Colombe," while another identifies "Translations," "I'd Just Like," "I Am Without You," "So Much More," and "Don't Know What You Want." Gene once boasted of a closet full of unreleased recordings, tapes, and acetates. "I got into a real poetic kind of writing," Gene revealed to Priore. "I was writing just to write during that period of time. There were two or three hundred unrecorded songs I wrote over that period, there's a whole drawer full of them, so I have no idea what I was thinking about, just images. I used to like to lock myself in my house and just work for days on songs. I had a little recording setup in one room and I would go in and put them on tape."

Sometime that same summer, Gene returned to the recording studio, this time Larabee Studio in West Hollywood, to lay down demos for the purpose of securing a new recording contract. An acetate of those sessions titled *Gene Clark Sings for You* was pressed up for distribution to other labels as well as to artists seeking material. The rough tracks, eight in all, some cut at Larabee, others at Gold Star, feature conspicuously crude backing from an overzealous drummer, bass player, and a mediocre lead guitarist. Over the intervening years this particular acetate, discovered in Liberty Records' vaults in the 1980s, has been mistakenly assumed to be the great lost second Gene Clark solo album and has taken on mythical proportions akin to the Beach Boys' *Smile.* In fact, it was nothing of the sort; its rudimentary arrangements and rough vocals suggest nothing more than a demo session. While one track, "That's Alright by Me," featuring a string accompaniment may be a holdover from the Leon Russell sessions, the others offer simple backing augmented here and there by calliope, a new Mellotron string simulator, and electric piano, the latter supplied by Alex Del Zoppo.

Alex was a member of the jazz-rock influenced band Sweetwater, a Los Angeles–based septet that bears the distinction of having been the first band to perform at the legendary Woodstock

Festival in 1969. Formed in 1967, the group had an unusual lineup of cello, flute, and congas—but no guitar. Tragedy struck Sweetwater when singer Nancy Nevins suffered a debilitating brain injury in a car accident and fell into a coma. She was not expected to live, but defied the odds and recovered.

"We were almost the house band at the Whisky for a while," states Alex. "We went in on a Tuesday night, then they held us over for a month or so and we would open for bigger acts or headline ourselves. All of a sudden one night I come offstage and I'm walking up the stairs and there's Gene Clark standing there. I was a big Byrds fan. And he says, 'Excuse me, I'm Gene Clark.' I replied, 'Oh, yeah, I know.' I was thinking 'Wow, this is great!' And he was just very casual. He said, 'I like the way you play piano and I would like to see if we can do some stuff together.' So we ended up talking up in the dressing room. A little while later he came by my house in Laurel Canyon and picked me up. What was remarkable was that he was driving this chocolate brown Ferrari coup. I said, 'I've seen this car before.' 'Oh, I drive around Hollywood a lot.' And I said, 'No, Steve McQueen has one exactly like that,' and he said, 'Oh, I bought it from him.' I thought that was pretty cool."

At Gene's house, the two listened to some of Gene's demo tracks with the idea of adding piano. "He only turned on a minimum of lights, then as we listened he turned them all off and we sat and listened in complete darkness. It seems odd now, but it wasn't in the context of those days. I think he wanted full concentration on the songs. I told him I thought I could add keyboards to some of them. He was quieter than I expected, but he was very gracious. I kind of expected him to have a giant ego, but he just wasn't like that. So many others you met in those days were egomaniacs. Gene was like a gentleman. I was a nobody, just some kid off the street playing piano, and he was very kind and treated me like an equal. I really appreciated that."

At the studio, Alex was encouraged to contribute his ideas to Gene's songs. "We tried a full piano but it was a little too overwhelming for the tracks, so I set up my Wurlitzer electric piano and we goofed around with that. I don't know what they kept or didn't keep. There were two sessions. The first session was just Gene and I alone. The next one had more players. He sang once and on a couple of tracks I overdubbed on existing tracks that already had drums and other instruments. It wasn't really produced. I don't remember a producer there or anyone from a record label. It was just Gene in charge of this thing. It seemed like demo sessions to me. Some of it verged on country material, but it was all still him. I don't even remember getting paid." Although Alex bumped into Gene a while later at the Troubadour, the two never again played together. "I have a photograph of me playing piano and Gene standing there looking at me."

Of the eight tracks on *Gene Clark Sings for You*, "On Her Own" is a fairly straightforward rock number about a free-spirited girl in San Francisco, encumbered by crashing cymbals and obtrusive, military-style drumming. "Past Tense" is another of Gene's Dylanesque excursions that includes Alex's electric piano flourishes and sounds vaguely reminiscent of Arthur Lee and Love's elaborate tempo changes. "Yesterday Am I Right" is the same song as the big band

Alex Del Zoppo records tracks with Gene for the Gene Clark Sings for You *demo, summer 1967.*

arrangement from the Hugh Masekela sessions only in a stripped-down form, a melancholy ballad with an aching vocal from Gene far more suited to sparse piano accompaniment than trombones and trumpets. "Past My Door" is similar in poetic vision to "Echoes" with an abrupt tempo change midstream and a powerful Beatles-inspired crescendo at the coda driven by a swelling Mellotron. Gene stretches to hit some of the highest notes within his range, almost falsetto verging on yodel. "That's Alright by Me" was a holdover from Gene Clark & the Group's live set and likely the oldest song on the acetate. Again the drumming is distracting but the song itself is strong, assisted by a small violin section. (Gene would revisit this song again a year later in sessions with Laramy Smith and those results would finally be released in 1998 on the British two-CD compilation *Gene Clark: Flying High.*) "One Way Road" boasts some unusual chord changes for Gene and is another song about an independent girl. The drummer appears to have some difficulties keeping the time together. "Down by the Pier" is a melancholy, 2/4-time, two-step shuffle expressing a longing for a girl who has left. Gene even manages to name-drop "Heartbreak Hotel" in the lyrics, while a circus-like calliope embellishes the track. The final cut,

"7.30 Mode," is the lone country-flavored song of the eight tracks and features Gene on harmonica and the unknown lead guitar player's attempting to contribute country licks. The song is similar in style and structure to Gene's work on 1971's *White Light* album.

Had the eight tracks on *Gene Clark Sings for You* been recorded properly, they might have made for a thought-provoking album. Despite the limited accompaniment, the songs continue Gene's exploration of abstract poetry in the lyrics. They stand in marked contrast to the music he had just released on *Gene Clark with the Gosdin Brothers* and his next official release, *The Fantastic Expedition of Dillard & Clark*, and represent a period in his career where he was further honing his songwriting skills and experimenting with new directions. Not surprisingly, Gene would never officially release any of these songs—he was so prolific that he simply abandoned them in favor of newer material when he returned to the studios.

Around the same time that Gene was laying down the *Gene Clark Sings for You* tracks, he began working with a group of young musicians he had met at the Ash Grove earlier in the year. The four teenage members of the Blokes were dedicated Byrds fans who included a Rickenbacker 12-string among their instrumentation and offered a healthy dose of Byrds songs in their live set.

Sunday night was talent night at the Ash Grove, when novice performers could take the stage. During a set by the Blokes, Gene joined them. As drummer Bruce Bowdin enthusiastically recalls, "The announcer welcomed us up on the stage. We started with 'Mr. Tambourine Man' and had the audience's attention. Sitting back on the drums, I noticed that Gene had emerged from the back dressing room and sat down at the table. I turned to Jim Groshong, our lead singer, and said, 'Let's do "I'll Feel a Whole Lot Better,"'" so Jim announced that this was written by Gene Clark and that if he was in the house it would be appreciated if he would come up onstage and help us. Man, this is the gods' honest truth: Gene put out his cigarette and literally ran up on the stage. He had the biggest grin on his face. He turned to me and John Noreen and exclaimed, 'You do Byrds better than we ever did.' Wow, that was a *big* compliment. I handed him a tambourine and we kicked off the intro. He was great. We rocked the place. After the song ended, the entire clientele stood up on their feet and gave us a standing ovation. I will never, ever forget that moment. We were all excited! Gene stayed up for two additional songs. He didn't want to leave. We closed with 'Eight Miles High.'"

Backstage afterwards, the group had the opportunity to meet Gene, who continued to heap praise on the young players. "I found him to be a very down-to-earth guy," recalls guitarist John Noreen. "I've met a lot of 'stars' and most of them are full of themselves. But he didn't come off that way at all. His interest in the band seemed sincere. He struck me as the type of guy who wouldn't blow smoke up your butt for any reason. So we were quite shocked when he said he would like to manage us. But that didn't work out. We all felt real comfortable with him, although we were pretty awestruck by the whole thing."

Gene's interest in the group was genuine and he followed through a couple of months later, after the group had changed its name to the Rose Garden and added singer Diana DeRose, by offering them some of his songs to record. "One time he came out to our house in Woodland Hills where we used to rehearse," John continues. "I was only about 16 and still living at home. He brought us a song called 'Till Today' and taught it to us. We sat around singing it. I think he just played it for us on his guitar and I taped it. He indicated that he had written it for us." Gene also offered the group a five-song acetate and some sheet music. The songs on the acetate included the folk-rockish "On Tenth Street," "Understand Me Too," an uptempo number with a slight country leaning, and the haunting, minor key, "Echoes"-influenced "Long Time." All three featured Gene alone on acoustic guitar and vocals, vaguely reminiscent of the tracks on *Gene Clark with the Gosdin Brothers*. The last two tracks are Gene on harmonica backed by a small ensemble comprised of drums, bass, and lead guitar. "Big City Girl" is a bluesy, rhythm guitar-heavy Jimmy Reed shuffle with Gene wailing away on harmonica, while "Doctor Doctor" is an eerie, rocky number that boasts a doubled vocal and strong backing harmonies (John believes Clarence White is playing Telecaster lead guitar). According to John, "He just gave them to us and said, 'If you want to do any of these, go ahead.' They were a group of published songs all written around the same time as 'Echoes' and stuff like that from his first album because I think it was a 1966 date on the acetate." Gene also offered sheet music for "Only Colombe" and "Down by the Pier." "We just picked out the songs we thought we could do," John notes.

The members of the Rose Garden got to know Gene a bit better. Bruce remembers a hair-raising ride with Gene in his Ferrari. "He invited me to sit shotgun and then he took me for the ride of my life down through the backside of Topanga Canyon with its hairpin turns and switchbacks. I do not know how fast the speedometer showed, but Gene had that Ferrari rocking back and forth with all four wheels drifting and sliding. To avoid going over the edge he would simply accelerate the vehicle to achieve tire traction once again. The ride was just like Steve McQueen's ride down the streets of San Francisco in the movie *Bullet*. We rounded the last turn and pulled across the PCH 1 and stopped. We lit cigarettes to calm down somewhat. He looked at me and just laughed. I said not a word. I was speechless!"

Shortly thereafter, the Rose Garden signed with ATCO Records and entered Gold Star recording studios to cut their one and only album. The group selected "Till Today" and "Long Time" to cover and Gene joined them in the studio to cut those tracks. "He stood by my drums," recalls Bruce, "behind the baffle and banged a pair of tambourines together throughout both instrumental tracks. He wore a pair of kid gloves on his hands and left a pile of sawdust on the recording studio floor." John claims Gene contributed to one track. "He came up with a guitar line on one of the other songs on the album, 'Coins of Fun.' He did that line. I couldn't think up a line I liked so he took my 12-string and figured out a line that became the signature riff in that song." The Rose Garden would score a hit single at the tail end of 1967 with "Next Plane to London" and their album, featuring two Gene Clark covers, would be released early the next year.

Despite what appeared to be a flurry of activity, Gene's career remained in limbo. He was without a recording contract and had severed ties with his longtime managers Jim Dickson and

Eddie Tickner. Following the Byrds' lead, he signed that autumn with Larry Spector, a former business manager who had an impressive roster of clients.

In another coup instigated by David Crosby, the Byrds had terminated their management agreement with Jim and Eddie in June 1967 and signed on with Larry. But by October, David had worn out his welcome with the remaining Byrds, having joined Buffalo Springfield onstage at Monterey for a controversial set (sitting in with other groups was still a no-no then) and had become increasingly demeaning towards the Byrds' own musical abilities. He was subsequently fired, leaving with a substantial settlement he used to purchase a yacht, the Mayan. Why did David receive a buy out and not Gene? "Gene quit, David was thrown out," answers Jim. "When David left, there was money; when Gene left, there wasn't any real money yet in the group. Gene was doing okay on his songwriting and publishing."

With bookings pending, including dates out East and two television shows, the Byrds turned once again to a familiar face. Gene Clark. Roger explains: "Chris called me up and said, 'We've got to do something. Without David we're not strong enough as a trio.' I agreed with him and he said, 'Let's get Gene back.' And I said, 'Oh man, do you think he can hack it?' So we called Gene up and he was receptive to it. He was into it right away. We asked him if he could fly and he said, 'Yes.' So we did fly."

Just why Gene opted to rejoin the Byrds is unclear. While he felt obliged to help his friends, his solo career had hit a brick wall. The security of being in a group again likely appealed to him, and sharing the same management would ensure a smooth transition. Unable to land Gene a new recording deal, Larry pitched the "reunion" idea to his client. Perhaps more significant, however, was the fact that the group was now the Byrds-without-Crosby, who had been Gene's chief nemesis.

But Gene's stated willingness to fly and his eroding confidence as a performer remained potential threats.

Before setting off for a three-night engagement in Minneapolis en route to New York, the Byrds taped two television appearances. On *The Smothers Brothers Comedy Hour,* a neatly coiffured Gene looked petrified as he mimed to the year-old "Mr. Spaceman" and the Byrds' latest recording, "Goin' Back." On *Where the Girls Are,* hosted by Noel Harrison, Gene looked a little more animated on "Mr. Spaceman" and a rendition of the Beatles' "Good Day Sunshine."

"We flew out to the Midwest and that's when he really kind of flipped out and had to take the train back," recalls Roger. "It was over at that point. We weren't going to try that again. It was a very nervous period for him." One Byrds associate on the tour even insists that Gene's singing was so off-key and his guitar work so out of time that the other Byrds instructed him to take Gene's performance out of the sound mix during the shows. Since Gene was only backing Roger and Chris, who were singing lead and playing loud as always, the audiences were none the wiser.

On the morning of their flight to New York, Gene bailed out, refusing to board the plane, visibly shaking and distraught. As the Byrds flew off to their next gig as a trio, Gene hopped a train back to Los Angeles, his return to the Byrds lasting all of three weeks.

While it is widely held that Gene did not record or contribute any songs to *The Notorious Byrd Brothers,* the Byrds album in progress when he briefly rejoined, in fact, he did both. Three members of the Rose Garden recall visiting Columbia Studios at Gene's invitation to witness him adding his voice to the vocal blend on Gerry Goffin and Carole King's wistful "Goin' Back," which had been recorded on September 5 and again on October 9, prior to Gene rejoining. John Noreen confirms it. "The last time I remember seeing Gene was when he went back to the Byrds briefly. They were doing some overdubs on 'Goin' Back.' None of the other band was there. Gene was putting on a vocal. The song was 'Goin' Back' because that was the first time I heard steel guitar and I went, 'What the hell was that thing?' because I didn't know." (John would later go on to become a noted pedal steel guitarist in Nashville and form country music chart toppers Highway 101.) Bruce Bowdin adds, "Yes, I remember the night of Clark's overdubbing. He had invited us down to Columbia's famous Studio A where all the Byrd albums had been crafted. We got there late and only heard the mixing effort through the playback speakers. They were blending in Gene's vocals. If you listen to the 45 through good speakers, you can hear Clark coming through." Suggests Roger, "He and I had a good blend, so why wouldn't we have kept him on the track?" Gene once remarked that he also added his voice to Roger's "Space Odyssey" track.

As for contributing a song to the album, Roger confirms that he and Gene co-wrote "Get to You," despite the label credit to the contrary. "The credit is wrong," he insists. "Gene and I wrote that song. Gene came over to my house on Alimore Drive. It was right after we had fired David. David had been accusing Chris and me of not being good enough musicians to play with him anymore. So I was going to show David: 'Oh, yeah? Well, I'm going to write a song in 5/4-time, man, and intersperse it with 6/8-time. I'll show you.' It was kind of my trying to show David that I was a better musician than he thought I was. So I was working on the chord progression when Gene came over and we started working on the song, the actual lyrics, making it about a trip to England like we did in 'Eight Miles High.' So, yeah, Gene and I wrote that song but I don't know how the credit got mixed up. The bureaucrats at Columbia Records got it wrong. I didn't have my hands on the credits." The eventual credit attributes the song to Roger and Chris. No change has ever been made on subsequent releases.

Upon his return to Los Angeles, Gene laid low. His insecurity and loss of confidence in his performing abilities troubled him deeply. He had already left his Rosilla Place abode and rented a tiny hillside house off Laurel Canyon Road. "Gene was living in a little rustic house on a side street," remembers Bernie Leadon, who would soon come to work with Gene. "It wasn't very far up the hill, but it was one of those houses that was built sort of into the hillside so that the garage was underneath the house and was right on the street, and there were one or two stories above that. It was a smallish house, but very tasty, a natural shingle-sided house." Gene had also taken on a personal assistant named Virginia Howard. She would come over every morning to handle Gene's business affairs: screen his calls, place calls on his behalf, book meetings and appointments, and sort out his various publishing royalties. She was not his maid, and although Gene treated her in a most professional manner, colleagues at the time believed that Virginia harbored affection for the singer.

In perhaps the most bizarre move of his career and under Larry Spector's direction, Gene composed an original score to *Marijuana,* an anti-drug educational short film targeted to impressionable high school teens. The film was produced, written, and directed by Max Miller and hosted by none other than Sonny Bono. Gene's music featured meandering blues and pseudo-psychedelic instrumental jams by a group called Things to Come, a Los Angeles-based band consisting of Bryan Garofalo on bass and drummer Russ Kunkel (who would later play on Gene's *No Other* album), with Larry Robinson, Michael Migilars, and Lynn Rominger on guitars. Gene may have contributed some harmonica to the tracks. Things to Come cut several singles in the late '60s and an album was recently reissued by Sundazed Records, but the film project was their only connection with Gene. "That was Larry's idea," confirms Russ. "We were both managed by him. Gene provided music for it."

Gene made a trip back to Bonner Springs in 1967 to visit his family for Christmas. In the New Year he returned to Los Angeles where he reacquainted himself with the leader of a Sacramento group that had opened for the Byrds when Gene was still a member. Larry Smith, better known by the stage name Laramy, was the lead singer and guitarist in the Fugitives, but had left the group in 1967 and moved to Los Angeles. (In mid-1966, the Fugitives recorded at Western Recorders under the temporary name the Grimfacqles, cutting several of Laramy's songs including "City of the Dead," later known as "Los Angeles.")

Laramy was hanging around the Byrds' *Notorious Byrd Brothers* album sessions when he met Gene. "I wanted to go more into original stuff, to be myself," he told rock historian Alec Palao, recalling his frustration with the Fugitives, "and everything that came back from the guitarist and drummer was, 'Oh, that doesn't sound like the Beatles.' I didn't wanna be the Beatles! At that point I had other designs, because I'd met Gene Clark."

In February 1968 things looked promising for Gene. Despite ceasing his business relationship with Larry Spector, he had managed to obtain a recording contract with A&M Records, whose office complex and studio facilities were located in the former Charlie Chaplin studio lot in Hollywood. The A&M lot would become a safe and nurturing environment for Gene over the next couple of years. "The artists were always welcome to come by, hang out, and visit with the members of the staff," recalls Jim Bickhart. "And also they had the recording studios there. That was the key aspect of things, too. That was a magnet for artists." The A in A&M stood for trumpeter Herb Alpert of the Tijuana Brass while the M stood for his partner, Jerry Moss. Jerry proved to be a major Gene Clark booster and offered Gene the contract. "Jerry Moss was a big fan of Gene's," confirms Eddie Tickner. "He thought Gene was marvelous. There was always a check waiting at his office for when Gene would show up."

With a contract in hand, Gene began assembling musicians to rehearse and record a second solo album. His first choice was Laramy Smith on guitar and backing vocals. Laramy suggested Fugitives drummer Wayne Bruns and a bass player acquaintance from Los Angeles, Richard Vandervordt (known to the others at the time as Aaron). Beginning in early March the four rehearsed at the A&M lot, working on a combination of material by Gene and Laramy. Gene took Laramy's "City of the Dead" and added a bridge, transforming the song into something less doom-laden under the new title "Los Angeles." He did the same with "Lyin' Down the Middle," later recorded by Dillard & Clark.

"Not all the songs were Gene's," admits Wayne. "Some of the material we were rehearsing was Larry's. He always had a pushy personality so we ended up doing some of his songs. In fact, that tune 'Lyin' Down the Middle' was more of a Laramy Smith tune. I remember sitting around with Larry when he came up with that line, 'I think that line down the middle of the road is driving me insane.' On that song 'Los Angeles,' Laramy had written the verse and then Gene wrote a bridge that I thought really improved the song. As a collaborative team they were probably pretty good together, but Larry's personality was sometimes hard to deal with.

The Gene Clark-Laramy Smith Group, March 1968: (left to right) Aaron Vandervordt, Wayne Bruns, Laramy Smith, and Gene Clark.

"Gene had this rehearsal hall right in the A&M studio lot," Wayne continues, "and we were rehearsing there five days a week. He put us on salary as well, which was nice because none of us had day jobs or anything. So that's all we were doing—rehearsing these tunes with Gene. People would stop in, like Bernie Leadon and the guy who wrote that song 'Rainy Days and Mondays' and 'Close to You,' Paul Williams. Herb Alpert was wandering around so it was really exciting for me."

While rehearsing with Laramy, Wayne, and Aaron, Gene rekindled his friendship with Douglas Dillard. Missouri-born Douglas had just left his namesake group over a difference of opinion with younger brother Rodney about the direction that the group should take. More of a purist, Douglas bristled at Rodney's intention to take the Dillards's sound into a more contemporary country-rock setting (a vision that would, in the end, elevate the Dillards to country-rock pioneers on their 1968 album *Wheatstraw Suite*).

The Dillards had formed in 1961 in and around Salem, Missouri. Long before the quartet coalesced, the two Dillard boys had grown up in a household filled with music. Their father, Homer Dillard, Sr., was a back porch fiddler and their mother, Lorene, played guitar. Both instilled a love of bluegrass and traditional Ozark Mountain music in their sons. With childhood friend John Hartford (who would go on to great success as a singer-songwriter, beginning with "Gentle on My Mind"), Douglas and Rodney progressed through a series of local bluegrass outfits that included the Ozark Mountain Boys and the Dixie Ramblers before forming the Dillards. The group featured Douglas on banjo, Rodney on guitar, Dean Webb on mandolin, and former Salem area schoolteacher and radio broadcaster Mitch Jayne on upright bass. In November 1962, the Dillards packed an old trailer and headed out for the bright lights of California. Debuting at the Ash Grove, their intermingle of virtuoso musicianship and homespun humor earned them an instant following and, after Jim Dickson spotted them, a recording contract with Elektra Records. A year later the Dillards became regular characters on the popular television sitcom *The Andy Griffith Show,* transforming themselves into the hillbilly family bluegrass band the Darling Boys. Between 1963 and 1965, the Dillards released three critically acclaimed albums and became the toast of the Southern California folk circuit, even branching out into nightclub engagements and supper clubs. All the while musicians by the truckload came out to be inspired by each player's individual talents, among them Chris Hillman, Stephen Stills, future Eagles Bernie Leadon and Don Henley, and the Nitty Gritty Dirt Band's John McEuen, to name a few.

Having already recorded a Bob Dylan song on the Dillards's second album, however, Rodney was itching to move away from the traditional base. The group had swapped their acoustic instruments for electric ones (Douglas playing his bantar) in 1965 and, sharing management with Dickson-Tickner, had toured with the Byrds. They had even recorded a bluegrass-flavored version of the Beatles' "I've Just Seen a Face" for Capitol Records. But breaking out beyond the now-declining folk circuit was proving difficult. It was at this point that Douglas opted to jump ship and go his own way rather than follow Rodney's direction.

A popular session musician, Douglas had already contributed to recordings by the Monkees and appeared onstage with Buffalo Springfield. In May, the Byrds invited him to tour Europe and enhance their own recent conversion to traditional country music (having enlisted Gram Parsons). Prior to that tour, Douglas had begun sessions for a solo instrumental record, *The Banjo Album,* for Together Records and had tapped Gene to play guitar and harmonica. The two found a mutual admiration for each other's talents and Douglas brought out the fun-loving side of Gene. Though Douglas was seven years older than Gene, the two developed an instant rapport on several levels. "There was a symbiosis that occurred between them," notes David Jackson, who played bass for what was to become Dillard & Clark. "They both liked martinis, they both liked pot, and they both liked acid. I can't remember really how much acid was taken, and I don't think it was anything resembling a daily, weekly, or monthly level, but there were some moments. Gene had a Ferrari at the time and Doug and Gene would take off. They were both relatively famous and could go to just about any bar or restaurant and be recognized and fawned over to some degree." For Gene, there was no pressure in working with Douglas. Just two Missouri boys pickin' and a-grinnin.'

Eddie Tickner remarks ruefully, "Doug and Gene were a match: two guys with a drinking problem teaming up." Songwriting friend Daniel Moore recalls, "Both of those guys were pretty party-hardy guys. They would go on for days. I couldn't keep up with them. I was good for one evening, then I had to go home and go to bed. But they would continue on."

Friends worried that Gene seemed to be relying more on alcohol than other stimulants to loosen up his usually tense demeanor. His drinking became public record on March 28, 1968, when he showed up at Derek Taylor's farewell party (appropriately held at the old Ciro's, now called It's Boss) visibly drunk and proceeded to take the stage during the Byrds' set. Laramy Smith witnessed the debacle and recounted Gene's mortification to musicologist Alec Palao: "Gene had been drinking heavily and we'd been driving in his Ferrari 275 and he was nuts. So there's the Byrds on this huge, huge stage. Everybody's there, all the originals, but no Gene Clark. So they start doing 'Eight Miles High.' There's a Gibson 335 up onstage and Gene decides to get up and play. Gene gets up, picks up this guitar, puts it on, but there's no cord. So he's gonna take Chris Hillman's cord. Chris is like slapping his hand but Gene is pulling on the cord and Chris is holding on to it and playing bass with one hand. And all of a sudden Gene falls right into the drums and everything goes all over the place. Me, I got up, hailed a taxi, and got out of there." Embarrassed, Gene quickly rose to his feet, with help from a Byrds roadie, and bid a hasty retreat into the night.

While by day Gene rehearsed with Laramy Smith and crew, by evening he would be at Douglas's Beechwood Canyon home engaged in a loose jam that gradually pulled in bassist David Jackson, mandolin player Don Beck, and guitarist/banjo player Bernie Leadon. "My remembrance was that the thing with Doug and Gene was an organic occurrence," offers Bernie.

"It just kind of evolved. The deal was that I was a banjo acolyte of Doug's and I was sleeping on his couch for about six months. Doug and I were playing every day and there was a little social scene in that building. It was a nice little community. Harry Dean Stanton was living in the apartment over the garage in the back. Harry Dean played music, too. Then Byron Berline showed up and he and Doug had played on a Dillards album before. And Dean Webb would come by and we'd have all-night picking parties, just playing music. So the evolution of Dillard & Clark was that Doug and I would sit around and play banjo instrumentals and make up songs that were banjo instrumentals—they had a verse, chorus, and a melody, but no lyrics. We had about ten or 15 of these things, plus sitting around playing the whole bluegrass canon of songs. Then Gene started coming over and hanging out and we would sing some of these existing bluegrass songs and we would play him these instrumentals. That's how I met Gene. And then Gene started coming back the next day with lyrics. We played him 'With Care from Someone,' that descending minor progression, and Gene came back the next day to another picking party and had the whole thing written. We would then sit there and add the harmonies. So that's how it all evolved."

Born in Minneapolis, Bernie had moved to San Diego as a youngster where he took up banjo and guitar, and in his teens was an ad hoc member of the Scottsville Squirrel Barkers, the local bluegrass outfit that included Chris Hillman. He later moved to Florida and played in rock 'n' roll bands before returning to Southern California at the request of Hearts & Flowers leader (and ex-Squirrel Barker) Larry Murray to join that band. Another pioneering country-folk-rock group, Hearts & Flowers folded in early 1968 and Bernie moved in with Douglas Dillard.

With Douglas off touring with the Byrds, Gene began recording with Laramy and company. On May 15 at Western Recorders they cut Bob Dylan's "I Pity the Immigrant" off his back-to-basics album *John Wesley Harding*. On May 21 they recorded "Lyin' Down the Middle," bringing in Bernie to add lead guitar. "I guess, after we had been doing it for a time, Gene, Doug, and I," Bernie explains, "then Gene knew more about my playing and said, 'Why don't you come down to the sessions and play on some stuff?'"

Further sessions on May 23 and June 3–6 found the group working further on those two songs as well as cutting "It's Alright by Me" and "Los Angeles" with Bernie again joining in. "Bernie used to come into rehearsal occasionally and he would play either banjo or guitar, though I don't think the plan was for him to join the group," suggests Wayne Bruns. "Gene had real serious country influences so I think that was kind of the direction he wanted to go, but he wasn't real positive at the time of the commercial viability of it."

Two days later Gene abruptly halted the sessions and abandoned the group. In the interim, Douglas Dillard had returned from the Byrds tour and Gene had come to realize that the Laramy Smith sessions were becoming less appealing than working with Douglas and Bernie. "Larry started having serious problems with his wife," recalls Wayne, "and it really affected him. The band was starting to sound fairly decent, we were okay, and had it continued, it may have even done something because we were doing that kind of country-rock sound. But Larry's wife wanted to divorce him and it really threw him for a loop emotionally. I think Gene got tired of the personal problems that Larry was going through because Larry would dwell on it. At rehearsals he would come in and he would be all down and out and talk about it and it got to the point where we weren't getting much accomplished. I think maybe Gene was working on a budget and I'm sure he wanted to get some work down. I think Gene just got tired of it eventually. I don't know if he wasn't happy with the tunes that were coming out or what, but eventually he just said, 'We're not going to do this anymore' and he went on to do the Dillard & Clark Expedition album."

Wayne believes that Gene intended on having the group perform live before knocking it on the head. "There was talk of that. He must have been planning that because he brought us all up to his house one day and had a hair stylist come over to cut everybody's hair."

In a whirlwind turnaround, on June 13—just one week after the last Laramy Smith session—Gene, Douglas, Bernie, Don Beck, David Jackson, and harpsichord player Andy Belling entered Annex Studios in Hollywood to begin recording tracks for *The Fantastic Expedition of Dillard & Clark*. That first session would yield "In the Plan" and "With Care from Someone."

"The stuff with Douglas and us was really happening," enthuses Bernie, "and I think at some point Gene just thought, 'Well, this is better than what I'm doing and certainly more fun than what I'm doing with those other guys.' Then I think Gene had to deal with A&M. Obviously Gene had taken Doug down to A&M and some conversations had taken place because labels have to approve these things. Somewhere after a couple of weeks the two of them became running buddies and bought matching Triumph motorcycles and came back and announced that Doug had signed with A&M too, and now they were going to be Dillard & Clark. And the rest of us thought it was this equal thing, so it was cool to us. The next thing was Larry Marks showed up and said we were going to make a record to basically document what we were doing. It all happened very fast, very organically, so it was a real labor of love and I think you can hear that in the music. And you can also hear how unified the whole album is. It was really exciting. We would be playing that music and laughing. Gene was obviously in a very creative period and writing several great songs a week. He was fulfilled and happy, laughing, smiling, and joking. That was the happiest that I ever saw him."

As Gene explained to Domenic Priore in 1985, "I had known Doug Dillard from before and at that time he was sort of working with Bernie Leadon and we just sat around and jammed a couple of times and then decided we would put together a group. That's really how it happened. It was really pretty much of a flow. We would sit around and someone would come up with an idea. That's all we did in those days, was ride our motorcycles or sit around and play music. That was it. We'd have jams almost every evening so things would come out of them. We'd end up in Beechwood Canyon where Doug lived, get the banjos and guitars, David Jackson would come in and play bass, and we'd just start pickin' and that's how all this stuff came out."

Musically, Gene was about to embark on one of the most satisfying and influential adventures of his post-Byrds career. On a personal level, however, his association with Douglas Dillard would exacerbate an already growing drinking problem. "When Gene got with Douglas Dillard, things changed," emphasizes Jim Dickson. "Douglas was amazing. He came into town on a vodka drunk, then discovered grass, and kept drinking and doing grass. Then he discovered acid and you would find Douglas drinking, smoking dope, and taking LSD at the same time. How he survived it, I have no idea. But he's fine now. Sweetheart of a guy, but he had an influence on Gene. While it didn't hurt Douglas because he didn't care, Gene was way too high-strung and too complex to deal with all that."

5

Full Circle

The notion of integrating traditional country and bluegrass music within a contemporary folk-rock context was definitely in the air in Southern California in 1968. The overblown excesses of psychedelia and acid rock freak-outs, all presaged by the Byrds' "Eight Miles High" two years earlier, had left many musicians feeling rather empty. In seeking a more fulfilling musical form they looked to an honest and purely American roots music with a direct kinship to folk: country music. Several key instigators in what would come to be known as country-rock by the early '70s began to make their initial moves in this direction in 1968, including Chris Hillman, Gram Parsons, Richie Furay, Rodney Dillard, Rick Nelson, and Gene Clark.

Gene had already demonstrated a genuine appreciation for the country music form on his 1966 debut solo album, *Gene Clark with the Gosdin Brothers*. With players like Clarence White and Douglas Dillard accompanying him, Gene had created a template for others to follow, on songs like "Tried So Hard" and "Keep on Pushin'." But his teaming with Douglas in the spring of 1968 to form the Dillard & Clark Expedition became a turning point in the evolution of country-rock. "Gene always loved country music," claims Douglas. "So he just combined all his knowledge of music and that's basically what he came up with." Visionaries far ahead of the pack, Gene and Douglas pointed the way to where traditional country, folk, and bluegrass music could be taken in a contemporary rock/pop context. In so doing, they created a unique sound that would influence dozens of artists, from Poco to the Eagles, and help define the entire alt.country/Americana/roots rock movement of the 1990s that featured artists like Victoria Williams, the Jayhawks, Gillian Welch, the Ghost Rockets, and the Coal Porters.

"There has to be something besides loud music," Douglas told *Los Angeles Herald-Examiner* reporter Michael Etchison in a November 1968 interview, "and a lot of people are finding out they can listen to country music." Added Gene, "There's something else happening. Country music is changing a lot. The Grand Ole Opry people—the Red Foleys, Lefty Frizzells, and Roy Acuffs—will be around a long time, but the young people, especially the ones that don't come from Nashville, are trying to change. Buck Owens, Merle Haggard, Waylon Jennings, all these guys are making those Nashville cats very nervous 'cause they're bringing in a whole new kind of fan."

Years later, Gene justified his motivations for pursuing a country and bluegrass direction at a time when others were beginning to tread a similar path. "It happened about the same time as [the Byrds'] *Sweetheart of the Rodeo* and [Hillman's and Parsons's] Flying Burrito Brothers came out of that. I had kind of the same idea in mind, but I had a little more ethnic idea. I had always loved bluegrass music, but hadn't had a chance to experiment. I met Doug and Bernie and we got together and started working with it. But it was one of those things that didn't really come about in the music industry until later."

Bernie Leadon emphasizes that Gene was simply returning to his true roots in the music they were creating. "Douglas was from Missouri and so was Gene. So we were sort of saying to him, 'Hey, Gene, you may have been a pop star, but don't forget you're a guy from Missouri who grew up with bluegrass and country music. Why don't you just play that? Doesn't it feel good?' And he just went, 'Yeah!' He responded to the stuff with Douglas and us with his whole heart and soul because it was embracing the totality of who Gene Clark was, his roots, and got to use his extraordinary lyric and writing ability but without having to try to invent a whole new music, which was what you were sort of expected to do in the pop world. Instead he was going back to the forms of the roots music of Scottish/Irish immigrant ballads, folk music, which evolved into bluegrass that European immigrants coming to Missouri experienced. Gene came out of that whole thing. It's a nice way to renew yourself, by going back to your roots."

After the failure of his debut solo album and singles, plus two years of musical limbo, Gene found salvation in collaborating with Douglas and Bernie. Up to that point Gene tended to write alone, but having lost some of his confidence in the ensuing years since leaving the Byrds, he found this new partnership energizing and fulfilling and it stimulated his creative juices. "It was really easy to write with Gene," acknowledges Bernie. "He would come in with a piece, he might have the chorus or something, and we'd just play it over and over for two hours without stopping, another instrumental jam, another chorus, another verse, play it some more and he'd start singing it again. Then maybe a new part would come into the instrumental thing and the next morning he'd come back with lyrics for that part. The lyrics were never written collaboratively. We were creating the music and Gene was bouncing off of that, reacting to what we were playing, coming back with lyrics, and we'd put harmonies in and a new section if someone had ideas. 'Let's do a new section, here's a new chord progression.' That's the reason I got a writing credit for 'Train Leaves Here This Morning.' My actual recollection is that I didn't do that much writing on the song, but I threw a couple of chords in that Gene thought were significant enough to merit a writing credit."

The formation of the actual group, the Dillard & Clark Expedition, was as spontaneous as the music being created at Douglas's Beechwood Canyon abode. Bass player David Jackson was enlisted after running into Gene at the Troubadour one night and receiving an invitation to drop on by. Before long he was showing up at Douglas's to join in the pickin' sessions with Gene, Douglas, and Bernie. David still marvels at Gene's creative process and the positive environment that fostered it. "Gene's ability to be a poet for these musical occasions, because the music would just sort of grow out of this poetry, was amazing. Gene would have a feel on a guitar and a basic sense of the chords usually, but sometimes Bernie would come in and say, 'No, that's the wrong chord. How about this one?' And Gene would say, 'Oh, yeah, that's better.' Stuff like that. I don't know if I would really call them jam sessions. We would just arrive together, but I always had the impression that we were doing something, that there was a direction as opposed to a jam, which is just sort of whatever's going on at the moment. But Gene would always have, almost each day as I recall, some semblance of a song, if only a line or two. And we might work on that or we might work on a song that we'd worked on previously, but we really worked on things as opposed to jamming."

David vividly recalls one truly magical moment when the four players' individual chemistries all aligned. "At some point down the line, we arrived at the house and Gene had a chorus and possibly part of a first verse. By two o'clock he had a couple of verses, three o'clock he had the third verse minus the third line. And the song really didn't quite gel yet. There was some spice or some thread missing. But because so much time had gone by and we had played it over and over and moved things around, the solo here moved to there, now by three or four o'clock we've got this thing pretty well together for the rest of our parts. But it's still missing that third line. So we start to play it from the top and the first verse is gorgeous, the second verse is gorgeous, and we all sing the chorus, and it's great. We do the solos. Now we come to the third verse. Gene sings the first line, he sings the second line, and 'boom'—here is the third line and the whole song just becomes a complete, usable, viable, beautiful entity. We sing the fourth line, go into the chorus and because it's now gelled like never before we sing this last chorus with such verve. Doug and Gene are sitting on the couch. Bernie is sitting in a chair at a 90-degree angle to the couch. I am with my upright bass leaning over the three of them. And when we sing this chorus and it is so beautifully executed, our eyes are closed and our foreheads are very close to each other. We finish the chorus and go to the outro. I raised my head up just a brief second before the last note. As we hit that last note a white puff of smoke was ever so present to my eyes from the joining of this musical quartet. It emanated from where those four heads touched. The moment had such great power. But we never, ever sang that song again. Dillard didn't remember it; it never came up again. It's as if it did its job, never to be necessary on the planet again, ever. That moment changed my life. I realized that music had more than the ability to sell something on the radio. It's truly a great power when done with the proper respect and reasons. Things like that would occur. There was a great symmetry and serendipity in the music we made."

Despite the obvious attraction of mentoring with someone as highly regarded as Douglas Dillard, banjo player and guitarist Bernie Leadon found himself drawn more to Gene as a budding songwriter himself. Like so many before him, Bernie was in awe of Gene's apparent ease

Pickin' buddies Douglas Dillard and Gene Clark, March 1969.

with songwriting. "I was quite mystified at the fact that Gene was so prolific and could sit around and jam with us, and mind you, that we were drinking beer as well. I would get to the point in the evening where I would be done for the day and would want to go to bed. Gene would go home and stay up all night and germinate this stuff. He would come back the next day with a completely intact song with a beautiful story, wonderful phrasing, wonderful lines, beautiful melody, the whole thing. I was just amazed. I had no clue how he did it. I was extremely mystified. His writing had a very Elizabethan kind of tone, very classic writing, in a way. What he often would do was put the verb at the end of the line, which was unusual. Gene is a very underappreciated writer. Seriously, people talk about Gram Parsons and others, but Gene was a very deep and mystical guy. He would write these vague-sounding lyrics that somehow had this very deep meaning. He was Dylan-influenced and very much in touch with being an artist."

Douglas, too, was astounded by Gene's remarkable gift. "Gene Clark was a very creative-minded person. One of the best writers I've ever seen, very prolific. I could watch him sit down and start writing a song and write a whole song without lifting his pencil from the paper. It just seemed like it came through him all of a sudden. It was really amazing."

One witness to the extraordinary musical goings-on at Douglas's house that spring was pedal steel guitarist Rusty Young. He had come out to Los Angeles from Colorado a few months earlier to guest on the final Buffalo Springfield album and stayed to form Poco with ex-Buffalo

Richie Furay and Jim Messina. As Poco was coalescing at Furay's Laurel Canyon home, Dillard & Clark were already in full flight. "They were further along than we were," recalled Rusty. "They had their band together and they were going to be real bluegrassy. I was blown out! If you took that early Byrds stuff that was real good and made it bluegrass, which a lot of that stuff was anyway, a lot of that singing and everything had real bluegrass roots, and the 12-string guitar that McGuinn used to play in that fingerpicking style. That was all played on the banjo instead of the 12-string guitar, so it sounded like bluegrass Byrds. Gene wrote great songs, there were Gene Clark's tunes and some of Bernie's tunes, all played by really fine bluegrass players and sung with that three-part Byrds harmony. It was terrific—we were knocked out. Boy, that was the closest thing to what I would consider country-rock that I have heard ever."

Throughout the spring, as an actual group began to emerge from the informal sessions at Douglas's, Bernie developed a friendship with Gene. While the guitarist continued to sleep on Douglas's couch, Gene appeared to be living in the lap of luxury in his well-appointed Laurel Canyon abode with his Ferrari and personal assistant, Virginia Howard. "Clearly Gene had money," maintains Bernie. "He always dressed well. He was a much snappier dresser than me and obviously had a much larger wardrobe. He was the type of person who took his jeans to the dry cleaners so they came back with a crease in them. He always had nice boots and nice jackets. He had this unbelievable red 1968 Ferrari. That was back when Ferarris were completely handmade. I think it was a V-12; it was a large one. I later saw one on the street about 15 years ago and I said to the owner, 'I had a friend who had one of these,' and he said, 'Really? They're worth about $750,000 now!' But at that time Gene had this car and when he was in the garage and would start it, because the garage was underneath the house, it would shake the whole house. But soon after he traded it in because he couldn't afford it. He then got a British racing green MG-GT, a 2.2 version of the MG. The GT was a square back. He drove that like a madman. I remember being squished up like a ball in the backseat because you could barely fit a third person in the back behind the front seat. Douglas would be in the passenger seat and Gene would be driving around Hollywood like a madman doing the gutterball. You come to a traffic light and pull over into the right turn lane and then jump the light and get in front of everybody and get back in the traffic lane. He drove it nuts. He drove it like he was still the Ferrari guy."

Despite all the accoutrements of fame, Gene remained distant from most people, even his new band mates. "He was an insular personality," Bernie stresses. "He was not extremely open. He had sort of a mysterious quality to him. I wouldn't say brooding but he was an introvert. In social settings he was introverted. He did seem like he had quite a bit on his mind and would often appear distracted. You'd say, 'Hey, Gene, what are you thinking?' and he would go, 'Huh? Oh,' like he was being brought back to reality. I don't recall seeing Gene with one woman. There were women around, but I don't remember a significant relationship or any particular relationship at that time."

David also found Gene's temperament contrary to his status as a bona fide star and recognized the duality in Gene's personality and the mood swings. "Fame puts you in a place that is not natural. So no matter where you came from, it just makes you wacky. Some people can handle it, some people can't. But Gene was fairly, I would use the word 'aloof,' but it's not really the word I mean. He was distant but, in retrospect, I think it was really shyness. I don't know if anyone knew Gene very well then. He was very quiet and had an odd sense of humor. Things would be funny to him that wouldn't necessarily be to others. I remember him saying something and laughing and I had to think about where the humor was in what he said that was so funny. He wasn't a particularly humorous man, but he was often lighthearted. I think there was a dark side there. But when he was happy and light he was just delightful, but unfortunately that wasn't too often. He seemed to be clouded by the trappings of stardom."

In mid-June, following the collapse of the Laramy Smith sessions, Dillard & Clark brought their folk/bluegrass/country-rock amalgam to A&M's Annex Studios' 8-track recording facility—a large, old, Hollywood-style studio a few blocks from the A&M lot—to lay down tracks for their debut album. "When Gene came over to A&M and we did Dillard & Clark," producer Larry Marks recalls, "that was a much more organic thing. Gene literally just walked into A&M and said, 'We've been doing some things—Doug, Bernie, and I—and I'd like to cut some tracks.' So I said, 'Well, let's go and cut them.' And that's how it happened."

Having honed the songs during their Beechwood Canyon sessions at Douglas's, the recording sessions ran smoothly, with few obstacles. "So when we went into the studio it was a piece of cake," maintains Bernie. "We knew the songs very well." The core of Gene, Douglas, Bernie, and David was augmented in the studio by Don Beck on dobro and mandolin, Chris Hillman also on mandolin, and Andy Belling on harpsichord. "We recorded in a circle, everybody sitting in a circle, all facing in," David notes. "I remember the engineer saying, 'God, this is awful. I'm getting leakage everywhere,' and Larry Marks replying, 'Well, that's what they want.' I was later told that it was because of those sessions that the Nitty Gritty Dirt Band recorded their *Will the Circle Be Unbroken* album in a circle. 'That's the way Dillard & Clark did it.'"

"I remember that in the batch of sessions for the first album there was only one day where there was a drummer," Bernie reveals. "The rest of the sessions we did acoustically with David on upright bass. I actually played like a sock rhythm [fretting closed chords and literally smacking or "socking" the strings in a percussive manner on the backbeat] on the guitar that sounded like a snare drum backing. That's how we cut those tracks. It was in an old-style studio in Hollywood where we would all be in the same room, sitting close to each other. Interestingly, Douglas pushed me to play banjo on a lot of the songs. So I play banjo on more songs than Douglas does, which shows how selfless he was in pushing me forward. 'With Care from Someone' is Douglas and 'Get It On Brother.' Pretty much all the rest are me. When I played banjo, Douglas played guitar."

A week and a half after that inaugural session, the group returned to cut perhaps one of Gene's best-known post-Byrds songs, "Train Leaves Here This Morning," written by Gene and Bernie. The song would reach a much wider audience four years later when the Eagles recorded it on their debut album. Bernie was a founding member of that group and brought the song to their attention. "I wasn't writing that much in the beginning with the Eagles," he explains. "One of the strengths of the band, to me, was that we had access to great outside writers with great songs, like on the first album with Jackson Browne and Jack Tempchin and later J.D. Souther. I did think that 'Train Leaves Here This Morning' was a great song and I did feel that Gene was an extraordinary writer. So I just thought, 'Well, I co-wrote half that song so I'll have half the publishing,' so let's try that out. And it worked well. 'Train Leaves Here This Morning' only made me money when the Eagles did it."

The Dillard & Clark Expedition took a hiatus until August 15, when sessions resumed with "She Darked the Sun" and "Don't Come Rollin'" and carried on sporadically into September as the group laid down the remainder of the album tracks. On September 13, Gene brought in one of his most personal compositions, an evocative glance back to his lost innocence in Swope Park titled "Something's Wrong." Gene and Douglas had taken a trip out to Missouri to shoot some photographs for the album cover (which appear on the back of the original vinyl album sleeve) and the idyllic setting had an impact on Gene; he longed for the simpler, unfettered life that he once enjoyed. But he could no longer have it. Too much had changed for him and the song reflects his nostalgic yearning.

At the same session, the group cut a rendition of the old bluegrass standard "Bonaparte's Retreat" that was not included on the album. The final session, however, marked a departure from all the previous recording dates and represents the only nod to a more contemporary rock sound from the group. On September 30 and October 1, the Dillard & Clark Expedition went electric, joined on the sessions by drummer Joe Larson and Jim Horn on organ, to record Gene's solitary composition "Out on the Side." Sounding very much like an outtake from The Band's *Music from Big Pink*—with its rolling organ, loping tempo, gorgeous mountain harmonies, and Robbie Robertson-like guitar licks—"Out on the Side" stood in stark contrast to the remainder of the album's acoustic tracks and confused more than a few listeners when it appeared as the opening track. "'Out on the Side' came from an entirely different session," David confirms. "Larry Marks was the producer and had a lot of input on that. I think it came from what the Beatles were doing at the time and it was more of a 'So-and-so is in the studio, how about we get him to play on this thing.' It was a little more haphazard, arty recording technique of that day."

Once the recording sessions wrapped up, the Dillard & Clark Expedition set its sights on preparing for live engagements. Michael Clarke, having left the Byrds at the end of 1967, was drafted on drums, now that the group had determined to go all-electric. The problem was that the group lacked direction. "Since there was no organization, I can't recall us having any formal management," sighs Bernie. "Eddie Tickner was nominally involved, but not really working with

Dillard. He might have been advising Gene loosely, but the upshot was that there was a record company but no management, no plan, no direction, no logistical support, and no money. It was Gene's deal, Douglas maybe got a taste, but nobody else got anything."

Organizing a live set and rehearsing with microphones were deemed unimportant. To Doug and Gene, the organic nature of the group would just flow out onstage. "The Dillard & Clark Expedition was not a very good live band because, exactly like the Flying Burrito Brothers, neither band had any ability to actually rehearse and be focused and organized about anything," allows Bernie. "With absolutely zero organization, none, we walked onstage without any prepared set list, without having properly figured out how we would begin and end songs. Without having really rehearsed the harmonies on microphone and be in some kind of balance. The result was complete noise and confusion; to come out looking quite cool and proceed to make absolute idiots of ourselves. Some of us, especially bluegrass musicians—banjo players and mandolin players like me and Don Beck—approach it very intellectually. To competently play bluegrass banjo, it's completely about organization and methodical thinking, analytical stuff. Yes, you want to play it with feeling, but it's very intricate and needs structure. Douglas had that part of his brain that he could do that, but he was also much more an instinctive-feel player and he would go completely over to playing on the vibe and the flow. And the others thought they could, too. When it absolutely all came together the thing would soar, but it was so lucid it didn't come together onstage. They would become self-conscious. In a room somewhere you could much more easily snap into that vibe and you might have one of those magical evenings sustain for several hours, amazing fluidity of creation. But as soon as you tried putting it onstage, you're now staging what had been occurring naturally in a room, only now there's an audience, a rather large audience, sitting there expectantly with drinks, waiting to be entertained on cue. Neither of these bands, Dillard & Clark nor the Burritos, had a clue how to do that."

The new electric Dillard & Clark Expedition, with Bernie on Gibson 335 electric guitar and David on Fender bass, returned to the recording studio to cut two tracks for a single prior to their public debut. For the session, Gene resurrected the Laramy Smith-Gene Clark collaboration "Lyin' Down the Middle" from the aborted sessions back in May, along with a rollicking cover of Elvis Presley's "Don't Be Cruel." Both are fine examples of country-influenced rock, the former dominated by Earl P. Ball's honky tonk piano, while the Elvis track boasts some unusual rockin' harpsichord from Andy Belling. Gene is in fine form on both tracks. "We started playing 'Don't Be Cruel' periodically," recalls David. "It would crop up in those early sessions before the recording of the first album. We'd be sitting around doing nothing and Gene would start into 'Don't Be Cruel' and it was a cool little version. It was recorded just as a by-product of us being in the studio. 'Hey, let's do that.' "

Sandwiched in between the end of the album sessions and the single's recording date, Gene returned to Annex Studios to lay down three tracks likely intended for inclusion on a movie soundtrack that never got completed. On November 14, with noted folk music session guitarist

Bruce Langhorne accompanying him, Gene recorded "Ribbons" and "Baptist Funeral," followed three days later by "Raymond the Clown," this time joined by Flying Burrito Brothers pedal steel guitarist Sneaky Pete Kleinow. No details of these sessions are known, except that they did not include members of the Dillard & Clark Expedition.

While the group would go on to play folk clubs like the Ash Grove and Golden Bear, the Dillard & Clark Expedition's Troubadour debut remains the pinnacle of their brief performing history—and a monumental disaster. Their album, *The Fantastic Expedition of Dillard & Clark,* had just been released, it was early December, and anticipation ran high for their Troubadour stand.

"It was a Tuesday night, the press is there, and it's literally the first night of the band, the first time we've stepped out to play in front of people, as I recall," David notes. "We go for sound check at three o'clock, I drive all the way back to Santa Monica where I was living at the time, take a nap, have a shower, dress up, drive back and get there at eight o'clock, and I say to the ticket-taker at the door, 'Have you seen Doug and Gene?' And she says, 'Yeah, they're next door at Dan Tana's,' which is an Italian restaurant next to the Troubadour. So I went next door. Doug and Gene, having left the sound check at three-thirty, have gone next door and started drinking martinis, and it's now eight o'clock. And, unbeknownst to me, they've taken acid. So now the lights go dark, it's now nine o'clock, the opening act has played, and the sound man says, 'Now, ladies and gentlemen, Dillard & Clark!' The lights come up and Gene is sitting on his amplifier facing the wall. Douglas is standing there with a massive grin, and he's got a world-class grin. He's smiling and holding his banjo. And literally just before we went on, Douglas said to me, 'Oh, you know, in bluegrass bands the bass player does the talking.' *Okay.* I was a fairly shy guy and I think I stuttered at the time, and I just panicked.

"So here we are," David continues, "Gene's facing the wall, Douglas is grinning with a smile much bigger than it should be, but somehow or other, I have no idea how, we got through the first song. In the second song, Douglas plays the fiddle. So he puts down his banjo and picks up his fiddle. Somehow we get Gene off his amplifier and he's back in front now and we play the second song. At the end of that song Douglas sets the fiddle on the stage, jumps in the air, and lands with both feet on the fiddle with a big smile on his face, breaking the fiddle. Don Beck is standing to my left playing mandolin and he looks at me and says, 'Well, I think that's enough for me,' and walks off the stage, never to return. He walked right off and never played the rest of the week. So then Douglas turns to me and says, 'Go ahead, say hi to the folks.' I tell you I don't think I shit my pants, but it sure smelled like it. Man, that was something! That was the degree to which Douglas and Gene could descend into the depths of both booze and drugs. It never again got that far out, however that set a tone for everything else we did."

For Bernie, the Troubadour debacle remains "one of the worst experiences I've ever had. Douglas and Gene completely became unglued. It just stopped working. Gene was terribly shy

Dillard & Clark debut at the Troubadour, December 1968: (left to right) Bernie Leadon, Michael Clarke, Gene Clark, and Douglas Dillard. (David Jackson is not shown.)

and spent all of the show mostly with his back to the audience. It all came to a screeching halt and they just sort of stared at each other and then exited the stage, leaving the rest of us standing there feeling like our pants were down at our ankles. I think I played a bit of 'Buckaroo' and left the stage soon after."

Following a sound scolding from Troubadour owner Doug Weston, the group managed to pull themselves together sufficiently to complete the week and earn a rave review from *Los Angeles Herald-Examiner* reporter Michael Etchison. He observed that Gene's voice "is even more lonesome than it was with the Byrds. Dillard and Leadon join him in a mix of high hill and flatland harmonies." Writer/publicist Jim Bickhart attended one of the shows and was suitably impressed. He also noted that Gene chose to ignore his past, as if to say, "It's what I'm doing now that matters." "He didn't do any Byrds songs with Dillard & Clark," Jim explains. "That's one thing I remember distinctly. He didn't even do anything from his first album with the Gosdin Brothers. They were mostly doing the stuff from the first Dillard & Clark album together. It sounded great. It was a little more electric than the album because they were performing with electric instruments, but it was very well done."

Michael Clarke bailed during the Troubadour stand (to join Chris Hillmn's Flying Burito Brothers) and drummer Jon Corneal, fresh from a stint with Gram Parsons's International Submarine Band, was literally plucked from the audience one night to fill the vacant drum stool. "I came back to California and I was hanging out at the Troubadour and Geno, Gene Clark, came up to me at the bar. We'd known of each other, but hadn't really met. You never knew who you'd run into at the bar there. He came up to me and asked if I had any drums with me. I told him I had a snare and a set of brushes. He said, 'That'll work. Do you want to sit in with us tonight?' They were playing the Troubadour that night, Dillard & Clark. So I said sure. That's how I ended up in the band. It was easy. We all liked each other. Doug and Gene liked me because I drank as much as they did."

Gene's aversion to flying and his unwillingness to stray far from his home base grounded the Dillard & Clark Expedition from the outset. Although the album garnered favorable reviews on its release at the end of November, without the ability to tour, the group stood little chance of gaining a wider audience for their fresh, innovative brand of country-rock. "Doug and Gene did some really good records that nobody paid attention to," laments Chris Hillman, an unabashed Dillard & Clark supporter. "That first album was fabulous, way better than anything the rest of us were doing when you measure it song-per-song. Better than Poco and the Burritos—consistent and lyrically brilliant." Reporter Michael Etchison declared, "They have the best country sound of any ex-rock group around." Even the album cover drew some attention. "They had the bad boy image on the motorcycles, passing that cigarette that everyone thought was a joint," laughs Rodney Dillard. "I got a big kick out of that." David grins, "That was who those guys were. Those two guys were pretty wild. There were some pretty wild times."

"Much is said about Gene's fear of flying," muses Bernie on Gene's often confusing and neurotic behavior, "but his fear of performing was legendary, too. His actual fear onstage of the audience was palpable and it was exaggerated by his use of alcohol or drugs. As a result of his fear he often drank or did drugs, which, of course, only increased his paranoia. You can't ignore his basic psychology of being afraid of all this stuff. It seems he wanted it so bad, success, but at the same time he was terrified of it. So I think that he may have been afraid of being a solo performer and so that's why he came over and hung out with us. I think the whole thing about 'What do I do now?' weighed on him along with peoples' expectations and his own expectations, the reality of life in Hollywood, which, of course, is not very glamorous. It's the whole issue of the artistic temperament. That whole thing of having to come up with something compelling artistically and then also make it commercially compelling, and also having a marketing team that can do something with it can be daunting. Gene was the sensitive artist guy who hadn't answered the question, 'How comfortable am I?' and the answer was that he wasn't comfortable doing it. So he constantly was in a situation where he had the intention of doing it but he had the counter-intention of, 'I don't know if I want to do this.'"

"I saw Gene years later at the Beverly Theatre on Wilshire when Rick Roberts was in the band," Bernie continues. "All these guys there onstage to support him and he did the same thing he did with Dillard & Clark, counting off a song and then standing with his back to the audience, facing the drummer, vamping on the intro for four minutes. He just couldn't make himself turn around. Everybody around him was doing body language like, 'Gene, man, go for it!' but he wouldn't turn around."

Gene performs with Douglas Dillard at the Troubadour, December 1968.

David Jackson agrees with Bernie's analysis of the dichotomy of Gene Clark the songwriter versus Gene Clark the performer. "Gene never felt all that comfortable just playing regular music with regular players. But I heard years later how he was playing a little coffeehouse by himself and would completely delight in sitting around playing songs with anybody. That was a part of Gene I never saw. He never seemed comfortable in front of an audience when I knew him. He seemed to always be trying to get to that place in his personality from which emanated the poetry. And that's not always that comfortable with an audience. They want to be entertained first or be allowed to arrive at that place. And he would never allow them the time to get there, he just started there. Gene just didn't have that kind of appeal. He was a more individual taste, like a fine wine. And not just anybody could appreciate that. I think he had a depth that was not conducive to mass appeal."

For all intents and purposes, the Dillard & Clark Expedition folded following their Troubadour engagement. Don and Michael left first and Bernie wasn't long in leaving, either. When the remnants of the group convened in February 1969 for a recording session to cut a new single ("Out on the Side" had been released in November to universal indifference), Bernie found himself out on the side. Douglas had hooked up with Donna Washburn, whose father was a prominent executive with the 7-Up soft drink company, and insisted she now join the group as the third voice, the role previously held by Bernie. "She was a lovely person, a very attractive blond young woman," recounts Bernie, "but she wanted to sing, too. She and Douglas were sort of an item. So Donna's there all the time and when we start singing she goes to the third part, which was the part I sang. So I figured I'm suddenly redundant. It was totally over for me, but it was clear it would never be a working band. So I opted out at that point. Donna had a big personality and was ambitious, but it was like if Yoko Ono showed up and started singing the third part and George Harrison's wondering what's going on. We tried it for one day and I just figured it wasn't working, so I left. There were only three parts in the harmonies."

"Donna sort of placed herself in that situation and Douglas allowed it," muses David. "Douglas allowed his women, all of whom were strong women, to be a part of his life in a fashion that he really shouldn't have. That's just his nature, just the way he is. I remember thinking there is no reason for this girl to be here. She's a delightful lady, but why is she ingratiating herself into this music that doesn't need this ingratiation? I guess there were some things that were better, some of the harmonies were interesting, but I personally didn't think that was of any great import to the needs of this music." Larry Marks agrees. "It was divisive in more ways than one. It didn't really work musically, but it wasn't going to go away. She was Doug's lady at that point. But she clearly wasn't out of the same briar patch as Doug or Gene. She always looked like Daisy Mae from Beverly Hills, dressing up in those kinds of clothes to be in the band. It just never quite worked because it wasn't real. Gene kind of lived with it, he accepted it, and everybody tried to make it work."

Without Bernie, who had moved on to join Linda Ronstadt's backing group, the reconstituted Dillard & Clark Expedition cut the exquisite "Why Not Your Baby," written by Gene alone and complimented by a lush string arrangement. Gene, Doug, and Donna harmonize together beautifully, suggesting the addition of Donna offered tremendous vocal potential. "Lyin' Down the Middle" had failed to chart when released by A&M a month earlier, as did "Why Not Your Baby" in May, a wholly undeserved fate for such a gorgeous record. This only compounded Gene's frustration with the music industry in general and A&M Records in particular.

Gene had severed his management ties with Larry Spector soon after the Dillard & Clark Expedition began recording their debut album, but there was some dust left unsettled from that business arrangement. A year or so after the dissolution of the Laramy Smith group, a former booking agent took legal action against Gene. "After that band broke up I kept rehearsing with another band and we went down to Palm Springs and were working a club down there," Wayne Bruns recalls. "Then I got a call down there from this agent. He had worked, in what capacity I'm not sure, with Gene. I can't remember his name, but we used to refer to him as 'The Weasel.' Somehow this guy had located me in Palm Springs and called me. He wanted me to fly up to L.A. because there was some legal dispute over the band. He flew me up and

I went into a courtroom and Gene was there. I hadn't seen him since the band folded and he seemed rather perturbed that I was there, although I never said anything to anyone or testified. What I suspected had happened was that this guy had possibly sued Gene for some money or something and told him that he had helped organize this band. I suspect that Gene probably said the band didn't really exist and just me being there wasn't particularly in Gene's favor. And I always thought there might have been some hard feelings over that, although that wasn't my intention."

Spector had worn out his welcome with Gene several months earlier, following a rather reprehensible incident involving Gene's younger brothers during a self-invited visit (without Gene) to the Clark home in Bonner Springs. David Clark winces as he relates the incident. "Larry was chumming up to our dad and going out and buying him drinks. They put Larry in the girls' room at the front of the upstairs and moved the girls out of their room and crammed them into our room and put a curtain up between us. In the evenings after everything would quiet down he would come and talk to us, each one of us. He was kind of interviewing us, seeing where we were at with things. He talked about screen tests for movies and played this whole thing up. He even talked about paying my car off so I could go out to California. But he was playing one brother off the other by telling us not to tell the others because we were the one he was interested in. He didn't bother talking to the girls. He was just interested in me and my brothers Rick and Dan. Gene got wind of this out in California and he called me. The three of us thought we were going to be movie stars. Well, Gene got so pissed off he went down to see Larry at his Malibu Beach home and said, 'What the hell are you doing?' And he picked Larry up and dropped him head first off his balcony onto the sand. Larry had a lot of power over Gene's career at that time and he killed Gene's chances for an album. I think Larry thought that had he gotten one of us in his grasp, then he had leverage over Gene. And, boy, when Dad found out I thought he was going to go out and rip this guy's head right off. And he could have done it."

Undaunted by the commercial failure of *The Fantastic Expedition of Dillard & Clark,* A&M called the group back to the studio on March 31 to begin laying down tracks for a second album. The first track recorded was a cover of bluegrass duo Reno and Smiley's country music hit "Stone Must Be the Wall" with ex-Dillard & Clark member Bernie Leadon guesting on guitar. The choice of a cover song over original material from Gene hinted at the direction the second album would ultimately take. Three days later they cut Gene's "Kansas City Southern," this time including pedal steel guitar from Sneaky Pete. Autobiographical in nature, the song derives its inspiration from the train trestle that crossed over Gregory Boulevard at one end of Swope Park. "Kansas City Southern" would remain in Gene's repertoire for the next 20 years and become almost synonymous with him. (Pure Prairie League later scored a minor hit with the song in the early '70s.)

Further sessions in April and May saw the recording of Gene's melancholy "Through the Morning, Through the Night" and a cover of the Everly Brothers' "So Sad," both pointing to Gene's mood and featuring lush harmonies. "That whole album was a lot more morose," avers David Jackson. "It wasn't just Gene. It was the time and the place the group was in. I remember there being some discomfort in the ranks, the feeling that this obviously didn't have the spark or the kind of feel the first album did. But it really couldn't because now there were a bunch of people hanging on and managers and stuff. I remember Eddie Tickner at the sessions just shaking his head and saying, 'Ah, this isn't happening like it should be.' Everything had taken a different turn. The personalness and the familyness of the first album was non-existent on the second one."

David feels part of the problem was the switch to electric instruments, which took away much of the innocence that informed the debut album, as well as the changes surrounding the group. "That album never really gelled like the first one did. The first album definitely grew out of us sitting around the couch at Douglas's house allowing Gene's poetry to grow. By the second album all of a sudden it's a different deal now. We're all electric. The press is talking to Doug and Gene, girls are around, and all of a sudden that quiet thing of not being inundated by the outside world and just playing music and being artful disappeared. Now we had to go out and play regular songs and be a band."

In June, the lineup of the group was further augmented by the addition of three-time national fiddle champion Byron Berline. A native of Oklahoma, Berline had first hooked up with the Dillards when the Missouri quartet played a gig at the University of Oklahoma on the day John Kennedy was assassinated. Impressed with Byron's facile fiddling ability, the Dillards invited him out to Los Angeles the following summer to guest on their traditional bluegrass album *Pickin' and Fiddlin'*. It was then that Byron first met Gene, at the Troubadour. Following those sessions, Byron returned to the University of Oklahoma and later worked with bluegrass pioneer Bill Monroe before serving a stint in the US army. He was stationed at Fort Polk in Louisiana when he received an invitation from Douglas Dillard. "Doug called me the day before I got out of the army," Byron remembers. "He said, 'What are you doing? Can you get away for a bit?' And I said, 'I'm getting out of the army tomorrow.' Doug said, 'Great! I want you to come out to California and record an album with me and Gene.' And I said, 'Man, I'll be there.'" Byron moved into Harry Dean Stanton's apartment next to Douglas's on Beechwood Canyon while Harry was away in Yugoslavia filming *Kelly's Heroes*.

With Byron on fiddle, the direction of the group's second album suddenly shifted towards a more traditional bluegrass sound. As Jon Corneal points out, "He played fast fiddle and in the right environment Doug can play real fast banjo, too. That's what happened, it ended up being a fast bluegrass group. At the time I think we played some of the world's fastest bluegrass. People couldn't believe it. The whole thrust was changing. It had become a bluegrass band. Gene was not happy with that. Originally they were going to be doing his songs and then all of a sudden they were doing a bunch of old Bill Monroe songs. Gene stepped back. Gene was trying to fit in and be a bluegrass rhythm player. It was such a waste. That had a lot to do with why he left the band. It was a shame. We should have talked it out and worked it out and maybe some good things would have come out of it."

David suggests, "Douglas was a pretty strong force in whatever circle he was standing by virtue of his personality and how we revered him, I think. So maybe Gene just succumbed to that."

The sessions now were based around bluegrass standards like "Roll in My Sweet Baby's Arms," "No Longer a Sweetheart of Mine," and a frantic cover of Boudeleaux Bryant's "Rocky Top." "I thought 'Rocky Top' was horrible," declares David. "Why it's there, is beyond me." As Gene later explained about the second album, titled *Through the Morning, Through the Night*, "It was schizophrenic in one respect, but in another respect it was something we were attempting to do, but we didn't have the time to sophisticate it like we had on the first album, where we took several months to rehearse things, talk it over, really get the arrangements and harmonies."

In the midst of the June sessions, Gene's brother David arrived for an unannounced visit. "Even as close as I was to him when we were younger," David Clark asserts, "I very seldom could track him down or talk to him or anything else. I got so tired of not getting a hold of him that I hitchhiked out to California in the spring of 1969 and spent almost eight weeks with him out there." David would witness the group recording and observe his brother as he went about the creative process. "Gene wanted Doug to have his day," posits David on his brother's reduced role on the second album. "He always thought that Doug had been overlooked as a serious musician and player and he wanted to give Doug that opportunity, but at the same time he had mixed emotions about it. To do that took the musical controls away from him. And then the stuff that was coming in, it wasn't that it was bad music, it just wasn't what Gene had in his mind to do. He was very unhappy about the way the album was going. It was such a departure from the first album. They were using too many cover songs and he wanted more original material, but nothing seemed to fit. The material he had was not in the real bluegrass strain where Byron and Doug were going. Donna was an influence that Gene didn't like over Doug. It wasn't that Gene didn't like her, but she was trying to push Doug more to the forefront. It didn't break the relationship down between Gene and Doug on a personal level because they were still great comrades, but it broke down their musical relationship. And with Byron coming onboard and going in a more bluegrass direction, Gene was not happy with where it was going. So he lost interest in it and when Gene loses interest in something he walks away from it. Although he was there and he contributed and there were some things that he even really enjoyed, there was a lot of it that he really wasn't that interested in and it was kind of a sleepwalk. He was already tired of it before the album came out and he sure as hell didn't want to go on the road with it. He was done with Dillard & Clark."

Living with Gene was quite an eye-opening experience for David, who found himself traveling in the fast lane and trying to keep up. "Gene was an enormous presence. I could not believe it when I saw it in 1969, the people that he had camaraderie with, like Steve McQueen, who was a good friend of Gene's. They were kindred in a lot of ways. They loved fast things, fast cars. Gene was an extremely wild driver, crazy behind the wheel from the get-go. He was always going way too fast. And that was his whole life. He was always going too fast and couldn't catch up with himself. That's what drove him. And people didn't understand that about him. We went to all the places. The Sunset Strip was the place to be. Gene was the guru at the Troubadour, I kid you not. If you went to the Whisky, Steve McQueen had a booth in the corner and everybody kind of worked the whole thing around Steve's booth. At the Troubadour, it was Gene Clark. At that time everybody kind of worked their way around to his corner to see what was going on. A lot of influential people passed through there, some I liked, some I didn't like at all.

"At the time, the only real concern I had about Gene was that he just seemed to be constantly going. There was no rest, day or night. On a typical day we would get up at two o'clock in the afternoon and from the time that he got up and got showered we were going. We very seldom stayed at the house. Once in a while I would talk him into eating an omelet before we would go. But generally we had anywhere from an hour or two hours before we got to the recording studio for his session and he always had things to do, places to go, things to pick up; he had all these irons in the fire. And there were some secret dealings that I was kind of shadowed out of. Obviously I wasn't that damn naïve; I knew what was going on, but I think he wanted to keep his little brother away from it. I was pretty hip to what was going on, though. Then we would go to the recording studio and I became the runner: getting coffee, getting beer, getting sandwiches, while this whole thing was going on. It was very interesting and educational.

"A typical hour when we came home," David continues, "was three or four in the morning, after we did the recording sessions, went out to dinner, went to the Sunset Strip, then went home. One night we came home, the sun was ready to come up, and he sat down at the kitchen table and started dragging pieces of paper, napkins, matchbook covers, and he laid them out on the table. He asked me for a pen and he asked me for some coffee. So I got the coffee on and he started writing. He would be working away and he would stop, sit back and look at it, scribble something out and write something else. This went on all night. It was a marathon. At one point he asked, 'Can you make me a sandwich?' So I made him a grilled cheese sandwich and he continued to down the coffee. It turned out what he was doing was working on three different ideas at the same time, flipping back and forth between them, taking things from one and putting them in another. By about noon I was completely fuzzy. I didn't need drugs; I was already spacey. But he kept on working. I said to him, 'You've got to get some sleep! You've got to be at the studio at two o'clock,' and he said, 'Nah, man, I've got to get these done. I'm just about done.' We were two hours late getting to the studio and had no sleep whatsoever. But he had finished what he was doing. He had completed these three projects together in the space of from about four o'clock in the morning until four in the afternoon after being up the day before at the sessions and up all night on the Sunset Strip with about three bites of a grilled cheese sandwich and about a gallon of coffee. He was just so focused. When he got into something he had to see it through the way he wanted it. He would not settle for 'that's good enough' and that's why he couldn't settle with what some people were doing in some of the bands he was in. He drove them nuts and they drove him nuts. It was a two-way street.

"Gene was a perfectionist. If you couldn't keep up, he didn't want you around. If you couldn't see the same vision that he was seeing, then he'd just as soon you go someplace else. He didn't want to be hateful about it, but people kept dragging on him and he would get violent. That's where that kind of reaction would come from. People blamed it on the drugs and alcohol, but he could be like that without them."

David inadvertently ended up contributing to the second Dillard & Clark album. "On some evenings after practice or a recording session they would sit around at a number of houses. I think it was at Harry Dean Stanton's house this one night and Harry had a reel-to-reel tape recorder going. There were a bunch of us monkeying around and the guys were toying with covers of several different things, all the way from country to pop-rock to spiritual. They were trying to find a filler track for the album. So we were sitting around that night just carrying on about this and that. Somebody was talking about a wife and said something about her being a dizzy bitch. I had some tablespoons that I was keeping time with and all of a sudden Gene lets out this big strum on the guitar and starts out kind of country, 'I once had a wife and she was dizzy.' And everybody just kind of went, 'Ah, cut it out' because he was kind of making fun of everybody. So I went vaudeville and replied, 'She was the love of my life and her name it was Lizzie.' So we got into this vaudeville thing, just kind of in your face 'this isn't working so let's screw it up' attitude. And that's how 'Corner Street Bar' came into being. I didn't know he was going to use it until I heard the album."

Between the completion of sessions and the release of *Through the Morning, Through the Night,* the Dillard & Clark Expedition, now featuring fiddler Byron Berline as principal soloist, set off on their one and only tour. They headed out in a two-car convoy (David Jackson was the only member who flew) on July 4, bound for Chicago. For Byron, performing with Gene and Doug would prove to be quite an experience. "I had heard from the other guys in the band some of the shenanigans that he and Doug did onstage, especially at the Troubadour, smashing Doug's fiddle and getting sloshed. But I hadn't been around them much. It was a big eye-opener for me. I had never experienced anything like this before. The first night we played, we were in Chicago at a little place called the Beaver's Club and I was wound up, ready to play. We had all this material kind of rehearsed up doing the album. The guy was giving us free drinks at the bar. Donna came up to me after we'd done the sound check and were standing around waiting to go onstage in about 30 or 40 minutes and she said, 'You better go get Doug and Gene away from that bar, they're drinking too much.' And I said, 'Oh, they're not either. They're alright.' So she said, 'I know they are. You just wait and see.' Sure enough, we got up onstage and they all but fell off of it. They didn't know where they were. And I thought, 'Good god, what is this?!' I was really disappointed and told them about it. I said if this was the way it was going to be, I was going back home. We couldn't play like that. It was a little better the rest of the tour. But seems like every time we played the Troubadour they did the same thing. Their bar bill was more than they made in a week—that's a fact. It's funny now, but they didn't care then."

On the way out to Chicago, the convoy stopped in Bonner Springs for an old-fashioned Clark family picnic. "Gene called his folks when we were about 50 miles out of Bonner," recalls Jon, "and by the time we got there they had a picnic for us—ham, potato salad, two washtubs full of beer. Just real down-to-earth people. Gene was just a country boy from Bonner Springs, Kansas." The moment was a turning point for Gene's younger brother Rick. "When Gene came through with Dillard & Clark, that was the first time I ever got to sit around with a professional band. Gene had given my dad his Gibson Dove, the red guitar he was photographed with after he left the Byrds, but I kind of finagled it away and it kind of became my guitar. In those days I was a very amateur songwriter and these guys were great. Douglas just sat there with this big Cheshire grin and listened. They all wanted to hear what 'the little brother' could do. That gave me confidence to keep pursuing what I was doing."

The new Dillard & Clark lineup: Standing behind Gene and Doug are (left to right) Donna Washburn, Byron Berline, Jon Corneal, and David Jackson.

The tour included a couple of dates in the Midwest before the group headed back home. On their return they were tapped to contribute to the soundtrack of William Faulkner's *The Reivers* starring Gene's buddy Steve McQueen. Lalo Schifrin was conducting and the group was offered a song by Alan and Marilyn Bergman, who had previously won an Academy Award for "The Windmills of Your Mind." The song was titled "The World Is Wide Open" and was scheduled as a single release for the group that would coincide with the movie's premiere. "Boy, I remember we worked hard on that, rehearsing on that song," recalls Byron. "And I'll tell you what, it really sounded good. We were all pleased with it, it sounded great. It was like the title song. We all got paid pretty well. I think they gave us around $3,000 to cut that, the band, and that was real good money back then. Then, all at once, we get this call and they told us they'd dropped everything. The producer didn't like Lalo Schifrin's music. So they hired John Williams to do it. We got caught in the squeeze. I have no idea what happened to the track we cut, but it was very good. I would love to hear it."

Released in September, *Through the Morning, Through the Night* was generally regarded as a disappointing follow-up to the groundbreaking *The Fantastic Expedition of Dillard & Clark* the year before. Seven of the 11 tracks were cover tunes (compared with only one on the first album) and although Gene posted some strong performances and the blending of his voice with Donna Washburn's presaged the pure country coupling of Gram Parsons and Emmylou Harris, the album was far less adventurous. "We kind of threw that one together quickly," surmises Douglas. "I like the first album the best. The second album was intermingled with a lot of different ideas. It was a little heavier on the steel guitar and drums."

Critics took particular note of one of the non-bluegrass covers on the album, Gene's soulful rendition of the Beatles' "Don't Let Me Down," citing it as the standout cut. Byron recalls the decision to record a Beatles song being serendipitous. "That was kind of a whim in the studio, working that one up. Gene just kind of had it in the back of his mind to do that one. Sneaky Pete was there, and Doug and I put some double fiddles on it and David Jackson played the cello. We worked up some string parts for it. It was just one of those things we worked up in the studio. Chris Hillman was in there playing mandolin." David remembers recording the track. "The 'Don't Let Me Down' recording was a special session, more of a spiritual feeling at that session than any of the others."

Disillusioned, Gene soon abandoned the Dillard & Clark Expedition. "Poor old Gene felt like he was being pushed out more and more," Byron explains. In a photo shoot around that time, Gene seems to be attempting to disappear from view, his disinterest and disillusionment barely concealed. "He'd bring a song or two to the band and it just kind of didn't fit what we were trying to do. I don't even know what we were trying to do. I wanted to play bluegrass and Doug did too, so once I got into the band Doug wanted to get into more bluegrass. And Gene realized that. He saw us going in another direction and didn't think his songs fit." That fall, Jim Bickhart, then a university student, booked the Expedition to play a concert at UCLA, only to discover that

Gene was no longer in the lineup. "What we were presented with was a bluegrass band who played little of their marvelous debut album," he laments.

"I think we made our mark in country-rock," offers Douglas. "We didn't make the charts, but we sure influenced a lot of people." While Gram Parsons's and Chris Hillman's Flying Burrito Brothers have been lionized as the founding fathers of country-rock, Chris reckons that Gene and Douglas deserve far more credit than they receive. "Some of Gene's greatest work was with Doug Dillard. We had the Burritos and there was Poco. The Burritos were hardcore country. I like Poco and they're wonderful guys and great musicians, but are they really country music to me? No. It's the Partridge Family of country music. But Dillard & Clark were really making great records. I'm telling you, that Dillard & Clark stuff was fantastic. The music was way ahead of the others, more conceptual and concise than the Burritos. The Burritos were really out of left field." The Nitty Gritty Dirt Band's John McEuen suggests, "If they hadn't been doing so many drugs and had been hungrier, Dillard & Clark would have been a major contender."

While teaming up with Douglas rejuvenated Gene's creativity and public profile—and placed him at ground zero as one of the prime movers in the integration of country music with rock—the two musicians became legendary for their drunken exploits. Certainly Douglas brought Gene out of his reclusive shell since leaving the Byrds, but the price Gene paid for that was dear. Indeed, their antics remain legendary. "When Gene hooked up with Doug, the drinking was ferocious," Chris insists. "Doug was a wild man. I knew there was trouble when I went to eat with them at eleven o'clock in the morning for lunch at Hamburger Hamlet on Hollywood Boulevard and they were having martinis. And I went, 'What? You guys are drinking that now?' I never was a drinker and I couldn't understand that. Gene wasn't much of a drinker in the Byrds or a heavy drug user. I don't think he liked pot and the rest of us did. Probably because it opened up all those dormant schizophrenia alleyways in his head and he felt he had such a horrible time on it that he just didn't do it. Alcohol was obviously something that he gravitated towards as an easier situation."

Friends tried to alert Gene to his growing problem. "I was always getting on him about drinking too much," claims Byron. "Things would get a little overboard a time or two, not only drinking, but drugs too. That's what killed all of the ones that have gone." Bernie confirms, "He was drinking a fair amount in Dillard & Clark. There was a lot of partying going on. I was sort of a beer drinker, but there was a lot of stuff going around between those two. I could hang to a certain point and then I would have to bow out. They would continue on."

The Troubadour remained Gene and Douglas's home base and many of their hijinks at the club have passed into legend, including the oft-told story of Douglas's girlfriend driving her car through the front of the club in a drunken attempt to run him over. Since leaving the group, Bernie had moved out to Topanga Canyon but would hear tales of Gene and Douglas's drunken reverie. "That was when they started doing stuff like trying to drive their motorcycles into the bar. From that point on when I would see those guys it was, 'Hey, there's the comedy team,' because they would usually be doing something silly together, often on their bikes." Even the un-flappable Byron had had enough. "I drink beer, but when it came time to do a show it's all busi-ness for me. But those guys would get right out there. I just couldn't handle it any more. I don't know how Doug is still alive, but he is. Amazing! They could have done real well if they had kept their heads on straight and wanted to keep doing it, but they didn't take it seriously."

After losing touch with Gene for a couple of years, Chip Douglas encountered the two partiers at a late-night recording session he was producing for Linda Ronstadt in 1969. "Gene and Douglas Dillard crashed a session we were doing. It was two minutes to midnight, about to go into triple time, and the two of them showed up having dropped acid or something. They got right into the middle of the room and Gene grabbed a tambourine and started banging on it, saying, 'Let's get this thing going.' I turned livid and kicked them both out. We were two takes away from finishing this song and I didn't want it to go into overtime."

Denny Bruce was a frequent patron of the Troubadour and would often see Gene holding court there. "I saw Gene get kicked out one night. He was with either David Carradine or Dewey Martin of Buffalo Springfield. They were pretty wasted. And the manager of the club, Robert Marchese, grew up in Pittsburgh and had been a football player and usually wore a Pittsburgh Steelers jer-sey to the club. He's the guy who threw John Lennon out of the club the night he had a Kotex on his head. So this night I happened to see Bob talking to Gene Clark. And Gene just wasn't going to leave, so Bob had to grab him by the arm, saying, 'Gene, come on, man. I don't want any trouble.' Bob walks Gene to the front door, Gene takes about ten or 15 steps down the street, turns around, and charges Bob, who's wearing his Steelers shirt. Bob not only tackled Gene, he body-slammed him onto the pavement. Bob turns to go inside as Gene walks away, then Gene turns around and goes at him again. And Bob again just tackled him and really threw him down."

"I'll never forget standing in front of the Whisky," notes John York, "and seeing Gene and Doug Dillard on small motorcycles at the red light waiting for the light to change and then revving up the engines and driving off, drunk out of their minds, and thinking, 'God, those poor guys are going to kill themselves.' Is this some sort of hillbilly fun or something? But in retro-spect, if I owned a record company, would I invest in people like that? There was this prevailing idea that artists were supposed to be bad boys. I think that if you believe in your own legend, you're in trouble. And, you know, I think at times Gene did. Other times he was just a regular guy. As he progressed through his career he developed very distinct segments of his personal-ity and the only way to survive in a band with him was to have a mechanism for dealing with each of those personalities."

Despite his well-known excesses, Gene was lucid enough that summer to realize that his self-destructive lifestyle in Los Angeles was detrimental to his well-being. He longed for a simpler way of life away from the public glare, where he could just be Harold Eugene Clark, not 'Gene Clark Rock Star'—a rural retreat akin to his childhood years in Kansas. He began driving up the California coast in an effort to escape Los Angeles and found what he was searching for. Little River is a remote yet picturesque spot on the Northern California coast, three miles south of Mendocino and bordering Van Damme State Park. Captivated by the tiny seaside community and its casual pace, Gene booked a room at the nearby Lazy Eye Motel (now the School House Creek Inn) and stayed for several days before returning to Los Angeles.

The pastoral experience remained with him and he continued to visit Little River and the Lazy Eye often, making the winding drive up the Pacific Coast Highway in his 1964 Porsche. On one such visit, Gene ventured into the Seagull Cellar Bar in the town of Mendocino, where he befriended proprietor-bartender Martin Hall. Gene became a frequent visitor to the Seagull and to his delight was treated no differently than any of the other locals or passersby. No one knew he was Gene Clark of the Byrds. Martin informed Gene that he had a cabin for rent across from the Andiron Lodge in Little River. Gene soon rented the cabin and, inspired by his rustic surroundings, begin writing a body of songs that represented a more basic approach to his muse—just acoustic guitar and voice.

Back in Los Angeles that autumn, Gene's life was about to take on more change. While he rarely lacked for female company and remained the object of adoration long after leaving the Byrds, Gene had not enjoyed a steady relationship for some time. Hardly characterized by friends as a womanizer content with a steady stream of one-night stands, Gene tended to seek out relationships with women even if they did not last long. Turning 25 that November, Gene believed it was time to settle down and soon found the right woman.

Carlie Lynn McCummings was born and raised in Evansville, Indiana. Following her graduation from Indiana State University in 1965 she moved out to Long Beach, California, where her grandmother owned an apartment house. Renting one of the units, Carlie began to check out the club scene in Los Angeles. "When I was in a sorority I used to go into the basement of our place and watch *Shindig* and *Hullabaloo* on TV and I would dance right there in that basement all by myself," Carlie remembers. "I lived to dance. I loved it. So after I graduated from college my options were to get married, go for my masters, or live at home with my parents. And I just thought, 'Ah, these don't work.' I had gotten a Chevy Impala for graduation and my dad was out of town so I packed up my car and drove to Long Beach. There used to be dance contests down there and I was in this club in Venice and I was dancing. This man came up to me and said he was a scout for Gazzarri's and would I like to come up to L.A. to audition to work as a dancer. I said, 'Sure! No problem.' So I drove up to L.A. and finally found Gazzarri's and it was this big club. I went in there like Little Annie Oakley and Gazzarri was there and I told him that his scout had told me to come up there and audition. He said, 'I don't have any scouts, but you can get up and dance on the break if you want. I'd love to see you dance.' So I got up there on the big platform, it was go-go dancing and the girls were all smartly dressed. There was a live band; it was Pat and Lolly Vegas. I was just having a great time. I thought this was too cool. I got off and he says, 'The last thing I had on my mind when you walked in here was to hire another dancer, but you have something I've never seen before. Would you like to go to work here?' And I said, 'Well, do you pay me?' and he says, 'Yeah,' and told me this wild amount. So I said, 'Okay, fine! I'll do it.'"

Relocating to Los Angeles, Carlie became a regular dancer at Gazzarri's. Her job allowed her the opportunity to socialize with musicians on the Strip. "The Whisky-A-Go Go was on another block and the Trip was right down the road, too. So I bought this little motorcycle. I would get up and dance, then on our break we'd go on to the Whisky where the Allman Brothers [then known as the Hour Glass] were playing. I'd get the dancers from there and we'd all go down to the Trip and Joel Scott Hill would be playing at the Trip, all these people who eventually got really famous, the Turtles and Johnny Barbata, were all playing at the clubs in L.A. So we would go club-tripping on our breaks and hang out together. I danced on *Hollywood-A-Go Go* on TV a couple of times and met Bonnie and Delaney Bramlett and started hanging out with them and Glen Hardin, J.D. Souther, and Sonny Curtis, who married my girlfriend from Indiana. So we all were hanging out together."

／ Carlie's exposure to the music business soon landed her a job with Bell Records in the production department, responsible for seeing albums through to completion and release. "One of the reasons I worked at Bell Records," she explains, "was that I had an ear for music, or I did at the time. I always liked Led Zeppelin, the Cream, Leslie West, and Mountain. Gene hated that stuff. He would break the albums." Bell's roster of artists at the time included Spooky Tooth, the Fifth Dimension, Seals & Crofts, Bobby Russell, Larry Williams, and Melanie. It was through Carlie's connections in the business that she met Gene in 1969.

"I had this thing where I wouldn't go out with artists. From where I was coming from, they weren't the most socially acceptable people. I was rather sheltered. As long as I was professional I could deal with them. Then I went to a party that Joanie Lowe had. She was the heir to the Lowe's theatre chain and her brother was a photographer that I used sometimes for openings. Gene was there and some other people. I was loving my job, I heard the best music in the world, had no attachments, no craziness. So Joanie calls me the next day and says, 'Carlie, Gene Clark has called me at least ten times for your phone number! Can I give it to him?' I said, 'Gene Clark who?' And she goes, 'Of the Byrds!' I said, 'The Byrds?' 'Yeah, you know the Byrds.' And I said, 'Oh, kinda,' because I really wasn't into them back in 1965. I'm sure I had heard them. So Joanie says, 'Can I give him your phone number?' And I said, 'Joanie, I really can't go out with artists. It's too confusing.' So she says, 'Well, will you at least come to this party he's coming to?' And I said, 'Okay, I'll go.' So I did and he was such a hood. He had his cigarettes rolled up in his T-shirt. I thought, 'Oh, my god!' But he kept saying to me, 'There's something special about you. I really like you.' So I thought, 'Well, okay,' but I wasn't sure about him. I don't know how he talked her into it, but somehow Joanie told him where I lived and I came home from work one day and he was sitting on his motorcycle with his legs crossed over it and he says to me, 'Do you want to go for a ride to the beach?' and I said, 'Okay,' and that was it. He looked like he had been ripped off the Sistine Chapel, let me tell you."

Smitten with the slender, blonde former dancer, Gene wanted to take her somewhere special. "We started dating and he said there was a place he wanted to show me. At the time I was about to become the head of West Coast operations for Bell Records, but they wanted to be sure I wouldn't run off in six months after they set it all up. I said, 'Ah, it won't happen.' A few months later I met Gene so I had to call Larry, my boss in New York, and tell him, 'Guess what, Larry? I'm moving to Mendocino,' because Gene said there was this place he wanted to take me to. I took two weeks off and we went on this excursion. We went to Big Sur and I had never seen sky so blue. Then we went to Mendocino and stayed for two weeks. Gene said to me, 'Would you like to live here?' and I said, 'Yeah!' So we came back to L.A. and packed up everything and the two of us moved into that little cabin in Little River."

In early 1970, with help from Gene's buddy "English Roger" Willis, Gene and Carlie left Los Angeles for Little River. "Before Gene met me he used to go up there and write," muses Carlie. "He'd just get a hotel room there on the ocean and write music. He'd never taken anybody there, he said, but when he found the girl he wanted to be with he would take her there. So off we went. We had this caravan with Gene's Porsche, my Ford Cortina, and Roger in the U-Haul and the three of us drove to Mendocino."

Today Mendocino is an exclusive, toney resort town dotted with Victorian-era houses along a sculpted coastline. The many restored inns, boutiques, and bed-and-breakfasts are popular destinations year-round. But before the Sir Douglas Quintet brought the community to public attention in the namesake hit song, Mendocino and its surrounding areas were home to a flourishing artistic community where the hippie ethic long outlived the rest of the nation. After World War II, many artists—painters, sculptors, and writers—had moved to Mendocino and the nearby communities of Albion, Little River, and northward up to Caspar. When Gene began visiting the area in the late '60s, it still retained its simple, unspoiled, rustic charm. (The movie *The Summer of 42* was filmed in the vicinity and the television series *Murder, She Wrote* used the town as a stand-in for Maine's Cabot Cove.)

Gene's brother Rick came out to live with Gene and Carlie in the summer of 1970 and was fascinated with the community's uncomplicated virtues. "When I first went to Mendocino there were a lot of hippies in the area, but it was a neat vibe, kind of like Haight-Ashbury got sick of the city and moved north. I remember they had a restaurant called the Pyewacket and there were goats going in and out and all these beautiful, pink-cheeked hippie chicks with flowers in their hair. You would be sitting there at a table having homemade bread and soup and all of a sudden a goat would wander through. People played music on the streets. I felt like I had died and gone to heaven. Everybody was so cool. I think that's probably what Gene loved about it. It was like the Summer of Love was still going and had simply moved north. Everybody was just happy. People walked around barefoot in restaurants. They had these big, old, redwood benches carved out and you could sit on the Headlands and watch the ocean, watch the whales go by. The forests were still pristine."

Named for a black cat in the book *Bell, Book & Candle,* the Pyewacket was a popular meeting spot that offered pizza, draft beer, and wine along with live music. Comments Carlie's brother Jim McCummings, now a realtor in Mendocino, "They had a band there known as the Mendocino Shuffle, a pun on the rather open sex life of many free-love folks at the time."

Not long after moving to Little River, English Roger took Gene and Carlie to nearby Albion to meet some friends of his. Philip and Ea O'Leno had fled Los Angeles for Mendocino in the spring of 1968. An accomplished woodworker and metalsmith, Philip was the son of a prominent Los Angeles attorney and had attended university with his good friend Jim Morrison of the Doors. Philip's wife, Ea, had been a popular hairdresser in Hollywood, styling the coiffures of many rock stars. The following year the two purchased some land off Albion Ridge Road in Albion where Philip set up his workshop. Ea had known English Roger and Gene years before in Los Angeles, so when Roger called to inquire if he might bring Gene by she was delighted. "Roger said to us, 'You'll like these people,'" Philip smiles, "and sure enough, we did. For about five years we were very tight, the four of us."

Carlie believes that Mendocino became Gene's refuge from the pressures of Los Angeles and the music business. "In Mendocino he was no one special. With Philip, Ea, and me, he was just one of the guys. The community would put up with anything because Gene was their local star. But he didn't feel pressure from them because they were just a bunch of hippies, basically. They would come over and want to play music with him so we always had a lot of people around." She feels that those first few years together in Mendocino were the happiest, most personally satisfying times in Gene's adult life. "I would say the person I fell in love with was as pure as I would ever see him again. Because he was feeling no pressure, he was getting just enough royalties to be comfortable, and he was writing and playing music for himself, which is why he did stuff with Doug, which was all fun for him and came to him like second nature."

Philip recalls fondly about Carlie and Gene, "They were real lovey-dovey, a real inspiration to anybody. It was just an ideal time with the four of us."

"I think a lot of it was his roots in Kansas and growing up there and all his family," suggests Gene's youngest son, Kai, on the appeal of the Mendocino community. "Mendocino kind of reminded him of growing up in Kansas. I think everybody wants that, some place they would like to return to from their childhood someday, where they were young with no stress, no bills, and no problems. Mendocino, for him, was his escape. And he could let out his wild side, too, and not get in trouble for it. There were many stories of my dad and Rick and David playing practical jokes. They were jokers up there. There's gonna be a few jokers in a family of 13."

"I think this area appealed to him because he grew up in the country outside of Kansas City, Kansas," Philip agrees. "Shortly after they were here I took him to get firewood with me and he took right to it. He had experience with it. He knew how to use a saw and buck wood and chop it. He said he had been making golf courses with his dad. That was no affectation for him to do country-rock; it was in him. He had strong country roots and it was his way of getting back to the land. He was more than a country boy at heart, although he was sophisticated. He wasn't a hillbilly, but he could be primitive sometimes."

Philip recalls that Gene was able to be himself in the Mendocino community. "We played cards quite a lot. There was no rock star stuff with us. He could talk with us because we knew Los Angeles. I was never around the music business. I left L.A. and except to visit I never went back. But I grew up there and knew a lot of what he was talking about and Ea had had a lot of friends in Hollywood. So he could talk with us; even if we didn't know a lot of the people involved, we knew the context. So that helped. Part of the attraction was the fact that we weren't in the business and he could just relax, but we understood what he was talking about. Every day when I would get done at my workshop they would come by and get us and we'd go out to the bars. He had his reputation, but in the community he was just Gene.

"Gene simply wanted to drop out. I know he had a tough time with the music industry, the people in the industry. He wanted to keep his career going and he thought he could do it from here. A lot of people can't. Unfortunately I don't think Gene was set up or established enough to do that. Dillard & Clark was real breakthrough music, but commercially it didn't do anything for him. So he kept going back to L.A. to make albums. He made three or four while he lived here. But when he lived here he was totally here, completely, except for when he was planning a new record. I spent many hours sitting up with him while he was composing, which was quite interesting."

On June 12, 1970, Carlie's birthday, Gene and Carlie were married in a ceremony in the front yard of Philip and Ea's rural home in Albion. Many of Gene's friends from Los Angeles came up for the wedding and the party lasted three days. The muddy lawn necessitated a second wedding dress for Carlie. "That wedding was like a typical country wedding," Philip chuckles. "We barbecued a big pig with plenty of beer and people slept all over the house. It seemed like hundreds and hundreds of people came to the wedding, a lot of L.A. people. Michael Clarke came to the wedding. David Carradine came. Chris Hillman was here." Laughs Ea, "Doug Dillard rolled three rental cars getting to the wedding." John Dietrich, son of Howard Hughes executive Noah Dietrich and a friend of Gene's, took the official photographs of the ceremony. Rick Clark was the only Clark family member to attend.

One month before the wedding, Gene had participated in a Byrds reunion of sorts at the Record Plant studio in Los Angeles instigated by their former manager, Jim Dickson. In an effort to kick-start Gene's flagging career, Jim had arranged for the other four original Byrds to back Gene on a single of two of his recent compositions, "One in a Hundred" and "She's the Kind of Girl," both composed in Little River. The momentous event, the first reunion of the original five since 1966, was kept from the public and media. Joining the group were percussionist Milt Holland as well as Bernie Leadon on guitar. Flautist Bud Shank overdubbed his part later. Not in attendance during the actual sessions themselves was David Crosby. Having gone on to scale the dizzying heights of superstardom with Crosby, Stills, Nash & Young, David's ego had become legendary and neither he nor the other four found it acceptable to be in the studio together. To his credit, David did agree to participate in the sessions, on his own time, to help out Gene. "Not everybody was prepared to be in the same room as Gene," notes Jim. "But they weren't against him. So I got them one at a time, though I think Michael and Chris did the basic track with Gene and I brought in McGuinn to overdub guitar and David to overdub harmony." Observed Roger, "Gene was a wreck at that point. He was really nervous during those sessions, like when he was on the airplane, but for the whole time."

The sessions continued on July 10, with further sessions the following February and April of 1971. These completed the two tracks, which, in the end, were not released by A&M and languished in their vaults until finally seeing the light of day in 1973 on a Dutch release, *Roadmaster*. All the trademarks of the Byrds sound grace both songs: that distinctive Rickenbacker jingle-jangle, loping bass, and smooth harmony singing (Gene and Roger in unison, with Crosby riding above them).

Gene's move up to the Mendocino area ultimately convinced other musicians to flee Los Angeles for the bucolic beauty and casual pace of the picturesque, ocean side locale—what became known in music circles as "the L.A. Getaway." Within the year, English Roger brought ex-Turtles and CSNY drummer Johnny Barbata up to look for property. Philip suggested they check out Comptche, further inland from Little River. "In Comptche many of the big ranches were being broken up and the prices were good," he states. "Within a very short while Johnny had bought a property and commissioned me to do the cabinet and millwork for the house. This all took place before Chris Ethridge, Joel Scott Hill, Booker T. Jones, and Ty Hill would be up here. Then Johnny found a great deal on a big piece of the Surprise Valley Ranch and needed partners to go in with him on the place. That was when he started getting his friends in L.A. interested in coming up. Pretty soon all the partners had their 160-acre pieces. That community lasted all through the 1970s and into the '80s. It was always good country party times with outdoor boogies out there. We loved those times." Eventually joining these artists would be the Grateful Dead's Bill Kreutzmann, Kris Kristofferson and Rita Coolidge, Taj Mahal, Journey and Starship drummer Aynsley Dunbar, and various members of the Doobie Brothers.

"It was such a party town," recalls Johnny Barbata. "It was like Carmel without all the people. It was a small town full of artists and painters, really cliquey. Gene loved it up there. You could be an ordinary person there. It didn't matter who you were. It was a Beatnik town, a lot of art galleries. Mendocino was a great place to go into to eat, party, hang out, and have a great time. Comptche was more inland so you didn't get all the fog. That was the place where they had big ranches and beautiful houses, vineyards, apples. That whole area was probably the best quality of life in California at that time." Johnny spent a lot of time with Gene and Carlie (he even purchased Gene's 1964 Porsche) and witnessed their close relationship. "They were real tight and very much in love. Carlie talked about their marriage lasting forever. She thought it was a lifetime thing."

"I think Gene and I were as close as you ever get to soul mates," reveals Carlie. "I think we had a destiny together. So there was nothing about his upbringing that ever bothered me, except occasionally when he'd make grammatical errors. I would just correct him. A lot of times he would ask me how something should be written properly and I would do it. He didn't mind that at all. Now my mother was a completely different story. She was a Daughter of the Revolution and she was from Kentucky and the Sons of the Kentuckians, that sort of thing. Her first question if I was dating someone was what kind of college he went to. The first time she came to visit Gene and I, Gene and my mom were like on two different planets. You would have thought that he had chopped off a finger or something because he left the toilet seat up. I think that she just scared him. I think her reality didn't include anything out of the box. When we lived in Mendocino out in the country, to her we might as well have been living on Mars. On the other side of the spectrum, Gene's parents were the complete opposite. Gene's mom went to church every day and had 13 children who slept four to a bed. And I just couldn't even conceive of that. I think he was a little embarrassed by the whole thing, his mom having 13 kids. I'd never heard anyone talk the way she did. She would call on the phone and it would be, 'Weeell, hello Coarlie gurl, how er yu?' They had never left the state in their lives. Until he brought her to Mendocino after we split up, his mom had never been more than six miles from her house. I never met his mom and dad. None of them came to his wedding. After we got divorced he brought them out. I talked to them on the phone, though. So I think that Gene and I left these two very different situations and landed in this place together. That was *our* space."

Carlie saw an innocence in Gene, almost a country-boy naïveté, as a result of his simple upbringing. "Just being around me he picked up things, and having me accept him and help him and teach him things that no one ever taught him, made him more comfortable in social settings. Poor guy. He didn't even know what fork to use. Can you imagine how uncomfortable those kinds of situations were for him? But it's not like I said, 'This is the fork you use, this is the knife you use and the side you put the glass on.' He just kind of picked it all up. Over the years he gained a new kind of grace. He watched and he paid attention. He didn't make grammatical errors when he spoke any more and he didn't use 'ain't' anymore. I would correct his grammar, but once I did, he never made that same mistake again. And he knew I did it out of love, it was never a degrading thing. I never made him feel any kind of social unequal, even though my mom definitely saw it."

Despite the exquisite literary nature of his lyrics, surprisingly, Gene rarely picked up a book. "Gene never read," Carlie reveals. "I read this lady named Madame Blavatski, who was a Russian writer in the seventeenth or eighteenth century who wrote this Edgar Cayce kind of stuff with all this incredible philosophy and the way things worked that was so before her time. It was mind-boggling to me. I would tell Gene what I had read and he would say, 'How do you think she knew that?' or 'What else did she do?' He was inquisitive. It was two volumes and the hardest reading I had done since college. I would get on these kicks where there had to be this consciousness-raising gem somewhere that would explain everything. So I would read this stuff. Gene was usually writing or playing his guitar, just doing his thing, and I would read. We never had a TV. I remember when the boys got older they used to walk down the road to this old grandpa's house that had some kind of antenna and they got cartoons on Saturday mornings."

And what music did Gene listen to at home? "His own," Carlie laughs. "He listened to his own records over and over again. I thought I would go crazy. I'm not sure if he was listening to it critically or whatever, but I think so. I used to go nuts. When he had finally recorded it and we got out of the studio after 23 takes, I was done. But the minute he got those test pressings he'd play them over and over. I'd go crazy. By then I was so done with that stuff. I'd heard it written, I'd heard it played, I'd heard it recorded, I'd heard it re-recorded, I'd heard it mixed. It was like a year. And then he had to hear it 24/7. It was one of the few things about his music that totally irritated me. He would say, 'Well, don't you like it?' and I would say, 'Yes, I like it! I've been liking it for days!' And he'd say, 'Well, I just want to keep listening,' and he would play it over and over. He liked Joni Mitchell, but you know what? He'd never buy it or bring it home. We would hear it over at Philip and Ea's house or when we would go somewhere, but there was no music in our house except his. He did like classical music. We used to play that sometimes."

Still determined to pull Gene's career from its slump, Jim Dickson encouraged Chris Hillman's Flying Burrito Brothers to record with Gene in January 1971. "There was sort of an on-again, off-again thing with Gene Clark and the Burritos," suggests Burrito Brother Rick Roberts. "Chris and Michael had been with him in the Byrds and Bernie Leadon had been with him in Dillard & Clark and they all wanted to try to help Gene get going again. We recorded two or three songs with him and he came and sat in with us on a few shows from time to time. It was always a very almost incestuous kind of relationship amongst us musicians." The Burrito Brothers backed Gene on his lovely country ballad "Here Tonight" and cut his "Tried So Hard" for their self-titled third album (although Gene does not sing on the track). "Here Tonight" had all the markings of a potential hit: a lilting country-rock gem with mellifluous pedal steel guitar from Sneaky Pete and sweet harmony backing from Chris, Bernie, and Rick. But it was inexplicably left in the can until its inclusion on the Dutch *Roadmaster* album two years later. "Gene was never a candidate for membership in the Burritos," clarifies Chris, scotching a long-held rumor, "but he was around and we worked together with him."

As Gene enlightened Domenic Priore in a 1985 interview, "During that period of time there was a lot of interchanging going on, people doing sessions with each other. You had the Burritos forming, Crosby, Stills & Nash forming, Roger with the other Byrds, the beginning of the Eagles coming out of Dillard & Clark; you had so much going on. People would be going in and out to other sessions. As far as 'Here Tonight,' that was just a time when I was there around the studios at the time, we were all signed to A&M, and we were just messing around in the studio or somebody asked if I'd do it. Those things would happen quite often."

Despite the collapse of the Dillard & Clark partnership and A&M's failure to release either his Byrds- or his Burritos-backed singles, Gene's contract with the record company still required two more albums. Comfortable in his new rural lifestyle, it took the direct intervention of one of the label's principals to motivate Gene to return to Los Angeles to record a new album. "Jerry Moss from A&M and his wife, they were our first visitors from L.A.," Carlie remembers. "He came up to say, 'Okay, you have a contract.' We had been up there about a year and he hadn't recorded or anything. He loved Gene. Jerry told him, 'You need to come to L.A. It'll be okay. I'll help you. Bring Carlie.' And we said, 'Okay, we'll come.' And it was okay the first few years, going back to L.A."

During the recording of *The Fantastic Expedition of Dillard & Clark* Gene had developed a friendship with guitarist Jesse Ed Davis. A Native American Kiowa born in Norman, Oklahoma, the same year as Gene, Jesse had come out to Los Angeles in the 1960s along with several fellow Oklahomans including Leon Russell, Carl Radle, and J.J. Cale, initially working for several years with bluesman Taj Mahal before branching out into studio work. Jesse Ed would go on to become an in-demand session guitarist for the likes of Eric Clapton, John Lennon, Rod Stewart, and Jackson Browne (Jesse's most memorable solo is on Jackson's "Doctor My Eyes").

Gene invited Jesse Ed to accompany him on his next album and to serve as producer. The two discovered a deep musical and spiritual kinship. "Actually those were some of the best times for Jesse Ed," acknowledges Carlie. "He was living with this gal, Patti Davis, down in Venice and we had some wonderful times with them. I think Jesse and Gene both brought out the Indian in each other. They made magical music together, I'll tell you that. They were incredible together. Ed knew guitar like Gene never dreamed of. Patti and I used to go to sleep, with them playing all night long. I think that's the first time Gene really aspired or felt the confidence to really play guitar, when he was with Ed. They made some pretty awesome music together." Philip adds, "Gene's friendship with Jesse Ed Davis made him identify more with his Indian side, Jesse being Indian himself." The two also shared a taste for alcohol and excessive behavior that, much like his teaming with Douglas Dillard, did not serve Gene well in the end.

"Gene and Jesse Ed got along well but they had their falling-outs, too," comments Rick Clark. "They were both men of similar habits at the time, like two peas in a pod at times and at other times they would go at it. They would both get loaded and go at each other, beat each other up. One time Gene had this little Porsche 914 that he bought and he loaned it to Jesse and Jesse disappeared with it and totaled it out. Jesse came back a couple of weeks later and Gene said, 'Where the hell's my car?' and Jesse went, 'Oh, man, that thing's totaled.' So they had a falling-out over that."

Before starting sessions for the album at The Village Recorder in Los Angeles, Gene demoed a batch of new songs, all composed in Little River. These included "The Waxing and Waning of the Moon," "Sweet Adrienne," "Only Yesterday's Gone," "The Sparrow," "Walking through This

World," "Back to the Earth Again," and "The First Time That I Saw," along with the nine songs destined for the album. He was searching for a style and an approach that reflected the inner peace
he was experiencing since leaving Los Angeles. He presented most of the songs in bare-bones
arrangements that prevented the instrumentation from cluttering the message of his poetry.

Clearly Gene found the tranquility of Little River both spiritually rejuvenating and emotionally inspiring. Songs like "White Light," for example, were borne out of his friendship with
Philip O'Leno. "The song 'White Light' was a description of this property," confirms Philip at his
home in nearby Albion. "My forge was just out here. I was pounding a lot of iron in those days.
It was a song for us." Philip witnessed the genesis of many of the songs that would appear on
the album. "It was kind of tedious the way he wrote songs because he would go over and over
them. Gene wrote on legal pads and he would write then scratch out lyrics. He would just compose lyrics as he went, he didn't note the music, he would just keep track of the lyrics. He was
writing all the time, pages of lyrics, and the song was in his head." Offers Ea, "You never knew
where Gene was sometimes. He would go out walking in the dark for hours composing songs.
He would just disappear writing songs."

When sessions began in March 1971, Jesse assembled a skeleton crew of supporting musicians including Gary Malabar on drums, John Selk on acoustic guitar, and bassist Chris
Ethridge, a close friend and associate of Johnny Barbata's (they would record *L.A. Getaway* with
Joel Scott Hill in 1972). As a teenager, Chris had come out to Los Angeles from Meridian, Mis-
sissippi, in 1965 to back Johnny Rivers at the Whisky-A-Go Go before becoming a founding
member of the Flying Burrito Brothers with Chris Hillman and Gram Parsons. By the end of the
decade he had moved up to Comptche and often socialized with the Clarks. "I knew him for ever
and ever," drawls the lanky Southern bass player. "We used to live close to each other when he
lived up around Mendocino. We would meet a lot of times back then. My wife Karen and Carlie were real good friends so Gene and me hung out a lot because of them, too. 'Course he was
gone a lot of the time back to L.A., but we still hung out a lot when he was up there."

Chris recalls the album sessions fondly. "Jesse Ed Davis was a great, great guitar player and
producer. I remember Bobbye Hall Porter, the little girl from Motown, came and played on it.
She played the regular trap set of drums along with the percussion, too. She told me that was
the first session she ever played the trap drums on and she was great, too." Keyboardists Ben
Sidran and Mike Utley were brought in near the end of the sessions to overdub piano and organ
respectively. "We had just got out there and the first place we stopped at was Jesse Ed's in Venice,"
recalls Mike of studio aces the Dixie Flyers. "So he said, 'You want to do a session?' It was that
quick. 'I need you to do an overdub. Be at Sunset Sound tomorrow at two o'clock.'"

The recordings went smoothly, Gene and Jesse very much in sync over the sound and di-
rection that the album was to take. The solo acoustic singer-songwriter era of the likes of James
Taylor and Neil Young was just beginning, so Gene was at the cutting edge of this phenomenon.
The only interruption came from an act of God in the form of the Los Angeles earthquake of

1971. "When the earthquake hit," Carlie points out, "Gene was in the recording studio and the echo chambers shook with the quake and you could hear it on the track just at the point where Gene sings, 'and the earth came trembling down.' That was not synthetic. It was the real earthquake." Chris Ethridge elaborates: "I had just left the studio. My brother from Meridian was visiting me so we had just left the studio. The guys told me what happened the next day. They were in there mixing and they had these big speakers up on these gray concrete blocks and they started wobbling underneath the speakers. And Ed Baker, the engineer working on the thing, stood up and hollered, 'Earthquake!' and they all ran down the stairs to get out of the studio. Gene said it was one of those rolling earthquakes instead of shaking. He said the telephone poles were literally slapping one side of the ground, then the other. Baker just took off running down the street and it was like waves in the ocean. And they said, 'Baker, where you going?' And he hollered back, 'I don't know!' and turned around and came running back straight towards them. They were outside during all of that. It was amazing. When they came back in and played back the tape, the earthquake actually came through on the tape. It was like the loudest bass drum you ever heard in your life. 'Boom.' I don't know how it could have done that, but it did."

As sessions resumed, Gene was called away to attend to another matter. He had been approached by his friend Dennis Hopper to provide a couple of songs for the soundtrack to a film Dennis was producing that would ultimately be titled *American Dreamer*. Having neglected to compose anything suitable, Gene was forced to scramble to come up with something for Dennis's project. "I'll never forget one night he was doing a soundtrack for some movie," Carlie recalls, "I think it was *American Dreamer*, and we were in L.A. to do it and he kept putting it off and putting it off. We went to this restaurant called Victoria Station and he sat there and wrote the soundtrack for this film on the napkins at dinner then went into the studio and did it and everybody loved it. He was just sitting there, I'm eating and he's writing on these napkins and went right into the studio an hour or two later and did it." As Gene told British writer Barry Ballard in 1985, "The day I was supposed to go in and record those things I didn't have anything ready because I had been working solid on the *White Light* album. When I wasn't in the studio I was spending all my time with my family. So I sat down with some cocktail napkins and I wrote the songs there and then. I just had melodies in my head, so I walked right in and did the gig. I had a picture of the film in my mind, what I was supposed to say and how it was supposed to come across. It was just one of those things, but sometimes it works well that way. It's a very funny thing that spontaneity can really happen, but it has to be right. Usually if you don't prepare something it's a drag, but in that particular case the spontaneity really made it work." The two songs Gene contributed were "Outlaw Song" and "American Dreamer," the latter also finding its way onto the soundtrack for another film, *The Farmer*.

When the completed album tracks were delivered to A&M, Gene and Jesse had chosen the title *White Light*, but upon its release the album bore the simple words "Gene Clark." Nonetheless, to Clark fans, the album is known as *White Light*. The front cover photo was shot on the roof of a building in Mendocino, while the back cover shot of Gene peering through a window with trees reflecting in the glass was taken at Philip's house in Albion. On its release in August 1971 *White Light* garnered unanimous plaudits from critics and reviewers, going on to top several Best Album of the Year lists and earning top honors in the Netherlands, where Gene retained a dedicated fan base.

With its emphasis on Gene's intensely personal poetry, *White Light* is a stunning work of sheer genius and Gene's highest watermark to that point. Jesse wisely let the songs stand on their own, Gene's voice strong and prominent. And his poetry in songs like the exquisite "Spanish Guitar," "With Tomorrow," and "Where My Love Lies Asleep" is delicately evocative. The album also includes a re-recording of "One in a Hundred" from Gene's ill-fated Byrds reunion sessions, in a sparser arrangement. Overall, the album reveals Gene at the top of his songwriting, buoyed by his new surroundings, new friendships, marriage, and the imminent birth of his first child.

White Light would prove to be Gene's most Dylan-influenced album. As *Rolling Stone* magazine reviewer Serge Denisoff suggested, " 'Spanish Guitar' is a first cousin to 'Visions of Johanna' mixed with 'Tom Thumb's Blues,' harmonica riff and all. 'Where My Love Lies Asleep' is even more Dylanesque, with bits of 'Girl from the North Country' penetrating it. Clark's use of word symbols is uncanny and invites many flattering comparisons to another side of Mr. Dylan— prior to *Nashville Skyline* days." Denisoff goes on to compare "With Tomorrow" favorably to Gene's Dillard & Clark-era ballad "Polly," before concluding that the album is "a fresh and innovative look at what came before in a new framework . . . to create one of the most interesting and exciting records of 1971." Like Dylan, Gene worked with simple chord figures, major and minor chords, no major sevenths or diminished fourths. For him it was the strength of the words and melody that carried the weight of the songs.

The album is not without its detractors, who consider the minimalist production and sparse, sometimes hesitant accompaniment to be weaknesses rather than strengths. Jim Bickhart notes, "I probably at the time would have preferred to hear something elaborate because I always thought Gene's stuff held up well under that. I liked the album, but I remember feeling that it was kind of under-produced. It didn't leave me feeling that if I were going to record an album I would go out and hire Jesse Ed Davis to produce it. Maybe to play some guitar licks on it, but this didn't strike me as something where Jesse brought a lot to the table. But maybe he and Gene got along well and were drinking buddies."

With royalties still coming in from the Byrds, Gene and Carlie purchased a large, stately, wood-framed, two-story house at the end of Middle Ridge Road in Albion, three miles inland from the coast, near Philip and Ea's property. Originally a stagecoach house in the 1800s, it had recently fallen into disrepair. The house was situated on 12 acres of land and surrounded by redwoods. Behind it were the Mendocino Headlands, which spread out westward before dropping off to the ocean. Prominent local logging family the Shandells, who owned much of the land nearby, had attempted to purchase the property, but the owner took a liking to Gene and Carlie and sold it to them for $28,000. The house is pictured in silhouette on the front cover of Gene's 1977 album *Two Sides to Every Story* and became Gene's dream home, the only house he would ever own.

"When Gene and Carlie first got married I was in contact with Gene quite a bit," notes brother David. "We probably talked with each other on average once every two weeks. I was living in central Missouri and things were starting to work for me. He was talking about Little River and how much he liked it there. One day he called me and said, 'I bought a farm out here!' And I said, 'A farm? In California? Where the hell do you buy a farm in California?' He told me, 'It's an apple farm out here on the Headlands in a little place called Albion.' I had to get out a map and look for it. 'I don't even see it. It's not even on the map!' And he said, 'Do you see Mendocino?' 'Yeah.' And he said, 'Well, it's just south of Mendocino.' He was real excited and he kind of got re-inspired there. He went into a whole different dimension at that time, very soulful, solo, acoustical."

"The place we had was just a magic place," enthuses Carlie. "It was right on the end of the ridge so in summer the fog would come in on both sides of you like these billowing clouds. At night we could lay in bed and we could see the ships going up to Seattle out on the horizon. It was idyllic. And Gene was like a little boy. We were totally innocent, living this reality that was ours. We were living the good life and weren't selling out. I used to cook on a woodstove and it took an hour and a half just to make coffee! He loved that part of it. I made my own bread. I was 'Hilda Homemaker.' We had nothing to do in those days. From the time we woke up until noon was breakfast. We hung out with Philip and Ea six out of seven nights a week and Gene would play music. The four of us were like four kids; we just had so much fun together."

Eldest son Kelly chuckles at the image of his parents as hippie nouveau landed gentry. "I actually equate my mom and dad with the very first yuppies. They were like back to the land, my mom was making homemade juice, but they were driving Porsches and Mercedes. They had a $3,500 juicer, for god's sake!"

"There were years when we made more money than we knew," allows Carlie. "That was from past royalties. We would get these huge checks out of the blue. The royalties always came in no matter what else was going on. Not only did he get the regular Byrds royalties, but also other artists were doing his songs. And in Europe he was revered. The boys are living off of something today, I'll tell you. They make as much as I make working."

In the turbulent times following the Summer of Love, seething with Vietnam War protests and a growing anti-establishment/back-to-the-land ethos, Gene and Carlie drew strength from their decision to abandon the city for the secure comforts of their Northern California retreat. "There was a time when Gene and I felt, and it was real, the whole world was changing," postulates Carlie. "We thought that. And for a while it looked like it was going to work, this back-to-the-land thing. We used to talk about when the shit hits the fan, when everything comes crashing down, we would just blow out the Albion Bridge and nobody could get to us."

Son Kai affectionately evokes memories of carefree times at the big house on Middle Ridge Road with his mom and dad. "Dad was into that lifestyle. He was definitely a mountain man in the old west. I kind of see my dad then with a smile on his face. I think he rebuilt the whole foundation of the house and I think he loved using his hands and getting his hands in the dirt. They cooked over a woodstove and had a well for water. My dad was fascinated with history and the old west and living off the land. There are still people who live that way in Mendocino. As if time stood still. When you live in the heart of L.A. you forget about those simple things like the trees or the wind blowing through the trees or a grassy field. Or not hearing a siren or a car, or having someone recognize you. My father was probably recognized everywhere he went in L.A. But in Mendocino, it was such a small place even if they did recognize you, they probably knew who you were, but it wasn't a big deal. 'There's that guy from L.A.' He loved it there. I have special memories of that farm. We loved it dearly."

6

Some Misunderstanding

Throughout Gene's entire career he was constantly disillusioned and frustrated by the fact that his records did not sell, which contributed to his increasingly self-abusive behavior. He was forever at odds with his record labels, whether CBS, A&M, or later, Asylum and RSO, for failing to adequately promote and market his recordings. "Gene bitched a lot about the executives and about the business," avers Philip O'Leno. "The A&M guys, there was another fuck-over. He really didn't like the treatment he got from those guys at A&M. He would express his frustrations about the music business and people from L.A." What Gene never understood, or more precisely, refused to accept, was that he needed to become a more public person—tour, do interviews, and perform—in order to get his records wider public attention. It wasn't just about writing a batch of songs, surfacing from his secure enclave in Laurel Canyon or the wilds of Mendocino to record them, and then retreating back into obscurity. But Gene did not want to play the game and suffered the consequences.

"They didn't have any way to market Gene," insists Chris Hillman. "How do you market him if you don't have him capable of being the public person to back that record up? You can't put a record out and go back to your cabin. Going on the road is what I'm talking about. He had to be a performer and although when he sang he had this very charismatic way about him, it wasn't strong enough to carry it. From the time he went solo on that first album through all the succeeding albums, they never developed him as a performer."

If Gene's public performances were scant in the late '60s since leaving the Byrds, they were virtually nonexistent following his move up to beautiful Albion on the Mendocino coast. Despite the stellar music on the album and rave reviews, *White Light* sold poorly. Once again, Gene presented his label with an outstanding effort, only to refuse to tour or perform in support of it.

"You have to understand that one of the reasons he left the Byrds was that he would not get on a plane again," cites Carlie, explaining Gene's deep aversion to touring. "It took four and a half years of our being together to get him on a plane. And I did it with two vodka and orange juices and two Valiums and I finally got him on a plane. It was only a 45-minute flight from San

Francisco to Ontario, California. He hadn't been flying up to that point. It broke the ice. He flew again, but he never loved it. You'd have to drug him before he got on the plane.

"You don't know what a fight it was to get him to appearances. In the Netherlands, I think, he was like the star of this big festival and I kept saying, 'Gene, we have to make some plans,' and he'd say 'Okay, we will.' I'm telling you, he did a no-show on this thing. There was no way of getting him on a plane. He wasn't like Sly Stone who was so screwed up he couldn't get himself together to get there, it was just that Gene was terrified to go to Amsterdam. 'What, you mean me go to Amsterdam and leave you here and I go onstage? No way!'"

Gene's dwindling confidence in his ability to face the public and perform was indeed a further factor in his reluctance to tour. He was suffering from a debilitating case of stage fright, which began after leaving the Byrds and manifested itself more and more in the intervening years. Eventually it became a battle just to get him to the stage, let alone to actually perform on it. Many close to Gene at the time assert that he exhibited the classic symptoms of panic disorder, an increasing anxiety not just about having to perform, but at the thought of having to go before the public. The sufferer becomes progressively more terrified of the fear response, which only exacerbates the growing panic. Certainly Gene suffered severe bouts of depression, especially since exiting the Byrds, and the thought of having to perform in that state must have been overwhelming. In that heightened condition it's no wonder Gene relied on alcohol as a form of self-medication. Unfortunately, with a history of alcoholism in his family, it became a dangerous dependency for Gene. "He was horrible," Carlie huffs. "I've seen him drink a whole fifth of tequila and walk onstage. Anyone else would pass right out. He needed it to perform in public. He hated it. He could not move. When he was at home writing songs or playing for Philip, Ea, and me he was so comfortable. But, boy, you put that guy on the stage and, oh, he was so stiff and uncomfortable. If you watch the films of the Byrds performing and he's playing the tambourine, he looks a lot looser because they were accepted and he was comfortable and they had done it enough." Additionally, in spite of his position at center stage, Gene was not the focal point of the Byrds. He had four others with him—the band was not under his own name and riding squarely on his shoulders alone. "Gene didn't have trouble getting onstage when he was surrounded by a bunch of guys who happened to be playing with him and singing with him and being successful," insists Eddie Tickner.

David Clark offers an insightful illumination into Gene's performance anxiety. "Getting him onstage was a battle. It was a war. It just ate him up. Before he went onstage people would get upset because they would come and see him and he wouldn't see them, even close family members. But I learned that when he was preparing to go onstage he would get into a zone. Nothing else was around him. He would avoid everyone, even other people in the dressing room. If there were too many people in the dressing room he would go out and sit in his car or go to a restroom and lock himself in. He had all this stuff going on in his head that he had to get so intent and focused on the performance so he could go out and do a reasonable job. Any

*Gene and Carlie's Albion friends Ea and
Philip O'Leno in the early '70s.*

interference whatsoever would throw him off track and he would lose his concentration. If
he went out and he screwed up the first song, immediately he would run for the booze, pills,
or whatever was handy. If he could get through the first set without making any blunders and
not getting too self-conscious, the second set he could put on a hell of a show."

On December 20, 1971, Kelly Eugene Clark, named for Gene's father, was born at Cedars
Sinai Hospital in Los Angeles. During her pregnancy, Carlie had been commuting regularly by
plane to Los Angeles to see her obstetrician, but in the three weeks prior to delivery, she and
Gene moved there temporarily, renting a modest house in Studio City in anticipation of the imminent birth. As she realized she was going into labor one night, Carlie woke Gene up. "He
freaked out and had to run around the house a couple of times in a panic before he could take
me to the hospital," she laughs. Following the birth, Carlie remained in the hospital for a few
days, but Gene was nowhere to be seen. Back at their rented house a steady procession of friends
came and went, celebrating the joyous event with Gene. With so much partying going on, when
it came time for Carlie and baby Kelly to leave the hospital, she had to call him several times
to get him to pick her up. She was left waiting with the baby until Gene got himself together.

Two weeks later, Gene, Carlie, and Kelly went with Philip and Ea to Philip's father's retreat at
Lake Arrowhead, California. Joined by Chris Hillman and a close friend of Carlie's, Annalise, the
guests frolicked in four feet of snow and celebrated the New Year.

After graduating from high school in Bonner Springs, Rick Clark had come west to hang out
with his brother and Carlie. During the *White Light* sessions, Rick looked after their rented cabin

in Little River while the two lived in Los Angeles. He eventually came to apprentice with Philip, becoming a skilled carpenter in his own right. (He later worked alongside Harrison Ford in Los Angeles before the master carpenter transformed into a movie star.) "After Gene left home he didn't hardly ever come back, so most of my brothers and sisters grew up not knowing him," offers Rick. "I introduced myself into Gene's life because I wanted to know him. I wanted to know who he was. At first he was a little bit annoyed about it, like 'Go away, kid, you bother me.'"

Rick had been performing in coffeehouses back in Kansas City and saw an opportunity to pursue a music career under his famous brother's auspices, and his presence was not welcomed by everyone. "Tell you the truth, I don't think Gene liked too much having Rick around," suggests Gene's friend Jason Ronard. "He would never say it. He was that kind of person, and kind is the word." Living in Gene's immense shadow ultimately would prove difficult for Rick. "Rick Clark wrote some interesting songs," concedes Gene's close confidant Tom Slocum, "but he could never get out from under Gene's shadow and it made him nuts." Carlie resented Rick's attempt to insinuate himself into their lives. "Rick was younger and I think that he wanted to walk in Gene's footsteps," she suggests. "But Rick had no idea of the enlightened soul Gene was. I just felt that he hung onto Gene's coattails." In the ensuing years, despite the apparent antipathy by some towards his presence, Rick would grow close to Gene, eventually moving in with him for a time after Gene and Carlie divorced. He would come to be one of Gene's confidants in later years and witness firsthand the tortured, conflicting personality his brother would become.

Whether by design or happenstance, Rick was nonetheless invited along when Gene entered Wally Heider's Los Angeles studio in April 1972 to record *Roadmaster*. In contrast to the spare, folk-based *White Light*, this new album was a return to a more laidback, country-rock style. Boasting the cream of the L.A. country-rock fraternity—namely Chris Ethridge, Byron Berline, Sneaky Pete, old friend Michael Clarke, pianist Spooner Oldham, and guitarist extraordinaire Clarence White—the sessions were fated to be cast in a country-rock mold. Since joining the Byrds in the summer of 1968, Clarence's star had been rising steadily, especially with the Pullstring Bender (or B-Bender), a device he and Gene Parsons (no relation to Gram Parsons) invented that attached to his Fender Telecaster and allowed him to simulate pedal steel guitar bends. (Clarence counted among his acolytes none other than Jimi Hendrix.) "We had a good time doing that album," enthuses Chris. "Gene had some really good songs and I had a great time playing with Clarence. Besides the Byrds stuff, that's probably one of Gene's best albums, I would think."

Producing the sessions was Chris Hinshaw, who had served as an engineer under Terry Melcher before being elevated to the producer's chair for *Roadmaster*. Chris's previous production experience included working with temperamental star and legendary partier Sly Stone. (Gene had initially approached former A&M Records producer Larry Marks to shepherd the album, but Larry had moved over to the motion picture industry.)

Gene and Terry had briefly entertained thoughts of recording an album together and rumors persist that they did, indeed, cut a couple of tracks, namely "Bed of Roses" and a cover of

Beach Boy/Melcher buddy Bruce Johnston's "Disney Girls (1957)," though no studio logs can substantiate the existence of these tracks. Drummer Johnny Barbata recalls Gene and Terry discussing a project that never came to fruition. "Terry Melcher was going to produce some songs for Gene and I was going to play drums on them. We went down to the Fairmont Hotel in San Francisco to meet with Terry and he didn't show up. That was around the time of the whole Charles Manson thing. That was happening at the same time that Gene and Terry were going to work together. Terry had promised [would-be musician] Manson he was going to do something with him and never did, and actually Manson came to Terry's house to kill him, but he was gone." Rick Clark says that Gene and Terry spent time together in the early '70s attempting to record an album, but their penchant for overindulgence got in the way.

Gene came to the *Roadmaster* sessions in April armed with another set of recent compositions, some more philosophical and soul searching in nature, such as "Shooting Star" and "Full Circle Song." These tunes suggested a leaning towards deeper, more spiritual concerns than relationships, a theme Gene had begun to explore on *White Light.* Other tracks, namely "I Remember the Railroad" and "In a Misty Morning," reflected Gene's nostalgia for simpler times. "Gene seemed to be real happy then, in good spirits," observed Byron Berline. "He seemed to be looking forward to the record. And I enjoyed the tracks; they were all good." The remainder of the completed tracks would be comprised of covers including bluegrass duo Lester Flatt and Earl Scruggs's "Rough and Rocky," the country music standard "I Really Don't Want to Know," Freddy Weller and Spooner Oldham's rocking "Roadmaster," and a pensive, dirge-like remake of Gene's old Byrds track "She Don't Care about Time."

From the outset the sessions were plagued with problems and would ultimately be abandoned in June, after only eight tracks were completed.

"We were having a lot of troubles at that time, everybody was, just getting the right things together," Gene told writer Domenic Priore in 1985. "The sessions were fun because I had great people playing on them, but it was hard to get it together the way I wanted it." According to Jim Dickson, who would eventually resurrect the *Roadmaster* tapes a year later, "Chris Hinshaw started that album, but he got too spaced out and it never got finished."

For brother Rick, the experience of being in a recording studio with the cream of the crop of L.A. players was memorable. He was even asked to contribute to the background harmonies on several tracks. "I'm doing a lot of the high harmonies like on 'Full Circle,'" he states proudly. "That's me doing the high part on that one. That was the first time I had ever been in a studio. Gene and I had started to play together in Mendocino." Other guests on the sessions included Clarence White's father Eric on harmonica and legendary folk session guitarist Bruce Langhorne. And Rick recalls one more guest in the studio. "Roger McGuinn came in and he and I sang harmonies on 'Rough and Rocky.' Neither of us was ever credited on that album." Roger's presence was, in fact, a harbinger of things to come and one of the reasons the sessions would ultimately be abandoned.

The other reason was Hinshaw's inability to maintain control. As Rick recalls, "We had a wonderful time except when Sly Stone came in and took over the studio when Gene was out of town. Chris Hinshaw invited him down for some reason during a session and it was on Gene's tab with the record company. He came in with an entourage of about 40 people in an RV and took over the studio. Clarence White and I were in there, and Chris Hinshaw, and somehow or other it turned into a real fiasco. They sat in there for a couple of days and brought all kinds of cocaine and ordered thousands of dollars worth of food from the restaurant next door. Then Gene came back into town and they had run up such a tab within those few days that it went way over A&M's allotted budget for that album. The record company was furious and that's what doomed that record. I blame Chris Hinshaw for all that because he was the one who called Sly and had him come down. It got really weird. Clarence and I got really disgusted, and he packed up his guitars and left."

A&M called a halt to the sessions and stored the completed tracks in their vaults with no intentions of releasing them anytime soon. With only eight tracks cut, the label had insufficient quantity to warrant an entire album. "It was a very misunderstood album," Gene reflected to Priore, suggesting that after failed attempts with Dillard & Clark and the Flying Burrito Brothers, the label was less inclined to back another risky country-rock venture, especially one as morose in tone as *Roadmaster.* "The record company didn't like it when I was finished with it. They didn't see any commercial value in it and they just sort of shelved it. But it was from troubled times. People were kind of going away from artistic things at that time and getting more into the heavy metal and hard rock thing and that made it kind of difficult in a way to do an album with really good material on it and get any kind of backing for it, sorry to say. But the album itself I was proud of, I was proud of the writing and proud of the bunch of people who played on it."

It would take the intervention of Gene's frequent benefactor and advocate Jim Dickson to eventually bring the *Roadmaster* sessions to the public a year later. "I ran across the tapes and there was some stuff on it that I thought was great," recalls Jim, "really good Gene Clark material, like 'I Remember the Railroad' and 'Misty Morning.' I went to Dave Hubert, who I knew from World Pacific days, and I told him, 'There's a lot of bootleg stuff out there.' I had just come back from Amsterdam and London where there were a lot of Burritos and Gene Clark bootlegs. I told him we had better versions of this stuff in the vaults and we should do it for Europe. He was handling the foreign market for A&M, so he got it authorized. I had just finished mixing the album when I got called in and told, 'What are we doing spending money on someone we don't even have signed anymore?' They were bitter because the costs were showing up on the domestic budget. I told them they were done and left it. We finished it up with Herb Pedersen overdubbing the harmonies and acoustic guitar."

In spite of the protest from executives, A&M licensed to their Dutch division, Ariola-Eurodisc Benelux, the eight tracks from their vaults plus the two Byrds-backed tracks from 1970–1971 ("She's the Kind of Girl" and "One in a Hundred") and the Flying Burrito Brothers track with

Gene ("Here Tonight") under the title *Roadmaster*. Import copies soon found their way to North American fans, who marveled at the quality of the oddly discarded tracks. Gene's soulful rendering of "She Don't Care about Time" was particularly noteworthy, and he had written a country-rock classic with the philosophical "Full Circle Song."

But while the songs themselves remain among Gene's finest works, the mixing of the album left much to be desired, with instruments disappearing and harmonies obscured. The original Hinshaw rough mixes had somehow been misplaced, and all Jim could do was what is called a "ruler mix," which basically means setting the levels just about equal and letting the tapes run, creating a rather flat, generic sound. (Nearly 30 years later, the Hinshaw mixes were discovered languishing in a tape vault and what they reveal is quite startling. The tracks virtually come alive: the drums are crisp, the guitars sparkle, and instruments previously unheard, like electric piano and Clarence White's intricate guitar, suddenly reappear. Harmonies that were essential to the strength of several tracks are now heard as they were meant to be. As one fan declared, *Roadmaster* was the "*Sgt. Pepper* of country-rock." At this point, the original mixes have yet to be officially released, despite the album being issued on CD in the 1990s.)

Jim Bickhart, who had worked for A&M's publicity department, ponders the label's decision to cut Gene loose. "I remember [publicist] Bob Garcia playing me that stuff and it seemed like Gene was doing good stuff, but he never seemed to get it finished, and when he finally did, it didn't come out in the US, which probably wasn't very helpful to Gene's frame of mind." Did Bickhart feel that the label had lost faith in Gene? "I think so. Not everybody, but some key people. You would think that if Jerry Moss was such a fan that he would just say, 'Fuck it, let's put it out anyway.' Especially after they had spent the money on recording. But there were obviously other business decisions being made. It didn't make sense to me."

In the midst of the *Roadmaster* sessions in May, Gene and Jim Dickson took time out to remix the tracks from *Gene Clark with the Gosdin Brothers*. To be reissued by Columbia Records under the title *Collector's Series: Early L.A. Sessions,* it boasted a retooled track list, detailed liner notes, an interview with Gene by Jim Bickhart, and the omission of the rather dated "Elevator Operator," the weakest cut on the original album. The remixed version of "Tried So Hard" brings Clarence White's superb guitar work to the fore, predating country-rock by at least two years. Gene's justification for the re-release of these tracks was that the recent elevation of country-rock to commercial acceptance through groups like the Eagles suddenly made the album relevant, especially since so few people had heard the original back in early 1967. As if to stress the point, the two overtly country-rock tracks, "Tried So Hard" and "Keep on Pushin'," are the opening cuts. In releasing the album, Gene earned some overdue recognition as a country-rock pioneer, even if the album was more folk-rock pop than country influenced. "We were all just a little ahead of our time," he told Bickhart in the liner notes.

By the time the *Roadmaster* sessions broke up in mid-June, Gene had already moved on. Serious discussions were underway with his four Byrds mates on the real possibility of a reunion, hence Roger's presence at the *Roadmaster* sessions. Negotiations centered around an album of new material from the five and a tour expected to be a massive affair involving the original Byrds and reunited Buffalo Springfield, with Crosby, Stills, Nash & Young as headliners. The timing seemed right. The Byrds were in the midst of a critical reappraisal in light of the success of Crosby's latest conglomerate. And they had advanced from golden oldies kings to pioneering heroes of the entire Southern California Asylum Records country/folk-rock pack, which included the Eagles, Jackson Browne, and Linda Ronstadt, not to mention CSNY and Neil Young. Everyone gave suitable deference to the role the Byrds played, not only in their own individual careers but in the sounds of early '70s denim-clad, cocaine-fueled, Southern California rock.

The media was all a-flutter with rumors of a potential gathering of Byrds. The tide of positive vibes seemed to carry the five along toward resolution of their various differences and the speedy recording of an album. First, everyone had to be available and free of contractual obligations to other labels. For Gene that was no problem, as A&M had given up on ever seeing a hit from Gene Clark and had cut him loose. Once that hurdle was cleared, Roger had to agree to put a permanent end to his own version of the Byrds, by then down to only himself and Clarence White, plus pickup drummers (like Miami-based Joe Lala) and bassists. (However, Chris Hillman would fill out the last of the Byrds dates.) Asylum Records mogul David Geffen then weighed in with a substantial offer to the five to record an album for his label. While the parceling of percentages was not necessarily equal, the terms were conducive enough to conclude the deal, and in September the five musicians—or as many as could be cobbled together at one time—assembled at Wally Heider's Studio No. 4 in San Francisco to begin sessions, with David Crosby as producer. Therein, regrettably, would lay the rub.

Few could have ever envisioned such an event. For Byrds fans it was a dream come true. That the five bickering Byrds could actually be in the same room—let alone record together—was beyond belief, given Gene's controversial exit from the group and David's firing. Michael had simply got fed up and walked offstage in late 1967, while Chris had left in a pique of anger in the fall of 1968 over finances and direction. Roger had recruited salaried players and continued to use the Byrds name, much to the consternation of David, who termed them "bullshit." "There were only ever five Byrds," he chirped. And here they were, together again. Expectations ran high. Too high.

From the outset there were underlying problems. While each songwriting member was expected to bring his strongest new material to the table, in fact a few held back their best with an eye toward solo deals spinning off of the much-publicized reunion bonanza. Furthermore, scheduling all five to be in the studio together at the same time given that three of them—David, Roger, and Chris—were still touring and/or recording with their own respective groups, would hinder progress on the tracks and the end results. Added to this was the presence of drugs (notably David's prodigious cocaine habit) and egos.

For his part, Gene was ready, willing, and able to make this thing work. He had the most to gain from a triumphant album, given the dismal state of his recording career at that point. He was the one who had failed to escape the ex-Byrds tag and establish himself in his own right. "We came straight from Mendocino," recalls Carlie, who, with Gene, stayed with Roger and his wife, Linda, during the sessions. "Gene was totally clear and excited about it and thought the magic would happen. He had high hopes and they all really got along well." Gene had had his own emotional baggage to overcome. "It had taken years for him to be comfortable around those guys again," reveals Carlie.

David recognized Gene's vulnerability and, surprisingly, acted accordingly. "I had a little more understanding," he admits today. "I had been away from Gene long enough to have gotten a little more maturity and have a little more sense of his value. He was a valuable guy. People could see there was talent there, but it just wasn't easy to elicit the response from him that you wanted because he was different. He was a different kind of guy. And I don't think that many of us really got who he was or how he made his decisions. At first when you encountered him you would think he wasn't really all that smart. He wasn't that well educated or deft or adept. There was very little polish there. But he had no lack of intelligence, he just didn't have it in the way that we understood it."

Designating David as producer (executive producer, some Byrds argue, given that each had a hand in supervising his own tracks) was the wrench in the works from the get-go. "The biggest problem was me," he readily concedes 30 years later. "I had by that time been in and part of the biggest group in the country and I was a raving success. And I didn't have the smarts to underplay that. Maybe I did, but I didn't do it enough. The way the chemistry works with the Byrds is that Roger's gotta be in charge. That's what has to happen; that's how it works. But I had chafed under that before and had wanted a bigger role and more of a say in how things went. So when we got together I came to it from that position. I don't think I was anywhere near careful enough of their feelings. Actually, we made a much better record than anyone gave us credit for, but there were mistakes in the making of it that I made, things that could have been done better."

Roger agrees that David's ego was a contributing factor to the failure of the album to live up to the Byrds' high standards. "The main reason was that Crosby was trying to prove that he had been the Byrds all along. That was the bottom line of it. He was successful with CSN and he was on a high, emotionally, drug wise, and financially, so he was the power man at the recording sessions and we all kind of submitted to that, unfortunately. He kind of had me on the run. I was intimidated by his status and all that at that point. And so he was producing it in such a way as to prove that he had been the real talent behind the Byrds all along and it was all going to come out now."

"Everybody was walking on eggshells," Chris explains, "and we needed somebody at the helm once again. We were trying to be polite in the sense of not opening up any old war wounds.

And Crosby was being the little king and bringing in this awful, awful engineer that worked on it. He was weird. You'd come in after doing a take and say, 'Can I hear that?' and he would freak out and snap back. It was unpleasant."

Roger points to an additional obstacle. "It was also too much of a party. David had this incredibly strong pot. Half a joint and you couldn't do anything. We were stoned out of our minds the whole time. I don't remember much recording. I remember just sitting around getting high." David's cavalier ingesting of cocaine presented temptations to Gene, who remained less inclined toward pot.

Regardless of the power plays, rampant egos, or drugs, Gene came onboard with two strong songs, "Full Circle" from the abandoned *Roadmaster* sessions, and "Changing Heart," a personal musing on the pitfalls of stardom. Both featured those glorious Byrds harmonies but, like the entire album, lacked the one absolutely distinctive and essential Byrds ingredient: Roger's chiming Rickenbacker electric 12-string guitar. In an effort to bring the group into the new decade and avoid being labeled as resting on their laurels, the Rickenbacker, while still present throughout the album, was mixed low to avoid any comparisons with the past. (That would prove to be a grave error in judgment.) And Gene was given lead vocal duties on two Neil Young covers, an acoustic reading of the electric guitar extravaganza "Cowgirl in the Sand" and a majestic "See the Sky about to Rain," which featured a glorious coda somehow mixed far higher in volume than the remainder of the album. "Gene's and the Neil Young songs were the strongest on that album," insists David, and correctly so.

Chris Hillman agrees with David's assessment. "'See the Sky about to Rain' and 'Full Circle' were probably the best tracks on the record. Gene's stuff was the best. The rest of us, I'll be honest, I contributed my worst material because I was getting ready to do a solo record, *Slipping Away*, and I was saving all my good stuff and contributed this throwaway stuff that was awful. Crosby's stuff was sketchy and Roger had 'Born to Rock & Roll,' which was terrible, yuck. But Gene's stuff was strong. His reading of 'See the Sky' was great. But we didn't have any direction, nobody at the helm." Roger adds, "I would agree. Gene came out the best on that album."

A further impediment to the album's success was the fact that the five had not played together beforehand sufficiently to gel as a unit. Instead of recording songs as a group, they cut separate parts piecemeal, overdubbing and constructing the tracks bit by bit. While 16-track technology facilitated this type of recording, and it had become the accepted standard of the time, it did not encourage a unified sound. "The thing was, the reunion album wasn't really a reunion," Gene concluded in a 1984 unpublished interview with Holger Peterson. "Chris was in Manassas, David was doing Crosby, Stills & Nash, Michael was building a house in Hawaii, I was recording *Roadmaster* at the time, doing a separate project, and Michael played on that. So we all would fly in and do our parts. We needed to get together and rehearse for about five weeks then go in and actually record together, rather than everyone flying in. Part of that Byrds reunion album is actually me and David Crosby and Neil Young and different assortments of

The Byrds reunite in 1972 for the highly anticipated Roadmaster *sessions: (left to right) Crosby, McGuinn, Clark, and Hillman.*

people on it." Indeed, according to CSNY drummer Johnny Barbata, he and studio bass player Wilton Felder played on "Cowgirl in the Sand," unbeknownst to Michael and Chris. "We never really got together, the five of us," Gene continues, "and seriously did a Byrds reunion. Never happened. Everyone telephoning in their parts. So it didn't have the essence it really needed. It may never happen again." Adds David, "Gene's right. We should have played more together before." Gene would later dub the reunion album the *Monkee Byrds.* "There were Byrds on the record," he told friend Tom Slocum, "but they didn't play together."

Released to great fanfare in February 1973, *Byrds,* boasting front and back cover shots of the group at the Troubadour with Gene front and center, moved quickly out of the chute on the way to gold status, only to stall when reviews carved it to pieces. "When I was sitting in the studio and they were doing it, I heard the magic there," muses Carlie. "But the magic that I heard sitting there I never heard on the album." And Chris laughs at the notion that it likely returned gold.

Plans for the much-ballyhooed tour were quietly dropped and the five Byrds went their separate ways. One can only wonder how Gene would have handled a high-profile mega-tour, given his performance anxiety. In a 1977 interview with UK writer Barry Ballard he characterized the reunion attempt as "having a fresh wound. You're still too sensitive. It's like having a divorce and then trying to get back together in six months. The underlying hurt and emotional things are still there and still very fresh."

Nonetheless, the only winner to emerge from the debacle was Gene. On the strength of his positive contributions to the album and critical praise for his songs and vocal performance, Asylum boss David Geffen offered Gene a solo contract for one album, with an option for more should the one prove successful. In anticipation of the recording sessions slated for the following April, Gene retreated to Albion and set about writing an entirely new body of music, which would become the album *No Other.*

But first he returned to the stage as a solo acoustic performer to open for Roger McGuinn on a two-week stand at Gene's home base, the Troubadour. By all accounts Gene managed to overcome his fears and turn in superb sets each night, introducing several recent compositions including "Silver Raven" and joining Roger onstage for a closing sampler of Byrds favorites. The engagement underscored the positive relationship between the two despite the recent failure of the Byrds reunion.

"Roger McGuinn and I and David Crosby are probably better friends now than we've ever been in our entire lives," Gene told DJ B. Mitchell Reed in 1974. "We went through a long time where we didn't know whether we were jealous of each other—now I'm being very honest with you—whether we were envious, whether one guy was more talented than the other. And, of course, we were very young. The falling out of the Byrds was really a mistake. It was not on purpose by anybody. All the way down the line, we're all good friends now."

Back home in Albion, Gene awaited the muse to imbue him with new songs. Local friend and drummer Andy Kandanes had a cottage by the ocean and offered Gene use of it whenever he felt the need to be alone to write. "Before I worked with Gene, I used to give him the keys to my place on the ocean on the cliff near Mendocino when he was working on the *No Other* album. He had the wife and kids and he used to go up there for the day to get away and write some tunes. I'd say, 'Here, go up to my place. Don't smoke up everything, but have a good time.' I would give him that space to write sometimes. I had a beautiful house on a cliff overlooking the ocean where the whales used to come in and rub their barnacles on the cliffs. It was right north of Mendocino in Indian Shoals, which is right by the Caspar lighthouse, a fantastic area that looks like a combination of the Cotswolds in England and Cornwall." Gene found the breathtaking setting inspiring and the contemplative solitude stimulating. In this environment he began an exploration of the essence of spirituality and the human spirit.

Frequent conversations with Philip on various religions, philosophies, and beliefs further stirred questions in Gene. An avid reader and explorer of the spiritual world in all its incarnations and guises, ancient and modern, Philip became Gene's guru and sounding board. Philip's personal library is impressive, reflecting a man on a quest for answers to the fundamental questions of life. "I always said to people, here was this amazing poet who's never read a book in his life," acknowledges Philip. "That's a fact. Gene never read. I'm a great reader and I study and Gene depended on me for some of that. He would ask me what I read about. We wouldn't get into conversations about it, but he would understand it. I would lend him books, but he wouldn't read them. He had a kind of moral and ethical viewpoint that wasn't spiritual or religious or anything like that, but he had a sense of right and wrong and he stuck pretty much close to that. Reality was very important to Gene, getting through the bullshit and down to what is meaningful, what is the truth. He was no abstract philosopher, but he wanted to get at the truth of things. To me it seemed as if he had an old soul, an innate wisdom beyond his being."

Gene's friend David Carradine introduced him to the precepts of Zen philosophy, and although he never read about it or practiced it, he was fascinated enough to incorporate its questions into his writing.

"He could never force it," Carlie recalls about Gene's songwriting process for *No Other*. "He either had to be open for it to be there and then it would just happen or not. I remember he was sitting in our house on Middle Ridge and there was a light coming through the window like a beam and it almost went right through his head and I thought, 'There it is. Now I'm sure you'll get something done today.' I don't know if you call it a medium or something."

Although Gene rarely spoke of himself as a poet, he *was* nonetheless. More to the point, what gave him pleasure was being able to sing his poetry, expressing lyrics that could, in his own words, stand the strength of strings: could be accompanied by guitar and sung melodically. His writing was rarely frivolous or superficial, even his songs about relationships. With his next album he would explore his poetic gift far more than he had ever before, and take great personal pride in being able to vocalize those concepts, ideas, and spiritual extrapolations in song.

Gene's friend Dennis Kelley remembers a conversation with Gene about his songwriting. "Being around him, he was sort of the typical down-home country boy; very laidback and easygoing. There was just no indication from his everyday speech that his writing could be so literate and poetic. During our conversation, Gene made the comment that he loved poetry and the way words and phrases could flow, and then he said, 'But to be able to sing those words is really where the beauty lies.' He said that to read the lines on paper is one thing, but to sing them really makes them come alive. As he spoke those words his eyes lit up with joy, he broke into a satisfied smile, and his whole face just seemed to be beaming with his love of singing. The look on his face, coupled with the almost reverent tone in his voice, made me realize that singing was truly one of the greatest joys that Gene could imagine. It was like he was a little kid on Christmas morning, walking into a room and seeing all of the presents under the tree. He was in heaven just thinking about the pleasure of singing. You had to be there to fully appreciate what I am trying to relate."

It has frequently been speculated that Gene's songs on *No Other* were drug-derived; that Gene conceived the eight songs in some cocaine haze, anointing Gene as the king of the Cosmic Cowboys. To this day, reviews of the reissued CD (2003) dwell inordinately on that bold assumption. The reality is much less beguiling: many of the album's themes derive from the Bible, while others examine the eternal conflicts between the inner spirit and the outer realities of life.

"Those songs were not conceived on drugs," contends Carlie, adamantly. "Mendocino was our cooling-out place and we had kids there." She insists that Gene was not a frequent recreational drug user at that point. In fact, she asserts, Gene didn't even like drugs. "Gene didn't do drugs well. He was way too sensitive to go to any valid or workable place with a mind-altering substance. I'm sure it was a great escape for him because he lost a certain amount of that intense reality or that intense consciousness or pressure. But it didn't go good. I can't say that I can ever remember him getting high and laughing and having fun when everyone else would be giggling and having fun. If Gene took a hit off of a joint he was really trying to be sociable because it wasn't his thing. He didn't like the way it made him feel. David Crosby had every kind of drug imaginable, but Gene would say, 'No thanks.'"

"Writers tend to read too much into the lyrics," Dennis Kelley hypothesizes. "We had been talking about the album and I mentioned that I liked that particular song 'From a Silver Phial,' especially the lines, 'Said she saw the sword of sorrow sunken in the sand of searching souls.' Gene himself told me the lyrics were inspired by the book of Revelations. I've read where someone said it was about a cocaine burn-out." References to needing a fix in "Some Misunderstanding" are not alluding to drugs but to the need for a bearing, a compass, some spiritual grounding of some sort, especially during the decadent "me-decade" of the 1970s.

Gene expounded to Domenic Priore in 1985, "People sometimes think, and I know they've asked this of Dylan, 'Do you write songs out of personal experiences or do you write songs like a novelist writes a novel?' Actually, in many cases you write them out of examples you get from watching other people or situations you see, or just dream up a situation. It is sort of like a novel writer. It's not always written because you went through a particular situation. A lot of times they are, but for the most part, most of the songs I've written are from observations. Something you see. Like you could be sitting at a coffee shop and see some guy arguing with his old lady or something and write a song about it."

To Steve Burgess in a 1977 *Dark Star* interview Gene confided, "'Some Misunderstanding' was written in a dream. I got up and wrote it down. I woke up, I was married at the time, and I told my wife, 'Look, I've gotta get up, turn on the lights for a moment, and write this down.' I wrote the song in completion because the dream was still fresh in my mind. I can't contrive a song."

One inspiration proved to be far more mundane in reality than oft speculated. In interviews, Gene would wax philosophical about the inspiration for his mysterious "Silver Raven" arising from a flying saucer, which he did indeed believe existed along with alien visitations to Earth. However, the silver raven in question was wife Carlie's favorite footwear. "I used to have these platform shoes, silver leather platform shoes made for me in the days of platform shoes," reveals Carlie. "I would dance with those shoes on and Gene called them my silver ravens." Confirms Ea, "The song 'Silver Raven' is about Carlie's silver platform shoes. She was a very good dancer and she could fly. She had them resoled and made those boots last."

In discussing the gestation of the songs for *No Other,* Gene told B. Mitchell Reed in 1974, "I spent a year of writing and analyzing the material on this album. I live at my ranch in Mendocino. That's where I do all my writing. I do maybe half of each song, then I fly down to L.A. and finish them. And then I use this energy to record them. So it's a balance to me of the two. It is not a San Francisco sound or an L.A. sound because one or the other is lacking in one flavor or the other. In other words, I get my clear head and my creative writing ability from the peaceful northern coast. But when I come to L.A. the energy hits me to inspire me to finish and to then give it the punch and to get all the way down. And also I have access to the finest musicians in the world. All the finest professionals are in L.A. at this time."

By the time Gene entered Village Recorder in Los Angeles in April 1974, he had assembled before him the A-list of studio aces who were ready, willing, and able to translate his lyrical revelations into musical form. With him on this journey would be a producer able to match Gene's grandiose visions pound-for-pound: elaborate arrangements framing Gene's exquisite poetry in musical mini-operas of wailing gospel choruses, screaming electric violins, swirling organs, and funked-up bass. In Thomas Jefferson Kaye, Gene had found his musical soul mate. Over the next five months the two partners would shape an album like no other in Gene's career.

"I would say probably that if any relationship was *the* relationship, it was Gene and Tommy Kaye," declares mutual friend and record producer Ken Mansfield. "I've never seen two people on such a wavelength as they had, and such good friends. These guys were like back-to-back buddies ready to take on the world. I actually envied their relationship in terms of how close they were."

Four years Gene's senior, Tommy Kontos was born and raised in New York where his career in music began at the age of 18 as head of A&R at Scepter Records. He adopted the surname Kaye shortly thereafter. Tommy enjoyed tremendous success as a producer, arranger, and songwriter for a diverse list of artists including the Shirelles, Maxine Brown, Jay and the Americans, Three Dog Night (he penned their hit "One Man Band"), Link Wray, and Loudon Wainwright III, as well as his own band, White Cloud, to name a few. Highly regarded in the recording industry, especially for his elaborate vocal arrangements, Tommy was just coming off producing the *Triumvirate* album with Mike Bloomfield, John Hammond, Jr., and Dr. John, as well as a controversial, colossally over-budget (reportedly $200,000 in costs), self-indulgent album for Dylan acolyte and road manager Bobby Neuwirth on David Geffen's Asylum label. (The album was rumored to be part of a deal with Dylan's manager, Albert Grossman, to get Dylan himself to sign with Asylum.) Talented, gregarious, well connected, and a partier renowned for his drug and alcohol excesses in spite of being a diabetic, Tommy was at the top of his game when he received a call from David Geffen to take on production chores for Gene Clark.

Some have insinuated that David foisted Gene on Tommy as an act of revenge for the costly Neuwirth fiasco. In his July 1997 column *The Blacklisted Journalist,* writer Al Aronowitz details the extravagant nonsense surrounding the Neuwirth sessions and Tommy's involvement with them. He also points out that David was, indeed, furious about the debacle. However, no one surrounding Gene at the time corroborates that assertion, and David has no interest in talking about Gene. It seems unlikely, though, that he would pony up $100,000 for Gene's album, an enviably substantial budget in 1974, merely as an act of vengeance on Tommy. Clearly, David was betting on Gene, anticipating he could deliver a quality, marketable product that could stand shoulder to shoulder with his other Asylum artists such as singer-songwriter Jackson Browne, whose sense of poetry matched Gene's.

In an unpublished 1991 interview with musicologist Ken Viola, Tommy Kaye recalled his initial meeting with Gene. "David Geffen asked me if I would like to produce Jackson Browne or Gene Clark and I said, 'I'd like to produce Gene Clark.' David thought that was really weird that I would say that. I told him Jackson didn't need a producer and I was always a Gene Clark fan from the Byrds. That's how we met. Gene was still on Asylum after the Byrds reunion album and David believed in him."

But the two did not hit it off at first. "David Geffen set up a meeting and I went up to Gene's house, my wife and I, and Gene was there with his wife, Carlie. He got drunk and he started in on me and kept insulting me. 'So what, you did Bobby Neuwirth! Fuck you!' Real nasty stuff. So I just split. The next morning he called me up and I said to him, 'Before you say a word, if you're going to say you're sorry, man, forget it. I'm going to tell you something. If this is any indication of how we're going to work together you tell me right now 'cause I'll call up David Geffen and I'm going to tell him where the fuck you're at and why I don't want to do your record.' And he went, 'Wow, no one's ever talked to me like this!' And then we became best friends. It was the most horrible night I've ever spent in my life. But he called me up, like a little kid that he'd do, the next day, and we became best friends. We argued, but we never got into it again like that."

Among the stellar supporting cast of musicians for the *No Other* sessions were bassist Lee Sklar, piano player Craig Doerge, and organist Mike Utley, who, unlike with the *White Light* sessions, was present this time from start to finish. Despite their individual track records for logging hundreds of recording dates as topflight studio musicians, all three agree that the *No Other* sessions were quite remarkable and memorable.

"It was a hard album to do," Lee notes. "I don't know where their heads met, he and Tommy, but it was a slightly arduous album to make. Each song took a while to sort out. I don't remember how much pre-production there was and how prepared Gene and Tommy were for it. It was just really a tough project just sorting through the songs. Gene was in great shape. He was a big, robust guy and was quite a presence. And I was such a Byrds fan that it was a kick to be able to work with him. I had worked with Roger McGuinn and Chris Hillman over the years so it was really a treat to get to work with Gene. He seemed to be in real good shape physically, musically, and emotionally. Everything was cruising. Gene was very focused on the project. It seemed very important to him. Tommy, too. Gene seemed fairly introverted and I think he was just real focused on the music. That was really dominating his mind. As much fun as it was to get together and play and hang out, the studio's not a hang out. Everybody was real focused on making the music."

Gene himself confirmed that the sessions were arduous in a 1977 interview with Steve Burgess in *Dark Star*. "Yes, it was a hard album to record. Not hard in a painful sense but hard in a sense of being so different to the musicians who recorded it. It took them a while to adjust to the approach Tommy and I were taking."

One feature of the sessions that the players found quite unique was the fact that Gene was present for every facet of the album's recording. "Gene was there for every minute of it," marvels Lee. "We constructed a vocal booth in the studio and he sang through everything, not like one of these absentee artists who comes in later and does their work. He was hands-on throughout the project." Archivist and reissue producer Andrew Sandoval, who supervised sound production for the expanded *No Other* CD reissue in 2003 for Warner Music, listened to all the session tapes, take after take, and noted that Gene was present for every recording, whether doing a scratch vocal for the musicians to follow or laying down a final master. "They didn't just do backing tracks and have Gene come in and do overdubbing of his vocals," enthuses Andrew. "They actually did live tracking with Gene. And Gene is the most consistent of all the players at the sessions. Everybody in the sessions made mistakes, but Gene really carried the sessions and was great throughout. His performances are spot-on each time. For example, 'From a Silver Phial,' there are a zillion takes and he's on all of them and they're all really good."

"There *were* a lot of takes," acknowledges Lee. "We labored pretty hard on it. It wasn't one of those projects where you just kind of nailed it immediately. I think there was a lot of looking for things. As I recall, on a lot of things we did a lot of takes, but from a developmental standpoint, not from making mistakes. It was 'Cut it,' then we'd listen to it and say, 'I don't know. Let's try this.' There was a lot of experimentation. There was a skeletal form to it, but then when it came to the track, people were then searching for parts. Gene may have had the melody and the lyric, but there wasn't the full structure. We would have to find parts. That was the luxury of that period where you weren't being pressed to like, 'Come on guys, look at the clock. We've got nine tracks to get today.' If you were in there all day and got a couple of tracks, that was great. That created personality in the music. It was given time to go through its formative state and then start to find some cool things that gave it its uniqueness. That's what I miss today. To me, that's what music was all about, that creative interaction. There was so much dimensionality to music from that period, and certainly with Gene's project, where each song was really a seed that then got to be planted and grow, as compared to now, where they come in 90 percent finished and you're just tidying up. I miss those days."

Comments Mike Utley, "Gene's songs were not your standard fare as far as the structure of the songs, like what you would get from a regular songwriter, two verses and a chorus, real structured songs. Even just the titles of the songs show they were pretty introverted. Even if they were love songs, you could never tell from the titles. That's the kind of writing he did. I had never worked with someone like Gene. You didn't know where the song was going to go. Eventually I worked with Jackson Browne and he was like that, too. Gene would come out into the room and play the songs for us like he was singing solo, a solo singer-songwriter. We would then make up chord charts and start working on them and he would describe the way he heard the song. With singer-songwriters, it's sort of like painting a picture. That's the way you look at it. It's sort of like a lot of color rather than just a feel or a groove, just getting into a groove and that's where you stay. With singer-songwriters, you listen to the lyrics. With me playing organ, I usually wouldn't come in from the top. I would wait until an appropriate time depending on what the lyrics said. The songs were great, but they were just so unusual. But that's typical of somebody that's singing their own material. They're writing it, so it's a little more personal rather than pitching it to someone else to sing."

Gene's friend Jesse Ed Davis was invited to contribute his distinctive guitar to the sessions. "For me it was a great session because I had never played with Jesse Ed Davis before," offers Craig Doerge. "I had heard a lot about Jesse. I was very impressed with him. Gene, of course, was nothing but nice. He was very cool and couldn't have been nicer to all the players. He was especially nice to myself and Lee. That was our one and only session with Gene. It was a pleasure to be treated so well."

Lee and Craig laugh about the time singer Joe Cocker crashed the sessions. "At one point we were doing this one song, we had been working on it for a couple of days, and it was finally coming together," Lee recalls. "We were in the middle of a take and Russ Kunkel and I looked at each other as if to say, 'This is it. We're finally getting it.' Joe Cocker was working next door in the other studio there. And at the time, Joe was pretty out of it. He was drinking real hard and whatever the hell else he was doing. He came wandering into the control room while we were working and got really into the song. He was sitting there behind the console just rocking back and forth, really digging it. He got so excited that he reached forward and hit the talkback button and let out one of his famous Cocker screams. It literally blew everybody's headphones off their heads. Gene knocked over the constructed vocal booth trying to get out to get at Joe. Joe's handlers dragged him out of the studio and rushed him down to the other room so that they could lock him in so Gene and Tommy wouldn't kill him. We went back and listened to the tape. You couldn't hear the scream, but you would have sworn someone had just taken a razor blade and cut the tape. The stop was so instantaneous because of the pain level of the scream that went down. It was just unbelievable. We all had to go home; nobody could hear anything. Everybody's heads were ringing. We had to come back the next day and start over again."

"I don't think I've ever seen a producer jump faster or to a higher extreme than Tommy," Craig chuckles. "We were happy not to be in Joe's shoes after that. I looked at Gene and he just looked so stunned. In those days nothing came into your phones except the Word of God, and that was the producer. Lee and I to this day still talk about that story. It was just priceless."

As for the oft-held contention that the sessions were dusted with excessive amounts of white powder, Lee disagrees. "Personally, I never did drugs at all and never drank. But as I recall, those dates with Gene were so kind of consuming and intense that I don't recall seeing anything going on there because there was so much focus. And Russ was really straight, Utley was really straight, Doerge, the list of musicians there, most of those guys were pretty straightahead. I don't remember seeing any blow or anything on those dates. No, Gene was very straight-up and very focused. That's the thing. There's always this kind of bullshit *Random Notes* mythology that all this stuff was real drug-oriented. Certainly there were sessions going on where there was a lot of drugs involved, but for the most part I would tend to say that when you listen to the quality of the music that came out you can't get that kind of recording done by being out of it. It's one thing when a session is over and somebody went out and partied, that's a whole other thing. But during the actual recording, most guys were pretty much intact. And if they got out of it and then they heard it afterwards, they were so embarrassed by it they didn't do it again. There is always so much mystique about that process and people always want to paint some sort of dark, weird, drug-induced atmosphere rather than copping to the fact that this was a creative process and it was a bunch of creative people getting together and making it the best they could. We were all well aware that this was our career. Every guy that played on that record—Utley, Kunkel, Doerge, Kootch [Danny Kortchmar], Bruton—is still working, with the exception of Jesse Ed and Gene. Everybody is still viable and busy, and you don't get that way by spending a career being out of it."

While the sessions themselves may have been alcohol- and drug-free, the after-hours gatherings were not necessarily as puritanical. With Gene and Carlie's second child, Kai Taylor Clark, born December 5, 1973, Carlie did not stay long in Los Angeles. She returned to Albion with the two boys while Gene finished recording *No Other*.

For the duration of the sessions, Gene and Carlie had rented a house in Los Angeles on Queens Road up above Sunset Strip. "We still had the place in Mendocino, but I thought it would be better if we had a regular home down there and we could go back and forth," Carlie explains. "That was when it started getting crazy. There were parties at our house 24/7. I would go to sleep at five in the morning and the boys would wake up at six and it was just too insane. I remember telling Gene, 'I can't do this. I can't live these two lives. I just can't do it.' So I went back to Mendocino. I took the van, we had this Dodge van, and headed out with the boys. He said he would just stay and finish up this album. 'Doug will stay here with me.' It was this huge house. I remember now what happened. I had gone to sleep one night and an ambulance came. Somebody had dropped Dexedrine or some kind of speed on the floor and some child, not my kids, had gotten it. That was it for me. I left. I was driving the van back to Mendocino and I got as far as the Burbank airport and I said, 'I'm not doing this.' So I got on a plane and flew to San Francisco and took a Greyhound to Mendocino. I got home and called Gene and said, 'You need to get someone to take you to the Burbank Airport and pick up the van. The keys are on the right front tire.' And that was it. I had had it with L.A. But he kept going back because he had to."

Douglas Dillard moved in with Gene for a while. Carlie recalls hearing of their antics. "One night Douglas and Gene were home and there was a movie being shot on the Strip below and the two heard, 'The house is surrounded!' They freaked out and ran from room to room collecting all their dope and flushing it down the toilet, then went outside waving a white dishtowel to surrender to the authorities. There were helicopters flying overhead and searchlights. Turns out it was a shoot for *The Mod Squad* or something."

By this time, Gene's running buddies included David Carradine and John Barrymore. "David Carradine is loony tunes," Carlie points out. "David is crazy. Another one that's absolutely loony tunes is John Barrymore. Oh, my god, another one of Gene's best friends. I quit going to L.A. with the boys. He would go from Mendocino to L.A. and it was like going from sanity to insanity."

While Gene had been managing to compartmentalize his two lives—L.A.'s ex-Byrd rock star/Troubadour habitué and Mendocino's back-to-the-land outdoorsman—the distinctions were starting to blur. He found himself increasingly drawn to Los Angeles to sustain his career. His friendships with the likes of Kaye, Carradine, Barrymore, Dillard, and Davis, all part of his Los Angeles drugs-and-booze persona, were beginning to overshadow his relationship with Philip and Ea and even with Carlie and the boys. Cocaine was the drug of choice for Gene's crowd and he succumbed to its allure. "Tommy Kaye, Jesse Ed Davis, and Gene really formed something of an 'Unholy Trio' in regards to their bad habits," postulates Dennis Kelley. "I am sure it was like pouring gasoline on the fire." Adds friend and actor Jason Ronard, "Tommy Kaye was just a beautiful cat, but did a little too much cocaine. We were very tight, Gene, myself, and Tommy. A very talented guy. These were remarkable human beings who put on the façade of drugs and couldn't take it off."

Following the tracking sessions, Tommy went into high gear on the overdubs and brought in a gospel chorus, Seatrain violinist Richard Greene on wah-wah violin, Chris Hillman on mandolin, ex-Butterfield Blues Band guitarist (and inventor of the Feiton tuning system) Buzzy Feiton, and percussionist Joe Lala. While Tommy's forte was elaborate arrangements and *No Other* shows his ability to cast Gene's songs in grand musical contexts, some insist that he overwhelmed the lyrics and melody. In a 1977 interview with Barry Ballard, Tommy even suggested the album was like "my answer to Brian Wilson and Phil Spector, as a producer."

The 2003 UK edition of *No Other,* however, is a revealing listen with regard to the impact of Tommy's ornate overdubbing. It includes six bonus tracks *without* the Phil Spectorish, "wall of sound" approach that permeates the official US release. In this stripped-down form, the songs have a more earnest appeal—most likely how Gene envisioned them. "That happens so often," suggests Lee Sylar. "One of the hardest things to do in this business is to know when to stop. Some people get so excited and so involved, they go, 'Jesus, I could have an orchestra on this!' Does it need it? Well, that question was never asked. Maybe a little quartet might have been nice, but the next thing you know they've got a 100-piece orchestra. That's always a tough call with so many producers, especially back then. It was a pretty indulged time where there weren't people sitting there staring at budget sheets and saying, 'Nice idea, but we really can't afford it,' which sometimes saves your album. If they had $100,000, that's a lot of money."

Regardless, Gene went along with the elaborate overdubs, and in the end, excessive or otherwise, he and Tommy Kaye had created a masterpiece.

It has been rumored for decades that *No Other* was originally conceived as a double album, Gene himself fueling speculation that hidden treasures cut during the sessions remained in the Asylum vaults. However, as Tommy revealed to Ken Viola, *No Other* was never a double album and the eight tracks were always the focus, although a version of "Train Leaves Here This Morning" was attempted. "Before we did *No Other* we went into the studio and did about ten or 15 things with just him and an acoustic guitar. A lot of those things were his new material for *No Other*. Gene might have meant that. We did do a lot of demos of our songs."

As befitting such a grandiose album, Gene and Tommy sought to package their masterwork in an equally elaborate sleeve. To that end they turned to Gene and Carlie's Albion companion, Ea O'Leno. "Gene asked me to do a cover that I felt was a feeling of his life that nobody else caught," enthuses Ea with great pride. "And this is what I came up with. Glamorous. We had him looking like a swashbuckler. He was totally okay with it. We were thinking glamorous movie stars, 1940s-type movie stars. If you look at the images, the prizefighter, it's very masculine. Everything is

Gene with producer/friend Tommy Kaye in 1974.

painted by hand. I think the images reminded me of Gene." But while Ea's rococo/high Holly-wood/silent film/Rudolph Valentino/art deco look was achieved on the front cover, the portrait of Gene on the back was, most fans agree, unsettling. There was Gene Clark, the handsome Kansas-raised folk/country-rocker from Northern California's redwood forests, decked out in women's clothing and makeup, his hand provocatively placed on his thigh close to a rather intimidating bulge. "Ea and I could talk him into just about anything," laughs Carlie. "It was like a dress-up thing for him. He was okay with it. He just let us play with him all day. Judy Hadash had this store, the Pleasure Dome, and she helped us with the women's clothes. Gene was in a mold in terms of his image that was very difficult for him and he really would have liked to be able to break out and be free. So he tried. The minute we were done, though, he was back to the way he always was."

Adds Ea, "I gave his hair a permanent and took him out and made him get used to those clothes. I put makeup on him and took him out to places like Dan Tana's for about four nights so he would feel comfortable looking like that. A swashbuckler was what he was supposed to be."

And what of that provocative pose? "When you look at this picture closely it leaves nothing to the imagination, if you know what I mean," Carlie smirks. "It drives Kelly and Kai nuts. 'Mom, how could you ever dress him up in drag like this?' Kelly and Kai hate it. We were trying to get some kind of change there for him. That photo was from when we were at Noah Dietrich's house up in the Hollywood Hills. He had this big mansion. It had all these fountains and all this stuff all over it so that's where we shot it." Ea defends her controversial decision to redefine Gene's image. "He's got a masculine pose with his hand on his hip. He loved the Barrymores and he liked that whole 1920s period."

Chris Hillman is far less generous. "Whoever directed him to wear that hideous makeup and drag queen stuff on the *No Other* album cover? It was like a guy walking over the abyss and someone telling him, 'Go this way.'" Mendocino resident Garth Beckington laughs, "Ea's a hair-dresser, but I've always been afraid to have her do my hair because I didn't want to look like that!" Fans remain firmly divided over the striking cover image.

When Gene and Tommy presented the completed album to Asylum boss David Geffen, they anticipated accolades from the label executive. Instead the response was hostile—David an-grily threw the album down, incredulous that $100,000 had been spent on a mere eight tracks. As Tommy told Viola, "Asylum was not behind that record. I got flack from David Geffen about how come there are only eight songs on the record after they spent all this money? But they were eight great songs and that was it. We were trying to make a real piece of art and we thought that David Geffen, being a really artsy guy, would get it. But he didn't. I think it even went over his head. Or he was maybe too busy with Cher Bono or something. The reason we had only eight songs on that album was because it was the vinyl thing and there was only so much time you could get on each side to get a great sounding record. That's why we went with the eight songs. They were very long songs." Another factor, in Tommy's opinion, was that Gene's manager at the time, Bennett Glotzer, who also managed Tommy, did not get on well with David.

For Gene, who had infused his very soul into *No Other*, it was a bitter blow, a personal disappointment and career setback from which he never fully recovered. Asylum released the album with a minimum of promotion and let it twist in the wind. "David just dropped it and wouldn't get behind it," Tommy informed Barry Ballard. "He wouldn't give us any money to go on tour, or to subsidize a band or anything. At that time he was thinking of going into movies and he sort of lost his desire." A near punch-out with David one night at Dan Tana's sealed the album's fate. According to Philip, "Gene went after Geffen right there in the restaurant. I don't know what he was going to do to him, but he was going to get physical. [Troubadour manager] John Desko got him outside. John had his heavy shoe on Gene's hand and said to him, 'If you continue to resist I'm gonna break your fuckin' hand!' And Gene was very protective of his hands, of course. They were sensitive because he played guitar. That was rage, more than just drunken rage."

"Gene burned so many bridges," sighs Chris. "But doing that to Geffen, that was a pivotal point. That shut it down for Gene. Geffen had the power then. He's a very powerful man. You can't do that to a guy like him."

Nonetheless, reviewers were staggered by the grandiloquence of *No Other* and heaped praise on both Gene and Tommy for their daring ambition, citing tracks like the darkly exquisite "Some Misunderstanding" and the ethereal "Strength of Strings" with its banshee-wailing backup voices as marvelous pieces of art. Inspired by Carlie, "Lady of the North" builds to a dense climax of searing electric violin. "Silver Raven" retains a haunting aura, while the title track is funked-up, propelled by Joe Lala's percussion and Jerry McGhee's fuzz guitar. Gene retained his appreciation for country-rock with the opening track, "Life's Greatest Fool," and with "The True One." Both were autobiographical ruminations on the price of fame, a theme Gene knew only too well. Fans and critics had a field day attempting to decipher all the hidden messages and inspirations in Gene's oblique lyrics.

Despite the critical response, the album only rose as high as No. 86 on the charts before disappearing. Many record buyers were confused by the apparent contradiction of cover image and music inside, while others found the album far too radical a departure from the acoustic balladeer of *White Light* or the bluegrass-country boy of *The Fantastic Expedition of Dillard & Clark*. As Gene later confided to Barry Ballard, "I thought it was a truly fine album and I felt very let down, very disappointed, that it didn't do better than it did. Almost to the point of depression, because I thought I'd finally found a niche with my own art that I could carry on into other areas." Surmises Bernie Leadon, "That album might be considered a masterpiece. It's certainly an ambitious album." In hindsight, some critics have recently suggested the album was too far ahead of its time, or merely out of its time, to be fully appreciated in 1974. Artistically, such a pronouncement is a high compliment. Commercially, it's the kiss of death.

Gene's frustration with the music business was only compounded by the failure of *No Other*. As Carlie muses, "The record companies were saying, 'Yes, they're great. But these need to be mixed different, they need to sound different, they're not commercial, they're too long,' which was a big one, you know. It was, 'If you want to continue in this business, if you want to continue to make a living in this business, you're going to have to whore yourself and give us what we want or we're not going to record you.' And that meant that he had to dance to another piper's tune, not his. It was the influence of the business. He had a vision of what his music was, and as time went on, the music industry had another vision of what was marketable. So the two never met."

From the perspective of his record labels, as well as his dwindling fan base, part of Gene's problem was his inconsistency—not in quality, but in style. While everything Gene released throughout his career was measured by the rigorously high creative standards Gene always set for himself, it was nonetheless incongruent from release to release. There was no instantly identifiable 'Gene Clark sound' once he had left the Byrds. Jim Bickhart offers up his assessment of the problems inherent in Gene's eclectic oeuvre. "With the exception of maybe a year with the Byrds, he was never quite in synch with his time. That may be what makes him distinctive in pop culture history and music history and what makes him worth remembering, but it also contributes to the melancholy memory I have of him. It could be said of Gene that the one thing he never did create was a consistent body of work stylistically. There was folk-rock and then there was the countryish stuff, then country-rock, and then whatever you want to call *No Other*. To those who were familiar with Gene Clark it always sounded like Gene Clark, but to Columbia Records or A&M Records or the *Tiger Beat* magazines or the program directors at the radio stations who liked to hear Rolling Stones records that sounded like Rolling Stones records, Gene Clark didn't qualify. In the abstract that was great, but for making yourself successful in a pretty brutal hit-making business, it just didn't work. It might work on a one-off, but it didn't happen for him. He needed more consistency, some stuff that sounded just enough like the Byrds to remind people of where he came from, and then to sound enough like itself over the course of a couple of albums that people would recognize who he was. And he didn't do that. It is kind of surprising that first Columbia Records and then A&M—in an era when there was still a lot more control over what artists sounded like—didn't exercise a firmer hand over his career."

Eschewing the high-flying touring luxuries of his contemporaries like CSNY or the Eagles, Gene assembled a two-man backing band dubbed the Silverados and set off in September in a battered Dodge van to play club dates across the highways and byways of the nation. Joining Gene were Duke Bardwell on bass and banjo, fresh from a stint in Elvis Presley's band, and Roger White on electric guitar. Gene was about to embark on the first of several low points in his life and career, with his failed masterpiece, a low-budget tour, a desperate need for money, increasing reliance on alcohol and drugs, and, as a direct consequence, a crumbling marriage.

"Gene was always a handful, but I thought it was an opportunity," offers Duke, the ever-ebullient Louisiana native. "I knew that he had played with the Byrds and knew about some of his songs, but as far as him personally, I really didn't know much about him. I really was quite surprised at our first public performance. It was quite honestly the picture of the way things were going to go for the next couple of years. It was at the Troubadour with Roger McGuinn and Odetta. It was the three of us, Roger White and I and Gene. Roger White and I had rehearsed with him a bunch in between the Elvis stuff I was doing. That night, on the way over there, Roger White had a motorcycle accident and broke his ankle so it was just me and Gene. Everybody had their own set—McGuinn, Odetta, and us—and there was going to be a thing together at the end. But Gene got so fucked up I didn't even want to get onstage with him. We had been practicing all this stuff with three-part harmonies and all of our parts, but the show must go on so we went on and did our part of the show. Afterwards he was looking for me at the end to get back up there with him and I went and hid in the corner. I'm serious. I didn't want to get back up there. I didn't know what to do. I think it was a combination of drinking and drugs, but it was mostly drinking. I didn't know until later when I realized he really enjoyed combining uppers and alcohol. He liked pills. And I was with someone else who liked pills. I was like, 'Gawddamn!' That was the first public show with him at the freakin' Troubadour in L.A." For Duke it was a portent of things to come. "This became a pattern for the next few years that we worked together. There were times that he would perform more sober. He never did perform totally sober, though."

Why, then, would Duke choose to leave Elvis Presley to go out on the road with Gene under these circumstances? "I was fascinated by his poetry," answers Duke. "I was really questioning his behavior at first, but the more that he wrote and the more of his lyrics that I heard and his melody structure, I was going, 'Where is this shit coming from?! It ain't coming from the Devil, I can tell. And if it's coming from God, then how come Gene's so fucked up?' My association with Gene Clark is what showed me that you could really take the language and bend it, twist it, mold it, and brush it like paint. It was like he was standing before a canvas and would create that canvas. I had never seen anything like that before and I was fascinated by it.

"I don't remember what song it was, but it was on that trip where we broke down and blew the motor in Chicago and we were stranded for the length of time it took to put something else in there and then we had to haul our asses down to Phoenix. It was that particular trip through the night where the moon was shining off of all these buttes and rock structures. Words started coming from him that were almost surreal. It was like he was tapping into a part of songwriting and poetry that I never even suspected, certainly in my own creativity. I would be driving and Gene would be ranting. It would be out of the blue. He would come out with these words and verses and it was like, 'I don't know what he means, but it sounds so good!' It was so amazing. To this day I would have to say that I will never forget watching genius and insanity go hand in hand like they did with Gene Clark."

Despite the austere conditions, spartan travel, and small nightclubs with unappreciative audiences expecting "Mr. Tambourine Man," Gene and the Silverados evolved a sound of their own as 1974 passed into 1975. They took songs from Gene's existing catalog, including numbers from *No Other,* and redefined them in Appalachian Mountain triad harmonies and country-flavored arrangements. In many respects the sound of Gene and the Silverados offered a logical next step from *The Fantastic Expedition of Dillard & Clark.* Songs like "Here Without You," "Spanish Guitar," "Silver Raven," and "Set You Free This Time" took on an entirely distinctive hue with the Silverados. In addition, Gene was inspired to write a collection of new songs all in a country-rock vein, including "Wheel of Time," "Home Run King," "What Is Meant Will Be," and "Daylight Line." Traditional numbers like "In the Pines" and "Long Black Veil" were given new life. In the fall of 1975 Gene expanded the Silverados with the addition of drummer Mark Singer and pianist John Guthridge, allowing the group to work up full-band arrangements of these new songs in anticipation of a January recording date for a proposed album. In preparation for those sessions, Gene and the Silverados laid down demos of a number of the songs at Mike Nesmith's Countryside Studios in Los Angeles.

"They did some great music together, but they got into some speed," laments Carlie. "The piano player they had was the best, so good. But Gene just scared that poor guy almost to death. He went running out screaming, 'I can't take this!' There was one night when they were driving and doing speed to keep going and this guy couldn't take it. It was really crazy."

The grind was grueling and Gene needed an extra push night after night in order to face his performance anxiety. "I think if someone is looking for a reason for him to get as fucked up as much as he did, then panic disorder's as good as any," muses Duke. "To this day I get sick to my stomach before I go onstage and I understand anything like that. The bigger the gig, the worse he'd get. So that may have some validity. It depended on the gig. One of the things that pissed me off the most was when we went up to where he lived in Mendocino, there was a venue there that allowed us to come play and it was like 'Gene Clark Comes Home.' And we went in to play that place and he got really fucked up before we went onstage. We had to cover for him a lot. I would have thought that if this was going to be a hometown thing that he was wanting to be sharp. But he wasn't. There was a show in Dallas where we realized we couldn't play together. We were like three songs into the show when Roger and I just got up and walked out. There was no way to play with him that night. He was so drunk. We couldn't monitor what he was doing or have any effect on what he was doing; he was the star and could go to the bar and drink what he wanted. And if he didn't find his balance between what pill he took, what he was eating, and what he was drinking, then it would incredibly affect the shows. Some of the shows were very, very good. There was a show at Ebbet's Field in Denver that was a good show, but there was another one in Berkeley where he was just so fucked up.

"I don't think he was comfortable with performing, but it was like a part of it that he really had to do. What else was he going to do? Sell cars? While we were together he had borrowed money from [Allman Brothers drummer] Butch Trucks to help save his 'farm,' as he called it. We knew he had gone to Butch for some help. Money was a problem. There wasn't much cash flow. At what age should somebody who has had a taste of success get realistic about whether they're going to have it again or not? Gene hadn't done anything else in his life.

"He was still being billed as 'Gene Clark of the Byrds.' But he knew that he needed anything that would get him in the door because there was Carlie and the two kids, and the mortgage, and he had to be out there making it. He was desperately seeking interest from a record label or somebody that could help him or do something for him. And it's hard to do it when you're carrying a band around. I have no idea what they were booking him for. We never knew what he was making. But there were some times when I felt it really wasn't anywhere near enough."

Out on the road, Duke and Roger were witness to Gene's dramatic mood swings. In deep depression over the state of his career, Gene would career from high to low. The daily ingesting of amphetamines mixed with alcohol only exaggerated his condition. "When you were with Gene you never knew where it was going to go," avers Duke. "For him to display any real form of levity was rare. There was always this cloudy, dark thing about him. I can remember seeing him rant or slam his fist into the dashboard of the old Dodge truck. It was such a roller coaster. I'm not sure if he might have been manic-depressive, but I think there was very likely some chemical imbalance because that kind of mood swing is usually diagnosed as manic-depressive and would have been chemically treatable. But I'm not sure what we would have gotten from him had he been treated. I'm not sure that the poetry would have come out the same. I can honestly not recall any single moment with him that I can remember as being one that was strewn with gaiety or levity. That just didn't seem to fit his nature. He was more dark than bright. It's not that it was all bad and draining and negative. I can picture him in my mind laughing hysterically, but it could just as easily have been at someone falling down the stairs."

Given the circumstances Gene found himself in while on the road, returning home and adjusting to any semblance of normalcy and family was often difficult. He brought his road persona home with him and was unable to disengage the two Genes. To Carlie and the boys, he was becoming a stranger. "Pretty soon he started to change," she recalls. "When he started going on tour he would come back and it was like his eyebrows were just sticking up and his eyes were rolling around in his head. It was just insane and I got to absolutely dread it when he was coming home because it would take two or three days to even know who this person was. He felt out of space, out of time, out of place. The real manic stuff was always when he had been drinking. He was the kindest, gentlest, most loving soul in the world as long as he wasn't drinking. Especially when we were in Mendocino and he wasn't under pressure. But he was getting progressively worse with his disease. The enlightening part of his life was becoming less and less; it was becoming obvious. Every time he went away he was footloose and fancy-free and felt no pressure and did drugs and got drunk and was Mr. Wonderful. And coming back there were responsibilities having a wife and kids and stuff."

Stabilized after a few days, Gene would get back to being a husband and father. "He was wonderful with the kids," Carlie smiles. "He adored them, just adored them. He used to sing to them. That was cute. He was in awe of them. They took him to a gentler place. He would sit and watch them a lot, not so much on the floor and playing with them or relating to them on their level, but just be in awe of them. They were beautiful."

"I have very few memories of my mom and dad together in Mendocino," sighs Kai. "I was too young when they split up. I always remember, though, my father being very loving, very caring, his touch was always very sweet. His scruffy face on mine when I was a kid and he would kiss me. The first thing I ever remember was he built a swing for us. It was a very special place, a 100-year-old farm with an at least 200-year-old apple orchard out front. Amazing old trees. We lived on the edge of the redwood forest, very dark and deep valley redwood forest, at the end of a dirt road with a pond and cattle land all around us. It was an amazing place. He built this swing out front in one of the apple trees, an awesome little swing."

"I definitely remember the farm," offers Kai's brother, Kelly. "And I really liked living there. When I was a kid I wanted to be an archaeologist and we lived by this gigantic cow and sheep field, acres and acres of that. And there were a couple of abandoned turn-of-the-century homesteads with all the stuff around. So I collected bones and all kinds of old stuff. That's great when you're a kid."

While Kai's recollections are of a serene pastoral life, all happiness and light, Kelly is more the realist, the pessimist, the darker cloud. In many respects, each boy grew up exhibiting a particular side of Gene's personality. For Kelly, memories of conflict remain as vivid as the redwood trees. "My mom and my dad fighting and my mom throwing plates or something like that, that's the first conscious memory I have of my father, unfortunately. That was when I was about three years old. There is a difference in people. I think that's why my mom and my dad were the perfect couple because my mom was a little more realistic about things sometimes and my dad was always in the clouds. I think that if people stick it out and there is no major trauma and they're both available enough, it can work for them. Like opposites attract and you accent each other well. Certain people handle things certain ways. But I think my father got complacent with my mother taking his shit, and my mother got to the point where she was tired of worrying about what was going to happen and she saw someone who was going to take care of her and pay attention to her, so she went with that. And I don't blame her. He left my mom in a 100-year-old farmhouse with two little kids, a woodstove, and all that stuff that's cute and fun when you're together and you want to do this hippie-yuppie thing. That's why I don't think everyone should be as upset about her leaving."

"There was a happy time for Gene up here, until before the end of his marriage when he and Carlie were fighting a lot and he was drinking more and more," recalls Philip. "It was kind of an ugly time, the last year of that. She was supportive of his career. She had worked in the business so she knew what it was about. She never drank until she met Gene. He got me into it more than

I would have been otherwise, I have to say. Hanging out with him, I drank more than I would have. But Gene started drinking more. His father drank. And then there was that Indian strain in him. There was the drunken aspect of him, too, a violent aspect. I have to say, though, any fights I ever witnessed between Gene and Carlie were shouting matches. I never saw him get violent with her. There wasn't any of that. But she was scared. Gene liked to throw knives and get pretty wild. He was good at it. He wasn't throwing them at her, but he scared her. He was not being a nice guy to her. He was being obnoxious, especially with his drinking and out in public he would make these scenes with her in town. Stories came back to me of the things he would say to her or the scenes he would make. We never saw it, but we heard about it. These people were telling me because they thought I should know about it. And I was thinking, 'No wonder she got fed up with it.'

"Gene had a dark side that I recognized, but I didn't know about manic depression or hear it called that. Somebody pointed it out to me and I said, 'Yeah, he did have a dark streak.' Now that we're more familiar with the term I would say yes, he was manic-depressive. There is a will to death, as Freud calls it, and it's an ugly thing when it gets the better of you. But some of that self-destructiveness happens that way, that's the dark streak. Not to harm others, but to harm yourself."

Was Carlie concerned that Gene might become physically violent? "I know that was in their family history," she states. "It could have been in Gene, but it doesn't have to be. Either you can go down that road or you can choose not to. Gene knew that even if he had seen it all his life it didn't matter; he knew that if he did, I was gone. He chased me, but I was faster than him. He was strong; he could do anything. I'm not saying that if I hadn't left it might have happened. I left because the way things were going, Kelly and Kai and I would not have been safe. I'm not so much saying physically safe, but emotionally and mentally safe."

Fearful that Gene's increasingly erratic behavior and drunken rages might harm her or the boys, on March 5, 1976, Carlie packed up and left Gene. Her destination for refuge was Hawaii. "I think it was probably the depression," reflects Carlie, on Gene's confused state of mind that hastened her departure. "Now in hindsight it's easier to see. If I had known a little bit more about what I know now, I would have managed to hang in there. Today there is no anger there. I know that if I had been able to hang on through a certain period when his true insanity was based on alcohol and drugs, we might have survived. I was no teetotaler myself at that point, so how could I know? It all was centered on my trying to control the sanity and the insanity. In L.A. he was still 'Gene Clark the Byrd' and all the groupies were around. I found out he was with someone down there. I was supposed to go down there and look for a house and the record company called and said it would be better for me to stay in Mendocino. I found out what was going on. He had this gal move in with him in the place when we were supposed to get a place and that was it. It was just too crazy. I locked the door, nailed the windows shut, put stuff in two duffle bags, and I knew that if he got drunk and found me he'd kill me, so I went to Hawaii only because he could not have gotten on a plane and managed to find me."

In a panic and with no money in Hawaii, Carlie called a friend in Mendocino, Mark Kimberly, who promptly flew out to comfort her. In doing so, Mark touched off a controversy that still divides family and friends. There are those who insist Carlie conspired to run off with Mark and leave Gene, while others sympathize with her impulsive flight to safety and calling Mark out of desperation. "Mark Kimberly went after her as Gene was pushing her away," maintains Philip. "Subconsciously, Gene was doing this. He was pushing her away. That was her way out, to go to Hawaii with Mark Kimberly, who owned the Little River Inn. She bailed. She took the two kids and was gone." So why did she leave Gene? Philip cites several reasons. "Well, the drinking, Gene's frustration with his work, Carlie's not understanding what was going on, maybe," he avers. "People get stubborn. Both of them were stubborn."

"Philip and Ea were mad at me," admits Carlie. "They thought I was totally out of line when I left. I never told them about any of the nightmare scenes with drunken Gene or any of the things I couldn't live with, with two children anymore, because I didn't think it was anyone else's business nor is it your business or anyone else's. He was a tortured soul and I'm sorry I had to see it. Slowly but surely I couldn't see anymore the gentle soul I had fallen in love with. It was more the manic person, unsure of himself, frustrated and drunk. Had it not been for Kelly and Kai I might have been able to manage to find a way to balance things out and stay. But it was impossible.

"Mark had told me that if I was ever not with Gene to let him know. Well, I flew to Hawaii and I had no money, no anything, so Mark flew right over there. I didn't go *with* him. It looked for all intents and purposes like it was all planned, but I knew what was going on. His family owned the Little River Inn in Mendocino and he had tons of bucks and I was in the middle of nowhere. We had a great time and there were times when we would all hang out and close the bar at their place in Mendocino. Yeah, it looked like we had run away together, but it was just my ace in the hole because I was in the middle of nowhere."

Gene was devastated when he discovered Carlie and the boys had fled. "When Carlie left, what did Gene do? He let it happen," Philip explains, his usually calm voice rising. "He didn't put up a fight, not just for the boys, but for her too. He just let it happen. And that might have been what he was criticized for. What would I do? Why not get on a plane and go over there to Hawaii and cause some hell or fight to get them back? But he didn't do that."

Rick Clark came up to the farm in Albion to console his brother. But while his sympathies lie squarely with Gene, Rick was unaware of the circumstances that precipitated the split. "He went through one of the worst heartaches of his life. Carlie ran off with Mark Kimberly to Hawaii and took Gene's kids. Then he ran out of money and she came back and tried to apologize, but Gene wouldn't take her back. She broke his heart real bad. She devastated him when she took his children and ran off with this guy totally unannounced. Didn't tell Gene or anything, just disappeared without explanation or any clue. And Gene went, 'What happened? I had this happy life and a young family and all of a sudden it's gone.' Up to that point Gene

thought everything was going swimmingly, then all of a sudden it went 'Crash!' It was right before the *Two Sides to Every Story* project. Right around that time. I held Gene's hand a lot. Gene
would just sit and cry, missing his kids and not knowing why it happened. He was a very sensitive man."

After a time, Carlie came back and attempted to reconcile with Gene. But it was to no avail,
and she returned to Hawaii. "I talked to Gene, but he was just too far gone," Carlie explains. "He
was too angry. It was like possessing me and that was not where it had to go. But I think because
of this whole thing that I ran away with Mark Kimberly, which was totally taken out of context, that hurt his ego. It hurt him more than it would if he had known that I legitimately left because it was too crazy for me to stay there with the boys. But he never understood that because
of this whole other scenario and all these stories. So when I got back from Hawaii, I made
arrangements to see him. But he was a maniac. If he could have locked me in a closet and kept
me there, he would have done it. He just had to possess me and that just wasn't healthy. If we
had a chance to stay together it would have had to have been healthier, but he was not in a headspace to even hear me."

In the intervening years, Carlie has come to terms with her time with Gene and the eventual
split. "I don't talk about it a lot. I'm not uncomfortable with it, but as time has gone on I know
that sometimes, once in your life, if you are really lucky, you get to experience that place that
Gene and I were at for a long time. Then something happened and it wasn't there any more. As
time gets between then and now, I look back on it as having been a precious place that I got to
experience that most people never experience in their whole lifetime.

"And I also happen to know that I heard music that most people would give anything in the
world to know; that I've actually sat there and had music transport me to another consciousness, and that doesn't happen very often. I was the love of his life and he was the love of my life,
too. Nothing will ever come close to that, nor would I want it to because I'm not sure that's so
healthy. He would call me sometimes after the anger was gone."

Carlie petitioned for divorce on June 11, 1976. Gene did not contest the petition nor did he
fight for custody of Kelly and Kai. "He never supported the kids," states Carlie. "Never did. And
I never pushed for it. He was supposed to pay the minimum child support, which was I think
$250 a month per child. But, you know what, Kelly and Kai were not a part of his consciousness.
One of the things he knew about me was no matter what he did the boys would be okay. And it's
true. When they started going to L.A. to visit him, there were so many stories. It was just insane.
But they needed to know their dad. I used to tell them, 'Some day your dad will have time just
to be with you guys, but instead of just making three people happy he's out there making hundreds of thousands of people happy.' So I kind of set them up."

Philip remains frustrated with Gene for not seeking joint custody of Kelly and Kai. "They
had wanted a family so Gene was looking forward to children. Then after the divorce, though,
he didn't spend much time with them or do like some fathers do in a situation like that and

demand time with the boys. Carlie would have given him everything he wanted. It wasn't anything they'd have to go to court over. She ended up with custody by default. He didn't contest it. He may have felt they would be better off with her, but he didn't want to be bothered."

Carlie and the boys lived with Mark Kimberly in Hawaii for two years, until the relationship soured. She and the boys then returned to the house on Middle Ridge Road in Albion (Gene had abandoned the house and moved back to Los Angeles by that time). "Mark Kimberly was more of a dad to me than any of the other men in my life at all," claims Kelly. "They were only together a couple of years, but I was five and I was just starting to notice and remember stuff. He taught me how to tie my shoelaces and how to ride a bike, the stuff my dad probably would have loved to do with me, but was too preoccupied with everything else."

Carlie was about to descend into a drug nightmare of her own. She met boyfriend Steve Solomon and for a time she and the boys shuffled between Albion and Steve's home in San Rafael, just north of San Francisco. A serious fall landed her in traction for six months, and Kelly and Kai went to live with their uncle Jim McCummings. "In that time my mom fell off of the Mendocino Headlands and got hepatitis on top of that so she was bedridden for six months," recalls Kelly. "Some other people looked after us and we went to summer camp for a long time, several months, and didn't see our mom." Upon Carlie's recovery, she and the boys moved in with Steve in San Rafael, where Carlie's drug use escalated to freebasing cocaine. "That's when the whole freebase thing started happening for her. This was kind of wacko because I was seven years old and I knew what freebase was and what was going on," Kelly reveals. "I think my brother was a lot more naïve to all that stuff. I was paying attention because it was affecting me and I was more interested in what the grown-ups were doing than in watching cartoons. And that's probably why I'm more of a jaded guy than my brother."

When the relationship with Steve ended, Carlie returned with the boys to the Mendocino area. She settled in Comptche with a French national and later had another child, Indiana. But the drug use continued throughout the 1970s and 1980s and the boys found themselves adrift, shuffled between parents and relatives.

"She was a totally loyal wife, devoted to her kids, when she was with Gene," offers Philip. "She got fucked up with drugs many years later, long after Gene. The late '80s and the 1990s were her drug years. She was not wild at all when she was with Gene. She didn't even drink much before then."

The emotional fallout of the divorce brought forth a rush of new songs from Gene that would inform his next album. "Sister Moon," with its line "You say you need my lovin' but you want to be free and you've made up your mind," and "Lonely Weekend," with its reference to Carlie leaving in lines like "I stepped into a world of living all alone, just a simple note that read I cannot explain why this must be" all point to a man coming to terms with his heartache in song, something at which Gene was already quite adept.

Reunited with Tommy Kaye (who had moved with L.A. socialite wife Hillary Hudson and daughter Eloise to the Albion property next to Philip and Ea) and financed by friend Gary Legon (who was married to porn star Marilyn Chambers) and Hillary's grandmother, Gene booked time at Artie Ripp's Fidelity Recording Studio in Los Angeles in January 1976. (Tom Slocum thinks Eddie Tickner may have also assisted with financing, after Gene leveraged some of his royalties.) Gene's initial plan called for the Silverados to back him in the studio on the songs they had worked up and road tested. As producer, Tommy had other ideas.

"We walked in there with all the Mike Utleys and everybody else and we thought we were going to record it the way we had been playing it and arranging it for the past two years out on the road," Duke complains. "But we got in there and we were way too opinionated for Thomas. I don't think we made it past two sessions before he fired us. I don't think we're on any of that album. It was obvious from the first song that Roger and I were going to teach everybody else how to play the songs, but Thomas Jefferson Kaye figured it was much easier for him to just can us and start from scratch. Gene had to be told what to do anyway. It's like it was a Thomas Jefferson Kaye album of Gene Clark songs. It was, 'Who's making the decisions here and why?' Not only that, but we went to him, Tommy Kaye, afterwards and told him that we had spent two years with Gene, sometimes in professional humiliation, and we had total respect for all these studio musicians that were brought in, but if you're going to let us do all the shit work and then can us then you're going to have to pay us for this. We wanted to be paid along with everyone else on the session. We actually threatened to take them to the union and shut the sessions down. We were so pissed. But we got paid. You have to understand the depths of what it is that we went through to get that far with him. Gene was not a part of all this, it was all Thomas Jefferson Kaye. We never played with Gene again. To be perfectly honest, I thought the stuff we had developed over that time period was raw, and good, and rhythmical, and suited the poetry well. And then they brought in all these slick players and just cleaned it all up. Oh well."

Recruiting seasoned studio players like Mike Utley, Jim Fielder (ex-Blood, Sweat & Tears bass player), Sammy Creason, and Jerry McGhee, and augmenting this basic backing with friends Douglas Dillard, Byron Berline, Al Perkins (from the Flying Burrito Brothers), and Daniel Moore and his brother Matthew from the Moore Brothers Band, the album sessions took on more polish as Tommy steered the ship. Emmylou Harris was invited to sing on two tracks as well. But regardless of the stellar supporting cast, Gene's melancholy frame of mind permeated every track. This time out, Tommy kept the accompaniment understated, though no less shimmering. "Gene wanted it to be a more country-flavored album," Tommy told Viola. "We didn't do the same thing we did with the *No Other* album. That album cost a fortune to make. I still love *Two Sides to Every Story*. It was just a different thing."

With no recording contract and no deadline, sessions ran throughout the year. Gene commuted back and forth between Los Angeles and Albion while Carlie was in Hawaii. Gene's brother Rick had moved in with Gene in Albion, and Tommy was a frequent visitor. "We called ourselves the 'Five Blind Bible Belt Boys,' a real bunch of characters," Tommy laughs during his 1991 interview with Viola. "One was an actor [Jason Ronard], another was Gene's brother [Rick Clark], this older guy, John Desko, a one-eyed, prince-of-darkness kind of guy, and Gene and I."

A newcomer to Gene's inner circle around that time was Tom Slocum. Born in Detroit and a descendant of famed explorer Joshua Slocum, Tom was raised in upstate New York. He had worked in Greenwich Village as an itinerant folksinger in the mid-'60s where he met and married then struggling singer Emmylou Harris, their brief marriage producing daughter Hallie. Always well connected, Tom moved in exclusive circles in both music and film, and his list of credits is impressive. Signed to Dylan manager Albert Grossman's Grosscourt Music, Slocum met Kaye and was with him during production of the *Triumvirate* album in the early '70s. "I got pulled into it more in the 1970s after I signed with Grossman's people," recalls Tom. "They signed me up on the strength of a four-song acoustic demo I did and then they tried to turn me into something I wasn't or I couldn't afford. They had Van Morrison's backup band, all these great players, and musically it was fun to do, but I just couldn't afford to keep those guys. So I couldn't do it. So Tommy Kaye called me up, it was 1975 or 1976, and he says, 'You've got to come back to L.A. and come up to Mendocino,' and it was all carte blanche, they sent the ticket. I had met Gene periodically before that, but never hung out with him. I listened to the Byrds records when I was a kid. But when I first met Gene it was briefly during the Byrds reunion, then I met him again with Tommy Kaye. I listened to the Dillard & Clark stuff in the 1960s when I lived in Nashville and I loved that music. The first album was groundbreaking. When people speak of this whole thing about Gram Parsons I just cover my ears. To me Gene Clark was there already."

Over the next 15 years, Tom and Gene would develop a close relationship, professionally and personally. "I would have people from time to time saying I was Gene's best friend," claims Tom. "I knew him and I pulled him out of some unusual spots. He was a good guy, basically, but he was complex. Part of the relationship that I had with him was based on the fact that he never trusted anybody, not really. It would take years for him to trust someone. I wasn't dependent on Gene Clark, I had my own life, so I wasn't preoccupied with him. I had no axe to grind or anything like that. Part of the reason I got along with these guys is they knew they couldn't con me. They also knew I didn't want to be in a band or be them. I wasn't dependent on them."

"Tommy Slocum is an amazing guy," laughs drummer Andy Kandanes. "When I was in the business, Tommy knew everybody. Tommy's job was to have lunch with everybody, from Clive Davis and Joe Smith to Stevie Wonder and whoever. Tommy was my guy about town; he was like my mouthpiece. 'Tommy, find a deal for me.' He's just an amazing guy. Nobody knows what the hell he does, but he's probably one of the best-known guys in the record business in Hollywood." Former Capitol Records executive Ken Mansfield adds: "Tell me somebody that doesn't know Tommy Slocum. Even when I was on top and you just don't have time for a lot of people, we always took Tommy's calls. Everybody would talk to Slocum and nobody knew why we all talked to him."

David Clark, however, remains wary of Tom. "I would say Tom Slocum was a very good friend of Gene's. Yes, they were very close. But he was a bit of a larcenist. To this day I don't think he's told me the truth about Gene. Him and Gene spent a lot of time together and they were buddies, but the way I saw it, he was Gene's 'Stepin Fetchit' for a long time. He thought there were big things coming from Gene. He befriended Gene during some tough times. I don't think it was all out of caring because he, too, was looking for something to happen."

As the *Two Sides to Every Story* sessions wound down, Gene began looking to assemble a band to go out on the road. He found what he needed right in Mendocino. Andy Kandanes was already working with a local R&B group known as the Mendocino All-Stars and Gene took the rhythm section from that group—Andy, bass player Peter Oliva, Willy James Shay on lead guitar, pianist Colin McNaughton, and a conga player—and christened them the Mendocino Rhythm Section. After a handful of local gigs around Northern California, Colin and the conga player were dropped and Tommy Kaye joined on rhythm guitar, and the group became the KC Southern Band. (The K, some suggest, is for Kaye, and the C is for Clark, though more logically it was a derivative of Gene's "Kansas City Southern," which he had re-recorded for the new album.) Initially Tom Slocum had been invited up to take the rhythm spot, but by the time he arrived, Kaye had stepped in. Rehearsals were held in the barn on Gene's Middle Ridge property where, for a time, many of the band members resided including Peter, a native New Yorker who migrated to Mendocino with Willie Shay. Peter first met a drunken Gene in 1971 when he staggered into Mendocino's Uncommon Good café and joined him onstage in a jam.

Peter recalls the Mendocino Rhythm Section's early incarnation attempting to find a signature sound: "The Mendocino Rhythm Section had some kinks to work out a bit. Some of the guys wanted to play freakin' mambo music or something. We had a conga player for a while and a piano player who was always on acid. It was just a little strange. We'd open up with a George Benson song and I just thought, 'You don't do this kind of music with a Byrd.' So we stopped doing that and we just started doing Gene's songs."

Ken Mansfield first met Gene at the Oaks Café in Yorkville, California, and was knocked out by his new band. He would become another of Gene's confidants. Ken's curriculum vitae is among the most impressive on the L.A. music scene. Working for Capitol Records in the 1960s, he became their representative to the Beatles' Apple Records before going on to produce breakthrough "outlaw" albums by country music renegades Waylon Jennings, Jessi Colter, and Tompall Glaser. Driving up the Northern California coast in search of property to purchase, Ken stopped in Yorkville. "It was pretty much just a café and a gas station at the time," Ken remembers. "We pulled in there to get something to eat and some guy comes over, sits down, and starts talking to me. It turned out it was Tommy Kaye. If you knew Tommy Kaye that was the kind of person he was. He never met a person he didn't know. Gene came over and we all started talking and it was just one of those things where everybody just kind of fell in with each other." Ken stayed to hear the band and was impressed. "This was one of the greatest little bands I had ever heard. They had that country-rock folk thing that Gene had with this real soul thing going through, almost like they had a black rhythm section or something." Ken ended up living close by later and became one of Gene's running buddies when he moved back to Laurel Canyon in the late '70s.

In the midst of rehearsing up at Gene's house, with various band members camped out hither and yon, Gene's parents came out for a visit. It was Kelly and Jeanne's first opportunity to witness their son on his home turf—and they were in for some surprises. "Mom and Dad went out to visit Gene in California one time and they were not happy with the results of that visit," reveals Gene's older sister Bonnie. "He had hangers-on and they were doing drugs and Mom was really bent out of shape about it. That was after Gene and Carlie had split up." Chuckles Peter, "I remember his dad looking like [noted elderly old-time Appalachian folk musician] Roscoe Holcomb." While Kelly took to the rugged rural setting and rustic charm of the 100-year-old former coach house, suggesting structural improvements, landscaping tips, and even going out to the local bars with Gene and company, Jeanne found it difficult to relate to her son and his friends, and her attempts at bringing any semblance of normalcy to the house were viewed as intrusive and unwelcome. "According to Mom, it wasn't much of a visit because she didn't see much of him and did a lot of cooking for a bunch of people," offers David Clark. "But Dad saw more of Gene. He was really more interested in hanging out with Dad and the guys." Slighted, Jeanne returned to Kansas upset and worried over Gene and his wanton lifestyle. Gene had successfully managed to keep his two lives—California and Kansas—separate, until now. "There was stuff going on that Mom didn't like and she was trying to be Mom and got on his case and he got kind of ugly with her," Bonnie confirms. "And I think there was a strain between them that never quite got patched up after that." Jeanne would also have to wait a little longer to meet her two grandsons.

Attempts to find a sympathetic record label for *Two Sides to Every Story* proved difficult. Gene's reputation in the music industry was widespread. "When we did the *Two Sides* album, he hadn't recorded in a long time," Tommy explained to Viola. "We did that record independently and we brought that record to every label—Columbia, Capitol, RCA, Geffen—we brought it to everybody. The last stop was RSO. At the time, RSO was the number one label and to get on that label wasn't easy. The president, Al Coury, and Robert Stigwood heard a song called 'Black Lung Miner' ["Give My Love to Marie"] and they said, 'Man, we want to sign Gene Clark.' They loved that song. That's what got him on RSO."

Released in February 1977 on the RSO label, then best known for disco acts (RSO stands for Robert Stigwood Organization, the man behind *Saturday Night Fever* and the Bee Gees), *Two Sides to Every Story* was a much more subdued effort than *No Other*. Somewhat of a dog's breakfast, the album careened from a weak cover of 1950s rockabilly chestnut "Marylou" (a mistake Gene later regretted, says Slocum) to the retro Conway Twitty/Floyd Cramer style of "Lonely Saturday," the subtle and delicate flourishes of piano and strings on Gene's highly personal and poignant "Past Addresses," "Sister Moon," and "Silent Crusade" (all metaphors for his current heartache), to a hard rockin' rendition of "Kansas City Southern, which, despite a more contemporary feel, pales in comparison to the original. As Tom Slocum notes, "Tommy and Gene thought that 'Kansas City Southern' had a more rock 'n' roll FM radio appeal, very CCR and John Fogerty. They wanted a hit. The record company wanted a hit. They thought 'Kansas City Southern' was it."

With far more impressive original compositions from Gene, such as "Wheel of Time," "What Is Meant Will Be," and "Daylight Line," the decision to include these tracks is bewildering. The schizophrenic nature of the album is also found in its style, part country-rock ("Home Run King" and "In the Pines"), part folk ballad ("Give My Love to Marie," "Past Addresses," and "Hear the Wind"), and part 1950s retread. Perhaps chastened by his *No Other* experience, Tommy exercises admirable restraint in his arrangements throughout the album, though his use of strings on singer-songwriter James Talley's "Give My Love to Marie" is slightly over the top. "I don't recall a strong personality from Tommy in leading those sessions," states Al Perkins, whose subtle pedal steel guitar work graces several tracks. "Gene was pretty much in charge." One wonders what the album might have sounded like had the Silverados been allowed to complete the sessions.

"I think it is more mature lyrically in one main respect, because the statements are simplified to where they are better understood," Gene revealed to *Dark Star*'s Steve Burgess in 1977, comparing the album to *No Other*. "I'm just saying that my feeling is that it is more mature lyrically in my own writing, in the songs that I wrote. The statements that are made are made without leaving an abstract question, even though it may contain abstract images, but the end result of that statement is what it means."

Once again the songwriting was introspective and personal, but for those who were privy to the recent upheaval in Gene's life, his wounded heart was clearly on his sleeve. Insists David Clark, "Almost everything he wrote was about a personal experience, a personal feeling, things around him, or an ideology, something that he believed in. For example, when he and Carlie split up, a lot of songs came out of that." If *White Light* was his response to the reclusive tranquility of the Northern California coast, and *No Other* his meditation on the meaning of life after becoming a father, then *Two Sides to Every Story* represents his stark reality check: a broken heart. Although, according to Carlie, Gene never wrote a song specifically about her, he was directing his writing her way on this album. "Gene was one of the people who couldn't sit down and discuss what he felt inside with most people," avers Rick Clark. "His pain came out through his art, his writing. And even though it was heartbreaking and very emotional, he created some of his most beautiful songs and work through expressing those feelings."

"Gene always had a broken heart," Tommy claimed to Viola. "He had a hard time with women. He was a romantic, very romantic. He was so sentimental and took everything so seriously. You always felt something was breaking his heart, whether a woman or a fantasy. He was this driven, heartbroken, emotionally beat-up guy. Gene kept everything inside him. He couldn't turn it around. The poor guy, he could never get to a place where he could be happy. He had a lot of fantasies and that's what made him such a great writer. He really believed his fantasies. He had this big thing for [actress] Sally Field. I lived through that whole Sally Field fantasy and he never met her! I had to watch the same movie with him ten times because she was in it. He had these fantasies about her and he actually started believing that him and Sally were going to get together. He would be talking like, 'Me and Sally are going to do this and that.' It was like it was really happening for him."

Perhaps most striking was the album cover of *Two Sides to Every Story*. In an effort to distance himself from the glam rock space oddity pictured on *No Other*, Gene is instead presented in full beard, blue jeans, cowboy boots, and flannel checked jacket, like some cosmic lumberjack or mountain man, in keeping with his Mendocino persona. The back cover close-up of a beaming Gene is as strangely off-putting as the glam shot on *No Other*. The setting is the house on Middle Ridge Road and the point is emphatic: this is the real me. The presence of toys and a picnic table are another message to Carlie: "I am the father of two boys who are no longer with me." Rick points out another clue to Gene's lifestyle: "In the photograph on the *Two Sides to Every Story* album where he's sitting on the picnic table, there are bullet holes in the table where we would shoot at cans and bottles from the back porch with Gene's guns. He had a Japanese army rifle and a Winchester that David Crosby had given him, an antique. You can see the bullet holes in the table if you look close enough."

Knife gouges are also visible in the table. "Gene and I became very adept at knife throwing," boasts Rick. "We used to do that at the house in Albion. We would sit in the kitchen and get out all the butcher knives and throw them at this plank wall beside the giant woodstove, to a point where we wore a hole from sticking all these knives in it that he had to cut a window into the wall. Later on when I worked with him and Pat Robinson and John York up in Topanga Canyon on the CRY [Clark, Robinson, York] stuff we would take breaks and have marathon dart competitions. And when we got bored with that we would take knives and throw them. Then Gene picked up this pick ax and just went underhanded and threw it and it stuck in the wall of Pat's studio. I'd never seen anyone make a pick ax stick in something. Gene could do that."

Reviews of the album were mixed. Barry Ballard, writing in *ZigZag*, voiced the opinions of most, declaring, "While *Two Sides to Every Story* is not likely to disappoint those of you who have eagerly awaited its release, at the same time it does not contain any real surprises, as did *No Other*, for instance." He goes on to praise Gene's voice, citing it as one of the finest in rock and Gene as "a songwriter of exceptional merit." Despite a more accessible sound than its predecessor, sales were meager and promotion spotty, especially after Gene reportedly insulted label head Al Coury. "Gene's drug and alcohol problems really burned out a lot of people," Peter Oliva notes. "He did that thing with Al Coury, the RSO guy."

As Tommy explained to Viola in 1991: "We cut the *Two Sides* album and Al Coury wanted to meet Gene, have dinner with him. He'd heard how crazy he was. So Al takes him to Dan Tana's and Al's with his lovely wife. I didn't go. Al's talking about Eric Clapton, the Bee Gees, and what RSO records is all about, trying to give him some insight into the label. All Gene had to do was be cool and we'd get $100,000 the next day. Gene's drinking martinis and all of a sudden he leans across the table and looks at Al. And Gene says to Al, 'All you want to do is fuck your wife in front of me,' and he's got his boots up on the table, that whole thing. I called Gene up later to ask him how it went and he tells me, 'Oh, man, I really fucked up.' I said, 'What'd you do?' and he tells me. I went crazy. 'You fuckin' lunatic!' The next day Al Coury calls me up and he says, 'Gene's really got a problem,' and I go, 'Uh, oh, there goes the deal.' Then Al says to me, 'I was going to give you a hundred grand but I'm going to give you $125,000. He's got a problem and I want to help.' Now *that's* a sweet man. That's how much he believed in Gene. That was the side that most people saw of Gene and said, 'Fuck him!' People didn't want to work with him because he could be like that to them. But he never meant that stuff. It was a part of that anger thing and that hurt thing he had and the only way he could get it out was to do that. There were really two sides to him; that's why I came up with the title. There was the side that I really knew. He was like the biggest teddy bear. But he could also scare a lot of people, too. When he got drinking he was one of those guys who got a little nasty. Never with me because I would collar him and I'm a skinny little dude." (The popular belief about the title *Two Sides to Every Story* is that it evokes Gene's recent split with Carlie.)

With an album to promote the KC Southern Band hit the road and stopped at the Troubadour in mid April before heading out to Europe—Gene's first overseas trip since the Byrds' 1965 UK tour. By the time the band hit the stage at Gene's old stomping grounds they were tight, confident, and their set list featured several recent collaborations between Gene and Tommy intended for their next album project together. These included "Forgive Me Girl" (later re-titled "Release Me Girl"), the dynamic "Taken by Surprise," "Crazy Ladies" (with a co-credit to Hillary Kontos), "Last of the Blue Diamond Miners" (a compelling, Neil Young-influenced collaboration between Gene, Tommy, and Bobby Neuwirth, who came up with the title and the line 'last of the red hot mainliners,' according to Tom Slocum), "Seventh Avenue Train," better known as "Hula Mula Man" (not Bula, as is often written), Tommy's "Shades of Blue," and "For Nickels and Dimes" (also known as "Denver or Whenever"). Recorded in demo form at Chappel Music and Fidelity studios in 1977, these new songs identified Gene and Tommy as a potent writing team, with Tommy bringing a whole new musical palette of major and minor seventh chords and elaborate choruses to Gene's insightful lyrics. Tommy told Barry Ballard he was initially reluctant to initiate the partnership: "I had never really wanted to play any of my songs for Gene because he was a writer and I didn't want him to feel I was trying to be pushy like a lot of producers are in getting their material onto albums that they're producing."

"A lot of great material was created during that time period," acknowledges Tom Slocum. "Those years when the band broke from Mendocino and went back to L.A. were very fertile and productive years from a songwriting, production, collaborative point of view." Regrettably, much of their music would never be officially released, but what exists in demo form, along with a handful of live tapes, reveals the KC Southern Band as Gene's finest backing band.

Andy raves about their Troubadour gig. "Everybody was there—Bob Dylan, Joan Baez. The place was packed. We did a phenomenal show, one of the best shows we ever did, and got a standing ovation. We walked upstairs to the dressing room and I'm standing next to Tommy Kaye and Gene, and Bob Dylan comes up and says, 'That was one of the best shows I've seen.' And he looks at me and says, 'Man, you're one hell of a drummer.' Then he turns and talks to someone else and Tommy says to me, 'Hey, that was Bob Dylan! That's worth a lot of money, man.' So I pulled out my wallet and Gene looks at me and says, 'Not yet.'"

Old friend Daniel Moore attended the Troubadour show and remembers being impressed with more than just the music. "Full house, a lot of people, the music was doing good. Gene was sounding fine. They did the first set and then they're getting ready to do the second set and they're going, 'Where's Gene?' Well, finally they found him and they get up and start their set. Gene sings half of a song and then he runs offstage and runs upstairs to the balcony. The band kept playing, Tommy Kaye's playing rhythm guitar, and they kept the groove going because they don't know where Gene is and they were waiting for him to come back onstage. Several minutes later, above the stage, Gene is up on the rafters, 20 feet high. And he's like an athlete, Tarzan, going from beam to beam, and the crowd went wild. It was one of the funniest things I'd ever seen in my life. And he got down off there without being killed, which was a miracle."

Following their triumphant Troubadour debut (Gene had displayed similar but less appreciated climbing antics at the Whisky years before), the KC Southern Band welcomed the rush of well-wishers, media, and friends backstage. Among those present to pass along their congratulations was a woman from Gene's past, Terri Messina (no relation to musician Jim Messina). Soon after his return from the European tour in May, Gene and Terri would embark on the most tempestuous, on-again, off-again relationship of his life—for the next 14 years. She would replace Carlie as the love of his life, but like that relationship, this one would see creative peaks punctuated by increasing chemical dependencies, abusive behavior, and irrational bouts. Gene's personal life was beginning to unravel just as his professional career was taking off in the company of old friends.

7

Past Addresses

Gene's return to public performances in the mid-to late '70s came at a steep price. His panic disorder, manifested in severe performance anxiety, and his manic-depressive behavior were only placated (and exacerbated) by an increasing reliance on alcohol and drugs. Months out on the road only intensified this abuse. The need to sustain a career from Los Angeles drew him more and more back into the lifestyle he had come to loathe and from which he had fled in the late '60s. Still reeling from the failure of his masterwork, *No Other*, Gene's career was in free fall and his marriage in ruins. The country comforts of his Mendocino lifestyle with his family and close friendship circle had all been supplanted by a whole new pack of associates, many with their own personal agendas for attaching themselves to the fading aura of the ex-Byrd. To them, Gene was still a legend, and the chance to share a bump of coke with a bona fide star was attraction enough to endure the increasing bouts of depression and violence he would often exhibit. But while many of these acquaintances could handle the pace, Gene couldn't. Their use of alcohol and drugs in his presence only intensified his own addiction problems. In addition, the new woman in his life would make hard drugs readily accessible to Gene, tipping him further into the abyss.

There are those close to Gene who submit that he had a fear of success and whenever it came close his self-destruct mechanism activated. "He couldn't handle fame at all," insists Roger McGuinn, who would team up with his former Byrd buddy in the late '70s only to see Gene blow it all off through increasingly self-abusive behavior. "He really had a problem with that. When fame would come he would do things to sabotage it for himself. He did that in McGuinn, Clark & Hillman and we had to let him go because of that, unfortunately." There is certainly a clear pattern throughout Gene's career to support this assertion. In the 1990s, following Gene's death, longtime fan Deb Johnson corresponded regularly with Jeanne Clark, who shared her reflections and insights concerning her son. "She often said that Gene could no more cope with fame and success than he could deal with failure," Deb reveals. "His life became a two-edged sword."

Record producer Ken Mansfield had seen similar behavior before, both in Gene and other artists. He suggests that Gene was better off away from celebrity and acclaim. "There was a pattern that Gene had and it's something I noticed and maybe others did, too. When he was not doing well in the business, success-wise, was when he seemed to do better as a person on his own. But the minute the success would start to happen he would get heavy back on the road and heavy into the corporate requirements of being an artist or of being a star—agents, managers, record companies, tour people—all this establishment stuff. Then it just seemed like it would freak him out and he would get crazy. A lot of it was that many of these people were not his kind of people and all of a sudden he was thrown into another realm, as far as who he would personally like to be with. When success would come, it meant going back on the road again and the road made Gene crazy, drove him nuts, the rigors of the road and the scheduling and all that. And when Gene got crazy he could get scary. He could be pretty volatile. You knew that if things started to happen for him he was going to take flight on you. That was pretty well known. He was too sensitive for the music business. That was the cowboy thing, the country boy thing."

In an effort to provide some family support in the wake of Carlie's departure, brothers Rick and David moved up to the property on Middle Ridge Road to comfort Gene. While Rick had witnessed his older brother's recent emotional decline and the influx of a new cabal of friends, David, who arrived in February 1977, was unprepared for the bacchanalian scene surrounding Gene. David's last visit had been during the recording of the second Dillard & Clark album, when Gene was king of the Sunset Strip.

"In the fall of 1976 I had just about had it with what I was doing," notes David, who had relocated to Missouri by then, "and I got talking to Gene and he said, 'Man, I really need you out here. You could help me rebuild this place.' He and Philip O'Leno had done quite a bit of work on the house getting it livable, but there were a bunch of old pumps and stuff and he was explaining some things to me. I was telling him stuff about them because that's my profession, machinery. So he said, 'Man, you've got to come out here.' We talked about it several times. Then at the first of the year in 1977, Mom and Dad had come out to visit him. That was their first trip out there and Gene had bought them a train ride there and back. I talked with Dad after they came back and he said, 'Well, it's a pretty nice place and he's talking about you coming out there and helping him with it.' So I loaded up my four kids and my wife at the time in a 1969 Ford Econoline van and drove out to Northern California to help him rebuild his farm. That was my intention for going. Well, it didn't take long for things to kind of disintegrate. They had a lot of problems and the drug usage was the mainstay of it. A lot of that was around everywhere. When we first got there, the first month or so, there were parties and one evening we had a big barbecue and Emmylou Harris was there along with several celebrities. My brother Kevin was out with us for a brief time because there were all these grandiose plans Gene had that all just evaporated. We spent a month making all these plans. We were living in the barn that I had refurbished. Rick was already there. I think Gene was trying to bring that nucleus of the family back around him. We were all playing some kind of desperados thing. We all had full beards and we had all kinds of crazy experiences." Those fraternal hijinks included terrorizing patrons at local bars with mock fights and hatchet throwing as well as playing pranks on local groupies.

"He was really frustrated at that point," muses David. "Here he was trying to put this band together, trying to get his career back on track, had an excellent album out, and he couldn't get these people together to even make a resemblance of what was on that album and that was frustrating for him." But did Gene compound the problems with his own habits? "Yes, always," David confirms.

Following their celebrated Troubadour stand, the KC Southern Band left for a brief tour of the UK in the company of Roger McGuinn and Chris Hillman, each fronting their own bands and performing separately. Gene, whose public profile was the lesser of the three, would open the shows followed by Chris and Roger. From a promotional standpoint the tour was a masterstroke, playing on UK fans' enduring affection for the Byrds collectively while each artist promoted his own recent solo project: Roger's *Thunderbyrd* album for CBS, Chris's *Slippin' Away* on Asylum, and Gene's RSO debut, *Two Sides to Every Story*. Despite the *New Musical Express (NME)* labeling them "repetitive and indistinctive," the KC Southern Band offered a solid set of astonishing new material like "Last of the Blue Diamond Miners," "Boll Weevil," and "Release Me Girl," all played with a raw urgency relying prominently on Willie James Shay's distorted lead guitar work.

There were, however, few familiar favorites from Gene's back catalog, as UK writer Barry Ballard suggests. "I recall a great disappointment and unfamiliarity with much of the material," he later recalled of the Hammersmith show, "with 'Silver Raven' and 'Sister Moon' being the only representatives of Gene's most recent solo albums. A 'greatest hits' portion of the set simply didn't materialize. For UK fans, who had waited so long to see him, it might have been more appropriate to substitute older, more familiar songs for some of the newer or unknown material." Reviewing the concert for *Melody Maker,* Allan Jones echoed the sentiment, saying that Gene's unique musical personality, evident on the songs "White Light" and "No Other," was "suffocated by his band," which he declared as brash and aggressive. The *NME* described Gene in his bearded mountain man guise as "the epitome of the slightly stumbling, overweight, bearded hippie who drank and smoked too much."

Despite a strong if unfamiliar performance, the band was already falling apart and any anticipated camaraderie between the three Byrds frontmen (touted in the media before the tour started—even suggesting a potential full-fledged Byrds reunion) never materialized. Opening in Dublin on April 27, 1977, the tour was fraught with problems as it made its way to the Hammersmith Odeon for two sold-out nights (April 30 and May 1, recorded by the BBC and later released as *Three Byrds Land in London*) before the wheels came off the cart altogether.

As KC Southern Band bass player Peter Oliva recalls, "Chris Hillman was picking at Roger all the time. Picking and picking at him. But Roger asked for it. He's like one of those guys that you pin stuff on their back in the school hall, like 'kick me.' He's just one of those guys. Hillman quit the tour. He was mad at McGuinn. All I know is that we got the promoter in our hotel room and we told him he wasn't going to leave except through the window unless he paid us something. So he did pay us something. That tour was actually going pretty good, but Hillman had a stick up his ass and Roger's just a dick, period. He's not a nice man."

On the opening night of the Hammersmith Odeon stand, the oft-speculated reunion did, indeed, take place. Following Roger's set, with heads wrapped in towels à la Bob Dylan's Rolling Thunder Revue, Gene and Chris emerged from the wings to join Roger for rousing renditions of "So You Want to Be a Rock 'n' Roll Star," "I'll Feel a Whole Lot Better," "Mr. Tambourine Man," and "Eight Miles High," much to the delight of the enraptured audience. Unfortunately the bonhomie was short-lived and no more reunions took place onstage. Unbeknownst to most at the time, the three ex-Byrds were contractually bound to present a Byrds mini-set at each concert. Several observers noted that the three ex-Byrds failed to take the obligatory onstage reunion component of the contract seriously. After a concert in Leeds, Chris abruptly quit the tour, citing inequities in the financial terms between the three headliners. "The agent had not paid us," he explained years later. "We didn't have travel paid for the next destination. I gave him 24 hours and then I said to Roger and Gene, 'I'm leaving.' This guy was taking advantage of us. They stayed for another couple of shows, and then they left."

Roger and Gene did carry on with the tour briefly, appearing in Glasgow on May 5, where Gene, visibly inebriated, staggered onstage to join a perturbed Roger for "Mr. Tambourine Man." Chris's departure appeared to dash any hopes of the speculated Byrds reunion and pointed to long-festering animosity within the Byrds camp.

Stranded in Europe with no money to get his band and entourage home, Gene called brother David back at the farm in Albion. David had already staked the band some seed money to get the tour off the ground. "I had put some investment money into it that I had gotten out of selling my business," he states. "When they first left, things were already kind of rough with the band. Tommy Kaye and some of the people weren't getting along and there was some rough weather. Well, it all came apart. Gene called me from Paris, France, at three o'clock in the morning. 'Where in the hell is the money?!' And I said, 'What are you talking about?' He said, 'I'm here in Paris, France, with an eight-piece band and there's no money here for us. We've got about six bucks between us.' What happened, or what I was later told, was that there was a joker in the deck that ripped off the funds for the tour. And there were other things that happened. Up until that point, it looked great. They wouldn't let them out of Dublin or Liverpool they played so well. They loved him over there. So I borrowed $5,000 to get them back to New York and never saw any of it because when they got back, it just got worse. I had gone out there in early February and I left in the middle of June with nothing. I had to get my children back home, back around people who could help us take care of them, until I got things straightened out."

Following a smattering of gigs, the KC Southern Band ground to a halt amid allegations of rampant drug and alcohol abuse and creative differences. The *Two Sides to Every Story* album had sunk without a trace and Gene again found himself without a record label, despite a war chest of spectacular new songs. He took the lull as an opportunity to pack up and move from Albion back to Los Angeles. He ceded the Middle Ridge property to Carlie and the boys and moved into a house on Stanley Hills in Laurel Canyon with his new mate, Terri Messina. For Gene, it was a case of out of the frying pan and into the fire.

Born into a wealthy family, Terri Messina's father was a prominent Los Angeles physician who raised his children in luxury and comfort, wanting for nothing. Her upbringing was everything Gene's wasn't—something Gene came to envy and a fact that she often played against the unpretentious Kansas boy. "Gene had all his brothers and sisters, 13 children in that family," states Terri, "and they weren't a wealthy family, so Gene never had any clue about money or investments or anything like that. I was raised quite differently. We weren't millionaires, but my father was a successful doctor and my grandmother was in real estate and had her own escrow company so I was very oriented toward buying and owning property, investment money, and all that sort of thing. So we were like night and day when it came to things like that. I always thought it was such a shame that he never had anybody that could help him with things like that at the beginning, when he was making a lot of money. It was all wasted away. He hated to take care of business, which was really too bad because when he did take care of business he was a really intelligent person and he could do things very well. It's just that he didn't like to do it. I used to tell him, 'Just because you're an artist doesn't mean you get off free. Nobody likes to pay taxes and keep records, but you have to do that.'" Indeed, Terri discovered that Gene was deeply in arrears on his taxes and arranged a schedule of repayment to eventually clear that up.

Following graduation in 1963, Terri enrolled in theatre arts at UCLA but left after two and a half years to act professionally, finding work in commercials and small productions while attending acting classes. She was sharing a house with three dancers in the Hollywood Hills in 1966 the first time she met Gene. "We had a New Year's Eve party and Gene came to the party and that was how I met him," notes Terri. "Gene and I started going out together after that party for about six months, very intimate and close, supposedly all in love and everything." The affair was brief, although Terri continued to harbor affection for the handsome, brooding singer-songwriter.

A surprising catalyst of the affair was mutual friend "English Roger" Willis (who later introduced Gene and Carlie to Philip and Ea in Albion). Roger had come to Los Angeles from London in the early '60s and worked in the film business, often as a stunt man and driver, when he befriended Gene at the Whisky-A-Go Go while tending bar. The two became close friends. It was English Roger who brought Gene to Terri's New Year's Eve party in 1966. (Ironically, before Gene and Terri hooked up again in the late '70s, Roger and Terri shared a house in Laurel Canyon, and Roger later lived briefly with Gene in Sherman Oaks.)

In the 1970s, Terri resided in France before returning to Los Angeles and rekindling her relationship with Gene. In marked contrast with Carlie Clark, the glamorous, diminutive brunette was far more enamored with the Hollywood lifestyle and less inclined to woodstoves and dirt roads.

"He kept the Mendocino property for a while," she confirms. "He was going through a divorce with his wife. He and I actually went up there and stayed once or twice, but it was really not my cup of tea. It was very, very funky. Even though my house in Laurel Canyon was rustic as well, I had a very together household and that place up there was a mess from my standards, and a little too rustic for my tastes. No one was really living there except for Gene's brother David, who was staying there with his wife. I think Carlie did live there for a while before it was sold. But when the divorce finally got settled it was part of the settlement. Really the only thing that they had financially left was that one piece of property. That was the only piece of property Gene ever owned in his life, which I always thought was a terrible shame."

"Terri was a very sophisticated woman," avers Tom Slocum. "She was the daughter of a doctor. She was a very smart person. She may have had chemical problems, but what attracted Gene to her was not the drugs. She had that aura of sophistication; she came from a good family. She was a very pretty woman in her youth. When the band broke camp to come back to L.A., I had a little place over on Beechwood Drive, Tommy Kaye and Hillary had a place in Laurel Canyon, and Terri had a place down the road from Tommy and Hillary. At that time Gene was staying with Tommy and Hillary, then suddenly he's living with Terri. We had good times. But the drug dealer trip caught up with both of them. She got cleaned up, but she got nailed too."

By the time Gene moved in with Terri in the summer of 1977, she was no longer pursuing an acting career. Laterally working in film editing, she was better known in exclusive circles as a supplier of cocaine. "My thing with that, talking about being a drug dealer, was mainly with friends," she clarifies, now clean and sober since the mid-'80s. "It wasn't like I was standing on a street corner dealing some drugs. To me it happened by accident because it just so happened that I got connected with people who had the things that people wanted and then people would ask me, 'Can you get me this? Are you gonna get me that?' At the beginning I was really not into it at all. And then I started doing it so much for favors that finally I decided I should make some money off of it because I was putting myself at risk all the time. So there definitely was a period when I was doing it and making money at it and doing so-called drug dealing." Asked whether she feels her access to drugs exacerbated Gene's own drug problems, Terri demurs. "That's a hard question to answer. Obviously, if I had them around and it made it more easy for him to get to them, then yes. But at the same time I, myself, was not the kind of person to want to see anybody screwed up and so I wouldn't be like just handing them out that freely to him. And at the same time, every time we ever split up he managed to get them all by himself without any trouble, without me being around. Many other people were using all the time. Certainly his drug problems were not just because of me, that's for sure."

Guitarist Garth Beckington was a friend from Gene's Mendocino period who worked with him off and on between 1981 and 1991. He later married Tommy Kaye's ex-wife Hillary and the two were known drug users. Garth confirms Terri's drug connections. "Yeah. She won't admit this, but she was involved in the supply side. They were together a long time. But consider the times. I don't think she introduced Gene to drugs. Gene was also not going to go out and cop drugs on his own. He wasn't that kind of gregarious guy, either. She made it very easy. It was always there. You can't say if he hadn't been with Terri, would he have gotten deep into drugs because, you know, that's a stupid thing. But she always had drugs."

Stresses Philip O'Leno, "When he left here finally and moved to Los Angeles and moved in with Terri Messina, he made the biggest mistake of his life because she was a coke dealer and had a lot of really good cocaine and heroin. And that's when he started going crazy, when he hooked up with her, what I consider crazy."

In Terri's company, Gene began to move in high-flying circles. The entire Laurel Canyon lifestyle revolved around cocaine and Gene fell into line, becoming a legendary partier. "That was the peak in Hollywood and for all of us, when the drug thing was just at the heaviest," admits Ken Mansfield. "When you said hi to someone, when they walked into the room, they'd say, 'Who's got the blow?' That was the whole thing. We all hung out at the Troubadour and at the Roxy on the Strip. We would just go out together. There was a real concentrated time when we would be out on the Strip almost every night. Someone would be playing someplace and it was that kind of word on the street thing where we would all end up hanging out together. A lot of it came out of the Troubadour because you would get your news from the Troubadour and proceed from there. It was a pretty hard-roaring group of people and Gene fit in well. Garth Beckington was around then too, in those days in Laurel Canyon. That particular point in my life, and most of us, was the craziest time of all, when we all were into drugs the most. Tommy's house was one of the houses we hung out at a lot. David Carradine was my neighbor in Laurel Canyon. Our two properties were side by side. David had a group called Water. I could tell you some wild Canyon stories. I had the old Lash LaRue estate up in the Canyon, which was a big place up there. Looking back it's not a nice memory. Even though we thought we were having a good time at that time, I don't think we really were. Shortly after Tommy's Kaye's little girl, Eloise, died in an unfortunate accident, it just seemed like everybody's life got dark and we all kind of lost hope there for a while. I think I had more of a survival nature and less tolerance for the way it was going down.

"Gene was a cowboy in a way," Ken continues. "He was kind of like the rancher who came in off the range and partied hard when he came in because he had to go back and work hard the next week. That's kind of what Gene was like, in a way. He could be very reclusive, too. Sometimes he had that combination of either not being available, or if he was around, he wasn't being a good guy—he was being a bad boy. So you had either he wasn't around, or if he was around, he wasn't being good. That's not a great combination. Gene wasn't like your social beings that got dressed up real nice and got there early and wanted to make friends. That wasn't Gene. Maybe he wasn't the life of the party, but sometimes he would be the center of attention. I'm not a psychologist, but it's possible that he was manic-depressive. That was part of his nature to be up and then down. He would come and knock out the club one night and the next day be so sweet to you. He was also that real nice, good-hearted country boy, too. That was the other side of him."

Ken recounts one of Gene's episodes: "I had an artist called Scarlet who had just got through a lot of hard work to headline at the Whisky as an unknown artist. That's how you broke out of L.A. and we pulled that off. And when you got to headline at the Whisky you got your famous friends to come down. That's what made your opening night a big deal. So Gene, because he was the famous Byrd and a close friend, was going to come down. But he got really out of it that night before he got there. He was used to coming in the stage door at the Whisky, which ran up along the side of the building in back. The stage door guy would always let him in, but this time he was stopped at the stage door by a security guy. Gene wasn't going to accept that, so he pushed passed this guy and started up the stairs and another security guy stopped him. The conversations got pretty bad and it ended up Gene starts to deck the guy. They get into a big brawl and the other security guy jumps in and pretty soon the whole thing rolls down the stairs into the edge of the stage area where people are sitting. The end result, because of the brouhaha, was that they closed us down that night and threw us out of the club. And afterwards, in his character like the old cowboy, the next day when he'd sobered up, he would come to you with his hat in his hand and his head bowed and say, 'I'm so sorry, man.' It was just so lovingly sincere that it was hard to be mad at the guy despite what he had done." And whatever became of Scarlet? "Nothing. That night with Gene may have been the turning point," laughs Ken.

In his 1995 autobiography, *Endless Highway,* David Carradine describes an altercation at his house between Gene and Bob Dylan during this dark period. An inebriated, belligerent Gene accosted Dylan, berating him as "a no-talent wimp" and claiming that he would have been nothing without the Byrds. David claims that Gene, wielding a pool cue, went after Dylan, but was intercepted. No one close to Gene at the time corroborates the story, though they do not deny that he was subject to drunken rages. Fueled by copious quantities of cocaine and other drugs, Gene and Terri's relationship was often explosive and the two frequently tangled. "She'd let him stay with her and sometimes she wouldn't," Garth notes. "He was always getting thrown out and then reinstated, then thrown out. You must have seen that kind of relationship before, the yo-yo kind of affair." On more than one occasion the confrontations turned physical. "That's true," admits Terri. "One time Gene did it and my brother came over and gave him a sock in the eye. He socked him; he didn't beat him up. He had a big black eye and my brother told him, 'Don't you ever hit my sister again!' That was one time. And then another time this very close friend of mine, my very first boyfriend from when I was 14, who had remained a friend of mine over the years, and he was a rough guy because he happens to be a Hell's Angel, happened to be at my house visiting me during a time when Gene and I were split up. And Gene came over to my house drunk, climbed over the fence, and broke the front door down. He came smashing in the house all drunk and started threatening me physically. And my friend beat him up. That time he really got beaten up bad. It wasn't something I advocated either. It was a horrible experience and I was screaming and yelling for him to stop. I, myself, called the police and tried to get them over there. But that wasn't my brother. My brother only gave him a black eye once." (Gene was hospitalized after the incident with the Hell's Angel.)

"Gene had an apartment that was under this house in Laurel Canyon and I had an apartment next door and we spent a lot of time together," offers drummer Greg Thomas, who was working with Roger McGuinn at the time. "Terri wouldn't let him live with her because he was kind of a maniac at the time and she had other dealings going on. It seems to me like he would spend a couple of days there and then leave for a couple of days, go home and crash, wake up a couple of days later and go back over there for a couple of days. She lived about five minutes away. He was insanely in love with her, possessed. He would drive himself mad if he had a fight with her. It seems like he was always over there begging forgiveness. It was a very volatile relationship." Adds Garth, "She was pretty much the woman in his life the rest of his life. I know that he asked her to marry him many, many times, but she never did."

"Terri was not good for Gene at all," insists Rick Clark. "She was a bad force in Gene's life, very bad for him. He loved her but it was kind of a fatalist kind of love."

In the midst of his tempestuous relationship with Terri, Gene returned to the stage as a solo performer at the Hollywood Canteen. The gigs, organized by compadre Tom Slocum, were low-key, in keeping with Gene's general discomfort with performing before an audience. "Gene was living in Laurel Canyon with Terri and looking for something to do," Tom recounts. "So I called him up and told him I had this place and he could come down here and play. He wasn't the kind of guy to go out and hustle to play. The Hollywood Canteen was down by the Improvisation on Melrose and in some ways it was a wonderful musical free-for-all. So I convinced him to come down and play like more than once or twice a week. This was before he got back together with McGuinn. Looking back on it now, it was Jean Ray of Jim and Jean, and myself, there was a young Garth Beckington, who at the time could play rings around anyone, a really wonderful guitar player. So I got Gene to come down and have some fun because music wasn't always fun for him. I tried to say, 'Look, there's no hype in all this. It's just going to be fun.' I could book the place, I could play the place, and I could have comedy for half an hour if I wanted, as long as I brought people into the venue. And that was McGuinn and Clark's first gig, when they decided to get back together, at the Hollywood Canteen."

Before that gig, Gene had accepted an offer from Roger to tour together as solo acoustic acts. "I was doing a tribute concert for some anniversary of the Troubadour," Roger recalls of the September 1977 show that precipitated his reunion with Gene. "Gene was in the audience and I invited him up to do 'Eight Miles High' with me. It went over great and afterwards Gene's friend Tommy Kaye said, 'Why don't you guys do a duo?' Neither of us was doing anything at the time. I was between bands and things and so was Gene. I asked my agent, Ron Rainey, 'Do you think you

Former Bryds Gene and Roger McGuinn tour as a duo, late 1977.

could book us as a duo?' So he checked out the situation and got back to me and said, 'Yeah, there's some interest out there. Do you want to do that?' And we said, 'Sure, let's go for it.' So we booked a tour as 'Roger McGuinn and Gene Clark' and it was great fun. We really enjoyed it. In fact Gene said later that was one of his favorite things, when we were just doing that acoustic duo."

Back in 1971, when he worked for the Agency for the Performing Arts (APA), New York-based Ron Rainey had been agent for the latter-day Byrds featuring Roger and Clarence White. The following year Ron relocated to Los Angeles, where he continued to work with Roger throughout his solo career. He also represented Roger and the Thunderbyrd band on the ill-fated UK tour in 1977. "At the end of the Thunderbyrd era, things slowed down for Roger and he wanted to do some solo dates. Around that time he told me he had been talking with Gene. I knew Gene a little bit. I had met him along the course of the way with Roger, and Gene had approached me about representing him with some of his solo albums, but I never did. I thought it was kind of a conflict of interest at the time. But I knew him. Then Roger asked if I could get them some gigs. And I did. I got them some local jobs around L.A., but didn't put them on the road at first. I always found that when something got Roger's attention it really got Roger's attention. He could be mercurial. He would change his mind. But when Roger got into this with Gene he saw it as a way of getting back to what he was, a folkie, and doing acoustic shows with Gene. Roger had been carrying everything on his back since the Byrds broke up—solo guy, and with the various incarnations of bands and Thunderbyrds—and the pressure on him was just too much. When Gene came around it was, 'Okay, here's somebody to share the burden with and someone who can contribute, write the songs, and we can tap into our legacy and we don't have a band to cart around,' so it was all positives for him. It was a good feeling for Roger. And Gene wanted to do it, too."

By October, Roger and Gene were touring nationwide. At a stop in Toronto, Gene expressed his delight with the duo to an interviewer at CHUM radio. "There is definitely a cycle happening. The fact that both of us feel comfortable performing a folkier show at this point and actually doing a concert set involving the audience in singing and participating in the show with us without electrified instruments—not that we have any prejudice against electric instruments—it's just that it's time to do this again, to stand up in front of people and sing and play and entertain people. And they're ready for it now." On December 7, Chris Hillman and David Crosby joined the two onstage at San Francisco's Boarding House for a rousing set of Byrds hits. Naturally, the media picked up on the good vibes between the four and once again hinted that a Byrds reunion was possibly in the wind. However, while a reunion did emerge, it was not the full Byrds.

Recently baptized as a born-again Christian and married to new wife Camilla, Roger had no desire to reconvene a gathering of Byrds. "The reason Roger folded the Byrds back in the early '70s," suggests Ron, "was that he pulled into a gas station in Malibu and he had 'Byrds 1' on his license plate and the gas station attendant looked at it and said, 'The Byrds? Man, whatever happened to them?' He said to me, 'Look, if the gas station attendant in the town I live in doesn't know that I exist, why should I be doing this?'" Nonetheless, Roger was interested in recording with his original Byrds mate, Gene Clark. "Roger was dissatisfied with Columbia Records and wanted to get a new deal when his deal was up with Columbia," Ron continues. "I went to a fellow named Rupert Perry, who at the time was vice president of A&R at Capitol Records. He was an English guy, a real nice fellow, and a Byrds fan, and he went for the Roger deal. We started putting a contract together right around the time that Gene was coming around. So I talked to Roger and asked him if he wanted to include Gene in this deal and see if we can get Capitol to take Gene and record the two of them as a duo. And Gene, of course, was all for it. As the thing moved along I started to feel like I was on a roll and then Chris Hillman entered the picture. I knew Chris's future wife, Connie Pappas, but I had never met Chris through all the dealings I had had with Roger and Gene and the Byrds. So I arranged a meeting, I think Connie set it up, and Chris was very defensive in those days. His initial response was, 'What would I want to do that for?' My reply was, '$25,000 in your pocket.' And Chris's reply to that was, 'Oh!' So I got Chris in and went to Capitol and said, 'What do you think? I've got three of the Byrds.' And Rupert Perry kept giving me another $25,000 for every Byrd I could deliver." Reveals Roger, "I wasn't that thrilled with Chris at that moment (I like him just fine now). I didn't think I wanted Chris in the band, but Rainey talked me into it."

Ron dispels the long-held myth that the teaming of McGuinn, Clark & Hillman was merely a failed attempt at a full-blown Byrds reunion scheme. "I don't think that was ever in the cards because I don't think any of them wanted to deal with Michael Clarke, and Crosby was a whole other story. I personally had no desire to get involved with David and I don't think anyone else did. I don't think that it was ever discussed. A full Byrds reunion was certainly not on my agenda, and it's safe to say I had a large part in putting this thing together. I don't ever remember talking to Roger about bringing David in." Confirms Chris, "We were so adamant against using the Byrds name yet we did Byrds songs. I think it was just that we were all desperate at that moment and it was just a chance to make some money."

Al Hersh had worked as road manager for Roger for several years before coming onboard the new conglomerate. He recalls wariness in some music industry quarters to take on the trio. "A lot of people were scared of their reputations, especially Gene, who was incredibly undependable. He had burned a lot of record labels. On the other hand the magic was there. Unfortunately, in putting them back together there were so many outside forces and influences that were trying to make them not be the Byrds at that time. My whole thing was, 'That's who you guys are. Be that. You don't have to go backwards, just pick up where you left off.'"

With no other recording prospects at hand, no management or direction, and desperately short of cash, Gene jumped aboard the new group. He had no residual negative feelings about the Byrds to color his decision to join with Roger and Chris. In fact, he welcomed the opportunity to work with them again and to take another shot at the big time, given the state of his career. But unlike the Byrds or Dillard & Clark, McGuinn, Clark & Hillman was a contrived coupling, a marriage of convenience, calculated rather than spontaneous or natural in evolution, and this would doom the project almost from the start.

"There was really nothing organic about it," insists Al. "Roger was floundering, Gene was beyond floundering, and they really kind of needed each other. Gene was pretty strapped for money and that was the main motivation. Roger didn't know what he wanted to do. He wasn't really writing any more and wasn't in a very motivated state. Hillman came onboard rather hesitantly. He wanted it to be McGuinn, Hillman & Clark. It got to be real petty. It was all about pettiness with those three guys. They had a long history of that from the Byrds. It's too bad because there was a lot of talent. All that pettiness and infighting was really what made a lot of the talent come out. I saw it happen. It was kind of a good thing, even though it was horrible to watch, and painful. Their whole careers were really based on that love/hate thing and jealousy. More hate than love. That's why putting that particular threesome together was so difficult. The timing was right, but there was never any plan. I was involved in the Byrds reunion in 1973 and it was such a disaster that there was never any thought of that ever happening again. It was another one of those horrible, painful experiences. That one was like pulling teeth and none of them was looking forward to that happening ever again, although Crosby was always hovering around at the beginning of McGuinn, Clark & Hillman. Michael Clarke was on the outs with

Firefall at the time and would occasionally show up, too. There were several times when all five guys would play together. Every time we played up in San Francisco, David would show up because he was living up there. There was a lot of accidental coming together."

"As a concept, it was fantastic," Ron boasts. "With the three of them, that was enough. Had there been a fourth one in there, God knows what it would have been like. Artistically it was wonderful. The absolute wealth of material was unbelievable. Each guy came out and did a song or two, then gave the stage to the other until all three were onstage and then they did their songs together. And they would do their Byrds songs, too."

On February 2, 1978, McGuinn, Clark & Hillman appeared at San Francisco's Boarding House where they were once again joined by David Crosby for a much-bootlegged set titled *Doin' Alright for Old People.* Further gigs followed, including the Golden Bear in Huntington Beach, before the group headed off in June on a tour of Japan, New Zealand, and Australia. They were accompanied by John Sambatino on guitar and ex-Poco drummer George Grantham filling in until Greg Thomas, Roger's former drummer in the Thunderbyrds, could saddle up.

The volatile nature of the three personalities emerged soon after that, on the Australian leg. "At one venue there was a strange dressing room situation," chuckles Al. "There was a big gap at the top of each dressing room. There were steel doors and walls, but you could actually hear everything that was going on in each room. And they were all bad-mouthing each other. Before the show I would come in and see each one of them and give each one a little tune up or pep talk. Roger said something about Chris and Chris could hear it as if we were standing right there. Chris had a real short fuse back then and he waited until after the show, then he hit Roger so hard he ended up in a urinal. He probably flew 30 feet before he landed. This was all a culmination of what happened years before, but Chris had a lot of resentment towards the other Byrds. He didn't take on Gene, though I saw them both a couple of times about to go for it. You could see them actually looking at each other and thinking about what would happen if they did. They both knew that one of them or both would end up dead. So they didn't try it. It came so close, though. It was real scary. I had my hands full dealing with those guys, 24 hours a day, seven days a week."

"Yes, I picked up Roger and threw him against a wall one night," admits Chris, "because he called me a little punk and 'Chris the bass player' and I wasn't Chris the bass player anymore. I said, 'Don't you ever do that.' Gene and I almost got into it one night because he was so out of it. And I just said, 'Don't do it, Gene. Don't even think of doing it. You're not going to win this one.' It was madness. But it was the drugs doing it to him. Poor Al. I liked Al and I thought he was a nice guy, but he had to do the cleanup. It was the 1970s and cocaine was everywhere. That was a heinous decade in this country's culture and society, a terrible time, and drugs made some people crazy or killed them."

"Touring was indescribable," sighs Al. "There were times when a lot of old ugly stuff was dredged up from the past and old debts settled from years and years ago. There was always a lot of tension. I made sure they all had their own separate dressing rooms because I never knew from one day to the next if they were going to be in love with each other or in hate. And it was usually hate. At any rate, I always had to be prepared to hide them from one another so that they didn't have any contact until after the show. It was funny because they would go out and sing all these peace songs and then right after the show they would be at each others' throats. They would turn around and beat the crap out of each other. It was a kind of controlled madness."

"They were professionally cordial with each other, but there wasn't a lot of warmth," observes Ron. "There were flashes between them when something good was done onstage or a particularly good show. There would be flashes of, 'Boy, that was pretty good' between them. But they weren't very warm to each other. As professionals onstage they were terrific. One night at the Roxy they started doing a show and McGuinn went to sing and nothing came out. Clark moved up to the microphone and picked right up where Roger would have been and sang the rest of the show, doing all of Roger's part, and did a great job. But, yeah, they weren't the kind of guys who would say, 'Hey, let's go out and have a beer or a burger together or something.' Professionally they did their work in the studio, they did their work onstage, but they weren't what you would call close."

Following the Australian tour, Gene and Terri vacationed in Fiji before returning to the US. Gene's relationship with Terri continued to be driven by obsession and drugs.

Despite the rocky start, McGuinn, Clark & Hillman entered Miami's Criteria Studios in November to record their debut album with noted producers Ron and Howard Albert calling the shots—fresh from reviving the flagging career of Crosby, Stills & Nash. Chris had worked with the producing brothers in Stephen Stills's Manassas, and believed that only they could ensure a contemporary sound rather than a dated Byrds retread. "The Albert Brothers consciously didn't want it to sound like the Byrds, which meant I couldn't play my Rickenbacker or sing," offers Roger. "So I was kind of benched for the whole project, but I got a couple of songs on there, ironically one of them became a hit. But I really didn't have much input into that first album."

Criteria Studios was noted for the sound of the Bee Gees on *Saturday Night Fever* and the overwhelming presence of that leviathan seeped into the sound and direction of the album. "The whole problem was disco and *Saturday Night Fever*," muses Greg. "The Albert Brothers were basically trying to take Gene, Roger, and Chris and turn them into the Gibb Brothers. You know if you just listen to that album. Just from the kind of music I was playing in the studio, it felt like a disco record. It didn't feel like what Gene was capable of doing. The Albert Brothers pretty much had the upper hand on the type of music that was going to be recorded and whose songs were to be recorded. They took Gene's songs and Roger's songs and Chris's songs and turned them into disco songs. I was playing a disco feel though it was a little more percussive than most disco records are. I kind of like what they did with some of the songs, but to me it wasn't a very Byrdsy type record."

Ensconced in an elegant, Spanish-style mansion on Pinetree Drive in Miami Beach owned by one of the Bee Gees, the three singer-songwriters found living under one roof almost as difficult as touring together. Rick Clark joined Gene as a roadie and witnessed the tense atmosphere. "Roger had a suite of rooms at one end of the house and Gene had a suite of rooms at the other end of the house and Chris had a suite upstairs. I stayed in the maid's quarters, which were plush. But at the time there was a riff between Roger and Gene to the point where they wouldn't speak to each other. I became their liaison. Roger would give me a message to give to Gene and Gene would give me a message to give to Roger and I'd walk back and forth from one end of the house to the other. And when they went into the studio there were very few times when they were all in the studio at the same time and the album suffered greatly as a result."

Tom Slocum visited Gene and Terri in Miami and was struck by the hostility in the air. "I went over to the house where they were all living in separate wings and it was like some kind of psychic combat going on." Greg lasted a day or two at the mansion before demanding to be moved out. "They stuck them in the same house and I finally said, 'I can't live in this!'" he recalls. "From the very first day there were blowups between them. So I told them they had to get me another place. First of all, Gene didn't sleep much. Roger was pretty normal at the time, but those three never got along. Doing the record was really a good time and everybody actually got along. I was playing drums so I was there all the time in the studio. But all three guys weren't together in the studio a lot. They were totally different creatures, all three of them. Gene was definitely the oddball in this case. I think it was mostly because of the drugs. It was a real heavy drug period for him."

As Tommy Kaye revealed to interviewer Ken Viola in 1991, "During the McGuinn, Clark, Hillman thing, Gene got very heavily into cocaine and the downtown [slang for heroin]. He was doing a lot of everything." According to Al, "The drug scene was huge down there in Miami. It was scary. There was also a lot of heroin going on then in Miami, too, besides the cocaine. Gene was into that big time. Terri had this little metal strong box. I never got to look into it firsthand, but there was a famous incident one night. They got into this horrendous fight, they were always fighting, and my recollection of it was the two of them running down the street stark naked with this strong box in this incredibly wealthy neighborhood in Miami and Gene tackling her right there on the street. I was pretty much always on patrol to make sure nobody got arrested, there was so much shit going on. It was like a 24-hour-a-day vigil. They were causing a lot of attention and I was always afraid we were going to get popped before the group ever got off the ground."

Rick confirms the rampant presence of cocaine. "At the time, Miami Beach was up to here with cocaine," pointing to his eyebrows. "The house, the studio, were swimming in it. I did so much that I got to the point where I didn't want to see it again. It became a divisive factor. The situation was bad enough as it was, but this just enhanced how bad the situation was. It was ugly. I didn't enjoy it. I told Gene I wanted out and got a plane ticket home. It was just a really bad vibe, the whole situation. It was the start of a downhill slide for Gene." Rick quit the sessions and flew back to California in disgust after one of the session sidemen asked him to score some hard drugs for him.

"We often had to wait for Gene," notes Chris. "A couple of days later he was back and he couldn't sing. He was out of control. It took poor Ron Albert hours to get a lead vocal from him, punching in syllables. He couldn't sing. It was the booze and drugs. I went up to their room while they were away and there was half-eaten food on the floor, a lizard in there, eating part of a sandwich. I thought, 'What *is this?!*' It was like Hollywood Babylon, so surreal. Gene was just *out there.*" Adds Roger, "Gene had Terri with him and she was kind of a destructive force, she kept him into drugs and stuff, they were doing heroin and fighting a lot, not a good scene."

Surprisingly, the group managed to pull an album out of the madness. Released in February 1979, *McGuinn, Clark & Hillman* climbed to No. 39, the best showing for any of the three principals since leaving the Byrds. A single, Roger's lightweight "Don't You Write Her Off," managed to hit No. 33 on the pop charts. Despite Greg's insistence that disco dominated the sessions, the album actually has a very 1970s pop sound, only slightly emphasizing the dance beat. Conspicuously absent is the Rickenbacker, but the playing and harmonies throughout remain strong, especially Chris's bass work. "It's sort of 'disco-y' in a way, very smooth," notes Chris, "but Gene wrote some great songs on it. Greg Thomas is a great drummer and he made that thing happen on those tracks. I sort of like that first album."

While Gene emerges as the strongest of the three songwriters, penning four songs that are far superior to his counterparts, he nonetheless suffered at the hands of the Albert Brothers' slick production, especially on "Release Me Girl." The demo cut with co-writer Tommy Kaye and the KC Southern Band two years before is an airy slice of aching melancholy as only Gene could deliver; the version arranged and recorded by Ron and Howard Albert is a funked-up, percussive disco travesty. As Gene bemoaned to writer Domenic Priore in 1985, "A lot of the songs during that time started out a different way. One thing about producers, when you get a producer for a record, sometimes they have their own view of how songs should be approached or how they should be recorded. In this particular case I would have liked actually to have seen the songs and material approached the way we were doing them, more as a group, than how people wanted them arranged as far as production. Even though it was a good record, I still think we lost our true sound, our true Byrds thing, because you had three Byrds there. I think if we had another approach to the production it could have been much more real."

"That record sounded like three guys each trying to do a solo thing," Tommy Kaye reported to Viola. "It didn't sound like a band at all. It wasn't a band. They didn't sing each other's backgrounds, they didn't write together. They did one of my songs on that album, 'Release Me Girl,' and destroyed it. Unbelievably bad. I just couldn't believe that record."

Tom Slocum observed the sessions and witnessed the lack of unity that clearly pervades the album. "At the studio with the Albert Brothers, who make great records, it was 'Okay, now we're going to do a Gene Clark song with George Terry and the Miami rhythm section of the Bee Gees.' Then it would be a McGuinn song with those same players. They did do some interesting jobs on things like 'Backstage Pass,' but I remember them listening to it and Gene wondering if it was like the Beatles' *White Album* where it was Beatle George and his band, then another track with Beatle Paul and his band. It was like Gene Clark and his Byrd people."

The song "Little Mama" was inspired by Terri, while "Feelin' Higher" bears her co-credit. Unlike "Release Me Girl," both songs work much better in a contemporary context, the latter boasting some tasteful piano from Paul Harris over a percussive coda provided by Joe Lala. "'Feelin' Higher' was written about flying saucers," reveals Terri. "Gene and I were totally into flying saucers, we totally believed in them." Al, who was given the task of driving Gene from gig to gig after the singer resisted flying, remembers the incident that sparked the song. "He and I actually saw what we perceived to be a flying saucer one night together. And he wrote the song about that incident. We were driving through New Jersey and we didn't say a word to each other about it when it happened or after it happened, but as it was happening we had a mind conversation where we didn't speak but we talked. It was one of the strangest things that happened to me in my life. And Gene was capable of doing that stuff. He was the kind of guy who couldn't really string a sentence together to talk to you, but he had a way with lyrics and was a very prolific songwriter."

"Backstage Pass" dates from the KC Southern Band's Troubadour engagement a year before. David Clark recalls the curious genesis of the song. "I saw him write out an entire song, 'Backstage Pass,' during a performance while it was going on," he marvels. "He would go out and perform, come back and write a bit, then go out and perform again, and come back and finish it up. It was at the Troubadour and they were working with lighting and spotlights to try to make Gene less self-conscious. Gene was uncomfortable about having the spotlight in his face. It bothered him. They had a spotlight behind the stage and it kind of came across and made a silhouette of him. That was the idea. But what it did was put a spotlight right down in front of the stage and there was this young girl who was gorgeous and she was dancing to the music. Gene used that as his catalyst for the song." Released as a single in August, the song failed to chart.

Critic Nick Kent savaged *McGuinn, Clark & Hillman* in his *New Musical Express* review, labeling the three ex-Byrds over the hill and bereft of inspiration. "McGC&H groans under the weight of its own tedium," he carped. "This is the kind of pablum one can see appealing solely to senile health food nuts . . . this desperate enterprise is aimed at the lowest common denominator, lower than the Eagles." In assessing the strengths and weaknesses of the album, writer William Ruhlmann concludes in the *All Music Guide,* "If the group didn't sound like the Byrds, they often did sound like the Eagles, the group that had inherited the Byrds' mantle in the 1970s. If the trio had an appealing sound, however, they lacked substance. The songwriting was pleasant but slight, songs of romance that were nowhere near the quality of the Eagles' or Crosby, Stills & Nash's material."

Despite the generally negative assessments of the album, McGuinn, Clark & Hillman remained a strong concert draw and set out on tour through much of 1979, including a jaunt across Europe where the Byrds franchise remained strong. The three never failed to deliver an exciting show. But what the others soon discovered was that Gene had not overcome his touring phobia, and it was not restricted to airplanes. "Everybody thinks that Gene had this fear of flying, but it wasn't just *flying*," emphasizes Al. "It was travel. Gene had this weird thing about traveling. It was actually painful traveling with him. I don't know what it was, but you could never really count on him to be there. Getting him on a plane to Australia wasn't easy, believe me. He could be in a car or on a bus, it didn't matter what mode of transportation, and he would freak. Really freak to the point where he couldn't do it. We had everything from private jets to motor homes and everything in between and he would freak on some level. Even in a car. We were in town cars driving across country and he would flip out. He would stay up the whole time you were traveling and he was always nervous. He always thought something horrible was going to happen. I don't know what the hell he was perceiving in his brain, but he was really scary. I actually had to hire a very giant black fellow to get him in a headlock to put him in a vehicle and get him to where he had to be once. But it was predictable. We all knew this was going to happen so nobody was surprised. We thought he might be hungry enough to bite the bullet and he

Chris, Roger and Gene reunite for McGuinn, Clark & Hillman in 1978.

did so on many occasions. I remember him painfully traveling from one place to another and putting up with it. But I was getting such a contact vibe off of him that was horrible. It was scary. There was some complex, weird shit going on in his mind."

As the touring regimen intensified, Gene began missing concerts, citing a variety of health-related excuses, most notably an abscessed tooth. The reality was less medical, but no less medicinal. "He said he had a toothache for the whole tour," offers Roger. "He was strung out." Once the new band hit the ground running, Gene took it as his cue to live the high life quite literally and, indeed, all the trappings of superstardom surrounded McGuinn, Clark & Hillman from the get-go. Flush with money for the first time in years, Gene went overboard on the rock 'n' roll lifestyle. After a decade in the wilderness, both personally and professionally, Gene, with Terri by his side, embraced the return to the limelight with gusto, propelled by alcohol and a mountain of white powder.

"I remember playing a club gig in Huntington Beach, the Golden Bear, and Chris and I were waiting for Gene and we kept looking at the door all night, but he never showed up," laments Roger. "That was the beginning of his not showing up. The whole tour went by when Gene wasn't there. It was okay, but it would have been better with Gene."

"Near the end Gene was barely able to finish a sentence, he was such a mess," claims Chris. "He wouldn't show up for shows. He was junked out. He'd come to a Capitol Records release party out of his mind on drugs. We were doing Dinah Shore's show live on television with Emmylou Harris and Ricky Scaggs and Gene's looking for his stash while we're sitting there on the couch. I kept saying to him, 'Stop that. Stop doing that. What are you doing?' 'I gotta get my stash,' he said. 'I think it's out in the car. I'm gonna go out to my car.' And I said, 'Sit down!' That's where we were clashing, he and I.

"I got to the point where I said, 'He's got to go.' I couldn't reach him. I would say things, but I couldn't talk to him like I used to be able to. I couldn't quite reach him and it would be hopeless. I would get angry, I was a very angry guy then, but I said, 'If that son of a bitch doesn't show up one more time. . . . How dare he do that?' I don't look at drug abuse as a disease. I look at it as a disease of selfishness. It's me first. That's where I draw the line. I'd been through that movie with Gram [Parsons]."

Al remembers, "I can't tell you how many nights I had to go up onstage and make announcements that Gene Clark wasn't here that night if anyone wanted a refund. Nobody did, maybe one person. But I had to make that announcement to some promoters who were well connected and I got threatened. It was scary, but it was also scary when he was there, too."

"He was called," Ron states about attempts to bring Gene back into the fold. "I know Hersh called him and I tried, but there was a time when Gene just disappeared. He left town and nobody could get to him. If Gene didn't want to be found, you couldn't find him. It's not like he called anybody and said, 'I don't want to be in this band anymore.' I don't remember him ever doing anything like that. He just didn't show up. He left Roger and all of us in the lurch by pulling what he did by just not showing up any more." Was Gene preoccupied with drugs? "Yep," insists Ron. "That became his full-time job. Those kinds of people become antisocial and that leads people like that to not doing shows.

"Chris told me one time they were playing an outdoor show and somebody yelled from the audience, 'Where's Gene?' and there was a plane flying overhead," Ron chuckles. "Chris pointed up to the sky and said, 'He's coming in now. He's a little late.'"

One band engagement Gene did manage to make was in front of his hometown crowd and family in Kansas City. Unfortunately his newfound drugged-out bravado fooled no one and only resulted in disappointment. In an attempt to give the folks back home the star treatment, Gene succeeded in driving a wedge between him and his family. "When he was here for the McGuinn, Clark & Hillman concert, that was a nightmare," sighs sister Bonnie. "He rented a limousine to pick up Mom and Dad. Mom kind of enjoyed the limelight and the little perks that came with it, but Dad was not comfortable with it in any way at all. He was not comfortable with Gene's chosen profession or with what he saw happening to Gene's life. I wouldn't say he didn't support Gene's career choice, but it was alienating to the family. Gene tried to shield the family from his public life, but it wasn't a hidden thing. We knew about his problems. I was very much aware of it, but maybe some of the family members just kind of put on the blinders and didn't want to see it.

"I could tell Gene was using drugs. We had a family gathering all set up with fruit trays and all this stuff. Gene got so upset that we couldn't stay there. The press was all over the place. So we went over to where he was staying and waited in the lobby for him for over an hour. When he came down he was wearing sunglasses hiding his eyes and he was playing the big star strutting around. And he made a scene at Trader Vic's, making them open the place back up so he could take the folks to dinner. It was very embarrassing for them. I think they knew, but they didn't want to know. Mom was just upset with his behavior, but I don't think she ever saw the domino effect: 'Your son is taking drugs and this is why he is behaving this way' because Gene's behavior was quite unpredictable any time. Mom was very disappointed in him because of his drug abuse and alcohol abuse. She knew. And he didn't hide it when they went out to California and he was hanging out with some rough people. I can remember him coming home a couple of times and having to make several trips out to the car during the course of the evening because that was in the period when Mom had banned alcohol in the house after Dad got his act cleaned up."

Rick confirms that Kelly and Jeanne had an inkling of what was going on with their son, but were in denial. "They just wanted to talk to their son, but Gene wanted to impress everyone back home. And Terri was into impressing people. They took Mom and Dad out to dinner and my Mom said, 'They kept getting up from the table every five minutes and running off to the bathroom and wouldn't eat their dinner.' They knew what was going on, but Gene was trying to hide it. It really saddened my parents. After that happened my parents just didn't want to deal with that anymore. They didn't go out of their way to ask Gene to come home."

By November 1979, as McGuinn, Clark & Hillman returned to Criteria Studios in Miami to record a follow-up album, Gene's presence within the group remained uncertain. As a result, his participation in what would become the album *City* was limited. He recorded two songs, then promptly left. "Gene kind of floated away and that's how he was depicted on that second album cover," Al notes. "He was literally floating away at that point."

In the end, the album was credited as "McGuinn & Hillman Featuring Gene Clark." He had gone from the powerhouse on their first album to merely an adjunct member by the second, all within the span of a year. "On that second album, Gene was there in body only," concludes Roger.

Released in January 1980, *City* barely managed to scrape to No. 136 on the album charts. Displaying a more characteristic Byrds sound with Roger's Rickenbacker restored, the album lacked strong songwriting. Of Gene's two tracks, the ironically titled "Won't Let You Down," with its Byrdsy 12-string guitars and harmonies, was the stronger; "Painted Fire" was an odd, 1950s–style pastiche driven by barrelhouse piano and, arguably, Gene's lamest lyrics ever. Al insists that "Won't Let You Down" was directed at Gene's two boys, Kelly and Kai. "Most of Gene's songs were addressed to women, but I think that song was more directed to his kids because he was pretty much an absentee dad." The song is more likely a paean to Terri Messina.

Despite the reduced billing on the album (the back cover credits barely acknowledge his participation), Gene managed once again to write the best song, topping his two partners. However, by the time of its release, Gene was gone from the group. McGuinn & Hillman carried on as a duo, releasing one more album before Capitol records bought out their contract after an unfortunate incident involving a Capitol executive and a group member at New York City's Bottom Line. "Pretty much what happened was what I thought would happen," Al maintains. "I didn't think it would really last as long as it did. I thought they lasted maybe one album longer than it should have.

"Gene never officially bailed out, he just stopped showing up. On that album cover, we actually came up with that concept of kind of having Gene morphing out of the picture, putting on a picture that looks like it's floating out of the building. This was just another one of those famous pictures they had, like the one where David Crosby was replaced by the horse on that Byrds album cover.

"None of us really realized, though, that Gene was sick," Al continues. "Nobody knew. He looked like he worked out every day of his life. You couldn't really tell. We knew that he was in psychic pain, but we never knew he had any physical ailments. Gene had to have an ulcer, at least one. The guy was on edge all the time. I can't remember him not being on edge, except when he was performing. That's the only time he seemed to be at peace, was onstage where he didn't have to deal with his pain. I think Gene was actually happiest, though he didn't know it, when he was onstage performing. He was a really good performer, even on his bad nights and he had some really bad nights. But the audience was very forgiving. But he was sick and we didn't know it. We couldn't really tell, but there was always something wrong with him."

Tom recalls meeting a distraught Gene around the time of the second album. "There are horror stories surrounding the McGuinn, Clark & Hillman thing. They were making those records and staying busy and I was happy to see them all working. When they were on the road I wouldn't hear from him much. Then I would get these phone calls. 'You're my best friend,' those kinds of calls. One night, it might have been at Barney's Beanery, he calls me up and says, 'Come on, let's go have a talk.' So I go and he's all out of sorts. He says to me, 'Sloc, they stole all the money.' I said, 'What do you mean? Who stole all the money?' And he said, 'I'm leaving McGuinn, Clark & Hillman. I did what was expected of me basically, and all the money's gone.' And I said to him, 'Wait a second here.' Only like three or four months before that everything was fine. Now he's saying he had no money?"

"Money was always an issue," admits Ron. "With musicians in general who aren't wealthy with lots of money in the bank, most of them have to work to support lifestyles and whatever. I always was looking out for Roger to make sure that Roger always had what he needed to make it through, and when I got the other guys, I did the same with them, although Gene didn't want to know. He didn't really want any advice. He could be a very bullheaded guy. When Chris and Connie came into the picture, Connie was pretty much the one we talked to, although sometimes Chris would want to be directly involved. Connie was a pro. Gene had Terri but Terri never really asserted herself into what I was doing. I wish I had spent more time with Gene, trying to make him feel more comfortable and make him feel at home and a part of something, if I had it to do over again. He was the one who needed it the most. Roger had Camilla, Chris had Connie, and even though Gene had Terri, I think he needed more. He needed more attention. I really liked Gene as a guy, he was warm and had a sense of humor and I always thought he was a great writer. I didn't like what he did at the end, but perhaps without the drug influence, perhaps this thing could have gone on to be a really big creative success. I wish things had been different."

Ron suggests that there was an element of mistrust between the three principals from the outset. "They were all looking over their shoulders to make sure that their end was covered. That's true." With so many stakeholders involved—artists, girlfriends, wives, agents, and personal managers—there was bound to be confusion, suspicion, and power plays. As Gene Clark told Jon Butcher in a 1987 unpublished interview, "The early part of McGuinn, Clark & Hillman was really magical. Roger and I had a great communication; we had a great partnership. But I think what happened was that there were a whole bunch of different managers that got in the middle of the thing. If we had been able to solidify the thing a little better, it might have worked. It was almost in a way a repeat of the Byrds reunion. We each had different managers and there wasn't any real leadership. Instead of the three of us spending more time together to shape and mold material, we were writing songs separately, which never has worked."

Gene placed much of the blame for the failure of McGuinn, Clark & Hillman on the aura of stardom that engulfed the group even before they had proven themselves. "We walked into a ready-made bet, just by our names only, and were spoiled with immediate limousines and Lear Jets, and with that kind of thing you don't feel you've earned your money, you don't feel like you worked for it. So, no, we didn't watch our money for that reason, because of being so catered to. It was like a big dinosaur where the head doesn't know what the tail is doing. There was too much involved in between. You couldn't just communicate with everybody involved and know what was happening."

Al offers an amusing aside to the McGuinn, Clark & Hillman story. "Tom Petty was a real groupie. I can't tell you how many dressing rooms I threw him out of. He was sending me music for years and I thought it was really good. I played some of it for Roger and Roger thought it was *him*. He actually said to me, 'When did I record that?' I was trying to get Roger to record some Petty stuff because no one was recording his stuff at the time and Roger wasn't writing shit. I thought it would be a perfect match. Tom Petty became what Roger could have been if he had continued to create. Instead he resented it. We ended up recording one of his songs, but it was a really tough thing to record it. Roger even changed some of the words. He always felt that Petty wouldn't amount to anything and was a cheap imitation of him. And we all know what happened."

Having walked out on Roger and Chris, once again abandoning a high-profile, successful group for an uncertain future, Gene was about to hit rock bottom. "Gene and I split up a few times," acknowledges Terri. "The main reason for the split-ups was that when Gene would drink, and it mainly had to do with alcohol and he used to do alcohol when he was doing drugs, the alcohol definitely had that Dr. Jeckle/Mr. Hyde effect on him. He would turn into a very mean and abusive person and he would hit me and abuse me physically and I had to get away from him."

Estranged from his girlfriend as a result of his increasingly unpredictable and sometimes threatening behavior, Gene was in the deepest throes of his drug addiction and made the dubious decision to move in with Jesse Ed Davis, a man battling his own alcohol and drug dependencies. Their partnership, in the company of a handful of other notorious substance abusers, only aggravated each other's circumstances. But misery loves company and the two musicians commiserated and careened from disaster to disaster. "The word on the street and among musicians was that Gene was trouble," allows friend John York. "The combination of Gene and those guys he was hanging around with, they were just trouble, and if you got involved with them your life would become a mess. And I'm sure business people felt that way, too. Musicians would say, 'Gene's gonna kill himself.'"

"He was pretty messed up, attacking patrons in bars and restaurants, picking fights, blaming anyone and everyone for the mismanagement of his life," Tom confirms. "Blaming everyone except the man in the mirror. It's safe to say Gene's mirror was unclear, beveled, and oblong and he was confused by the shape within the images. His violence knew no bounds. He more than frightened his friends as well as strangers. One night in Dan Tana's he took a swing at the maître d' and he got intercepted by a big Scot contractor who promptly knocked him on his ass, picked him up, and threw him out the door. When Gene drank and got out of control he was a scary son of a gun."

According to Rick, "Tommy Kaye, Philip O'Leno, John Desko, me, and some other people like Roger Willis were always loyal to Gene and would try at times when Gene was being led down a disastrous path by people he thought were his friends, these very few people who really *were* his friends would try to step in and would end up getting hurt themselves, one way or another. I got hurt by Gene when he wasn't in his best state of mind. We had a couple of knock-down, drag-out fights."

During this period, what some writers term Gene's 'lost weekend,' Gene made a number of informal tapes of recent compositions, many recorded at friends' houses. One such tape, known to its participants as the *Glass House Tape* (having been recorded at David Carradine's Laurel Canyon abode that sported floor-to-ceiling windows), features Gene and Tommy Kaye on acoustic guitars, Rick Clark, lead guitarist Garth Beckington, and Jon Faurot on bass, with vocal arrangements by Tommy. The six tracks on the tape are loose and a bit swaggering—likely befitting the mood of the gathering—but they represent an intriguing glimpse into Gene's career at that point.

"Shades of Blue," a song by Tommy later recorded for his own solo album and cut by Gene several times but never released, bears a striking resemblance to Neil Young's "Hey Hey My My," while "Crazy Ladies," a Clark-Kaye-Hillary Kontos Kaye collaboration, features Tommy's finesse with vocal arrangements. "If I Don't Have You" is a waltz-time, country-flavored ballad reminiscent of the Skyliners' 1950s tearjerker "Since I Don't Have You." "I'll Change Your Life" is early Beatles pop. "Midnight Mare," a rare collaboration between Gene and Rick, features tasteful guitar work from Garth as well as the superbly blended voices of the two writers, who even add some saucy whinnying. "Gene and I would just sit in the living room with a little 4-track and just sit and write songs off the top of our heads," Rick recalls. "We wrote that one down at Newport Beach when I was down there building homes. Talk about harmonies—Gene and I were like the Everly Brothers. He and I could sing so tight. Some really beautiful stuff got recorded. Gene and I actually collaborated on quite a few things, but a lot of them never got recorded. Some of them were on tapes that we made just sitting around in his living room. A lot of those tapes disappeared when Gene died."

David believes his younger brother Rick's career aspirations never managed to emerge from beneath Gene's larger shadow. "Rick had the opportunities, he had the offer and the inroads," maintains David, "and if it hadn't been for his habits and his laziness he would have been able to go a long ways in that industry. It wasn't that he wasn't talented. He had talent. I tried to convince Gene and Rick in 1977 how to make this work for them. Gene was not a stage presence. He didn't like being the stage presence; Rick was the stage presence. He was the actor, the performer. He had that type of persona. He wasn't the powerful writer or the great musician that

Gene was, although he did some pretty good work in his time. If Gene would have stayed in the background, wrote and produced, and let Rick front and take the band on the road, it would have worked for them. And let me manage them. That's my forte; I'm a manager. That's what I do well. But they could not get beyond the ego. Gene's ego would not let Rick go onstage. Gene talked about a lot of things, but when it came down to getting him over his insatiable ego, his desire to be the one and only, it crippled him as much as the drugs or anything."

The real treasure on the *Glass House Tape* is "Communication," which offers Gene's strange musings on alien beings and religion, implying that Jesus, angels, and other Biblical references were, in fact, alien visitors to Earth. He writes: "Talk about your prophet, what kind of man was he? The alien savior walked on the waters of the sea. From where did he originate? What kind of power took to elevate him? What was he trying to communicate? What in heaven do you think halos are?"

Backed by spare acoustic guitar, handclaps, and an ethereal chorus, Gene reinterprets several Biblical tales in an *X-Files* context. The song is eerily stunning, even in rough form, despite what are clearly borderline paranoid ideas. Recalls Peter Oliva, "I remember we were in Hollywood and Gene says to me, 'There they are up there, man! Do you see them?' And I said, 'What are you looking at?' And he goes, 'Up there on that roof. Space guys. Space guys are up there!' I'm going, 'What space guys?' He was listening to this Tom Pacheco song ["All Fly Away"] about the sky being full of ships and people staying up and watching the sky for space men. He would play that record over and over again. I don't know where he got those ideas from, but if you take enough speed and do enough coke that stuff happens."

Among Gene's current retinue of hangers-on was Joanelle 'Jody' Romero, a young Native American actress and budding singer-songwriter. Joanelle came from an acting family (her mother, Rita, had worked in several Elvis Presley movies and her brother, Robby, was a noted actor) and got her break as a teenager starring in *A Girl Called Hatter Fox* in 1977. She starred in 1989's *Pow Wow Highway* produced by George Harrison, and founded Spirit World Productions in 1991 for Native American films, music, television, and live events. As a founder of Red Nation Records, she became the first American Indian woman to perform at Lilith Fair, in 1998. An associate of Jesse Ed Davis in 1980 when she met Gene, Joanelle was hanging out with The Band's Rick Danko and blues man Paul Butterfield. She was also acquainted with Gene's acting buddy Jason Ronard, who introduced her to the singer. "They all—Geno, Butterfield, Danko, and Jesse Ed Davis—took me under their wing as far as music goes," claims Joanelle. "I was really young. Not only were they my best friends but also my musical mentors. I was discovered by Leonard Cohen as far as singing goes, but these guys were like my drinking buddies, my music mentors, my best friends, and I was like this young girl musician who hung out with them. We bonded real closely."

With Joanelle, Gene embarked on a lengthy drinking binge sparked by the shocking murder of one of Gene's personal heroes, John Lennon, on December 8, 1980. The news of John's death threw Gene into a tailspin of emotions salved only by excessive alcohol abuse. "I remember Geno and I and Dean Stockwell and my brother, and whoever else floated in, when John Lennon died, we rented a hotel room on Sunset and we locked ourselves in this room and it was outrageous. We drank his passing away and just got really loaded and flipped out over that. And then after that Geno and I went to Dan Tana's and we were in this illusion that we were John and Yoko. We were both aware of what we were doing, but we were really fucked up. It was mostly booze.

"There was one time that I slept with Geno," she admits, "but it was more like a sister/brother relationship, more on that level than a sexual or romantic relationship. If we were sober it might have gone there, but because we were so out of it, it never went there. But I was madly in love with Geno. It was like a fantasy thing because we were more like a brother and sister. There was a total soul, total karma deal, that we had. I always felt safe with Gene. Even through all the drunkenness I always felt safe with him. He was always very tender with me and very loving and nurturing, always, as an artist and as a young woman. He was very sensitive. He never pulled any of that guy stuff on me. But the whole time he was in and out with Terri. Oh, god, yes, he was madly in love with her, madly, madly in love with that woman. And she messed up everything. All of us tried to get him away from her, all of his closest friends like Jason and Butter, everyone that cared anything about Geno. I never liked her. I thought she was very evil. Even through my drunkenness and explorations with drugs as a young artist I always felt she was awful, not a good person. She wasn't cool."

Gene encouraged Joanelle to write and perform songs, even joining her onstage and inviting her to participate in jam sessions with his friends. "I have old tapes of him and I singing and writing. I performed with him. We performed at the Improvisation. We did a lot of little gigs here and there. I even have footage of us on tape performing, me and Geno, Garth and Tommy Kaye. Geno taught me everything I know about phrasing and harmony. His career wasn't happening at that time. Gene was very frustrated with his career. I remember there were these other people, we all used to hang out at their house and write songs and get loaded up, Hillary and Tommy Kaye."

Joanelle finally saw the light one evening on a binge with Gene. "The last moment I drank, my last run, was with Gene Clark and Jesse Ed Davis. I was 22 years old, and I remember going to this store on Santa Monica Boulevard, a drug store like a Safeway, and none of us had any money and we were filthy dirty. We had been on a run for like a month, just drinking and singing and writing songs and being locked up in a room. We had the shakes really bad. We went to get a big thing of malt beer to take away the shakes. And I remember—and this is a conscious moment in my drunken haze—looking at Geno and looking at Jesse and thinking, 'They've had their careers. They've had record deals and they're legends. And I'm 22 and I have a future and I want my dreams to happen.' And I remember consciously saying, 'I'm going to get sober after today.' They dropped me back at my apartment and Jesse Ed gave me his grandma's conch belt, which I still have to this day. They dropped me off and then they went on their way. That was in 1981. And I've been 22 years sober now."

For Gene, the nightmare wasn't over quite yet. In free fall, he had yet to hit bottom. A memento from his family back home in Kansas would serve as a wake-up call to clean up his act.

"In the early '80s, when he really went on the skids, he would very seldom call home," recalls brother David. "I almost lost contact with him for a while. Once in a while I would call him up and ask him what's up and he'd say, 'Oh, nothing much, just trying to get it together.' And you could hear all this noise in the background and he'd say he had some friends over. Another time I would call him and he wouldn't say anything, just be completely out of it. He would recognize my name, but he didn't know who I was. It was really spooky.

"Mom and Dad had their fortieth wedding anniversary party in May 1981 and Mom still did almost all the preparing for that one. She made a cake that was a replica of their wedding cake. But with it she made all these little heart-shaped cakes, each one with the name of one of her children. Gene didn't come. Rick came home for it. I was headed out to Montana at that time. After that, Rick and I ended up in Southern California and I took this heart-shaped cake with Gene's name on it up to Gene's. And that's when I found him the way he was. I barely recognized him. He was in absolutely miserable condition. I thought he was going to die then. I told him then, 'Man, you have *got* to do something about yourself. You need to check into a hospital.' He was swollen and yellow from jaundice, hepatitis-looking stuff. At that time he was playing his Long Riders role with his Indian hat and feather in it. When I walked onto the balcony of that West Hollywood apartment, I did not know who he was right off. He had just swollen so much and was in such bad shape.

"He was hanging around with these really gross characters who were just a bunch of burnouts and he wasn't much better," David continues. "Cathy Evelyn Smith was there, the girl who was involved in John Belushi's death. They were all flopped around the place and there was a bottle of Wild Turkey Gene had and an old pizza lying around. I finally said to him, 'Can I talk to you a minute without all this?' So we went outside and sat on a curb and I said, 'Would you quit hitting that shit?' meaning the Wild Turkey, 'I want to talk to you.' And he said, 'I really don't want this. Got any beer?' So we walked down to the package store and got a six-pack of tallboy Budweiser and sat there on the curb and drank it. I went out to the car and got the cake and handed it to him and said, 'I don't know whether this will mean anything to you or not, but Mom wanted me to give it to you.' I never saw anything tear through him like that. He just broke down right there. He looked at me and asked, 'Do I still have a family?' And I said, 'Not if I ever see you like this again. I don't want to even *claim* you like this.' That whole thing just gutted him right there in the street. It all came crashing down on him. He walked over to me, took a couple of steps and looked at me, and I reached over and hugged him. He started crying and said, 'I don't want to be like this.' And I said to him, 'Then get yourself some help and quit this crap before you kill yourself. I don't want to have to come back and bury you.'"

Shortly thereafter, Gene and Jesse Ed Davis fled Los Angeles for the island of Oahu in Hawaii, to Lanikai, a small community right on the ocean, ostensibly to clean up from the heroin and cocaine. Gene always insisted he was in control of his body. Healthy and robust as a young man, he was convinced that if he needed to get clean he could do it simply through sheer force of will and his own physical strength, without rehab or any programs. Determined to rid his body of the toxic substances he had been pouring into it, he set himself on a cleansing regimen in an environment away from temptation. "He thought he didn't need rehab," Terri explains. "He would say, 'I know I can get clean when I want. I've done it before and I can do it this time.'" It was a scene that would play itself out several times over the next decade.

As Gene told interviewer Jon Butcher in 1987, "I found it quite necessary to get away at the time. I really needed to go do some thinking. I moved to Hawaii for a year, just stayed there and lived anonymously. Did a lot of walking along the beach, thinking, meditating, and getting myself back into some kind of feeling until I was ready to come back."

Settling into a tiny bungalow, Gene and Jesse found solace in their music and alcohol. During their stay on the island the two became fixtures around the community, even forming a short-lived group to play at a local watering hole. "They played at Anna Banana's on South Beretania," remembers resident Damian Paul, whose friend Wade Cambron played bass for Gene and Jesse's band. "It's a club and it's still there. Gene did some old Byrds tunes like 'I'll Feel a Whole Lot Better' and a lot of material from his solo albums and the other musicians did some solo spots. Wade did a solo with 'Pretty Woman,' the Roy Orbison song. It was actually kind of a fun, loose group. They were all professional musicians and they were able to get together and probably rehearse a little bit in between getting high and put on a decent show. It was Jesse Ed Davis on lead guitar, Gene on rhythm guitar, Wade on bass, and I can't remember who the drummer was, but he was probably a local. It was obvious to me that Gene had a drinking problem because they were really putting it away. I would assume they were doing drugs. I know Jesse had to be. Jesse had a heroin habit. I don't know what Gene's drugs of choice were. The rumor through the coconut wireless was that they were here to get clean from heroin. Gene seemed very relaxed. He seemed to be in a pleasant mood and enjoying himself.

"I think Gene was here a couple of months. I was good friends with Jesse Ed Davis. The last time I saw Jesse he came by my house and wanted to borrow twenty dollars. He was drunk and driving, and walked into my house with a bottle of Southern Comfort he was drinking right out of the bottle. He offered me the bottle and I said no thanks. That was the last time I ever saw him. He left shortly after that and I'm pretty sure Gene left with him."

By the end of 1981, claiming to be clear of heroin and cocaine though still drinking, Gene was ready to come back to the mainland and resume his career. He placed a call to one of the few friends in the music business he had left, drummer Andy Kandanes. "I was producing

Tommy Kaye when Gene called me," Andy recalls. "He was in Hawaii and was having a real rough go of it. He was hanging out with Jesse Ed Davis and they were getting into some serious drugs. He wanted to come back and see his kids for Christmas, but he really didn't have the cash so I loaned him a few thousand dollars and he flew back and spent Christmas with his kids. Then he came and stayed with me and he asked me if I would like to collaborate with him on an album. I talked to Tommy and he said, 'Yeah, let's put my album on the back burner for a while and let's pursue this thing with Gene. It'll be like the old days. It'll be fun.' So all three of us lived in this very large mansion-like house I had in Santa Rosa and proceeded to do a lot of writing and going to the studio and recording. That's how the whole thing started. To work with Gene you had to kind of live with Gene. He wasn't the kind of guy you just showed up at the office with, you know what I mean? Gene had lived with me for months and months and so had Tommy. It was a whole different ballpark. It was kind of like a Fellini movie in a lot of ways."

Armed with a truckload of songs and a renewed sense of purpose, Gene, Andy, and Tommy—plus the rhythm section from the Mendocino All-Stars augmented by Chris Hillman and Herb Pedersen—began recording what would become *Firebyrd* in early 1982. Shuttling between studios in San Francisco and Los Angeles, sessions would continue into the following year.

Initially, Tommy was set to produce the album, but early into the project he bowed out for medical reasons (a diabetic, his drug use was especially detrimental to his health) and Andy stepped up to the plate. "Tommy Kaye was one of my best friends," asserts Andy. "He was a tremendous producer and I was his protégé. Tommy taught me everything I know. Not being a real orthodox kind of guy in terms of work ethic, Tommy was able to work around Gene's idiosyncrasies and eccentricities, and because of that he was able to pull some of the best stuff out of Gene. When we started the *Firebyrd* album Tommy got sick and just couldn't carry on, but the groundwork was set. Tommy and I had collaborated a great deal on the game plan and the three of us had sat down and written a lot of tunes together."

Two other familiar faces from Gene's past came onboard for the album. "Eddie Tickner handled the publishing and I got Jim Dickson involved from the aspect of helping me get some studio time in L.A. and I thought maybe he could help in securing a record deal," Andy explains. "Artistically, he really didn't have any input. Jim Dickson really wasn't a producer. His name went on it, though. But he did get me a couple of session people when I needed them and they did really well that way. He brought in Herb Pedersen, who was great, and Buddy Shank, which I regret." A further Clark associate, Ken Mansfield, ended up remixing the album in the 1990s for distribution in the UK as *This Byrd Has Flown*—a tongue-in-cheek title, no doubt, and perhaps a nod to the Beatles' *Rubber Soul* gem "Norwegian Wood (This Bird Has Flown)."

As Jim recalls, "The second time that Gene lived with me was when he had been through lots of disasters, marriages, failed careers, all that. He was back on the street and had been involved with junk. I hadn't seen him in a long time. While we were doing that Andy Kandanes album and going up to San Francisco to record, Gene lived with me all that time." Jim felt it necessary to lay down the law with Gene. "I told him, 'You drink or do any drugs, Gene, and you're out of here and I'm finished with you.' He would drink about a half a pound of coffee a day and pace the house like a maniac. The day I got that album finished he got out of there and went out and got drunk. He had a bigger drinking problem than drugs." Andy had to lay down a similar threat. "One time we were in the studio and he kind of fell off the edge. I went back to my house, packed my bags, and said to him, 'I'm going to Jamaica. I'll be back Tuesday. Either be clean or be gone. You make the choice whether you want to finish the album or not.' And it worked. I usually didn't have to get that heavy with him. I was able to reason with him."

Andy and Gene collaborated on three tracks on *Firebyrd*. "I was mainly an R&B writer, but I learned a lot from Gene," he acknowledges. "I learned a lot from him, but at the same time I was able to contribute and open up new things for him. We were pretty prolific and a lot of stuff still hasn't been recorded. We just didn't have time." One of their tracks, "Rodeo Rider," had all the earmarks of a country music hit with the right push behind it. "That was about a friend of ours, Sandy Pinkert, who is also a great writer," reveals Andy. "He wrote 'Coca-Cola Cowboy.' He was a pretty well-known guy and quite a character, a real wild man. He rode in a rodeo and the tune is about Sandy. I thought it was a good single or a good cover for some of these new country guys. But it didn't get any exposure. No one ever heard it."

Gene made the decision to re-record one of his best-known Byrds songs, "I'll Feel a Whole Lot Better," in a more 1980s rock context. "Although redoing 'Feel a Whole Lot Better' wasn't strongly in my mind at first," Gene told writer Barry Ballard, "so many people had asked me to do it that I figured it would probably be a good thing to do, so I just said, 'Well, OK.'" He also cut an expanded version of "Mr. Tambourine Man" with all the original verses intact. It was a bold move, given the song's immediate association with Roger McGuinn, but back in 1964 it was Gene who had been the Byrds' original lead singer. "I had always wanted to record that version," he informed Ballard. "I started messing around with it in the studio. Everybody picked up on it and so we went ahead and did it. There was so much poetry in it that I always wanted to do a longer version to capture some of it." Jim brought in Herb Pedersen from the Dillards to harmonize with Gene on the track. Eschewing the Rickenbacker 12-string guitar, Gene's arrangement relies primarily on piano flourishes. "We sat down and did an arrangement and thought it was pretty damn good," boasts Andy. "That was Ossie Ahlers from the Mendocino All-Stars on piano. That was Gene's idea to do that. I thought it was one of the better Byrds tunes and if anyone deserved to do a cover of it, he did."

The other cover on the album is Gordon Lightfoot's folk-pop ballad "If You Could Read My Mind," which, in the end, may have been a questionable choice. "These two guys had a parallel career," Andy insists. "Gordon had stayed up at my place in Mendocino. There's a picture of my house on the back of one of his albums. Gordon was pretty fond of Mendocino. Even though those two guys had never collaborated, they were kind of like soul brothers. They were so much alike it was amazing. Gordon was quite a prolific writer and so was Gene, and they were both poets. I think Gene just wanted to pay him a little tribute and kind of say, 'Hey, man, I know you're out there.' That was Gene's idea and I thought it was a great tune."

As the *Firebyrd* sessions carried on sporadically through 1982, Gene was wooed away to participate in another project: an ex-Byrds, country-rock dream team that never really took flight. On July 7, Gene, Chris Hillman, Michael Clarke, banjo player Herb Pedersen, and dobro/pedal steel guitarist Al Perkins of the Flying Burrito Brothers and the Souther, Hillman, and Furay Band assembled at The Alley rehearsal hall in North Hollywood to pool their talents and create a potential new group, dubbed Flyte. "I remember us thinking of names that had to do with the Byrds," notes Al, "but not using the Byrds name. Since the Byrds name had a 'y' in it we thought that might be a pretty cool way of doing a similar name. The first working or tentative name was American Standard, then it changed to Free Flight before Flyte." Al had been recording with Chris on his *Morning Sky* album, a return to acoustic-based bluegrass music, at Criterion Studios in Los Angeles when he was recruited for the new project.

On July 10 the new group entered Criterion Studios, returning on July 21 to cut a five-song demo: Gene's "I'll Feel a Whole Lot Better" (arranged in a country-rock mode instead of the rockier take on *Firebyrd*), the Box Tops hit "The Letter," Gram Parsons's "Still Feeling Blue" and "One Hundred Years from Now," and Rodney Crowell's "No More Memories Hanging 'Round" all produced by Jim Dickson. Oddly, no original songs were attempted. Following the sessions, Chris and Al went out on tour as a bluegrass duo while Eddie Tickner hustled the demo tape in Nashville, to no avail. No one was interested in Flyte. It's not surprising, given the mediocre cover versions, generic sound, and lackluster performances. Despite the topnotch players involved, Flyte seemed to lack a distinctive sound.

Al recalls that Gene was on his best behavior for the Flyte rehearsals and sessions. "I didn't notice anyone out of line. I think Chris was sensitive to that kind of thing. I didn't go to the bar and drink with them, but I remember a lot of people coming and going because we were in L.A. and they had a lot of friends. But I'm sure Chris would have tried to dissuade any of that kind of thing from going on. That was likely one of the stipulations. I'm sure Jim, who was always the mediator, probably encouraged Chris and Herb that Gene was in good shape to do this and at the same time probably warned Gene not to try anything. I think everybody at the time was in good shape because I wouldn't have wanted to be involved in anything dodgy."

Flyte reconvened in late November to rehearse for an impending two-night engagement at L.A.'s country music bastion, the Palomino, on December 17–18, opening for another of Eddie's artists, Emmylou Harris. By this time, Michael had bowed out and the group had transformed from country-rock to acoustic bluegrass. Gene was relegated to supporting status, performing "If You Could Read My Mind," "Train Leaves Here This Morning," and a duet with Chris on "Mr. Tambourine Man," while Chris took the lead, debuting several new songs from his recently released bluegrass-flavored album. Despite a positive reception, Flyte folded soon after, doomed from the start by a lack of direction and commitment. "It was a pretty good idea for a group," Gene acknowledged in his 1985 interview with Domenic Priore, "but Chris was headed in one direction and I was kind of headed in another. It never really came together." It's likely Gene wouldn't have stayed long after the group shifted direction to a more acoustic bluegrass sound, nor would he have settled for being second fiddle to Chris.

"I don't remember how it came to an end, but I elected to go with Chris," states Al. "Chris had a real strong urge at that time during the recording of *Morning Sky* to get back to bluegrass music and go out acoustically. That was the purpose in recording that album. I have a feeling the Flyte thing was worth a try, but I know he was disenchanted with what had happened in McGuinn, Clark & Hillman and it weighed heavily on his mind that Gene had left the group, whether it was fear of flying or drugs. I think that influenced his decision to go out acoustically rather than the electric thing. We were already doing acoustic gigs as a duo before that." Concludes Chris, "Flyte really wasn't anything. That was just Dickson goofing around. They've got some bootleg thing out and it's awful. Once again it was just spinning our wheels."

In anticipation of the release of *Firebyrd,* Gene assembled a new backing band in March 1983 dubbed the Firebyrds including Andy on drums, bassist Mark Andes (on hiatus from Heart) and his brother, Matt, on guitar (both had been in Jo Jo Gunne), and newcomer Trace Harrill on second guitar. Mark did not stay long and KC Southern veteran Peter Oliva was called to step in on bass. After just a handful of gigs and before the band took a jaunt up to Edmonton, Canada, Andy left and was replaced by Michael Clarke.

"One of the highlights of Gene's first trip to Edmonton when he was leading the Firebyrds was getting him a gig on a show called *Sun Country,* which Ian Tyson [of Ian & Sylvia fame] co-hosted," points out Edmonton journalist Peter North, who was involved with production on the show. "That was Halloween 1983. The house band was a damn fine unit, better than Gene's group, actually. Usually guests would get two songs, but both Ian and I felt someone of Gene's stature should get three, if possible. Gene ended up performing Rodney Crowell's somewhat prophetic 'Ain't Livin' Long like This,' the Dillard & Clark/Eagles' 'Train Leaves Here This Morning,' and 'Rodeo Rider' from the *Firebyrd* disc. Gene looked good and sounded even better on the day of the taping. The vocals were live. Ian was most gracious on all the intros and obviously really pleased to have someone he connected with on the show. 'If you think this next song is a cover of the Eagles classic,' Ian announced, 'Well, it's not. This is the man who wrote it.' And Gene nailed it. I would suspect it had been some time since he had appeared on a television show that paid him good money and treated him with the respect he deserved. The house band was always thrilled to have someone they admired and listened to devoutly on the show, so someone was always asking Gene to talk about the Byrds, Dillard & Clark, his solo work between breaks. Ian and Gene reminisced about the days when Ian & Sylvia played L.A. and all the Byrds would be hanging out listening to their harmonies. Gene considered Ian to be one of the greats and was honored to be on the show. I remember it as being a sincere mutual admiration society."

Prior to taping the show, the Firebyrds played three nights at Edmonton's Ambassador club, where Peter caught their sets. "The band was average at best," he remembers. "They had a guitar player who wanted to look like Ron Wood and have Keith Richards's lifestyle [Trace Harrill], so there were some memorable moments. The set list included 'Kansas City Southern,' 'Through the Morning, Through the Night,' the Everly's 'So Sad,' a couple of early Beatles tunes, 'Tears of Rage,' 'I'll Feel a Whole Lot Better,' and 'Eight Miles High.' The group was supposed to do two 50-minute sets, but couldn't pull it off without repeating a few tunes. When they did hit the nerve on tunes like 'Feel a Whole Lot Better' and 'Kansas City Southern' there was a decided shiver factor through the crowd. Gene had charisma to spare and looked like he was born to be onstage. He'd sit with folks and chat after the night was over, signing autographs on every album he ever participated on. The band came back just over a year later and it was a much better outfit. I booked them into a place called the Penthouse in the Sheraton Hotel for a one-night show and they worked hard and had obviously been touring and rehearsing in a focused manner. The crowd loved them. It was sold out, 350 seats. They had most of the Firebyrd disc in their repertoire and I remember Gene did a short solo thing that was well received. We all stayed up until five in the morning listening to the stories that only Gene and Michael could tell."

The Firebyrds toured sporadically through the year as Andy, Tom Slocum, and Jim Dickson worked to find the *Firebyrd* album a label. In the end, tiny independent label Allegiance/Takoma picked up the album and released it in early 1984. "A lot of people didn't want to touch that album because they were afraid that Gene wasn't stable enough," admits Andy. "That they would put money into it, promote it, and then Gene wouldn't go out on the road. Clive Davis told me, 'I don't think you'll get a record deal.' I asked him why and he said, 'The guy's a genius and a great artist, but I don't think anyone wants to touch him.' So I said to Clive, 'All I can do is try.' I talked with Bob Krasnow from Warner Brothers and Bob said the same thing, 'Man, if you get him a deal, give me a call. I'll give you a job.' It was quite an adventure. Gene had burned a lot of bridges, let me tell you. David Geffen was one of the biggest ones he burned." Confirms Tom, who helped broker the contract, "This little label had a nice little roster. They had Spencer Davis, John Fahey, Bert Jansch, Pentangle, that kind of stuff. As far as the deal went down, there was no hype involved. The idea was to just get the record out. Nobody wanted to touch him because of what happened with Capitol Records [McGuinn, Clark & Hillman's label]. 'He's a lunatic, he's this, he's that,' and he wasn't. He was branded as trouble, no doubt about that."

The limited promotional abilities of the independent label ensured that *Firebyrd* received scant attention. "The label was owned by the guy who used to be the head of marketing and promotion at Capitol before opening his own label," continues Andy. "It was supposed to be a really hot item, but they didn't promote anything. They just catalogued it and that was the end of story."

As Gene confirmed to Barry Ballard in 1985, "The *Firebyrd* album has so far been received really well, but it's not being pressed any more. I don't know the reasons and I can't understand it because I know that all the copies sold out and there were some back orders that weren't filled."

Reviews were mixed. Some cited the commercial sound on the album as a good thing for Gene, while others viewed it as a sellout of his artistic integrity. Whatever the opinion, while hardly as adventurous as *No Other* or as slickly produced as *Two Sides to Every Story, Firebyrd* was a worthy release for Gene. "I've had pros and cons on it," sighs Andy. "There were great reviews when it was released. Then after awhile there were those opinionated people who decided it was too commercial. Everybody's got to eat, you know." Commercial-sounding tracks like "Rain Song," "Made for Love," "Blue Raven," and "Something About You Baby" are all paeans to Terri, who Gene was trying to woo back. "Gene's songs are all about 'the jones'," avers Jason Ronard, "about Carlie or Terri giving him a hard time. If Gene just broken up with a girl, like he did with Terri every other month, he'd have another song out of it." The album's Tommy Kaye song, "Vanessa," is a treat—a haunting track driven by some shimmering guitar from Greg Douglas and Tommy's genius for vocal arranging.

The standout track by far is Gene's stunning reinterpretation of "Mr. Tambourine Man." Claims Ken Mansfield, "Bob Dylan said that Gene's solo version of 'Tambourine Man' was the single best version that was ever done of that song. When he starts out you think it isn't going to happen because it starts out on piano but, boy, when he starts singing, it just melts you." In an interview with KMET radio, Gene offered his justification for the rearrangement. "I went to Hawaii a couple of years ago and stayed in a Japanese-Hawaiian neighborhood. I spent about four months just staring at the ocean, wondering what I was doing. These little children used to walk to school in front of my house every day and they would chant as they walked. Somehow one day I just thought it was sort of like a pied piper or a tambourine. So I took the rhythm, their cadence of their particular walk, the little Japanese children, as they sang. They walked in a row every day past the house and sang and did their little dance. I took that rhythm and took the verses to 'Tambourine Man' and re-recorded it that way, with that feeling of those children. That's how that happened."

What could have been a stronger track, "Blue Raven," a slight poke at "Silver Raven" and Carlie, is marred by an annoying flute part throughout from Bud Shank. "That was Dickson's idea," insists Andy. "Bud's an icon, but it was not my choice. I would rather have had sax player David Sanborn." The later reissue of the album boasted three additional tracks. One of these, Tommy's "Dixie Flyer" (also included on Tommy's solo album *Not Alone*), was supposed to be included on the original *Firebyrd* release, according to Gene, but was somehow excised from the album.

By January 1984, Trace Harrill, a controversial member of the Firebyrds from the outset, was ousted from the band and replaced by Texas musician Mike Hardwick on guitar and pedal steel. Peter recalls, "Michael Clarke told us, 'I've got a guy named Wickie, man, you'll love this guy.' So we got Wickie up there and that was a great band. He's a rock and you need that in a band. When he played steel, it was really a lot of fun. I enjoyed playing with Wickie."

The Firebyrds lineup in 1984: (left to right) Michael Clarke, Matt Andes, Gene Clark, Peter Oliva, and Michael Hardwick.

"I had been touring with Jerry Jeff Walker for several years and I had roomed with Michael Clarke on the road," offers Wickie. "He drummed with Jerry Jeff. Michael had quit Jerry Jeff and moved back to Los Angeles. I heard he was playing with Gene and I thought that was great because I was a Gene fan from the beginning. So what happened was, they needed somebody at the last minute for this tour they were getting ready to go on. The band was Matt Andes, Peter Oliva, Michael, and Gene and they needed somebody on short notice. So Michael Clarke called me up and I jumped at the chance to play with Gene. Three days later I was in Los Angeles at a rehearsal hall learning the songs two days before we left."

It was a baptism by fire with the Firebyrds for Wickie. "We did a brutal, nine-week tour. We left Los Angeles and drove to the first show in Santa Fe, New Mexico. We were pretty much playing the same places Michael and I had been playing with Jerry Jeff. Then we went down to Austin for two nights, then Houston and Dallas, and then the guys went home for a week or two. Then we started up again and they came through and picked me up in Austin and I think one of the first shows was in Kansas City, because I remember meeting Gene's mother and father and his brothers."

Wickie found in Gene not only a talented musician, but a mentor. "Gene was really good to me. I was about ten years younger than the rest of them. When I went out there to play with those guys it was by the seat of my pants. They barely had management; they barely had bookings. I got paid a lot of money with Jerry Jeff and I just walked away to play with Gene and Michael, no guarantees, just something I wanted to do. I just thought, 'Man, I'm ready.' I had already worn out two copies of *No Other*. We started rehearsing in this funky little rehearsal hall and it was pretty much on me. I had to learn these songs really fast, so I was taking notes and trying to listen and pay attention. I had to learn like 20 songs. After we were done with that portion of it, we took a little break. And Gene said, 'Well, I need to do some of the old stuff, too.' So he started pulling out some of his older songs and I knew them. I was all over them and the other guys had to learn them. And he just kind of grinned and he was laughing as if to say, 'Thank you for showing up. I guess Michael was right, you are the right guy.' That made me feel good.

"I know I was present during certain problems, he had his problems and I was there when some unpleasant things went on and everybody has lots of stories about Gene, but I was also there and I saw a real goodness in Gene. I have to say I learned a lot from Gene, not just musical things; I'm talking about just gentlemanly things, how you should act, and in some ways, he was kind of protective of me. What he told me at certain times I listened to and paid attention to, and some of that I still carry to this day. He had a good heart. I remember we were loading out in Santa Fe, the very first show, and he grabbed my amplifier and he's carrying it out behind the club and he almost slipped in the snow. And I said to him, 'Oh, you don't need to do that. I'll carry it,' and he goes, 'Ah, I don't mind.' And I'm thinking, 'Here's Gene Clark of the Byrds carrying my amp out, loading out after the club's closed, stomping around in the snow.' The other guys were all inside having drinks."

Working with Gene Clark was nonetheless an eye-opener for Wickie, who was used to better treatment under Jerry Jeff Walker's employ. "That brutal nine weeks was in a van. We had a local California rental on that van that wouldn't allow it to be taken out of the state. I found out about that after we were already in Toronto. We pulled a U-Haul trailer with our gear across the US, went to New York and hung a left and went to Boston, then up to Toronto. We got as far as Ottawa and started working our way back, driving across Canada in February. We went all the way to Vancouver and over to Victoria on the island. That's when we found out what we were all made of. We had one guy with us as road manager and driver. At that point we were exhausted. And the gigs started falling through and we ended up not getting paid on a big part of the tour. I was used to making pretty decent money and here we were out there just scrambling around. The booking agent would call and the dates were falling out left and right and they're trying to put dates together on the road as we went through. We played some pretty funky rock clubs, but it was pretty darn good every night. It came down to everyone saying, 'We're not gonna quit on this one. It's too much fun. If we just hang in here, maybe things will get better.' That's pretty much what kept everyone going."

"Gene was actually in a good place," insists Peter. "He was holding it together. He was out there on the road and he wasn't drinking, he wasn't doing anything. Well, one incident—and that was almost at the very end of the tour. We were in Nanaimo, British Columbia. We had been out about three months or something and somehow he got to drinking and he emptied out this whole place. But that was it. We had a stern talking-to with him and then he stopped that. He punched a few people. And we punched Gene a few times, too. We had to, at certain times, to get him in line when he was drunk. Gene and I roomed together on that tour because nobody wanted to room with him—he would talk to people that weren't there in the room. He had his spaceman stage, his mafioso stage, where he'd say, 'Scuz a me.' Then he'd start yelling at people who weren't in the room. I'd go, 'Jeez!' This was my life with Gene. Drugs? We had no money for drugs. Gene didn't drink that much on that tour, not enough that he got crazed.

"When Gene was straight he was a really likeable, nice guy," Peter stresses. "I didn't see him fall into any slumps, no more than anybody else. You have your good days and your bad days. But when he would get drunk I always felt he was holding down a lot of stuff. He felt guilty about his kids and he used to cry, 'Oh, my poor little babies. I love my babies. I never see them.' He would go on like that. He had a lot of issues to deal with." Wickie recalls, "I know there were maybe a few shows where everybody in the band got drunk, but we probably outnumbered the people in the audience on those nights. But there were some nights when Gene was just amazing. Yes, we all got frustrated, but we all dealt with it our own way. People got drunk, but nobody got arrested or got hurt and there were a couple of stinker shows. But most all of them were pretty darn good and special to behold."

Despite the arduous conditions out on the road, Wickie especially remembers the compassionate side of Gene's character, the part few ever saw through the media's glare. "When we were driving into Edmonton the night before the show we had been traveling all day and it was way after dark. Somewhere out in the middle of nowhere, about three hours out of Edmonton, there was a crossroads with a flashing red light for the traffic to stop one way while the other keeps going and there had been a terrible car wreck. We came driving by immediately after it happened. The police weren't there yet. There was maybe a car or two that had stopped. We all got out of the van and Gene and Michael went down to the crash site. And there were some that were severely injured in this car wreck. There was this girl who had apparently been sitting in the front seat who hadn't been wearing a seatbelt and had been thrown into the backseat and was busted up pretty bad. Those two guys tried to render whatever kind of aid they could while waiting for the ambulance to come. This woman was seriously injured and Gene stuck his arm into the car, reached in and grabbed her hand. He was holding her hand and telling her it was going to be okay. And he stayed there with this young woman for about an hour or so before the authorities came and then the ambulance came. We probably stayed around another half hour after they got the people out of the other car that had turned over and rolled several times down the embankment. And I know that the next day he called the local hospital to see if everything was okay."

Matt Andes left the group soon after the accident and Wickie assumed all guitar duties, relying more on Gene's acoustic rhythm guitar to fill out the sound. Wickie's pedal steel added a new dimension to songs like "Train Leaves Here This Morning" and "Silver Raven." "I was real pleased with that four-piece lineup," Peter smiles. "I remember Michael Clarke wanted a screaming rock 'n' roll band, but Wickie played real nice, tasteful stuff. I just felt that Gene was a guy who needed to get onstage and shine and the band needs to chill. We're there to make him sound good, but basically we want to highlight this guy and what he does. He doesn't need some guitar player jumping in front of him and taking long leads. The thing was to enhance Gene. The Firebyrds was a good band that maybe could have done something."

Before Matt left the group, though, Gene took the Firebyrds into Skip Saylor's tiny studio on Larchmont Boulevard in Los Angeles where they laid down basic tracks for two songs: a cover of the Beatles' "She Loves You" and a newer number, "Into the Night," by songwriters Liz Anderson and Jeff Rollings, who were signed to Criterion Music at the time. "Gene liked 'She Loves You,'" Peter notes. "Matt Andes was playing an 'Every Breath You Take' kind of guitar part on it. It was neat." Tom Slocum, who financed the sessions, suggests, "I was under the impression they wrote 'Into the Night' and Gene may have changed something later. I remember Gene and Liz, this gorgeous redhead with a fake leg or foot, going over the song, rehearsing at his house. There were only live guide vocals done, very rough, on 'She Loves You,' and a semi-terrible, buried vocal on 'Into the Night.' We never re-recorded or overdubbed because Gene either hit the road, was working, or was out of gas. At the time Gene was really active into live gigs." The recordings were never completed. The tapes were later stored with Barbra Streisand's producer, John Arrias, and have since disappeared.

Despite the use of cover tunes, Gene was still writing. And Wickie was struck by Gene's unique creative process. "I had come out of Austin and at that time in Austin there was quite a singer-songwriter scene going on, kind of a country-rock thing. So by being around Jerry Jeff, I was around Guy Clark, B.W. Stevenson, Townes Van Zandt, Billy Jo Shaver, guys like that, regularly. But Gene was on a whole other level. And it wasn't because he was a Byrd or was hooked up with the Burritos and that whole scene or Doug Dillard. He just found the way, and he was doing it. His vocals were tremendous and his songwriting was amazing. He would write songs real fast. He wrote a song or at least finished a song while we were driving in the van going to a gig in Texas. The song was called 'Gypsy Rider,' which has turned out to be one of his classic songs [recorded in 1986 with Carla Olson on *So Rebellious a Lover*]. I was used to seeing guys working on bits and pieces and taking a while to put it together. But it just came out of him; it just flowed. I watched how those other guys wrote, I was around them doing demos, but I had never seen anything like Gene. And tell me where those melody lines came from? Completely original. And the way he phrased and put the words together? This was from a guy who had an incredible gift. I don't remember him really reading anything. We might have a newspaper in the van and Matt would read it and Michael might read something, but I don't remember Gene reading. Yet he was a man of words. Where did it come from? It was a gift."

Peter lays part of the blame for Gene's stalled career on the lack of constant and consistent support. Gene did not enjoy the luxuries of someone like Neil Young, whose manager, Elliot Roberts, stuck with Neil through thick and thin and allowed him to follow his muse without distraction from the business end. There was no Elliot Roberts, David Geffen, or Albert Grossman to guide Gene's career. "He didn't have proper direction," asserts Peter. "He needed somebody to direct him, but there was nobody around in his little sphere of friends that was reliable or upright. They should have done with Gene what they were doing with Steve Goodman or John Prine, people like that. There were guys back then that were doing the same thing basically in the same sphere and Gene was as original as any of those guys were and could have been out there doing it." But Peter also points to Gene's lack of business savvy and cutthroat edge as a further liability. "Gene didn't have it in him to be a scoundrel. He was not a conniving person. He didn't connive. He was really an innocent. This is something a lot of people don't know, but Gene was really an innocent. He was kind of like a kid wandering through a department store and forgetting about his mommy. I guess we all have that, but the thing is he had a lot of people that came up and used him the wrong way. And that is the real crime. The people that got a hold of him didn't help him; they ruined him in a lot of ways. I think with this whole singer-songwriter thing that's happening in the last ten years, Gene would have flourished and that's really where he should have gone."

By the summer of 1984 the Firebyrds were running out of steam. Still, commitments remained. Wickie bowed out and the band gigged for a while as a trio. "I remember Wickie said, 'I'm out of here,' and I said, 'You're not going to leave, are you?' He said, 'Peter, it's gonna get ugly.' He was right, but I had nothing to lose so I stuck around. We did some gigs with just me, Michael, and Gene. That was the strangest thing. We picked up this guitarist in Providence, Rhode Island. We said, 'Hey, man, you wanna play with Gene Clark?' And he goes, 'The guy from the Byrds?! Oh yeah, man. Sure! When's our first gig?' I told him, 'In about a half hour, man.' Gene and Michael go, 'You gotta teach this guy the songs, Peter.' So I took him into a back room and I'm trying to teach him the songs. He doesn't know what's going on. We burned him out after about three gigs. So then we did some more gigs with just me, Michael, and Gene, and they were the worst gigs, just terrible."

Before that last ignominious tour, the Firebyrds appeared in June at Madame Wong's West club on Wilshire Boulevard in Los Angeles. The gig would be significant not for the performance, but for who was in attendance.

Near the end of the group's set that night, Tom Slocum invited singer Carla Olson (of punk/country-rock young guns the Textones), who was there with her manager and boyfriend, Saul Davis, to join Gene onstage. "Saul and I intentionally went to see Gene that night actually because we had never met him," explains the Austin-born singer-songwriter. "We just decided kind of at the last minute we were going to go to the show. We sat down at a booth with

Textones singer Carla Olson joins Gene onstage for the first time at Madame Wong's West, June 1984.

another friend of ours and were enjoying the show. Then Gene's friend Tom Slocum came over and sat in the booth with us during the set. I didn't know Tom, but he recognized me and introduced himself. He said, 'I really like the Textones. You should get up and sing with Gene on the encore.' I said, 'That's okay, Tom. Don't worry. I'm just here to enjoy the show.' And Tom said, 'No, you should get up and sing with Gene. They're going to do "Feel a Whole Lot Better." You know that one.' He kept pushing and pushing me. When the show was over with and they started to do the encore he literally grabbed me by the hand and pulled me up on the stage and threw a tambourine at me and said, 'Sing!' In the middle of the guitar solo, Gene leaned over and said, 'Hi, I'm Gene Clark.' There's a photo, actually, of that moment, the moment we first met. Then after the show we went backstage and talked with him."

Carla Olson's Textones were among a brand-new breed of country-rock traditionalists. The early '80s Paisley Underground revival of 1960s power-pop in Los Angeles had spurred a healthy country-rock/Americana roots scene. This would ultimately spawn the alt.country movement, spearheaded in the late '80s and early '90s by such artists as Lucinda Williams, Gillian Welch, Victoria Williams, the Jayhawks, and Son Volt, among others. These performers took as their guiding inspiration the works of doomed country-rock pioneers like Gram Parsons, the Flying Burrito Brothers, the *Sweetheart of the Rodeo*-era Byrds, and Dillard & Clark.

"I didn't really get hip to the Burrito Brothers until Elvis Costello made such a big deal about Gram Parsons being his favorite songwriter," explains Carla, who, despite an early preference for British rock, was well familiar with groups like the Byrds and Dillards. She had come to Los Angeles in 1978 with friend Kathy Valentine, and the two formed the punk-inspired Textones the following year (Kathy soon departed, later taking a spot in the Go-Go's). Carla's big break came when she appeared alongside Bob Dylan in the video for "Sweetheart like You" from his acclaimed *Infidels* album. She would later team up with Rolling Stones guitar great Mick Taylor.

"You couldn't easily find a Flying Burrito Brothers album because they probably didn't print a lot of them," she continues. "Don Henley and his band were the ones who turned me on to the country-rock revolution. Gene was a legend. I was aware of who he was, certainly with McGuinn, Clark & Hillman. I wasn't so much aware of the stuff he did with Vern Gosdin or Doug Dillard, but I had known the Dillards from Texas. They used to play in Dallas all the time. Gene was always kind of the serious guy in the Byrds. He wrote the most beautiful melodies, the most haunting. The charisma he had onstage was so different from what Roger was projecting. He was so aloof and cool."

When Carla's gregarious manager Chicago-born Saul Davis inquired who Gene's manager was, the singer replied he currently had no management and followed it up with, "Why don't you be my manager?" As Carla notes, "So it just kind of blossomed from there that Saul started working with him." Gene was already beginning to look elsewhere, realizing the Firebyrds band had just about run its course. The failure of *Firebyrd* to reignite his career, and the paucity of gigs, signaled it was time for a change. In August he performed alongside Roger McGuinn at McCabe's in Santa Monica, then made a guest appearance on "Ivory Tower," a track by nouveau country-rockers the Long Ryders, and joined Carla and the Textones in the studio for their debut A&M album, *Midnight Mission*.

Wickie remembers with some malice Gene's transition from the Firebyrds to becoming involved with Saul and his stable of associates. "The last show I played with Gene, we played the Country Club in Reseda as a four-piece. That was the night that Sid Griffin's band, the Long Ryders, opened up for us and we met them and their manager Saul Davis. It's funny looking back on that night because we had no idea how things were going to unfold. I kind of remember seeing Sid trying to talk to Gene and asking him specific questions about certain records and stuff like that and Gene being nice, but looking uncomfortable with the whole thing. We knew Peter Oliva was getting ready to maybe leave and we needed a bass player and thought their bass player was really good. So we thought, 'Maybe we could get him to go out on the tour.'

The next thing I know, Saul was managing Gene. I don't think Saul had much use for the rest of us. I think Michael Clarke and Saul didn't get along. Gene needed a manager and Saul filled that role for him and paired him up with his girlfriend, Carla Olson. I was kind of bitter about that."

The arrival of Carla and Saul at that particular point in Gene's life and career, while certainly serendipitous, would prove fortuitous. It gave Gene the chance to return to a more roots-based, acoustic singer-songwriter format—always his strength—and offered fresh, new associations that would recharge his creative batteries.

8

Day for Night

The year 1985 would prove to be one of Gene's busiest since leaving the Byrds. Following low-key engagements in New England, Gene folded the Firebyrds in January and joined forces with Michael Clarke and various associates for what was initially billed as a "Twentieth Anniversary Tribute to the Byrds" tour (remarkably, Gene would carry the Byrds banner on the road for the next four years). In March, Gene embarked on a much-anticipated UK solo tour supporting British folk-rockers Lindisfarne, capped off by a spectacular headlining set on April 4 at Dingwall's club in North London. Later, back in the US, Gene would forge two musical alliances that would, albeit briefly, re-energize his songwriting and return him to the spotlight: he began a productive songwriting partnership with Pat Robinson (in association with Byrds colleague John York), and teamed with Textones singer-songwriter Carla Olson in the studio to create an exceptional roots album.

Despite the flurry of activity in his career, Gene's home life experienced a stability not found since the early months in Mendocino. In the mid-'80s, after living on and off with girlfriend Terri in and around Laurel Canyon, Gene settled into a small, two-bedroom bungalow at 14747 Otsego in Sherman Oaks. Owned by Ray Berry and his wife Jean, a retired actress noted for being Flash Gordon's sidekick in the old serials, this would remain Gene's residence until his death. "Ray and Jean kind of adopted Gene," suggests brother Rick. "They lived in the back house and Gene rented the front house from them. Ray was kind of a cantankerous son of a bitch who loved scotch." At times Terri, English Roger, Michael Clarke, and various band members resided with Gene at the house. Kelly and Kai would also come to live with him for a while.

Since the late '70s the boys had spent several weeks each summer with Gene in Los Angeles. "When we first started to visit him, he was living in Laurel Canyon, him and Terri Messina, I always remember the smell of the place, the ivy and all that," reflects Kai. "A lot of famous people lived in the area and we would go to other people's houses and swim in their pools." (One pool the boys frequented belonged to actor Kurt Russell and his then girlfriend, actress Season Hubley; Gene was a close friend of theirs.) "He wasn't a hands-on father, I don't think he knew how to be that," Kai continues, "but I think in a way he felt bad because he wasn't there all the time for us because he was trying to build his career. I understand that now, and am sensitive to that situation as a musician. We missed him and we didn't ever get to know him enough. We would be there for a summer, then we would go away.

"I remember we were so into *Star Wars* and all the little action figures," Kai enthuses, recalling one particular summer with Gene. "My dad would buy us all the cool toys we couldn't get up in Mendocino. He really spoiled us. But this one particular summer my dad was very poor. All he ate was brown rice with soy sauce and butter on it. He was poor, but living in this nice house with a hot tub. We called that the 'brown rice summer' because we ate brown rice every day for months. My dad was hilarious then. Most people don't know the sense of humor that he had, especially around us kids. He would tell the funniest jokes and you just couldn't help but laugh until you cried. He was a very funny guy when he wanted to be, but he had to be very comfortable around anyone to bust those jokes. I just remember him always making me laugh that summer.

"So *The Empire Strikes Back* came out that summer," Kai continues, "and of course we had to see the premiere. Dad takes us to the movie, then out to dinner at the Howling Coyote in North Hollywood, a big Mexican restaurant. This was a special occasion because this was the brown rice summer and he took us out to a nice restaurant. We're sitting there eating and who comes along but Mark Hamill—Luke Skywalker! My brother and me flip out. Turns out he's a big fan of my dad's music so he sits down with us. We're going, 'Luke Skywalker's having dinner with us!' We were beside ourselves. So my dad brings him back to our house and they're having a drink and a good time. And my brother and I decide to act out the scene where Luke gets his arm cut off by Darth Vader. 'Luke, love your father.' It was hilarious. My dad was cracking up.

"He definitely gave my brother and I a hundred percent of love when he was around. And that's what counts. And if we needed some money or clothes, he would look after us. When our mother sent us to him he definitely tried to do the best he could to take care of us and support us. As a father he wanted the best for us."

Not surprisingly, older brother Kelly's recollections of that period are far less rosy than Kai's. "I'll tell you about the summers. We were with my dad for about four days. All the other days we were with my Aunt Victoria, Uncle Rick's girlfriend. My dad didn't have the time, the money, or the ability to take care of us. He didn't know what to do. And I also think that he didn't want to have us watch him do whatever he was up to because most of the time he was pretty messed up. My earliest memories of my dad are the Laurel Canyon days when he lived in the elf house with Terri Messina. There was absolute craziness going on there. Terri and my dad were doing a lot of cocaine. He got to the point once where he got kind of nuts and threw stuff out the top window. They were way out of their minds. I remember all the cool toys and hanging out with my dad, but I also remember he was not very available most of the time. He slept late; they were out a lot. I just remember lots of babysitters."

"There were some hard times," concedes Rick. "The boys would come down and stay with Gene when he was going through a rough time. Gene would try to kill his pain like any other tortured soul does and the boys witnessed some stuff that they shouldn't have had to, and it hurt them. It hurt Gene, too, that they had to see some things that weren't so great. I can't say that it totally alienated them, but they tended not to come around as much when Gene was going through some very tortured times."

Resurrecting the Byrds moniker was a humbling experience for Gene, though one borne of necessity. Promoter Michael Gaiman had approached Michael Clarke with the anniversary tribute concept and, given the dire circumstances surrounding the last Firebyrds gigs, the money on the table was simply too hard to resist. Clarke then brought Gene in. In doing so, however, Gene was acceding to the widely held music industry opinion that he had failed to rise above the shadow of the Byrds in his solo career. Dogged by the legacy of that band, Gene swallowed his pride and signed on. "I said to him, 'Why are you going out and being the Byrds?'" recalls friend Pat Robinson. "It would have been enough to say 'Gene Clark *from* the Byrds.' But he had to make a living; he had to pay his bills. That was the sad thing about it." Like many members of name bands who had struck out on their own, Gene could command far more money by using the more recognizable band name than his own. The sum was always greater than the individual components. "At first, he hated doing it," insists Tom Slocum.

While McGuinn, Crosby, and Hillman were approached with the anniversary tribute concept, no one involved expected them to jump onboard what was perceived as a cheap cash-in. From the get-go this would be an ersatz Byrds plying the lucrative nostalgia circuit where the presence of one or two original members in a name band was sufficient to draw in the baby boomers. Recruiting ex-Firefall and Burrito Brother Rick Roberts, Beach Boy associate Blondie Chaplin, and several members of The Band (Rick Danko, Richard Manuel, and, for a time, Garth Hudson), the Twentieth Anniversary Tribute to the Byrds (also known as A Celebration of the Byrds) hit the road in early 1985. In an effort to pump up the Byrds' credibility, latter-day Byrd John York was added to the team.

"I think that Gene had a lot of really ambivalent feelings about that," notes John, recalling how the band initially came together. "Everyone till the day the earth is gone will be trying to reunite the Byrds and the Beatles. Let's face it. So it was another attempt to try to get some kind of Byrd thing going. I went to the Palomino club to hear some friends of mine, the Textones, play. I was friends with the drummer, Phil, and Gene was friends with Carla, who was fronting that band. Michael Clarke was there also. And the whole club was buzzing. 'There are three Byrds in the room! Maybe they'll get up and play.' Michael came up to me and said, 'Would you go out on the road again?' And I said, 'Well, yeah, I guess so. It depends on the conditions.' He said, 'We need three guys to use the name. We're going to call it a Twentieth Anniversary Tribute to the Byrds. We're not going to call it the Byrds. We need one more Byrd.' So I thought 'Yeah, sure, I'll do it.'

"One night I drove out to where they lived, Michael and Gene had a place together, and brought my guitar and sat down and played with Gene. And Michael told me that that was the moment that Gene decided to do it. Michael thought that if he pulled me in, Gene would go for it. I think Gene really wanted to be accepted as Gene Clark, but this was, in his mind, an interim step in his career. Because when we had chances to sign a contract with a manager, none of us wanted to do it. There wasn't one of us that actually wanted to keep that Byrds situation going. Everyone had their own idea of what they really wanted to do and this was just sort of a thrown-together thing. It wasn't seen as long-term in any way."

John found some justification in his decision to sign on. "Initially I thought it was a good idea because I thought that if anybody is going to play that music at least this is an authentic representation of guys who either did play that music or were around at that time. You think, 'God, there's only a handful of us left who really know how to play this music like this. We're the real guys.' So there was some of that feeling of 'We ought to do this! This is authentic.' And a lot of these young bands were going, 'Yeah, the Byrds!' and they had never actually seen a bunch of guys who are twice their age who can really play like that. When you think about it, imagine somebody seeing Rick Danko, Richard Manuel, Gene, Rick Roberts, Michael, Blondie, and my-self. That's quite a collection of musicians."

For John, invoking the mighty Byrds name is a sacred trust that should never be treated lightly. "The music of the Byrds is very powerful. And we all try to serve that music. Once you confront it in your life, you have to face the question: what does it mean to have spent time in that folk-rock army? I was only enlisted for a very short time, but I've had to face the same question: what does that music mean? That music is greater than any of us because when we're all gone, people will still be playing 'Turn! Turn! Turn!' So how do we serve that music? I think the answer is that we get out of the way, personally. If people want to hear that music, then we play it, and we understand that we're keeping it alive. And I know there were times when Gene felt that way because he used to talk about how his mission was to save the world and the music was a part of it. And other times I have no idea what was really going on in his mind because he would just be somewhere else."

Gene rationalized his use of the Byrds name as a stepping-stone in a 1987 interview with Jon Butcher: "First of all, we're not wanting to try to be the Byrds after the Byrds were such a powerful, innovative thing, but the fact is that people still are calling it the Byrds. Now the next step is that I have interest from record companies, major record companies, who are saying 'Now that we know you guys are good . . .' but they wouldn't have even looked at us had we not done this. That's the weird part of the story. 'Why don't you change the name and cut a new album?' That's the natural progression of events. That's how it came down. That's what I favor and I know the other guys do, too. We don't want to be categorized as a nostalgia act and it isn't the original Byrds and we do know that. But it is guys who really are Byrd people so it has a very authentic spirit to it. The way we've learned to get around it is that we really don't play the songs true to the original form. We play them in kind of an updated manner, the way we feel they would be played now."

From the start, the Twentieth Anniversary Tribute to the Byrds tour was in trouble. Byrds fans expecting a polished show were in for a surprise. The presence of a number of bona fide rock luminaries lent the whole production an air of aloofness that permeated the stage. "I remember there was only one rehearsal for the Tribute band," John recalls. "Immediately a couple of the guys came up with the idea that, instead of creating a show, first one guy would come out and do two songs, then another guy would come out and do two or three songs, and that way half the show was covered by presenting these guys each in a solo spot. And, of course, we presented it as something wonderful. 'Each guy's gonna come out and you're going see what we do as individuals.' But really, as Danko used to say, it was a cheap theatrical trick. Nobody had the work ethic to put together a decent show. Then we would all come together and do the hits back-to-back and it was over. There was no effort to put it together in such a way to make it an interesting show. Nobody had that work ethic. It was just this attitude. It's not enough that you're merely there. You have to involve the audience. So it was frustrating for some of us." Despite John's misgivings, Gene's solo spots were generally well received, allowing him to present several songs from his solo career in stripped-down form.

Reflecting on the Byrds' mini Rolling Thunder Revue, John notes, "To me it was like being on the road with a bunch of pirates. We have these romantic ideas about pirates as incredible characters. But there is also a possibility that things could turn into a nightmare in any situation at any moment. Doesn't matter if you're just going to get a cup of coffee or you're onstage. You would have these glorious moments where somehow miraculously it would all pull together. I remember maybe two gigs out of three or four months of gigs that were just magic. Usually, depending on where people's bloodstreams were on the level of what we called 'achieving blend'—where you reached a certain point where everything was wonderful and you stayed there—then it was great. But if anyone goes over that line, then the monster comes out. And that can happen at any moment.

"So, for instance," John goes on to explain, "let's say you're contracted for two performances in a night—two sets. Everybody gets high and drunk for the first set and the first set is wonderful. And then there's a break while the other band plays. Then the next set is a nightmare because by that point the cohesive factor is gone and everyone is off in their own reality. I can't speak for Blondie, but it was a nightmare. You had guys with great hearts—sensitive, wonderful people—who for some reason created these personalities that were in a certain sense larger than life. So dealing with them on a day-to-day basis was almost impossible. You couldn't just have a real relationship with somebody because you had the person that they really were and then at any time that person could start to fade and this sort of monster would evolve. And depending on where they were in that arc that they would travel in, it could be fun for a while, then it could become not fun."

Gene and Michael were comrades in arms with a long history together. Their camaraderie, however, could often get out of hand and contributed to the swaggering nature of the ensemble. "They were like brothers; they had a tremendous mutual appreciation for each other," muses John. "And then at times they would be at each other and it would be, 'Stop the bus! Stop the bus!' and they would go outside and have a fistfight. Then they would come in and be laughing, 'You bastard, you knocked my tooth out, ha ha ha.' It was just surreal. Just like pirates. Throwing firecrackers at each other on the bus, stuff like that. They were like backwoods kids sometimes."

Several members of the group had serious alcohol and drug habits, and Gene soon fell into line. The personal humiliation of having to resort to being a Byrd once again only exacerbated Gene's excesses. "When Gene was clean he was very professional—on time and watching how long the show should be and this song follows that, all that stuff," John notes. "But when he was not, I remember doing shows with Gene and Rick Danko and the coke dealer would walk in. We'd see him come in the door and we knew that this meant that either the set would be cut short by a couple of songs so they could get to that guy or they would walk offstage in the middle of a song and we'd be left figuring out what to do now. And then they would come back. What was the most important thing? It certainly wasn't the music. And we were lucky that we got the music that we got.

"There were some people who really loved those shows and others who didn't because they could see behind the scenes. I remember one show in Corpus Christi, Texas, and Gene had spent the day in the bar with Danko. So by the time we started the show there was no hope of any kind of a show. You know, when you go into some of these communities there are guys who served in Vietnam who, when they heard 'Turn! Turn! Turn!' or they heard the Byrds' music in Vietnam, it gave them hope. These guys, some of them in wheelchairs, would be weeping when we played 'Chimes of Freedom.' They took this music real seriously. You have to know that when you're playing to people that are having an emotional catharsis because you're playing this music that saved their lives. So at this gig in Corpus Christi the promoter walked up out of the audience and started to apologize to the audience. He took the microphone and says, 'I'm really sorry for this. I thought this was going to be something great for you people. If you want your money back, it's okay.' And Danko comes over and grabs the guy away from the microphone and dances him into the audience. He made it into a joke, like it was all a joke. Danko saved that moment. But a guy came up to me from the audience after the show and he handed me a note. 'Give this to Gene Clark.' I opened it and it made me cry. It said, 'I was in Vietnam for four years and your music kept me alive. A lot of my buddies feel the same way. We came here to see you and you're just a fucking drunk. Stop playing that music.' I couldn't give that note to Gene."

John pauses. "It worked for awhile, but then the nature of the gigs just kept dropping. I think what was happening inside the industry was that promoters were saying, 'Well, I hear these guys are just a bunch of drunks!' There were some shows that were just horrendous. There was no focus. And the rest of us would be left wondering, 'What do we do?' I remember one night we were playing in New Orleans and Gene was just out of it. We were singing 'My Back Pages' and we started the first verse and then Gene just didn't sing the second verse. Michael Clarke was going, 'Johnny! Sing it!' I know the song in my sleep, right? So I go up to the mic and I start singing and Gene comes up to me and he says, 'You want to be Gene Clark? I'll fucking kill you. I'll rip your throat out right now!' And I said, 'Gene, relax man! Just sing the song. If you don't want to sing the song, I'll sing it. I don't care who sings it.' Then ten minutes later he comes over and he's putting his arm around me like it never happened. It was the demon, it wasn't Gene. And that could happen at any moment.

"I remember those days when Gene would go over the edge onstage and you'd be thinking, 'Oh, my god. We've got 20 minutes to go in the show and he's like on another planet.' He'd start leading the audience in a sing-along. He didn't have like a persona where he wanted to connect with the audience, but underneath his normal way of performing there was a guy who really wanted to be that entertainer. He would go into 'Stand by Me' and try to get the entire audience to sing along for 15 minutes. He'd become a nightclub entertainer or something. I think that was the progressive compartmentalizing of his demons in his personality because it was easy to see what mode he was in. We all just got to recognize what place his mind was in."

Gene's discomfort with flying remained an issue for the Byrds tribute band. "I do remember in the days when he was not sober that he would go to the bar and get pretty drunk to get on a plane," confirms John. "And then there would be the worry: is he going to be loud, is he going to be destructive, or is he just going to fall asleep?" Adds Michael Curtis, a later Byrds tribute member, "I sat next to him a lot of times and he would white-knuckle it, grabbing a hold of things. The plane would shake and I'd say, 'Gene, it's okay, man. It's just a little turbulence.' He didn't like it, I could tell. I already knew that about him, but when you're sitting there next to him you realize there's real fear there and you're flying for two or three hours in the air. Gene would basically be gripping the armrests and be uncomfortable until we landed."

Road manager Carlos Bernal recalls the difficulties involved in dealing with all the excesses. "I remember with Rick Danko a couple of times we had to take the tour bus several hundred miles out of the way in one direction, then bring it back in the right direction and reconnect with the trip, all in order to see 'Lou the Guru.' He was the guy who was going to make the shows go well for the rest of the tour. He was like the bagman of some sort." Gene, in particular, presented a particular challenge. "Sometimes there was a combination of the Italian and the Native American Indian in him and we called him the 'Awopaho.' We had to double up sometimes on the rooms and sometimes he would be chanting like an American Indian. He had an Italian girlfriend for a long time and had some Indian in his background, so there you go."

John offers, "We used to make a joke. We used to say that Gene was Apache, Irish, and Italian, and if you had those three guys in an elevator they would kill each other. He had these multiple personalities. There were times when I had to room with Gene on the road and I would come back to the room and I would be knocking on the door and Gene was in his Italian mode. He'd get on this thing where he thought he was the Godfather and he would talk like his idea of what the Godfather would talk like. I would be knocking on the door saying, 'Hey Gene, it's John,' and Gene would be saying, 'Eh, donna bother me, eh? Go away, eh?' So finally I got it in my head that if I talked like that, 'Hey, Geno, hey, it's a me, Johnny. Hey, hey, open da door, eh?' it would work like a charm—and he would open the door. But I had to know who he thought he was in his fantasy at that moment. This was definitely exacerbated by the drinking and drugs. This was not a normal thing. When he was straight, he was wonderful."

According to Rick Roberts, "We actually sent Gene home at one point. We were out and it was October. Gene had been drunk every night for two or three weeks and was not doing very well onstage. We sent him home for about ten days until he could get himself straightened out enough to perform and the band performed without him during that time. His doctor told him he had to get straight and so he did. And he came back on the road and did okay, but then after awhile he went right back drinking."

What may have begun as an earnest tribute was quickly corrupted by promoters who cared more about filling seats than about celebrating the Byrds legend. "The problem was that promoters kept billing it as the Byrds," sighs John, "and we were all really upset about that. Roger was upset about it, and Chris, and rightly so."

Rick Roberts stresses, "The funny thing was it started off really legitimate. I called up Hillman and asked if he had any objection to us doing this. Chris was like my mentor. And he said, 'No' he had no objections, although he later said to the *Los Angeles Times* what a bunch of assholes we were for doing this. I objected to that and told him so. Nonetheless it was supposed to be one tour, but it just kept going on and on. But as it went on it stopped being the Twentieth Anniversary Tribute to the Byrds, to a Salute to the Byrds, to just the Byrds. And I was going, 'Uh, uh, this is wrong. I don't like this.' We talked to a couple of promoters about it and they said the reason was that they didn't have room on the marquee for the whole name. Then one night we pulled up to a venue and the marquee said, 'Tonight Only: The Original Byrds Performing Just for You.' So they had room for all that! It got real bad and the whole thing fell apart. I talked to Gene about it and told him we had to call it something else. In fact, I suggested we called it Phoenix, which is the bird rising from the ashes. Gene said, 'No, it would make it too hard to get gigs.' He recognized that he needed the Byrds name there. I told Gene and Michael that if they couldn't rename it, if they were going to keep it being the Byrds, then I couldn't do it. My honor won't allow it. And they said they were going to keep it the Byrds, so I walked. I had some pride, professional pride, and I did not think it was right."

Following Rick Roberts's departure, the tribute Byrds lineup remained fluid over the next couple of years. Rick Danko dropped out, replaced first by ex-Byrds roadie Carlos Bernal and later by Michael Curtis, a noted songwriter in his own right, having penned "Blue Letter" for

Fleetwood Mac and "Southern Cross" with his brother for Crosby, Stills & Nash. (The Byrds tribute band performed "Southern Cross" in their set.) For a time, the group expanded to include Greg Harris on banjo and guitar along with former Burrito Brother Sneaky Pete on pedal steel. Billy Darnell came onboard on lead guitar for Blondie Chaplin, and former McGuinn, Clark & Hillman drummer Greg Thomas eventually replaced Michael Clarke. Another latter-day Byrd, Skip Battin, also appeared with the group on occasion. By 1987 the lineup had solidified around Clark, York, Darnell, Thomas, and Curtis (and remained so until the group disbanded in early 1990).

While on one of several hiatuses from the four-year Byrds tribute tour, Gene entered his longtime demo studio of choice, L.A.'s Criterion Studios, accompanied by Carla Olson and the Textones to lay down six tracks: "Gypsy Rider," "Why Did You Leave Me Today," "Day for Night," "Jokers Are Wild" (written by Pat Robinson and Dick Holler, who wrote Dion's hit "Abraham, Martin and John"), "Lover's Turnaround" (co-written with Tommy Kaye back in the late '70s), and "Winning Hand." All were cut in a contemporary country music vein embellished by pedal steel guitar from ex-Linda Ronstadt band member Ed Black. The intent was to use these tracks to score a recording deal for Gene. The chemistry between Gene and Carla in the

The Twentieth Anniversary Tribute to the Byrds band, July 1985: (left to right) Blondie Chaplin, John York, Gene Clark, Carlos Bernal, Rick Roberts, and Michael Clarke.

studio convinced manager Saul Davis to consider a joint effort and he approached Demon Records in the UK to fund a Clark-Olson album.

Attending the sessions was Pat Robinson, a songwriter affiliated with Bug Music, a song publishing company operated by Dan and Fred Bourgoise that included Del Shannon, Moon Martin, and John Hiatt, among others. Gene had recently signed on with Bug. Pat had penned songs on albums by Martin, Joe Cocker, Laura Branigan, and Glen Campbell. Encouraged by Saul, Pat and Gene began collaborating on songs and formed a close friendship that resulted in Gene's songs taking on a more contemporary veneer. A Los Angeles native, Pat had embarked on a career in music at age 15, backing rockabilly legend Johnny Burnette before forming Fenwick. With that band, and later with Back Pocket, he nurtured an association with Stan Ross and Bob Keen, producing demos at Gold Star studios in the 1960s. As a result, Pat knew his way around a recording studio.

"I met Gene when he recorded 'Jokers Are Wild'," recalls Pat. "That was a really good little tune and Geno loved it. Saul got it to Gene and then I think Gene asked me to come in and sing on it. Saul was my manager. It was always a courtesy for the writer to be invited to the session and be on the track. For Gene to do an outside song it had to be pretty striking to him. And it is a striking song. He did a good job with it. And then Geno and I went on to write together, real solid. Everybody at Bug was always encouraging Gene to work more because they knew that would keep him sober, he was good at it, and it would make everybody money, too. It would make him money, which he needed to get out of that compromise thing of doing the Byrds."

Affable and ever upbeat, Pat complemented Gene's frequent morose moods. "Gene's reputation, even though he was considered a huge star, was that he was a little hard to work with," notes Pat. "And I was considered real easy to work with. So we were kind of opposites. I don't know if he was late for appointments or if he would just blow people off, but when I used to come over to his house, he was a very organized guy. When people say he was like a flaky guy, that's nowhere near the truth. I would see his little pad on his coffee table, everything in his place, with his list of things to do. He would rewrite all our lyrics to our songs meticulously. He had very nice handwriting. His was too neat, very anal."

Although Pat, too, had his wilder side, he was nonetheless good for Gene—a structured, positive influence that kept the focus on Gene's songwriting. "I've co-written with a lot of people, I was a very active co-writer, and Gene, I was really impressed with him. But he was wild. He had something definitely on the spiritual thing and he really loved doing stuff with the Bible. My whole family was raised very strict Catholic. Gene was very into all that stuff, Ezekiel's Wheel and all that. We had songs, tapes of really outrageous songs that no one's ever heard, including one called 'Ezekiel's Wheel.' Gene wasn't a reader, but he would have the Beatles album *Yesterday and Today* out and he would be listening to that. He really loved the Beatles and he used to study their music. He would pull the old records out and that impressed me. I thought, 'Wow, this guy knows where he's going.' He really had a commitment to the Beatles. What I was impressed with was that they were so melodic. You can study the Beatles even today and you can learn a lot about melody structure and things because they were very good writers. And Gene just knew that that was a source of good writing. So he was a pretty smart guy."

Pat also witnessed Gene's other personalities. "See, here's one of the biggest problems, to get right to the base of his problem. When Gene would have a few beers he would get a little arrogant. He'd get a little bit insecure and when you get insecure you start asserting yourself a little bit. I used to watch him piss people off and it used to really hurt my feelings because I would feel bad for him, and I would feel bad because he was putting the wrong impression out, that he was putting his wrong foot forward.

"There were three phases that Gene would go through when he was playing along with us. I think the first one was Reggae Man. He would be playing along and he'd be drinking a few beers and then everything he would do on the guitar would slip into this high reggae rhythm, that high cha-chink chink thing. We'd go through a bunch of songs and everything he played was this little rhythm. So we'd say to ourselves, 'Oh, Geno's Reggae Man now.' Then he would howl for a while after he did his Reggae Man thing. He would be the Indian. Then he would turn into Italian Man at the very end of the evening. Everything would go from cha-chink chink to diddle iddle iddle iddle, really high up on the strings like a mandolin. It was so funny. That was some of the stuff that was so wild. He would slip into 'Stand by Me' as he was playing. He did that all the time. He went into 'Be My Baby' right in the middle of "Immigrant Girl" while we were recording that and we had to fix it.

"He used to slip into these dream states, which I thought was really amazing. He'd go into these dream states and lay down on the couch and go, 'I'll be right back, Patrick.' He would start talking to imaginary people in a dream. He would go, 'Would you let her go? I'm gonna come after you! I've got my bow and a bag full of arrows.' He would be laying there with his eyes closed talking to somebody and he would create these scenes. It was really wild. I'd never heard anybody do that. Of course it was the alcohol kicking it in. They used to call him Uncle Cherokee. He would howl for a while. I would sit there and wait until he was done. It might be 20 or 30 minutes, then he would pop up and we'd write some more. 'My Marie,' 'Washington Square,' if you listen to those words, they're pretty amazing. They were all true stories about friends and Chelsea and Washington Square back in New York. He really had an imagination.

"We used to say to each other, 'We're a couple of tough hombres,'" Pat admits. "And we would throw knives. Gene taught me how to do it, to reduce your spin as you throw it. We did this thing where we had two hatchets, six knives, and a battle ax, and we would walk towards the door throwing them as we walked. Voomph, voomph, voomph, one after the other. As quickly as we could get to the line and get all the knives stuck without going over the line was the winner. We would stand up one of those big telephone cable reels and throw knives at that. Geno would walk into my house and pick up a paring knife and go 'whip' and it would stick in the wall. Anything he could grab, he'd throw it. This one time he took this big pick ax and someone could have been killed. He almost killed a few people, too, by throwing knives. I think he almost hit Shannon O'Neill with a knife. So this big pick ax came right through the wall of the studio, into the inside of the studio. Amazing! I used to have a woodstove and we used to have the fire going. A very rustic setting and Geno loved that—fire and knives."

What began as a loose collaboration soon evolved into a parallel group alongside Gene's Byrds. When he was off the road, Gene, Pat, and John York would write and record demos of their songs at Silvery Moon studios. What emerged from this was CRY—Clark, Robinson, York. Also laterally associated with CRY were brother Rick (who co-wrote "Dangerous Games" and "Somewhere after Midnight" with Gene and Pat) and pianist-to-the-stars Nicky Hopkins. "The process at Pat's studio was to sit around and brainstorm, come up with an idea, start throwing ideas back and forth, write it down and record it," Rick recalls. "There's nothing more fun than having a real good collaborative thing going on. It's kind of a magical thing." Did Gene find the collaborative process invigorating? "Oh, yeah! You could see a twinkle in his eye. There had been a period of time where Gene didn't have that spark or twinkle in his eye. But it wasn't there like it was on that album cover photograph [*Two Sides to Every Story*]."

"He loved it when I just took control," smiles Pat. "I would get a track going, a drum groove or something, and he'd say, 'Patrick's gonna get everything going great!' He would get things started and he loved building the productions. I would do the basic drum programs and he would program all these little fills and tambourine things. He loved building the songs. And by the end of the night, we'd be done with our song. We'd usually finish a song a day. Then he would want to hear it eight times as loud as we could play it and it would be four in the morning.

"He used to love my sense of humor because I could crack him up. I like to dink around and I could get Gene in a good mood in a matter of minutes. That was one of the good things about our relationship. He was very introverted. But the alcohol covered up a lot of his insecurities and shyness. He was very shy, as a matter of fact. Me being the Aries and the more easily assertive, I was always the guy to lighten things up and get things going, and Gene needed a guy like me in his life. And I needed a guy like Gene."

In retrospect, John regards the CRY experience as a nurturing environment for Gene, a rejuvenation. Gene was still on top of his game as a writer. "Oh, yeah. The CRY thing was designed to be a haven from all the demons—that he could still be creative if you could provide the environment without the demons. A lot of these guys that get messed up, they think they're not creative when they're not high. To me that doesn't make any sense. Creativity is so much a part of your nature if you're a creative person, it doesn't disappear. No, this was a haven up in Topanga Canyon, which is kind of rustic. Pat Robinson maybe someday should get sainthood, I don't know. He had a studio in his house and he tried to create a workshop environment where they could write together. No hangers-on, no one was allowed to come there who was drinking or doing drugs or anything. No distractions. CRY was a really good thing. The thing that we had to deal with was that when Gene was not in his right mind, he could not tell the difference

John York, Gene Clark and Pat Robinson of CRY, 1987.

between music he was writing and music that already existed. His songs would always become [Ben E. King's] 'Stand by Me' and we'd have to say, 'Gene, no, that's 'Stand by Me.' That was always the big joke."

As if keeping the Byrds tribute on the road and getting CRY off the ground weren't enough, in early 1986 Gene and Carla Olson began sessions for their duet album, *So Rebellious a Lover*, at Control Center studios in Los Angeles with drummer Michael Huey producing. Michael had previously drummed for Glenn Frey, Juice Newton, Joe Walsh, and Chris Hillman when Saul approached him with the offer to produce Gene and Carla. "I came of age in the 1960s with the Byrds," gushes Michael. "Never in my wildest dreams did I ever imagine I would be in a recording studio producing Gene Clark. He was one of the fathers of modern rock 'n' roll. And lo and behold he's out in the studio with Chris Hillman! That pretty much blew me away, personally. The engineer and I just kept looking at each other all day long going, 'I can't believe it!' It was pretty amazing to have these two guys there. Gene was such a wonderful man, too. Never aloof or arrogant, a pretty down-home kind of guy. He had the aura about him, but he never played on it. He was just a very charismatic guy in a kind of quiet way.

"Actually it was the four of us—Gene, Carla, Saul, and myself—who steered that album through. We ploughed through a lot of material before we picked those songs. We knew that the album was going to be rather dark because that tended to be Gene's style. There were some uptempo, happier, rockier songs, but they just didn't seem to fit on that album. He really, really loved those down songs. That's what he listens to, that's what he writes, that's what he plays. Great songs, but any time we had something uptempo, he didn't like it. He just didn't like fast songs or to rock that much. And that's truly the way he was. So we knew it was going to be kind of a dark and introspective album and we decided to go with it because it seemed to fit. That style wasn't so much Carla. That was more Gene, as far as the direction, more of a Gene vibe, although Carla had a lot of input."

Using a stripped-down, back-to-basics approach and framing the songs in a rootsy folk/country context, Michael managed to create the perfect setting for Gene and Carla's songs. While Gene dominates the material, Carla holds her own, contributing such compositions as "The Drifter" and "Are We Still Making Love." "We got together quite often at Gene's house for business," she recalls, "and I would hang around while Gene and Saul did business or we were waiting around for Gene to make these huge dinners. He used to love to make these big meals. He was a great cook. He made steak and salad and potatoes like you wouldn't believe. So I was just sitting around feeling like the fifth wheel and Gene would start to play guitar and other people would come over like Tommy Slocum and we'd all be playing guitars and singing. I can't remember who came up with the idea of recording this stuff. I have always hated my voice and I felt so honored that Gene allowed me to sing with him. He was just so totally giving that way. He never looked down his nose at anybody that was singing. He never put anybody down."

Two songs destined for the album emerged out of those impromptu kitchen sessions. "One time I remember we were sitting there," Carla recalls, "Gene and me and Saul, Michael Clarke, and somebody else, and we got on this 'Hot Burrito' kick. Gene just started playing it on acoustic guitar. I just was singing harmony under my breath. He played something else, too, then he said, 'I've got this great song that my brother wrote. Listen to this.' We thought it was a Woody Guthrie song from the 1930s. We just fell in love with it. He and Rick wrote it together." The song was "Del Gato," one of the highlights of the album, a poignant tale of early California history. "When we were living in Mendocino with Gene," Rick explains, "we didn't have a TV. That's how we ended up writing 'Del Gato' because I was reading about the early history of California. That's how the idea for 'Del Gato' came about and we wrote it in one evening."

For *So Rebellious a Lover,* Michael assembled a solid backing band whose talents complemented Gene and Carla's musical vision. "We had pretty much an all-star rhythm section," he states. "In Los Angeles musicians' circles they were quite well known. We had Otha Young on acoustic guitar from Juice Newton's band, and Skip Edwards did a lot of keyboards on it. He's now with Dwight Yoakam." Long Ryders guitarist Stephen McCarthy added dobro and lap steel. Michael provided the drums. Chris Hillman (who appeared on almost every album Gene released throughout his career) guested on mandolin on several tracks.

Despite the stellar supporting players and stressless studio vibe, Gene endured considerable hardship throughout the sessions. As Michael remembers, "He was going through heavy stomach problems and intestinal problems and he was in pain a lot of the time we were recording and had to be taken to the hospital. He was popping a lot of aspirins and Tylenol and drinking monumental amounts of coffee and smoking. I think that helped to speed up his death because all of that stuff pretty much ate a hole in his stomach. But he wasn't drinking alcohol. He was on the wagon, or at least he was not drinking around me. He had to, because of his stomach. He would double over in pain."

Terri had recently joined AA and, clean and sober from both alcohol and drugs, encouraged Gene to get straight. In deference to her, Gene began attending AA meetings and made an effort to mend his ways, though his commitment wavered over the next five years. "When Terri went into AA, Gene never completely cleaned up," Pat Robinson maintains. "I was drinking with him the night before he went in to pick up his 30-day chip. He was just wild. He made his own rules up. Terri went in and became a counselor, but I consider that kind of candy-ass. I'm all for cleaning up, but you don't go from major drug dealer to preacher, or totally freaked out and in fear. I guess that makes sense if something has almost killed you, but she used that against Gene, too. She tried to keep him in AA as much as she could. That doesn't work with Gene, that organized thing. Obviously if he's out drinking the night before he accepts a 30-day chip, he wasn't honest enough."

"When I was around Gene, especially during the CRY period, Terri was very active in helping to keep him on the straight and narrow path," acknowledges John York. "I have no doubt in my mind that he really loved her. As far as I could tell she was a good influence. I didn't know her in her drug days. We would write songs on the road and he would want to write about her. He would use the name Marie because it was easier to sing than Terri. He had a lot of songs with Marie in them."

"The number one and two causes of ulcers in the stomach are coffee and aspirin," stresses Carla. "And that was the case with Gene Clark. At one point he was going to AA meetings and drinking coffee like it was going out of style. All they do at those AA meetings is drink gallons of coffee and smoke. And Gene had his gums scraped two or three times because he had peritonitis and he was taking aspirins for the pain. So there you go: aspirins, coffee, smoking, and booze. That's a prescription for a hole in your stomach right there."

Back out on the road with his Byrds tribute, Gene's stomach pain was becoming unbearable. "We were playing in Reno or Tahoe and Gene was in tremendous pain," recalls John. "His stomach was in so much pain, his organs were shutting down, his digestive track was shutting down. And we said, 'Let's cancel the gig, it's not worth it,' and he said, 'No, no, we've got an obligation. You guys need the money.' So we had oxygen offstage for him. After the last night we immediately took him to the airport and flew him home and checked him into UCLA hospital. Greg Thomas called the hospital and they told him that if this guy had gotten there maybe a day later, he would have been dead. They said it was the largest trench ulcer, where the bottom of your stomach is one big ulcer, they had ever seen. And they took the entire bottom of his stomach out. They said, 'This guy has been in incredible pain for years.' So I know that physically, when he stopped drinking and stopped using drugs, he was in tremendous pain." Rick Clark notes, "He had an ulcer that blocked his colon so that every time he would eat he would throw up. He was losing weight to the point where I could practically put my index finger and thumb around his wrist."

Terri's father, a prominent Los Angeles physician, facilitated the operation and arranged for Gene to pay it off later since he had no health insurance. "That was during the time when he finally got clean and all," clarifies Terri. "He almost died. He was getting ready to go on this tour and it was going to be rather gruesome doing a show almost every night and he was sick. I kept saying to him, 'I don't think you should go. I think you're too sick. At least let's go find out what the hell's going on with you.' He hated going to doctors. I told him, 'I'd swear you have an ulcer because my dad had an ulcer when I was growing up so I know what it's like to be with some-one who has an ulcer.' So he goes on this tour and he might have seen a doctor up in Tahoe, but when he came back from that tour he was deathly ill. He had lost weight and was in the worst shape I had ever seen him. My dad told him straight to his face, 'You're dying.' He didn't even know everything that was going on. He just looked at him and said, 'Whatever you're doing, you're killing yourself. You look almost dead to me.' And it scared Gene. So he agreed that he had to see somebody. My dad had an ulcer and was treated by the head of the gastrointestinal cen-ter at UCLA Med School, so that's who we set Gene up with. They said that he had the worst ulcer they had ever seen. If he had started treating it earlier they could have done it with med-ication and he wouldn't have had to have the operation. Nowadays they're able to treat it with medicine. But his was something that was extremely let go for a long time. He used to have a huge bottle of aspirins and he would be tossing down all these aspirins all the time. After the operation 11 doctors lined up in his room at the hospital and told him that if he ever went back to drinking and drugging, he was going to die. There was no question in their minds. No way was he going to last through this kind of behavior again."

It was a wake-up call Gene was not likely to heed. Even in recovery, Gene remained him-self. "I've never seen anyone in my entire life bounce back from surgery so quickly," marvels Tom Slocum. "This was when Gene still smoked and he's lying on his bed and he's booking gigs in Vegas and he says, 'Sloc, you got a cigarette?' And I said, 'You're not supposed to smoke in a hos-pital! You're gonna get in trouble.' Gene says, 'Fuck it.' "

With Demon Records in the UK already behind the Gene and Carla album, Saul was busy trying to land a US recording contract and running into roadblocks. "Gene had so thoroughly destroyed his name in the music industry by the time that we knew him that it was really difficult to get any opportunities for him," laments Saul. "You can just look at it his-torically. He made more than one solo record only with A&M. Every other record was with a different label. Only Jerry Moss and Herb Alpert [A&M] hung in for more than one album. Otherwise it was one record for Geffen, one record for RSO, one for Takoma. Whatever the specifics were, he just couldn't quite get that consistent support." Saul remains circumspect about Gene's stature in the business. "One of the clichés I have about artists is that it's almost better to be ten percent less talented, if you can spare that ten percent, and have ten percent common sense or ability to do business. You don't want to be ninety-percent businessman, but you don't want to be zero-percent businessman. Even if you can be nutty to the public image-wise, you still have to be able to do business, whether you do it directly or you have someone represent you. And Gene had so thoroughly made a mess of his business career and his reputation, it was really impossible, in spite of his great songs, his looks, his voice, and the people who had recorded his songs, for him to really make the kind of career moves that he should have been able to make based on his talent.

"The other problem with Gene's solo career," Saul notes, "is that there was never a hit in his own name. If he had had one rock radio song that had been Top 20, even just some AOR turntable hit from one of the records so people could have known the name Gene Clark—that would have been different. But that moment never happened. Okay, here's a guy who had been in Dillard & Clark, had these solo records, was in the Byrds and he's written songs that other people have recorded, but they send out 500 of his records to radio stations and people don't know who the hell he is. Are they going to go, 'Oh, wow, here's a new Gene Clark album. Didn't we have something Gene Clark that we used to play the hell out of eight years ago?' That never happened for Gene. The difference between having one—let's just call it a 'hit,' for lack of a better term—and having none, is huge. The difference isn't one; it's like a thousand. That was awfully tough for Gene."

"There was some estrangement going on between Gene and a lot of people during that time," Huey Michael postulates. "Gene was coming out of a real drunk period and Saul had really worked him quite a bit and brought him back career-wise. He hadn't really been straight long enough for a lot of people to know it yet and people were still kind of afraid to be around him. This was kind of like the coming out for Gene. I took it at the time that this was the first step in a long-range career plan, a comeback. We would do this album and the next one would be a little more rock. All this to try to bring him back."

In the end, Rhino Records, best known at the time for reissuing the Monkees and comedy albums, picked up *So Rebellious a Lover* and released it with minimal promotion in the spring of 1987. Standout tracks include the hauntingly exquisite "Gypsy Rider," "Del Gato," and an aching "Why Did You Leave Me Today." The sympathetic, unobtrusive backing allowed the strength of the songwriting to shine through. Gene's vocal performance throughout is both compelling and heartbreaking, especially on the tender Gram Parsons-Chris Ethridge classic "Hot Burrito #1." While the record heralded Gene's return, it is as much Carla's album as Gene's. She proves a more than worthy partner to his rich, melancholy, full-voiced delivery. She contributes several compositions, including "The Drifter" and "Every Angel in Heaven." Together the two harmonize like a folk version of Gram Parsons and Emmylou Harris on "Fair & Tender Ladies" and their duet on "Are We Still Making Love" is pure honky tonk heaven.

"When we released *So Rebellious a Lover*," avers Carla, "the only category they could put us in for a Grammy was the country category because there wasn't a category for acoustic music and for some reason it didn't register to people as folk music. And country at that point was pretty much awful stuff except for people like Steve Earle and Lyle Lovett. There was such a Las Vegas thing in country music then."

Critics unanimously heralded the album's rootsy feel—a precursor to the entire Americana/alt.country movement—and acknowledged the return of Gene to the public eye. Sales, however, were slim. "It got wonderful critical acclaim, great reviews, but it didn't sell many," Michael laments. "It was toward the late '80s and the groups on the radio were a lot of tight pants and hair, Duran Duran and that Euro pop/rock/disco thing, and this album went against every grain of commercial success you could possibly do at that time. There was no such thing as Americana or roots rock at that time and also it was prior to unplugged, that MTV show. A year or two after we did the album, for artists to go on MTV and do acoustic versions of their material was a new and exciting thing, so we were ahead of the curve. But there weren't a lot of marketing dollars behind it." The album would be Gene's last official release. (A reissue from Fuel 2000 Records in 2004 added six bonus tracks to the album, four of which are from the 1985 Textones sessions.)

"If Rhino Records had gone to town on 'Gypsy Rider' and serviced it to country radio, that might have turned into something," Saul points out. "Or if Willie Nelson had looked at 'Del Gato,' 'Spanish Guitar,' 'Gypsy Rider,' or 'Set You Free This Time' and cut a Gene Clark song. Emmylou Harris for some weird reason has never done a Gene Clark song. The songs that Gene had, his moments where he had success, happened either from songs that had a life of their own or real early in his career, even the Ronstadt song was picked off of one of the Dillard & Clark records, same thing with the Eagles. The songs that were covered, whether by Tom Petty, Roxy Music, or Husker Dü, were all his main two or three songs, like 'Eight Miles High,' 'Feel a Whole Lot Better.' So no one of major stature later in the 1970s or 1980s or since came across 'Gypsy Rider' or 'Del Gato' or any of these other songs and made them hits, which may have revitalized his career." Adds Carla, "Gene definitely had the potential to write commercially if he put his mind to it."

"Maybe in the right genre of music, I guess country, Gene could have had some kind of a hit country ballad," suggests Saul. "I've got a stack of rejection letters where we sent out demos. Gene's reputation unfortunately hurt him. You would think objectively, in black-and-white, here's a guy who had been in one of the biggest American bands of all time including a couple of No. 1 records. He's had songs cut from people like Roxy Music and Tom Petty to the Eagles and Linda Ronstadt. He looks great, he writes great songs, good image, and great voice. Obviously he got shafted for a record deal, when you look at it objectively. But then you add all that other stuff surrounding him. So it doesn't work as scientifically or arithmetically as you would think."

Ken Mansfield places part of the blame for Gene's stalled career on Gene's suspicion of the music business and those who ran it. "His songs weren't getting out there to other artists to record. Those are the operative words: 'getting out there.' Gene had such an incredible distrust of the industry and signing deals and publishing companies, record companies and everybody that went with it, agents, managers, and everything else, to a point where he just didn't really facilitate things getting out there. I'll tell you what, if he didn't like you and you were the biggest recording artist in the world and you liked his song, he wouldn't give it to you." Adds Tom Slocum, "Gene hated Bug Music. He was ready to walk out on them before he died, but he didn't. They didn't do enough for him. If you are going to have a publishing administration deal, you want to get something out of it. His catalog didn't get promoted. No one was aggressively representing his songs and that's what he was upset with. Whatever the residuals have been since he died, he still wouldn't have been with Bug Music."

In an effort to promote the album, Gene and Carla undertook several performances together in and around Los Angeles, and traveled to Nashville to appear with cantankerous host Ralph Emory on TNN's *Nashville Now.* "That was pretty pathetic," huffs Carla. "Gene was sick, I was sick and didn't know it. The band sounded great, they learned the songs really well and played cool parts, but everything was sort of not totally all quite there." Emory spent more time asking a bewildered and increasingly uncomfortable Gene about his time in the New Christy Minstrels some 25 years earlier than discussing his current album.

Tom Slocum, Fred Bourgoise of Bug Music, Carla Olson, and Gene Clark backstage at Madame Wong's West, June 1984.

Simultaneous to the recording and release of *So Rebellious a Lover,* CBS was readying a compilation of Byrds outtakes serendipitously unearthed by Tom Slocum. "I found the tapes to the *Never Before* album," Tom confirms. "I was doing some work at Wally Heider's studio, which Dickson had worked at 25 years before. José Feliciano's wife had taken over the studio and Jana Feliciano was producing this girl, a real poppy British thing, and she wanted me to fix this thing. I used to fix things. So I told her I had to have access to things including their library. And it was in that library that I found the alternate versions of 'Eight Miles High' and 'Why,' 'Triad,' 'The Day Walk,' and all those tapes. These were the sessions Dickson did outside of Columbia's studios. I told Dickson about it and he almost had a heart attack. I wasn't on a Byrds mission; I literally stumbled upon this stuff."

Gene himself informed interviewer Barry Ballard as far back as March 1985 about the discovery of these tapes: "I don't know how many hours there are, but I've heard that there is somewhere in the neighborhood of 100 hours of tape that has never been released: outtakes, takes that we didn't put on albums, cuts that we didn't have time to put on albums. Things like the stereo version of 'She Don't Care about Time.' The original 'Eight Miles High' cut at the RCA studio, some things like 'She Has a Way,' a song of Crosby's called 'Psychodrama City.' Sometimes we'd cut maybe 15 or 16 sides for an album and choose the best ones. There's just so much and I don't even remember some of the songs myself. Most were cut when I was there. So what we're going to do is go in and listen to all this stuff and mix it all in stereo for some volumes that are going to come out."

Titled *Never Before* (after a song at the time believed to be one of Gene's last sessions with the Byrds and later identified correctly as "The Day Walk"), the album was released in late 1987 by CBS Special Products subsidiary label Murray Hill. It garnered considerable attention, more so than Gene and Carla's recent album, revealing once again the commanding shadow the Byrds continued to cast over Gene. (*Never Before* was later issued as an expanded CD with bonus tracks.)

While the original Byrds recordings kept the group's legacy alive, Gene ran afoul of his former band mates, who weighed in to put a halt to the use of the Byrds name. "Gene called it a Byrds tribute band, but then that's when all the trouble started with Roger and David over using the Byrds name," cites Rick Clark. "Then Michael did it after that, and Roger and David sued Michael to stop using the Byrds name, too. Gene actually won in court the ownership of that name. When Roger and David were suing Gene for using the name, it went into litigation and Gene won the right and ownership of the title and could actually use the name the Byrds. But Gene, being a nice, honorable guy like he was, didn't want to offend the other guys, so he called it a Byrds tribute band. Then the promoters would cut the tribute word off and bill it as the Byrds and that caused a lot of animosity that wasn't necessary and never needed to happen. It was awkward for Gene. He would always try to go out of his way with those guys not to do anything that would cause them to be offended. But inevitably, no matter what he did, one or the other of them would take some offense."

Adds road manager Carlos Bernal, "A circuit judge in Florida declared that in the usage therein lies the ownership, so you can definitely have the Byrds name and those others can't. And the Constitution says you cannot deny a person his right to work at his profession. Crosby, Chris, and Roger got back together again to play and say, 'We're the Byrds, they can't use this name.' Gene went back and forth on it, but Michael was the one who ended up with the name. The others argued, 'But you're just the drummer.'" In the end a lengthy and bitter legal case was settled in Michael Clarke's favor, granting him the use of the Byrds name. Gene wisely remained on the sidelines during the protracted battle that pitted Michael and manager Steve Green against Roger, David, and Chris.

"People didn't come up to him and say, 'Hello, Mr. Byrd,'" Tom Slocum wisecracks. "He was always billed as the ex-Byrd. I think he sensed that as a recording artist he broke away from that. But in the public persona and how he interacted with the public, no, he hadn't broken away from the Byrds. He also had a joke for himself. He called himself Lester Byrd. During all the wrangling over who was going to own the name Gene told me, 'Guess what, Sloc? I've got a new act now, Lester Byrd' because the lawyers told him he was the lesser Byrd in the band and therefore shouldn't have control of the name. So he would refer to himself as Lester Byrd. He was obviously humiliated, yet he turned that pain into Lester Byrd."

In an effort to strengthen their claim, Roger, Chris, and David performed as the Byrds in June 1988 at the stately Wiltern Theatre in Los Angeles for a benefit concert in honor of the Ash Grove club. Gene attended, but was not invited to perform. The following January the three, backed by Chris's Desert Rose Band, undertook a series of three concerts billed as the Byrds at the Coach House in San Juan Capistrano, the Bacchanal in San Diego, and the Ventura Theatre in Los Angeles. Once again, Gene was not asked to participate. "I don't know why," concedes Chris in retrospect. "Gene had gone on some television show as the Byrds and they were awful. David saw that and went nuclear. That's when he wanted to get some lawyers and play some shows. And actually the shows we played were pretty good. We should have called him up, but we didn't. We were mad at him. I take blame for that, too."

"Chris is not a forgiving or warm and fuzzy guy," offers David. "He is a very tough guy and is hard on people. He expects a lot and if you can deliver, then he has respect for you. But if you are not up to specs, he is not forgiving about it. And Gene came in kind of a square peg in a round hole in the first place and then went downhill. So I'm sure that Chris was hard on him."

"Yeah, we were ticked off with Gene for that," Roger admits. "There were hard feelings at that point because of Gene's participation with Michael on the Byrds knockoff band, the tribute to the Byrds, or anniversary celebration. But that's kind of a mistake. I think it would have been nice to include Gene. I always liked Gene after that. I wasn't angry with him personally. I think it was mostly David's thing. David was really the most offended by Gene and Michael doing the Byrds." Does Roger regret not asking Gene to join in, especially when he was seated in the audience? "Yeah. That's too bad. I regret that. It was not a very sporting way to behave." But while

Chris now feels that the three should have let Gene and Michael use the name in order to make a living, Roger remains adamantly opposed to their resurrecting the Byrds name. "Well, I disagree. I think they should have done something else. The name was our group thing. I had made an agreement with David that I wouldn't use the name any further unless all of us did, and I thought if I was going to make that commitment, they should too." Roger has steadfastly resisted attempts over the intervening years for a full-blown Byrds reunion, even rebuffing his fellow Byrd mates' requests. "It wouldn't be the Byrds," he asserts. "Paul McCartney had battled people who were saying 'Let's get the remaining Beatles back together' for years, and he replied, 'You can't reheat a soufflé.' And I think that's appropriate."

David still harbors a dream to perform with the remaining Byrds, but reluctantly accepts Roger's stance. "I know I would still like to do it. But that's not what Roger wants to do. Roger has always been in the driver's seat. It can't be the Byrds without Roger. So if he doesn't want to do it, then it's a dead issue." Adds Chris, "All the times I was upset with McGuinn when we would get offers to go out as the Byrds again for lots of money, but in his wisdom, Roger was right. Because it's best to keep those doors sealed shut. You always will remember that person as they were, not who they are now. It would never have worked. And we can't bring back that memory and Roger has a valid point: Gene and Mike are dead. What's the point? Those reunion things never work out. We don't look the way we used to. It becomes an oldies thing. But years ago I used to think, 'Why doesn't he want to do it?'"

In the 1980s, the advent of classic rock and the viability of several other major reunion tours by high-profile 1960s artists encouraged promoters to pursue a Byrds reunion. Million-dollar offers were placed before each of the five, and while Gene relished the opportunity not only to make some legitimate Byrds music with the rightful heirs to the legacy, he also desperately needed the money. "I remember sitting in on the meetings for the US Festival and the Byrds were offered a million dollars by Steve Wasniuk to re-form for one night," Tom confirms. "But Camilla [McGuinn] and Roger had become born-again Christians and wanted nothing to do with anything that might possibly be misconstrued as anti-Christian. It was nuts. The sabotage that went on was just nuts. There were huge amounts of money offered. I was listening to all this and hearing all the lawyers' points of view. It was incredible. Had they gotten back together again and allowed themselves to play, they could have smoked. Who was their competition then? The Eagles? The Bee Gees? They would have smoked 'em."

Terri recalls Gene's valiant efforts to resolve the differences between the other Byrds in order for a tour and album to go forward. At stake for Gene: a million-dollar payday. "They were offered really good money, a tour of all the major cities here and in Europe, but Roger and David wouldn't hear about it. They were totally not interested in hearing about it. Talk about a humbling experience, Gene went over to see David at his house and almost begged him to do that tour, telling him how badly he needed the money. But they just totally shut Gene out. And this was before he started fucking up and went down the tubes, before he went back to the drugs and alcohol. But they liked to do that, point the finger at Gene whenever they were upset at him for one thing or another. And they did a lot of real tricky-dick things, so I am not a big fan of the rest of the Byrds from my own personal experiences of being around them and what happened over the years. Gene had really some bad feelings about what went down with those guys in their time together."

Amid this highly charged atmosphere of resentment and recrimination, CBS Records was preparing a four-CD Byrds retrospective box set to be released in 1990. With Roger acting as consultant to the project on behalf of the Byrds, Gene was about to discover just how deep the ill will ran.

Carlie Clark's drug problem had worsened by the late '80s, and in a moment of clarity she sent the boys to live with Gene in Los Angeles. For Gene, having to raise two teenage boys—sons he barely knew and who barely knew him beyond the occasional summer visit— was unnerving. "Gene had this tiny, two-bedroom house and that was a lot of pressure on Gene," insists Carla. "He had to set an example for his kids, but he was still Gene Clark. How do you be Dad when you've stayed up for three days writing songs with Pat Robinson?" Compounding the anxiety was the presence of Terri as surrogate Mom.

"It was terrible," maintains Terri. "It was terrible for both of us. I don't think it was great for the boys and they already came from a bad situation. At least they came to a healthy situation when they came to us. Gene and I had cleaned up, gotten back together, made a commitment to stay away from all the drugs and alcohol, and were going to AA meetings at least three times a week. I already had two or three years clean. Then we get a phone call from the school up there in Mendocino saying that these kids were not being looked after and that the mother was in outer space, totally not capable of taking care of them. And they said we should come and get them and do something about it because they were almost like living without any parental care at all. So there wasn't anything else to do. They had nowhere else to go, so we took them in. But Gene was going on the road; we were not rich at the time and only living on a small amount of money and just barely making a living in a teeny little house. And now we're going to have two teenage boys living with us? Just your imagination and intelligence can tell you what kind of situation that was. And the boys weren't happy about the situation either! They had all their friends up in Mendocino; they liked Mendocino. And now I'm trying to exert some kind of discipline into the picture, too, because Gene was really lax in that area. He did nothing.

"He didn't know how to be a parent and I didn't know how to be a parent. I've never been a parent. I just know that at a certain point you have to lay the law down and show some discipline. The both of them were flunking out of high school. The older one, Kelly, he had already left school and the younger one had gotten straight Fs in the last semester. And that's only because they weren't taking it seriously—they're both very smart boys. The older one totally was not going back to school, that was not even a discussion. He just was not going back. The younger one, he was going back to school. So we went and enrolled him and talked with his teachers. We tried to tell them about the situation he was coming from and to hang in there with him and please let us know. And I would work with him with his homework every night. I spent every night trying to work with him and get him back in line."

"My dad really liked having us there," recalls Kelly. "It was cool. But we would hear Terri nagging to my father for an hour in their bedroom. It was a small house; my dad lived very simply for the last ten years of his life. And he would come out and he would holler at us about nothing. He would feel bad, but I think Terri just bitched at him so much about why he had the kids when we're trying to do this and that. I don't know what Terri's deal was."

Kelly's own alcohol and drug problems intensified an already stressful situation. "Kelly was getting into alcohol and dope then, smoking pot, and Gene sure got on his case," recalls Carla, who visited the house on Ostego frequently. "Man, I was over there one time and he really lit into Kelly for smoking pot in the house. And Kai was like angelic compared to Kelly. He was the kid who could do no wrong and, of course, Kelly could do nothing but wrong." Comments Philip O'Leno, "Kelly started right in high school getting totally drunk at kids' parties and he would be throwing up and being an asshole drunk at 16 years old."

"He already had a drinking problem that had started up there," Terri continues. "Now, it wasn't anything real troublesome that I thought, but I knew that he was having his moments and I heard about it. He got a lot of driving under the influence tickets. And Gene paid for them all. He paid for Kelly to go 'alcohol school' and all those things they make you do. It had already been a few thousand dollars out of Gene's and my pocket for this kid. At first we didn't know how to deal with it. Gene and I discussed it and decided he had to go into rehab, that was all there was to it. He wasn't getting the message yet. And it just happened that this guy Carlie had run away to Hawaii with was a counselor at an alcohol youth rehab center. He said he wanted to help us with Kelly. So he got a free place at a very expensive rehab facility, a free bed. That was a gift. And we said to Kelly, 'We're not bailing you out this time. You have to go to rehab and we've taken care of it for you. The only thing we ask you is go there and stay for 30 days.' Gene had to say that to him. At the time Gene was not drinking or using. Kelly refused to go there. He got very upset. To this day, we don't speak. Those two boys have nothing to do with me and they hate me because they knew that I was that influence."

Mendocino had held little attraction for Kelly—and too many temptations. "When I was a little kid, I liked Mendocino," he muses, "but I've really taken to be in the city. My brother still has that affinity for Mendocino, the countryside, the woods and all that. I don't have that same affinity. Mendocino was kind of a vacuum for a lot of people that I cared about. More so than it is now, Mendocino had a very underlying dark side. There were way too many drugs, way too many freaky musicians and artistic people all in one small community, and way too much black money rolling around from the marijuana trip. So there was a lot of drugs and a lot of stuff going on, a lot of strange, dysfunctional behavior. I actually spent a month and a half in the county jail shortly after my eighteenth birthday. I was 95 pounds and I was five foot six and was in jail with guys that had killed people. It was freaky for me. That was kind of the beginning of the end of my party time." Declares Carlie, "He saw it in his dad. He knows it's a family disease."

Realizing his life was in a downward spiral, Kelly pulled back, joined AA, and turned himself around. "He pulled out of it," Philip O'leno acknowledges. "By the time he was 18 he was in AA and hasn't touched anything since then. He saw it in his father and grandfather and he just completely stopped that pattern right there. That's why Kelly caught himself. He didn't want to go that way." Did Kelly ever feel that Gene was being a hypocrite in criticizing his drinking and drug use? "No. My dad was sober at that point, so I didn't think it was hypocritical of him. My father really got me close to going to meetings a lot earlier than I actually did. He sat with me and really took an interest in us, unless Terri was around nagging at him about how much money it cost him to have us there."

The strain of living with their reluctant father was not without its bright moments for both boys. "His favorite place was in the kitchen," smiles Kai. "That was his place to write songs and his cowboy boots would be tapping on the marble all night long and drive me crazy. I would hear him writing songs all night. Sometimes I would wake up and come out and he would make me some hot chocolate and we would sit and talk late into the night. We would talk about stories and he had some great stories to tell. One was his fear of flying, for sure. He told me how they were coming over the mountains once and the plane must have dropped a thousand feet, just no gravity. It's funny because my uncles don't like to fly, my dad didn't like to fly, and my grandparents never flew. I think maybe it's growing up in the plains where you can drive to wherever you need to be. It was frightening for him to fly and it drove him crazy and I think he drank a lot, too, because of his flying. You can't be a rock 'n' roll star and not fly in a plane.

"He loved the old west. He seriously wanted to be an outlaw. He would buy the six-guns and holsters; his whole house was decorated like the old west. He loved the stories and he loved the Native American beliefs. He was captivated and fascinated by that imagery of the old west and some of his songs reflected that.

"There were some funny times," Kai continues. "We got to see a side of our dad that we never did see. For us it was very special to be there. I was so close to becoming a really close friend of my father's before he passed away. I was 17 and becoming a man. We were just developing that father/son thing, that bond. That's the most painful thing for me, especially when I see those father/son movies. Every young man longs for that bond between father and son, taking you fishing, throwing a ball in the yard, or playing music. If only I had gotten the chance to play with him onstage. But I like to look at it as he *is* playing music with me, he *is* in me. He's part of my inspiration, his gift.

"He had a little studio room in one of the bedrooms and would have everything patched all over, cords plugged in everywhere, and I would trip over a cord and he would say 'Oh, no. I've been working on that all night.' He would get the studio all set up just to record one song, then pack it up. He would turn that into a bunkroom when Kelly and I would come and stay. Then when we moved in, he set it up in the living room. He would pack it all away, then all of a sudden he would pull it all out and hook it all up, wires everywhere. It was his passion.

"My father was haunted by some demons," muses Kai. "In later years, towards the end, he would have really bad nightmares. He would wake up in the middle of the night screaming and I would be there to calm him, which was nice for me to be there for him. I don't know what he had been through in his life that could torment him like that. I think he definitely had a sense of some sort of premonitions of death."

Kelly sees a lot of himself in Gene. "When I was older and I was living with him, I used to watch him deal with his daily thing. My father, like me, used to drink way too much coffee and smoke tons of cigarettes, totally wound up tight. I'm wound up tight all the time. I can't sit still. But he was funny. He would be hilarious. He could never sit still, either. He was the biggest kid you ever met. He always bought us the coolest toys way above our age level. We had pellet guns before we could walk, which wasn't a good thing. We would always shoot them in the house.

"He didn't let us down. When we were with him, he was there for us. But I think he didn't know what to do with a kid if you don't have them around. It takes a lot of practice."

"A lot of people are divorced," Kai adds, "and they're always thinking that first person is their love, but they know they can't get along together, talk to each other, or live together. That was my mom and dad. My mom and Gene loved each other. She was the love of his life and he hers. They knew they would never love anybody else like that. My dad loved Terri, of course, but I think Terri was more of a soul mate and friend as well as a lover. She was someone who was there when he needed someone to confide in, hang out with, or drink with, or celebrate with, because my mom wasn't there. My mom and dad weren't together a whole long time, but the time that they were together was very special, and the result was the two of us."

Like her son Kelly, Carlie turned her life around after hitting rock bottom. "My mom had a really tough time and I'm so proud of her," Kai enthuses. "She basically had to start over again at age 50. That's really hard to do when you've lived a whole life of money and fame and all that and go right back to square one and start over again."

The grim specter of death confronted Gene in the mid-'80s, first with a longtime buddy, then a family member. "There was a period around 1985 when Gene and Jesse Ed Davis were getting back together and talking about projects," recalls Rick Clark. "Leon Russell was interested in doing some work with them. And then Jesse died, really sadly, in a Venice laundromat, of a heroin overdose. I went over to Gene's house and said, 'God, Jesse, man. I can't believe it.' Gene was trying to hide his emotions about it and was kind of cavalier, which surprised me. He went, 'Well, you know, these things happen.' He didn't want to talk about it. I thought at the time that he was being really cold, but then I realized it affected him really deeply and he couldn't handle talking about it."

On October 2, 1987, Nancy Patricia Marconette, Gene's next-youngest sibling, died of complications related to medication she was required to take for her lifelong mental condition. The news hit Gene hard. "That was a shocker," sighs sister Bonnie. "We knew she was in trouble, but I don't think any of us believed she was dying. And when she did it was just utterly unbelievable. She was very bipolar and had a whole lot of problems." At the time, Bonnie maintains, Gene had isolated himself from the family and had little contact. Nevertheless, Nancy's death stunned him. "He got the news out of left field much like the rest of the family," confirms David. "He called me up and he asked me, 'What's going on?' He heard all this stuff about a drug overdose and I told him Nancy was a professional nurse and she had a lot of physical and emotional problems. She knew she was supposed to be taking medication for her condition and she didn't do it. She had a case of blood clotting all the time from some operations and she wasn't taking her blood thinners and she suffered a blood clot in her heart and it killed her. It was tough on Gene."

Gene confided to friends like Pat Robinson that his sobriety was more for Terri's sake than his own and he continued to drink behind her back, though not to the excess of previous years. Touring with the Byrds tribute band afforded him the opportunity to bend the rules, though Greg Thomas did his best to keep Gene in line. "Greg was able to say to him, 'No, no, no, you're not going to do that,' and take the drink out of Gene's hands," Michael Curtis confirms. "I'm pretty sure Greg was instrumental in keeping Gene clean for long. After his stomach operation his skin color came back, he was strong, he had been working out, and he was happy, maybe for the first time in a long time. The good part for me was that he laughed and he actually had fun. It was a joy to be out doing music instead of being so dark and worried about his health."

Gene's sense of humor and penchant for practical jokes returned. "Billy [Darnell], Gene, and I got into this thing on a tour on the East Coast, this weird comedic daily rap," chuckles Michael. "Gene would do the voice of John Wayne, Billy would do the voice of Richard Nixon, and I would do Jack Kennedy. And we would have these rolling conversations that were just hilarious because they were just whatever came off the top of your head using those characters—and what kind of rivalry they might have had, all in one room together. It went on for days and days and probably drove Greg nuts. Gene was in a really happy state and I was thrilled, as was everyone else around him, because he was laughing. He had that kind of farm boy cackle when he laughed and I'm not sure if a lot of people ever heard him laugh. We had a pretty good time.

"There was another funny little thing because we were all into the hilarity thing at that point. Gene, of course, was Harold Eugene Clark. We were in some sort of trailer before a show and one of the handlers was in there with us. John goes into the back to use the restroom facilities and yells out, 'There's no toilet paper in here.' So this guy gets on his radio and yells, 'Hey, John York of the Byrds needs some butt wad! Get some butt wad over here right away.'

Gene, Darnell, Greg, and I are all laughing. Finally somebody delivers some toilet paper, but somehow Gene got the nickname Harold Buttwad, pronounced 'Boo-twaud.' So when we were in airports killing time we would go and page people. So Harold Buttwad would get paged because you'd have to spell it out to them to see if they would say, 'Harold Butt Wad' or 'Harold Boo-twaud, please come to the white courtesy phone.' And everybody would crack up. Just something silly to kill the tension."

Gene's Byrds worked regularly through 1988 and 1989, touring with other retro acts on promoter David Fishoff's Classic SuperFest tour as well as performing regularly at the Harrah's hotel chain in Las Vegas, Reno, and Lake Tahoe. "Mostly we had a Harrah's contract in which we would do three of the four Harrah's hotels," recalls Michael. "Every three months we would do two weeks at each one. Those were always great. The Harrah's deal was probably $12,000 to $15,000 a week. Each of the four of us got $2,000 a week and the agent would make something and Gene would get the rest. Some of the bills on the marquee would say, 'The Byrds Featuring Gene Clark'."

During an East Coast tour in autumn 1988, Gene returned to perform solo on *Nashville Now* and was once again dogged with questions about the New Christy Minstrels. The tour resumed in Kansas City at the Midland Theatre where various family members got the chance to see him. This time out he was fit and sober. "Gene was the best onstage I had ever seen him," recalls Bonnie. "He was relaxed with himself and he was wonderful. After the show he came out and was with the family members. That was the best memory of Gene performing I have. When I saw him on that McGuinn, Clark & Hillman show he had looked so uncomfortable onstage. He has never been a good stage personality until I saw him with that Byrds Celebration and he finally looked comfortable onstage. There were times when he could come completely unglued before going onstage. I think that fame was very hard for him to handle, I really do."

Off the road, Gene maintained his parallel activities, making demo tracks for a follow-up album with Carla Olson and working with CRY, which had expanded to CHRY with the formal addition of Nicky Hopkins. CHRY recording sessions had been bolstered by support from Gene's Byrds sidemen, Billy Darnell, Greg, and Michael, as well as Carla. Having accumulated an impressive backlog of strong tracks, some written for films including *The Karate Kid* and Dennis Hopper's tough gang movie, *Colors,* CHRY went in search of a recording deal. Denny Diante at CBS was interested and meetings were set up to pursue a possible deal with CBS. "We had a meeting with the four of us, CHRY, and Gene's manager at the time, David Bendett," John recalls. "We offered it to him. David was the guy who got a song on the *Welcome Back Kotter* show for John Sebastian, which changed Sebastian's career forever. Then Bendett found Gene. So in every situation we would get in, Bendett would not want a band. He would want Gene to have the contract and everyone else to be a hireling. So we had a meeting and we said to him, 'This is the band: Gene, Pat Robinson, Nicky Hopkins, and me. No drugs, no alcohol, we are all seasoned professionals, we all write, we all know exactly what we're doing.' 'No. Gene is the star. No deal.' It could have been incredible, an unbelievable band."

Pat Robinson remembers the end of CHRY with a touch of bitterness. "They would be offering Gene his own deals. 'Gene, we've got a movie deal that's gonna launch your career,' and we were constantly being ignored. They tried to divide us and treat Gene like the star. Now that didn't help Gene because Gene needed us, the camaraderie and sensibility that John and I and Nicky brought to the deal. And that's one of the things that people misunderstand about Gene. He appeared to be arrogant and cocky, but you have to understand that he was being offered all these things and people were constantly telling him all these things. He could have done it if he had the discipline. He was always around the corner from getting the discipline. That's one of the things people have to understand about how he used to make people mad. He was a sweetheart and he just got arrogant a lot, especially if he had a few drinks. That covered up his insecurities."

With CHRY on the skids, the CRY and CHRY tapes cut over the last couple of years were abandoned until 2001, when Pat resurrected them and negotiated a deal with UK-based Delta Music to release a double CD titled *Under the Silvery Moon*. It featured 29 unreleased tracks, including five alternate versions of songs that appeared on *So Rebellious a Lover*. Gene's name and likeness were prominently displayed in the packaging with no reference to CRY or CHRY specifically. For all intents and purposes, this appeared to be a legitimate Gene Clark release of long-lost tracks, and anticipation among Clark aficionados and collectors ran high. The only problem was that despite possessing all the original tapes and having produced the sessions, Pat failed to secure the rights to release the material from Gene Clark Music (operated by Kelly and Kai and administered by their attorney, Scott Johnson). It was a costly error for Pat, who found himself served with an injunction and a cease and desist order for the double CD.

"It was great stuff," Pat insists. "*Silvery Moon* was the title because I rented Silvery Moon studios for the summer from my friend Gary Stern to finish up all the projects I had. I would go in every day and build the tracks I was working on. That's where we cut that stuff. After Gene died, years went by and no one talked of Gene. That was about eight years. I couldn't listen to Gene's voice for four years without breaking into tears. Carla, too. So no one talked about doing anything with CHRY, but everybody knew we wanted to do something with it. My attorney told me that I didn't need any approval from anybody. I just needed to pay a fair royalty. I owned the masters, I co-wrote the stuff, and I paid for everything. I had a right to grant a license for the songs. My lawyer put the deal together, took a commission and everything. Then he said, 'Oh, I didn't know that we needed the approval through the estate first. We're going to pay a fair royalty, definitely.' And I was going to split the advance with the estate, with the boys. That seemed fair. So we were off and running. It came out, they came after me, and it was a big stink."

Talk of replacing Gene's vocals and carrying on with Carla as the "C" in CHRY was dashed by John. "It was Saul's idea to bring Carla in," states Pat, "but John stopped it. John York is a real shy guy, but really assertive and firm in his ways. He just said, 'Patrick, Gene's work belongs to us.' He stopped it. He wanted CHRY out, he just didn't want Carla involved. I was caught in the middle. I just thought it was a good excuse to get it out. It had been seven or eight years. But

John went 'No,' which I'm glad he did, actually." John explains, "We realized that Gene would never have wanted Carla or anybody else to be a part of it. No offense to Carla, but it was the three of us [plus Hopkins], that was the whole idea, and we would be going against the original ethic. If Gene had wanted Carla on it at any time he could have invited her."

In September 2003, Delta Music released a single CD of 14 CHRY tracks, this time sanctioned by Gene Clark Music. Fans who had long wondered about these recordings were thrilled to finally hear tracks like the autobiographical "Mary Sue," "Immigrant Girl," inspired by the checkout girl at the AM/PM convenience store around the corner from Gene's house, "Carry On," written for *The Karate Kid 2,* and "My Marie," an ode to Terri Messina. The CD reveals the strength of the Clark-Robinson songwriting collaboration and Pat's ability to present Gene's songs in a contemporary musical context. One can only speculate what might have come from this teaming had Gene insisted on keeping it a group project and had a major label backed it.

"You have to understand the classic rock star situation," John points out regarding Gene's naïve trust in the wrong people to guide his career. "All you have to do is be the rock star and everything else is taken care of for you. You think of Elvis and Colonel Tom Parker. And if you believe that, then you're susceptible to people who are really going to take you for a ride. And it's true; the artist can't do everything, so you find yourself in a situation where you are really vulnerable. There was a side of Gene that was very naïve and very vulnerable. He would get around people who would tell him all kinds of stuff that he would believe and it would get him in trouble. I remember trying to tell him that, and he just would not listen to me and got very offended. Then later on down the line he figured it out. But it was a thing where he would take on someone as an advisor, or even in the world of party buddies he would pick the wrong people. It's what we used to call 'the monster and his friend.' You get one guy who gets drunk and gets messed up on drugs and you put him together with another guy like that and they're worse than either one of them could possibly be alone. Gene used to be surrounded by these people. There was one guy who used to phone him up and say, 'Gene, you're my star. How's my star?' "

Gene's next move was to record several solo demo tracks to secure his own solo record deal. Studio engineer John Arrias had been involved in the CRY and CHRY sessions and he, Terri, and Gene hatched a plan to cut some demos at the studio he operated for Barbra Streisand, B&J Studios, in the basement of the Lion's Share building on Beverly Boulevard. John Arrias's credentials were solid gold, having engineered 13 Streisand albums as well as records for a diverse roster of artists including Hall & Oates, Barry Manilow, Johnny Mathis, Bob Seger, Chris Hillman, Patti LaBelle, Kenny Rogers, Diana Ross, Little Feat, Donna Summers, Jeff Beck, Marshall Tucker Band, Cher, and Glen Campbell.

"The year 1987 was when I think I really started working with Gene," John reflects, "just hanging with him and working out tunes, coming up with some ideas and stuff like that, and 1990 is when we finally got in the studio and recorded." Gene's previous recordings with Pat

Robinson had been cut at home studios; he wanted a more professional-sounding recording quality and that's what John Arrias offered. "We did those tunes with his touring band, the Byrds: John York, Billy Darnell, Michael Curtis, Greg Thomas, and Gene. We recorded them at Bill Schnee's studio in the Valley. Bill's an old engineer who worked with Richard Perry in the Carly Simon days. Then I took them into my studio, B&J, and we finished the recordings and mixed them there. Jeff 'Skunk' Baxter was involved. We did some work at Baxter's house, actually. In fact, 'My Marie' was cut at Baxter's house. We re-cut 'My Marie' several times, could never get it right until we did it at Baxter's house in the hills with a Roland 12-track. That was all around 1990." Four master tracks were completed: "I Don't Want to See You Anymore," "Mary Sue," "Look Who's Missing Who," and "Shades of Blue."

John believes "Shades of Blue" was one of Gene's best masters in his latter years. "That song had an arrangement that we came up with in the studio on the fly that was just incredible. We had backward guitar on this amazing intro, almost a minute long, before you got to the song. That's why we worked with Tommy Kaye. Tommy brought that song out. That was the only song that wasn't Gene's that we did. I insisted he do it because I loved it so much and we came up with that arrangement that was very cool, a very different arrangement."

Despite Tommy's initial involvement in the sessions, he was soon sent packing. "He was so blown out you couldn't make sense out of him," insists John. "He brought a bunch of tapes out, stuff that he had recorded. But he was so out of it. Somehow, I can't recall if it was Gene or Pat, but we decided we wanted nothing to do with him. Tommy was bad news at that point." Tommy explained the situation to Ken Viola in a 1991 interview: "I went out to do that project and I was let go because Gene was so clean and straight. It was like doing a rehab record and the rule was no drinking and I was still drinking and it was making him upset."

"John's talent is really as an engineer," offers Terri, who had a financial stake in the sessions but did not attend. "He is a great technician. But he doesn't really have the soul. He wasn't a producer. That's what I felt was lacking. His stuff was really well-done tech stuff, but I don't get the soul part out of it. Tommy Kaye has the soul part. We wanted Tommy involved because we thought, 'What a great combination, Tommy and John,' because we'll get these technically well-done tapes and at the same time have Tommy, and we both admired his talent because he works from the soul. So we told Tommy, 'Gene and I are both sober. This is our lifestyle now. So if you want to come and work on this you have to stay clean.' We told him that up front. 'If you don't think you can do it, then just don't do it.' Then he starts telling us, 'I've been sober for so many months and I've been going to all these meetings' and blah blah blah. So we sent him a ticket, he flew out here, and he was only here a few days when he got all fucked up. So we fired him. That was rough because he was a very close friend to us and we dearly loved him. But we were trying to do something serious."

John recalls that Gene was focused and clean for the sessions. "Absolutely, he was in great shape. He was taking care of himself because he was busy. He was doing something; he was working on his love, the music. He was doing some light stuff but nothing to the extreme that he was doing later. No, he was in great shape."

Brother David remembers speaking with Gene during this period. "He got a lot of his health issues in order, he was cleaning out his legal house, his taxes and business affairs. He worked really hard to clean that up and he worked hard to get his career back on track, but nobody wanted to touch him. He had already alienated so many people. Nobody would back him. He was a bad bet. Nobody wanted Gene Clark coming into their office and pointing a gun to their head, playing the Godfather or smashing the windows out of their car or threatening their families. There was that side to him. He had many violent episodes along Sunset Strip and in Los Angeles and San Francisco. He picked many physical fights. He alienated almost everybody and anybody who could be of any help to him. But he was actually repairing that damage. At this time the hangers-on were pretty distant. He was really alone and he re-evaluated his whole life. He called me up during that time and he said, 'I've just realized what a mess I've made of my life. I turned around and looked at what I piled up behind me and it scares me to death.' And I said, 'You got a hell of a pile of shit behind you man, but you're the one that's gotta shovel it. No one can do it for you, you gotta do it yourself. And it's going to be a long hard job.' He said, 'Yeah, you're right.'"

John Arrias shopped the completed tracks to various labels, but came up empty-handed. "There were a few people interested but they just weren't knocked out by it, I guess. The tapes turned out okay, but I wasn't thrilled with them." Any attempts at further sessions evaporated after a falling out between Terri and John over financial arrangements. Terri expected John to kick in one-third of the costs, including musicians and flying in Tommy. John thought otherwise. "I supplied the studio! I told her, 'You know what? If I charged you for what the studio costs, it would be ten times what you put in.' What did she put in, a couple of thousand dollars? I supplied the studio, my engineering services, all my people, all the tapes, everything. I supplied thousands of dollars of time and energy and everything. 'And you want me to supply money, too?' That's what I told her. That was my falling out with Terri. Gene and I never had a falling out. We were like brothers. It was the three of us, me, Gene, and Pat. That was it. We were a team." The tapes remain in John's possession.

"I think Gene felt over the barrel with John," posits friend and record producer Shannon O'Neill. "I do remember that. He didn't feel good about it. That was Gene's modus operandi at times. He'd get paranoid or get it out of perspective. A couple of the songs they did sounded great. They were really good, a lot better than the stuff Gene did with Pat. If you've got a good song, then you've got something to work with. But Gene was saying, 'I just don't like this. I don't like the vibe and I want to get out of this. This is the end of this. I want you to come in and maybe we'll get Pat involved and we'll do some good stuff.'" Saul Davis does not mince words in assessing the John Arrias debacle: "He was always holding out all this stuff that he said was happening, but it was all jive."

As far back as August 1987, Gene was contemplating a possible future for his Byrds tribute group beyond rehashing "Eight Miles High." In an interview with Jon Butcher he envisioned bigger things for the quintet. "The group has really gotten to be excellent and we're wondering if being the Byrds is the right thing to do or whether we should maybe be the Silver Ravens or something. We could go on to something that's like the next thing because the group is excellent and the camaraderie is there. The guys are like brothers now, Greg, Billy, John, Mike, and I. We've been together for over two years and really feel close and our playing reflects that. We have a lot of new songs that we're working up, so that helps, too. Most of the time, when we're booked as the Byrds, people come out to see us for the nostalgia, but a lot of new fans come out too that are Byrds fans now, young people who are into it. A lot of it has to do with people like Tom Petty, the Bangles, even Springsteen, who refers to the Byrds being a major influence."

After attending one of the Byrds shows featuring just Crosby, McGuinn, and Hillman in 1989 and joining the trio onstage at the Ventura Theatre, Tom Petty was inspired to record a Byrds song on his debut solo album, *Full Moon Fever*. His choice came not from the pen of those three, however, but from Gene Clark, the Byrd left out of the concert series. Released in May 1989, Tom's supercharged cover of Gene's Byrds classic "I'll Feel a Whole Lot Better"—the only cover on the album—earned raves from critics and fans. It also reinforced the long-held notion that Gene had been the strongest of the Byrds songwriters. With the publishing held by Tickson Music and sales in excess of four million copies, Gene stood to pocket in excess of $150,000 in writer royalties. Having lived hand to mouth for more than a decade, this windfall only brought out the worst in Gene—and spelled the beginning of the end.

I t was a familiar scenario, played out several times throughout his career. Gene simply could not handle success or money. "I guess maybe there were three Genes," suggests Saul Davis regarding the transformation in Gene following Petty's album. "There was down-and-out Gene, hard on his luck. And regular Gene, the humble guy. Then there was the money-flowing Gene. And that meant trouble, and that's when he was drinking, and that wasn't good whatsoever. Gene was one of these guys who was better when he was down and out than when the money was pouring in. When the Petty money started rolling in he went out and bought a Cadillac and a motorcycle. But by the time he passed away, which wasn't that much longer afterwards, I think all the money that came in had just evaporated."

Rick winces as he describes his brother's rapid decline. "Gene was in such a vulnerable position. Right towards the end he probably weighed no more than about 130 pounds. He never quite completely recovered from the stomach surgery. And Gene had been struggling financially. He'd been doing small tours, he'd been working, but he was physically ill. Then all of a sudden Tom Petty did 'Feel a Whole Lot Better' and this big royalty check shows up and all the bloodsuckers and cockroaches came out of the woodwork. 'Gene, let's party!' and Gene footed the bill. 'Hey Gene, you're the greatest! Let's go get some more booze and drugs!' And Gene was generous to people to a fault. He was never really sure of people's sincerity because he had been told what a great buddy he was by people, then to have them turn around and stab him in the back so many times that his heart had been broken. So he was very wary of people. They hung around for about a month until the money was gone and then they all just disappeared again and I get a call from Terri Messina saying, 'Your brother's out of control. You gotta do something about him.' So I went into L.A. and Gene was so skinny and so gaunt and just broken. I told him, 'Man, I want you to go to a hospital,' and we got into a big fight. 'Get out of my house!' and I said, 'Man, I'm just trying to help you.' That was a falling out right before Gene started to disintegrate to the point of death."

Flush with money and surrounded by sycophants feeding his ego while looking to drain him dry, Gene began drinking and snorting cocaine again. He eventually moved on to smoking crack and freebasing cocaine and heroin. "During our heaviest drug-using days together," remarks Terri, "and everyone was doing drugs in Laurel Canyon and we were in the middle of that whole Hollywood scene, I'm sure he did smoke coke. Someone handed it to him and he did it. But he wasn't into it. Now, all these years later, after we've cleaned up our act and gone through everything, he is getting back into the drug thing and he's smoking crack every day, all day long. I had to leave. I was with him at the beginning but I had to leave. I gave him several chances and he made promises and then it would happen again. Probably after the fourth or fifth time it was getting worse and it was doing a terrible thing to me, too, because I start using. So then I went, 'That's it. I've got to get out of here.' So I left him and I moved in with my parents. I loved him so much, I didn't want to break up with him. But I couldn't be with him when he was mean and nasty or when I knew it was bad for my own personal health, too. I could only take so much of it, but I was miserable. I was in absolute hell."

Some suggest that Terri herself enjoyed Gene's newfound wealth. "They weren't living together at the time and when he got all the money from the Tom Petty album Terri decided to move into Gene's house, which she wasn't living in, and totally redecorated that house," offers Carla. "They spent thousands and thousands of dollars redecorating Gene's house in all this adobe shit, this southwest motif. Spent that money as fast as Gene got it in. She even told me, 'I just bought a $500 bedspread.'"

With no immediate need for cash, Gene let the Byrds tribute band slide. He was too busy with a self-destruct free fall. Even a highly anticipated UK solo tour advertised to begin on October 4, 1989, was abruptly canceled after Gene claimed he had suffered a shoulder injury. The reality was that he simply had no need or desire to fly to the UK.

"There were plans to do other things, but by April and May of 1990 Gene was pretty much out there again," notes Michael Curtis. "He had new buddies. I don't know who these guys were, but I just heard there were some other guys he was hanging with who were obviously joining in the party. The fact that you have to join the party to be in the band, I was just not into it at that time, nor was anybody else. That's kind of when the downfall started going on. I didn't talk to him for a couple of weeks, then he would call me at three in the morning. 'Curtis, get up, man. Come over here. Let's work on something.' And I'd tell him I was sleeping and had to get up in the morning and he'd be yelling at me. 'You son of a bitch, get over here!' I'd say, 'What are you doing up at three in the morning?' 'Come on, man, I've got something for you.' I just thought, 'Oh, man, don't be getting back into that shit again.' So for a couple of days he'd call. I'd go over during the day but you'd get a call at three in the morning and somebody's raving on the other end of the phone. The point is I knew what would happen. I would go over there, he'd lay out some lines, and I'd probably do them."

For Carla, witnessing Gene's decline into an alcohol and drug abyss was particularly painful. "My father was manic-depressive and I saw the symptoms in Gene. His highs were very high without drugs or alcohol, and his lows were very low. I think drugs and alcohol only exacerbated that in Gene. I think they were genuine malfunctions of the brain and body. If Gene walked in the door and if he wasn't drinking, he would be absolutely fine and his face was sort of conservatively pleasant. But if he had been drinking, he would be cackling outrageously and talking loud and you knew you didn't want to spend a lot of time with him. My father was an alcoholic, too, and died of alcoholism and when I would see Gene like that it brought me really to reality. When Gene was like that I didn't want to be around him, but there were times when you had a gig or a rehearsal and you just had to get through it. One night we rehearsed for that McCabe show that became the *Silhouetted in Light* album [recorded February 3, 1990, and released posthumously in 1992] and, god, Gene had been up for three days. He was three-sheets-to-the-wind. I'm surprised we even got through the songs in the rehearsal because he was so out there. And there were times also when you would look across the stage and there would be this absolutely majestic human being who nothing could change no matter what, whether he was fucked up or not, nothing could change what he had to contribute in this world as a singer and poet. Just his incredible presence."

Gene always believed he could pull himself out of any tailspin. He had done it before, he could do it again. But now over 40 and no longer in his best physical shape, going cold turkey would not be easy. "Even though I wasn't living with him I was talking to him on a daily basis, trying to get him to go into rehab," insists Terri. "And he wouldn't do it because every single time before he got himself clean. He never went into rehab. So he didn't think he needed rehab. He thought, 'I know I can get clean whenever I want. I've done it before.' And I was trying to say to him, 'Maybe you can't do it this time. Maybe you need to go somewhere and just lock yourself up and do it because this is really serious.' So I was going through all this with him."

Close friend Jason Ronard remembers Gene's reluctance to seek help. "I've seen him get bad before and I've seen him come out of it. He always used to say to me, 'Jas, don't worry. I know how to get out of this,' and he always did. But not this time. I knew he wasn't getting out of it and it made me too sad. There was no helping him. He wouldn't have gone to rehab without a fight. You'd have to tie him down. He was a beautiful human being that was caught under the drugs.

I drove him up north for a gig with Leon Russell around that time and he took the glove compartment lid down and poured a mountain of cocaine out and another mountain of heroin and took a hit off of each pile all the way to San Francisco. Figure it out? I couldn't believe he was doing that."

Terri made one last attempt at an intervention with Gene in November 1990. Her parents owned a vacation home in the ski resort community of Mammoth Lakes, northeast of Los Angeles. Terri and Gene had spent time there in the 1980s with members of the Firebyrds and more recently with John Arrias and his family. This time it would be just the two of them in an attempt to get Gene clean and sober. "It was a nightmare, a total nightmare," laments Terri. "We were going to spend a month away from everybody. We didn't even know anybody who had drugs in Mammoth. So he couldn't get anything. We were just going to be totally healthy and clean. So we get up there and there was, in the cabin, a bottle of liquor that my dad had just for entertaining. Liqueurs or something you make the hot drinks with, I don't know. Gene wakes me up in the middle of the night and he's drunk on something he's found in the cupboard and acting totally crazed. Totally crazed! And speaking in tongues, he was that nuts. It scared the shit out of me. I had to pack everything up and get out of there. I left the house in such a hurry. I called home and I was scared and I was crying and told my mom, 'Gene's getting all drunk and I'm scared to death.' I never left that cabin unless it was spic-and-span. You don't use my parents' house, then leave it a mess. But I couldn't clean it up; I had to get out of there. My mom said, 'Just jump in the car and get out of there.' So I threw a few things in the car and drove back. And because I didn't do the house right, all the pipes broke. Cost my dad $5,000 to get all the pipes fixed. That was one of Gene's bullshit things."

For Terri, the incident was the final straw. "Rather than bringing him happiness, if that money had come through, say, six months or a year before, I think that it would have gotten invested in a piece of property and there would have been nothing like that going on. I had all these plans. All I could think of was doing something where we could invest in something that would set us up and we would never have to worry about security for the rest of our lives. But the Petty money started coming in when he had already started using. It contributed to his problems. And so now after having returned to that, with the money he was having a terrible time climbing out of that hole. Terrible time. It was bad timing. You don't know what little money Gene and I lived on. And then he picks up something like a quarter of a million dollars. Of course, they don't just give you a quarter of a million dollars, but he was getting nice, generous checks for so many thousands of dollars coming in. When he gets high and he's off like that he spends on all kinds of nonsense, like a kid with toys, and then he smashes it all. Cars and motorcycles. He spends a fortune fixing it up then he smashes it. So he buys another car and smashes it. Then he buys a nice motorcycle and smashes that. Insane! It was absolutely insane."

Back in October 1984, Gene had articulated his thoughts on money, fame, and the pitfalls of living the rock star lifestyle to CBC interviewer Holger Peterson: "A few years ago, I was secure.

I had everything covered and had myself set up. But by making foolish investments without really knowing that part of the game, and also the price of a divorce, these things are just a reality, and not having properties and finances set up in such a way, I found myself starting from ground zero again. And actually I don't mind that because there is something about doing it that way that makes it really worth it when you get it. And I know damn well this time that it will make a lot more sense to me to put it in the right place. But the problem is that you think you have to keep up with Stephen Stills, that you have to keep up with so and so. I had three Ferraris, I had maids, a large home in L.A., a ranch in Northern California. The overhead was staggering. You never stop to think you can live a lot cheaper than that. When you are a rock 'n' roll star, one of the downfalls of it is having to keep up that image. You don't have to do it that way. The advent of expensive showmanship in Los Angeles—limousines, parties, things like that—you were spending hundreds and hundreds of dollars a day. And that's really where a lot of it went for us. A lot of my friends would not deny that, including my friends Stephen Stills and Roger McGuinn. We've all had it happen to us. We've all made a tremendous amount of money and then somehow, if you're not used to handling it, you lose it. I came from not a poor family but a farm family from the Midwest and I didn't know anything about handling large amounts of money. That is one of the reasons why most of us today don't have the finances we should. We made millions of dollars. Had I listened to the people who were trying to guide me in those days, I would have been a lot better off. Taxes caught up with me. A lot of us have gone through it. I like to see those people, though, who have gone through it and snap back from it and keep on going."

For 45-year-old Gene Clark, snapping back would not be easy.

9

No Other

From his earliest childhood days, Gene Clark disliked going to the doctor. A healthy, strapping boy in his youth, he had an unflagging conviction that he alone could heal himself of whatever ailed him. But following decades of alcohol and frequent drug abuse, his health began to fail. A heavy smoking habit ravaged Gene's vocal cords, leaving him with a persistent cough. His stomach surgery left him weakened, and recurring gum disease caused him great discomfort. Alcohol and drugs left him pale and gaunt. "I would see Gene here and there in later years," muses friend Byron Berline. "I lived in the same area. He just never did look well. Lots of times I'd see him and he looked real shaky. He'd always try to be nice and cordial, but I could tell he didn't seem too healthy. Once you hit 40 years old your life changes a little bit. Your body starts warning you that you can't do things like you did when you were 20 or 30. Gene ignored the warnings. The rest of us had enough sense to stop. That's why it's sad. I wish we could have done something for him. Back in those days, the 1960s and 1970s, everyone was young and stupid. But it's all up to the person, there's nothing you can do."

Gene was scheduled to record a version of "Silver Raven" for a film soundtrack, but dental problems hindered attempts by John Arrias and Pat Robinson to get a satisfactory take. "He had terrible problems with his teeth," notes Pat. "John and I, we put that together to have his teeth fixed, and then he knocked them out again. We sent Scott, who was John's assistant engineer, to go with Gene to get his business together. Gene was driving down Ventura Boulevard and smashed into the back of a guy and he hit the wheel knocking his front teeth out. Gene spit his teeth out on the street—he was bleeding all over himself—and went out to talk to the other guy. Scott, who was about 19 at the time, couldn't believe it."

"There was a lady by the name of Daphna, she was a film producer, and she wanted Gene's song, 'Silver Raven,' for the title of this movie," recalls John. "One night in early 1991 at about three in the morning he called me up and said, 'I've got to get this thing on tape.' So we went over to the studio with another guitar player friend of his [Garth Beckington] and the two of them sat in the booth, just two guitars and Gene singing live and it was just the most amazing recording of this 'Silver Raven' song. And then he did a second song, 'More Than That Now,' and that's all we did, no overdubs, just two guitars and a live vocal. This was not his final recording of that song when he called me up at three in the morning; he just wanted to get it on tape. So we never got the definitive recording that she wanted for the film before he died.

"That night that he came in, his voice was about two octaves lower. He was feeling something. A week or so before that he had gotten into a car accident and busted his two front teeth out. He was supposed to do some live gig and he could hardly talk with no two front teeth. So I sent him to my dentist who did a hurry-up job and put in some teeth for him. When he talked he had this little lisp thing and a whistle. So when he sang 'Silver Raven' he sang with this whistle and this low voice and I think that's why Daphna didn't want to use it because it didn't sound like Gene. She called me after Gene passed away and she says, 'I still want that song, but I've got someone else who could record it.' I said, 'Well, who do you have?' And she said, 'I've got Harry Nilsson.' 'Fantastic!' So I met with Harry and played him Gene's version and it blew his mind. He thought that was the most incredible thing. So Harry and I went into the studio with Pat Robinson and re-recorded the song on acoustic guitar and Harry did it exactly like Gene. We were going to put a piano on it and drums and fix it up, but a month later Harry died. I put the song in a closet and said, 'I'm never pulling that song out again!' And that's where it lives, in my closet."

John was dismayed at Gene's state. "He was looking pretty bad. He was bleeding from the ears. I kept telling him, 'You've got to go to a doctor! I'm taking you now. You look terrible.' And he would say, 'Nah, I'm going out to the desert and I'm going to clean out.' He would go out there and clean his brain and everything else out, his body, and live healthy for a couple of weeks, then he'd come back and do it all over again."

For a man who had always prided himself on his well-groomed appearance, friends were shocked to see him neglect his hygiene. "That's what everybody told me," recalls Terri Messina, about Gene's last months. "He hadn't taken a bath, his hair was all greasy, he was all dirty and funky and he was out of it."

Only a few close friends knew that Gene had been suffering throat problems and, on the recommendation of Tom Slocum, had agreed to see a specialist. The prognosis was throat cancer. "I was with him when he came out of the doctor's office, a throat specialist," sighs Tom. "Gene had been trying to stop smoking. There was this sense of fatalism he had after he had come out of the doctors and called Terri to tell her something about his health. I think he was really fatalistic about the cancer. He started getting fucked up after he heard from the doctor."

"When he got ill in the last year, his voice was really going," Tommy Kaye noted in his 1991 interview with Ken Viola. "He had throat cancer, a malignant growth, a polyp on his vocal cords. This was really fucking his head up. He started drinking heavily and getting into the drugs. I asked him to quit drinking and smoking. I had been in the program for two years." Adds Jason Ronard, "He just turned into Keith Richards. I think it might have been more self-destructive when he found out he had throat cancer. That's what really did it. Gene was dying six months before that. I told Garth, I said, 'Gene will be dead in six months.'"

Seventeen-year-old Kelly Clark had attempted to reconnect with his father during this period and knew of the cancer. He also witnessed how his father dealt with the news. "I was aware of that, yes, I was. A couple of months before my father died I went to see him on my own. I showed up at his house and you had to wade through the empties and there were cigarette burns in the furniture. His car was crashed. And my dad had always been very anal about being freaky clean. I went there to get the last of my stuff from when I was living there. He had said he was going to give my brother and I a couple of hundred dollars each because we were broke. He was passed out and when he woke up he told me to take him to the liquor store. He bought a six-pack of cheap beer, a gallon of wine, and two fifths of vodka. Ever see *Leaving Las Vegas*? We're talking about *Leaving Las Vegas* times here. He slugged probably half of that bottle of wine, then proceeded to slug a lot of the vodka, then cracked a beer. He then went and vomited for about an hour and then came back out and was drinking more. I was completely disgusted and upset. I stayed at a friend's house, came back the next day, and packed up my stuff and left."

Shortly before Gene's diagnosis, he had enjoyed a brief moment of glory when the Byrds were inducted into the Rock & Roll Hall of Fame on January 16, 1991 in a glittering ceremony at New York's fabled Waldorf Astoria Hotel. (Ironically, it was the same night that the Americans began their air strikes on Baghdad in the Persian Gulf War.) The event would mark the first time since 1973 that all five Byrds had stood together. It would also be the last.

In deference to the honor, Gene attempted to straighten himself out before the trip to New York. "It was probably one of the biggest thrills I've ever had in my life," he admitted modestly in an interview weeks later, "because the respect that they showed us at that place, I didn't know that we were thought of like that. I really didn't. It came as a shock to me. When we walked onstage, those people stood up, and you're talking about almost every record company president and most every news agent, everybody of any kind of real importance in the business, and they were on their feet for ten minutes nonstop. I looked down and there's Tracy Chapman, and Bonnie Raitt, and everybody standing there smiling and it made me feel so good."

Accompanied by Terri, Gene played it straight. Michael Clarke, however, was still battling his demons (he died nearly two years later of complications brought on by decades of alcoholism). David Crosby had recently come through the other end of his own personal drug ordeal and was feeling paternalistic towards his former band mates, an attitude that did not sit well with Michael. "That's the good part, the fact that we were all there together," Chris Hillman offers. "I ran into Michael earlier in the day and he was just soused, drunk as a skunk. I just thought, 'Oh, boy, here we go.' Initially it was Crosby, Roger, and I at one table, then Gene came over and sat down. Mike was over sitting with Don Henley. Mike was really out there. So we brought Mike over and we all sat together. I'll never forget David looking over at Mike and saying, 'If you ever want some help, I'm here for you.' And Mike says, 'What are you talking about?' David replies, 'Your drinking. I'll help you do whatever you need,' and Mike says, 'I got no problem.' So David says, 'Okay.' Mike's was typical of the alcoholic response: I can handle it. On the plus side, Gene was straight that night, but he had this palsy. I remember his hands shaking. But he was nice, he was sweet and subdued. I looked around and there we were, the five of us together. And I thought it was a fitting closure and we were being honored for that one particular part of our lives when we really peaked as a unit, not the Skip Battin era, not the McGuinn, Clark, Hillman thing, but the 1964 to 1967 period."

"It was a bittersweet moment," offers Roger McGuinn, who suggests that the camaraderie was superficial. The other Byrds were still bitter over the legal battle with Michael for control of the Byrds name. "Michael was drunk, but Gene was being good because David was there, and David being a total teetotaler, into AA and everything, nobody was drinking at the table. There was wine on the table and we weren't touching it because of David. But Michael had had a couple of bottles of wine at that point and he was out there. And the animosity between Michael and David had always been there and it was really magnified at that point. I really didn't dislike either Gene or Michael permanently. I would get upset with them for things, but I always liked them and I was glad to be there with them."

During the obligatory jam session that followed the formal induction, the five Byrds performed "Turn! Turn! Turn!" and "Mr. Tambourine Man" before closing out with Gene on lead vocals for "I'll Feel a Whole Lot Better." "That was a great ending to the whole thing," stresses Chris. "Especially when you consider groups like Creedence where John Fogerty wouldn't let the other two guys up to play with him. Ninety-nine percent of all those bands they induct aren't speaking to each other. But we did. We sat at one table together and we got up and did the thing. It was a really nice evening."

While Gene may have been outwardly magnanimous towards his former band mates and basking in the glory of the moment, he, too, harbored some residual bitterness over the release three months earlier of the much-anticipated Byrds box set, though he was far too much of a gentleman to raise the issue. In attempting to rewrite the group's history and redefine the roles of others in the Byrds recorded legacy, Roger had clearly slighted Gene's considerable contributions to the group by omitting from the box set several of Gene's key compositions, such as "Set You Free This Time," "Here Without You," and "I Knew I'd Want You" in favor of clearly inferior tracks from the latter-day Byrds. And Roger, David, and Chris had cut four new tracks for the album months earlier in Nashville and neglected to invite Gene (Michael's nonparticipation can be explained by the recent lawsuit over the Byrds name).

"I think that box set was slanted way too much toward Roger and not enough towards me, Gene, or Chris," insists David. "I think that's definite. And I don't think Roger thought twice about it, he just did what he wanted to do. He is a very selfish guy." Jim Dickson agrees. "McGuinn doesn't think Gene was as important to the Byrds as he was. That's why he put more of his stuff on it." Stresses Saul Davis, who fired off a pointed letter to CBS/Sony complaining of the slight to Gene, "There are tons of errors in that box set, besides the songs that were left off and the money not being divided right. Not in McGuinn's section, which they went over with a fine-tooth comb, but in Gene's and the rest of the guys. They were so pro-McGuinn at Sony. And those new recordings, that was obnoxious." Chris maintains that the box set is an embarrassment rather than a crowning achievement to the group's career. "The artwork on those four CDs looked like new age massage music. Also, the choice of songs was abysmal. It was totally unfair. Roger had a consulting fee and got to put it together with someone at Columbia. Some of those gems from Gene were not included. I was misquoted in the booklet. I couldn't even give that box set to my mother because the guy put in words I didn't say."

Recent attempts at a revised Byrds box set have met with demands for input from the two other surviving Byrds. "Crosby and I were not involved in that first box set," insists Chris, "but David and I will be involved this time. There will be more of Gene's songs. I'm not trying to undermine Roger, I wish him all the best, but let's be fair here. We'll fix it."

Having gigged with him occasionally during Gene's heavy bout with drugs in 1981, guitarist Garth Beckington returned to the singer's inner circle in late 1989. Garth had hooked up with Tommy's ex-wife, Hillary Kontos, and moved up to the Mendocino area. A wealthy and powerful woman, Hillary was a force to be reckoned with.

"Garth was a really good musician at one point in his life," states Tom Slocum. "He could really play. He was also a really nice guy. I knew him from when he first came in from North Carolina. Garth came from a very well-to-do Southern family." Nonetheless, Tom believes that Garth and Hillary had ulterior motives. "By thinking they were hitching their horse to Gene's wagon they were thinking they were going to get to be a part of something bigger. That was so unrealistic, it goes beyond being naïve. It gets into manipulation and there are a lot of horror stories as far as the Garth and Hillary deal goes."

By 1991, Hillary and Garth were living in a comfortable Hollywood Hills home on Adina. Jason Ronard came to live with them around that time. "I never knew that Gene was doing crack until after he was dead," Jason reveals. "He would never do that in front of me. He would be too embarrassed. Gene didn't get into that until the end when he was trying to do his Keith Richards thing or whatever he was doing then. He was freebasing and I didn't even know that.

"Garth would like to think he was a friend of Gene's, but Gene was never warm with Garth or Hillary," insists Jason. "Gene needed a good guitar player and Garth was a great guitar player. That's probably the only reason that Garth was pulled back into that little circle. Every time I would ask Gene, 'What do you gotta do with Garth?' He'd go, 'Well, man, I don't know. I don't want him really, but I need a guitar player right now.'"

Gene needed little encouragement to get involved in hard drugs again. "People have wagged their fingers at Garth and Hillary and I've known them for many years," states Terri, insisting that while the two may have been involved in serious drugs, it was Gene alone who chose to use again. "They're not the best influence, but you know what? They're not any worse influence than anyone else around him." Tom suggests, "I think Gene was just so tired inside his body and his soul he just didn't care anymore. Possibly it was the medical news. I think he had given up to a certain degree. There was nothing I could do."

Tom contends that Gene's bankroll had come to an end by early 1991, yet the drugs were still around. "As he was running out of money there was no way he could afford whatever he was doing. And I would say that to people who would call me up. 'Whatever he's doing with these people, I don't want to be around. I don't want to see it or get in the middle of it.' I couldn't be around it. I said to him, 'This is wrong. You can't do this, Geno.' He'd drop little hints like, 'I really don't feel well, Sloc.' His pain was tremendous." He recalls episodes where Gene was out of control. "I got a call from the LAPD one night and they said, 'Would you come over and pull Gene Clark out of jail?' So I got him out of jail. He had been going 120 miles an hour down Chandler Boulevard on his Norton motorcycle, all fucked up. The cop said to me, 'That guy's walking on fumes, man.'"

Gene's last formal master recording session took place in the months preceding his death, when longtime friend Shannon O'Neill arranged for him to cut a track with ex-Burrito Brother Sneaky Pete Kleinow. The track was "All I Want," composed by Gene and Tom in Gene's kitchen in 1986. A native of South Carolina, Shannon had known Gene since the late '60s when he hung out on the A&M lot with the country-rock fraternity. In 1990 Shannon and Gene were talking about cutting an album. "I tried to get him a deal shortly before he died, but it was just about impossible," he offers. "Even though he was very talented, people didn't want to get involved with something that could possibly be a problem because he was kind of a wild guy."

While recording an album for Sneaky Pete, Shannon suggested Gene cut "All I Want." "That was originally going to be an instrumental for a Sneaky Pete album. I used a stellar cast of musicians including Albert Lee, Jai Winding, Herb Pedersen, and Sneaky Pete. I had already cut the track for Sneaky's album, but I felt the song would be much stronger with Gene's vocal. Gene came to the sessions, so we ended up putting him on it. There was a pitch problem in one spot, Gene had some problems, and so I put it in ProTools and got it back up. Herb Pedersen is singing backup because Gene was dead by then, so I asked him to sing it just like Gene. And he did. Herb told me that Gene was the only singer that ever intimidated him. He thought Gene was the best singer he ever heard." (Sneaky Pete's album, *The Legend & the Legacy,* was released by Shiloh Records in 1994 with liner notes that Gene had written years before.)

"All I Want" ultimately appeared on the 1996 album *This Byrd Has Flown,* the UK repackaging of Gene's 1984 *Firebyrd* album that offered three bonus tracks issued by Monster Music under Ken Mansfield's aegis. The other two date from the *Firebyrd* sessions (and served double duty on Tommy's solo album).

"That was Ken Mansfield's idea, to add those tracks," claims Andy Kandanes, the original producer of the *Firebyrd* sessions. "That was kind of a controversial thing. I told Ken I wasn't really in favor of that, but he felt that we really needed to do that to get a decent distribution deal. But those three tracks didn't really fit. Two of them were Tommy Kaye songs ["C'est la Bonne Rue" and "Dixie Flyer"], which I did on Tommy Kaye's album. But I was told in no uncertain terms that I needed three more tracks on that thing [*This Byrd Has Flown*] if we were going to get it distributed in Europe. I think Tommy Slocum got 'All I Want' and it's pretty good."

Gene and Shannon continued to toss around ideas for an album including a slow country rendition of the Beatles' "From Me to You" with Carla and Gene dueting. "I remember he had played it for Carla and she felt it was too country for her," Shannon recalls. "So I may have a version of it with Gene's vocal alone. It was cut in March of 1991. Gene wanted me to get together with Pat Robinson because he had been working with Pat and he liked Pat. Gene liked working with his friends."

On Tuesday, April 12, 1991, Gene began a five-night stand at the Cinegrill. A smallish nightclub that had seen better days, the Cinegrill was in the stately, Spanish colonial Roosevelt Hotel on Hollywood Boulevard across from Grauman's Chinese Theatre in the heart of old Hollywood. The Roosevelt had been the site of the first-ever Academy Awards ceremony in 1929 and had a long history as the rendezvous spot for the movie crowd and 1940s-era glitterati. When Gene played the room, it was in the process of reinventing itself as a hip nightspot after decades of jazz music.

Gene regarded the engagement as a comeback of sorts—a return to former glories after years in the shadows—and anticipated a house packed with music industry insiders, celebrities, media, and friends. In the end, the Cinegrill shows confirmed the rumor that Gene's career was, indeed, all but over and his days on this earth were numbered.

In preparation for the gig, Gene assembled a backing band consisting of Garth on guitar along with Garth's longtime bass player friend, Jon Faurot. Both had worked with Gene briefly back in 1981. Jon recruited studio drummer extraordinaire Rick Schlosser and Rick, in turn, recommended keyboard player Stewart Elster.

Rick Schlosser had worked with hundreds of artists including Van Morrison, James Taylor, Nicolette Larson, Juice Newton, Nitty Gritty Dirt Band, Art Garfunkel, Burton Cummings, and Linda Ronstadt throughout a career spanning almost 40 years. Although he had never worked with Gene, Rick had toured and recorded with Tommy Kaye. "Gene and Tommy were sort of like two peas in a pod," notes Rick. "That's why I understood Gene, because I understood Tommy. They would just get really fucked up and think they were out there doing something that was important and unfortunately they were kidding themselves. Maybe there was a time when you could do that in this business, but many people died trying to get away with that. And I could see why those two guys could be friends. Gene reminded me of Tommy Kaye, but even in worse shape than Tommy. And I saw Tommy in pretty bad shape at times. It's difficult for me to be around people like that. You want to reach out and help, but you realize this person is on their own path, whatever that is, and you can't always help people like that. He has to help himself. The people he had hung with and done all that stuff with would be there still doing it and they would want him to be a part of it. And he probably had very little willpower to change."

Jon Faurot hadn't seen Gene in several years and was taken aback at his transformation. "I went over to his house and when I went in, I was shocked. Gene looked awful. He had lost some of his hair, his skin looked bad, he was gaunt, he had sores on him. I thought he had AIDS or something. I thought he was really sick. He was kind of like drooling. I was shocked because it wasn't the Gene I knew. When I had known him earlier, he was a big guy who was healthy looking. I was just stunned. He looked like someone who was doing heroin. I've seen a lot of people like that and it just destroys you." But Jon found working with Gene again rewarding. "I started playing with Gene in his kitchen. That was a really interesting time because I really got the feeling of what a tremendously talented guy Gene was. I was trying to write songs and I learned a lot of stuff from him, subtle little things about songwriting that I just never knew. He was so gifted. I learned not to second-guess him; he always had a plan. He had some kind of road map in his head. Plus he could still sing, even though he smoked about a zillion cigarettes a day. Working with him in the kitchen with Garth was just a lot of fun."

Rehearsals for the band convened at the Alley, a well-known rehearsal room in North Hollywood. Like so many aspects of Gene's career, what started out promising, soon fell apart. "Gene was very together and everything was going well," Jon recalls, "but on the last day of rehearsals, which was the day before the gig started, a well-known folksinger was there upstairs. So Gene went up to see him and he had some heroin and gave Gene a bump of heroin. That threw the whole thing off. Something happened to Gene. He came down and he was different. That started this whole thing.

"That night he had a radio interview at Pasadena City College and he came to get us, Garth and me were at Garth's house in Cahuenga Pass, and he had been drinking a lot. He had this big Lincoln town car he was driving and Gene had this thing, when he got into a car he would suddenly become Steve McQueen. Garth was in the front seat and I was in the back with Tom Slocum and Gene's honking his horn, flashing his lights, and driving wild. So we got out to City College and Gene couldn't find the radio interview so we drove back. Garth and I decided we'd had enough and got a cab back to Garth's house. We didn't want to drive with Gene. What happened after that was that Gene got arrested and thrown in jail that night. Tommy knows the details of that. I don't know what he got arrested for, but he got out because he knew all the cops there.

"The next day we had a sound check at the Cinegrill, the afternoon of the gig. We had gone down there to set up the gear, and Gene was not in good shape," Jon adds. "I just don't think the Cinegrill knew what they were getting into with him. They had no idea. They just thought, 'Gene Clark of the Byrds!'"

Rick was used to working in a professional environment and found Gene's ramshackle approach unsettling. "The shows were very much off the cuff, even though we had rehearsed. I had always tried to pride myself on showing up for the gig ready to play and be completely there. I wasn't drinking or doing drugs. I was just really trying to make it as good as I could. There were quite a few people who came out to see him, so you want to be professional. And it was a little bit embarrassing having someone like that not being as professional as the band. I don't remember it as being a real pleasant experience because you really didn't know which Gene was going to show up. I was around him a few times when he was really quite lucid and sober and then at other times he would be really difficult to work with because he wasn't all there. It was like working with a drunk.

"Having been a session drummer where it was so important to maintain the feel or the tempo, Gene had a real tendency to slow things down and I just wasn't going to let that happen. But I think that was just his heart rate. We did 'Eight Miles High' and he did it at about half tempo. Then all of a sudden Gene announced, 'Okay, Rick, take it,' and he left the stage for me to play a drum solo on a tune that was so slow. It was a dirge-like tempo. I felt so open and naked sitting there thinking, 'No, don't leave me now!' But he did."

Gene is joined by Rick Schlosser, Jon Faurot, and Steward Elster at his final gig at the Cinegrill, April 1991.

Garth confirms Gene's unfocused approach to the Cinegrill performance. "The first night was kind of weird because he got out there and started playing a bunch of songs that we'd never played before. I was caught way off guard by that one. So I was just completely lost. Usually I can anticipate changes and stuff, but because Gene had his own rules it wasn't like the blues or country music, exactly, where you know the form. Gene would take a complete left turn when you were expecting a half right."

To say the performances were loose is an understatement. Gene appeared each night in jeans, gray cutaway tuxedo jacket with tails, black or white shirt, and Western string tie, face un-shaven, hair unkempt, and clearly under the influence of either alcohol, drugs, or both. His on-stage patter tended to meander off into a mumble and during instrumental breaks he would leave the stage to sit at the front table with friends like Shannon and enjoy a drink and a ciga-rette. His backing band was competent, with Stewart's fluid keyboards dominating the instru-mental passages while Rick kept as tight a reign on the tempos as possible. All the songs, however, took on a laconic, plodding gait. Gene mixed familiar numbers from the Byrds and his solo albums with a few surprises like "Don't Let Me Down" and The Band's "I Shall Be Released," introducing Stew's organ solo in the latter by saying, "Take me to the church." He performed "Mr. Tambourine Man" on the final night only. And topping it all off, having gotten corrective dentures a few months earlier, Gene had again knocked his front teeth out just days before the gig. His vocals, already in a lower register and frequently slurred, were plagued by a slight whis-tle. Friends and associates were appalled at what they were witnessing.

"The Cinegrill was a disaster," Saul declares. "He looked terrible, his nose, his mouth. He had a car accident a few days before. We went the first night because he had asked Carla to come up and sing with him, but we didn't go another night. Part of the deal was that Gene got a hotel room, a suite, at the Hotel Roosevelt, so instead of going home every night he would stay there. We went up to his room the night we were there and all of a sudden he thought it was 1965 all over again. He had money from the Tom Petty cover and he had this gig and it was totally like awful. When we were leaving, Taj Mahal was coming in to see the show and we ran into him in the lobby. We stopped him and kind of warned him about the gig."

"There were many, many magical moments with Gene," allows Carla, "but that wasn't one of them. I just shrugged my shoulders and got through the show. The only thing, in retrospect, that I'm pleased about is that he gave me a peck on the cheek as I left the stage after we sang 'Num-ber One Is to Survive.' In retrospect, that was as if it was the last time."

"I thought the performance wasn't too good," comments Shannon, who likened the engage-ment to watching a train wreck. "He didn't seem to have great musicians hanging around. Garth was pretty messed up, as I recall. I'd seen Gene going in and out of stages in his life. He wasn't looking great; he was looking pretty weathered. I'd seen him messed up in the 1970s and 1980s and I'd seen him pull it together and look great. This Cinegrill gig was okay, but this wasn't one of his better groups. The only one that impressed me was Rick Schlosser. The other guys were not of the same caliber. If he had had a really smoking band, it might have been a different thing. He may have been depressed about that."

"People were calling me up who were there and saying, 'Oh, my god, man. You just don't want to know!'" recalls John York.

Tom Slocum pleaded with Gene to cancel the remaining shows, but he wouldn't listen. "The Cinegrill gig was a mess," he laments. "It was tragic. It was beyond a disaster and I told people that on the phone. He had a terrible problem with his teeth. He was going to have to have it corrected because he had this clack going on. I told him it was a disaster and he said, 'Sloc, it doesn't matter anymore.'"

"I was there for every one of them but one, and he flipped the night I wasn't there," claims Jason. "Jon Faurot and all those guys said, 'Jason, you gotta come' because Gene wouldn't fuck up too much if I was there. He wouldn't do that shit in front of me. He would never want to see me seeing him not being a pro. So Faurot called me and said, 'Jason, he's up onstage and he's singing and then all of a sudden he starts leading the band and he goes into the audience and sits at a table.' I said, 'What?! I'll be there tomorrow night.'"

Despite the intervention fiasco at the Mammoth Lakes ski resort months before, Terri had not given up on Gene yet. And word filtered back to her about the Cinegrill: "I was talking to Gene every day and the second or third day I could tell he was all fucked up. I could always tell right away. He was asking me, 'When are you coming back? Are you going to be back for the show? We've got a hotel room and we can stay here and it'll be really neat.' And I said, 'Oh, god. You're not going to do this show high are you?' And he said, 'Oh, no. I haven't touched a thing.' And I'm going, 'Yeah, right!' He knew better. He stopped calling because he knew I was busting him, or he would call first thing in the morning when he was sober enough to get away with it. Finally the whole thing was bothering me so much that I told him, 'I'm not going to go to that show. I'm not coming back to watch you make an ass of yourself and get up in front of everybody when you're trying to make a comeback and get people to believe in you again.' So I didn't go. That's why I wasn't there, because I knew he was fucked up and had been on a sprec for days. I was talking to other people and I would get the reports from everybody saying, 'Oh, he's been up every night. He's been up partying. I don't think he's slept once this week.' And that's how he was."

"I don't remember which nights were bad, but he got through all five nights," concedes Jon. "Some nights were better than others. He just wasn't together enough to do anything. We were exhausted after each night because you couldn't relax. You were never sure where he would go. But he also had some really good moments. There were nights where he was better, a lot better. So there were a couple of successful nights. But it really was his last hurrah."

One person who managed to find something redeeming in the shambling performances was son Kai, who, seated at the mixing board at the back of the club, witnessed for the first time his father perform. "A mentor of mine who was a big fan of my dad's up in Mendocino said,

'You've never seen one of your dad's concerts. You should really go and see one of his concerts.' Of course, it was his last show, at the Cinegrill, which is kind of ironic that I ended up going to his very last show. This mentor had taken me out of high school and said, 'You gotta go fly to L.A. and see your dad play.' So I went and I ended up taking care of him for a while after that. I ended up staying with him. And it wasn't his greatest performance. He wasn't in the greatest condition right then, I could see that. The alcohol and things were coming back. We had a lot of great talks and stories late at night. He had a room at the Roosevelt and a lot of famous people came in and out. It was real exciting for me because I think I was 17 at the time and I had been playing music for about three years, so it was really important to see my dad and have him see me play guitar. It was funny, because he was saying, 'Wow, you're getting good. I'd better step up to keep up with you.' It was sweet, a great father-son kind of thing."

A recent confrontation with his brother kept Rick from attending the Cinegrill gigs. "Gene and I had some unresolved issues. Then he called me and we started talking again and he said, 'Man, I'm really sorry. I know you were trying to help me, but I wasn't in a state of mind where I was receptive to that. Everybody else was hanging around and sucking the blood out of me and I didn't realize it.' He called me up right before the Cinegrill shows and he said, 'I want you to come down. I'm doing a series of shows at the Cinegrill.' I was still nursing my wounds from the situation that had taken place so I didn't go, because some of the people that were his backing band were the people that were sucking the energy out of him. They always had heroin around."

Though Gene was often accompanied by Rita Romero, actress and mother of drinking buddy Joanelle (Gene first invited Rita to the Rock & Roll Hall of Fame induction but changed his mind at the last minute in favor of Terri), there was another woman about to enter his life, just days into the Cinegrill disaster.

Karen Johnson was vice president of artist relations at Private Music, a small, musician-driven record company whose claim to fame was new age phenomenon Yanni. Private Music had expressed interest in signing Gene, but label boss Ron Goldstein wanted assurance that Gene was in good shape. Karen attended the Cinegrill shows. "I met Gene exactly 46 days before he died," she reveals. "It was a very condensed period of time because I got to know him very well. At the time we were focusing on musicians who had had past careers, such as Taj Mahal and Etta James, as well as new musicians. I went and it was obvious that he was in terrible shape in terms of his health. He sang beautifully, he performed beautifully, but he stumbled and he headed to the bar frequently. Later I was invited to come up to his room to chat with him. We sat around and Gene obviously was very drunk that night. He asked me to come over for dinner the next night. In the morning his son Kai called me and said, 'I know you are coming over to see my father,' he was about 17 at the time, and he said, 'Is there anything you can do to help him?' I was at the time 11 years sober and I said, 'The only way I can do something to help your father is if he asks me for help.' So he put his father on the phone and Gene said, 'Will you help me?' and I said 'Yes.'"

Karen went to dinner at Gene's house that night. "He had tried to clean the house a little, but at that point he had been sleeping on the couch and vomiting into a bowl at the side of the couch," she recalls. Over the next six weeks, Karen would spend just about every day with Gene until his death. She admits she was attracted to him and insists the affection was reciprocated. While there is no doubting that Karen became a key player in Gene's final days and in the months that followed his death—an angel of mercy in some eyes—not everyone close to Gene at the time agrees that they were becoming a couple. "I lived at his house often," she reveals. "I slept in the same bed with him. We didn't have sex because I felt he was too sick and that wasn't our relationship. Our relationship was a loving relationship, but it didn't involve sex. He got dressed up one night and took me out to dinner and told me it was time for me to be taken out and sported around. He was very tender and gentle in those ways. He had no money at the time. He had dribbles coming in, he was in debt, he may have been behind in his rent, but he was behind on everything. And there were sycophants around him galore. That was one thing I was really trying to protect him from.

"He was starting to get sober. The help that he wanted from me was to get sober. He didn't like Alcoholics Anonymous meetings but he agreed to go to one, more to please me, I think, and he sat through it. He stayed sober until about the third to last day that I knew him, until the third day before he died.

"When we talked about business, I told him he needed a lawyer because there were too many people around him who wanted things from him. It was at the time when the copyright laws were changing. I told him that there was only one person in this business that I totally trusted to give him advice, even for no money unless you can work something out, and that was Scott Johnson, my ex-husband, a music attorney in Baltimore. I told Gene that I didn't solicit for Scott and Scott refuses to solicit for clients as it's unethical, but as a human being that was the person I could suggest. So Gene agreed. I called Scott and he was coming out here for a vacation. They had a meeting set up and Gene didn't show up for that meeting. That was the second night before he died. He was out drinking that night."

Friends confirm that Gene was making an effort to clean himself up in his usual manner of going cold turkey and embarking on a regimen of extreme physical activity. He would be out working in his garden or vigorously shooting hoops in the driveway. This time, though, his body couldn't take the abrupt change. "I told him that it didn't look good that my record company could sign him and, at any rate, it was important for him to get his health back," says Karen. "I suspect that he suspected that he had cancer because he used to talk about the fact that he wanted to go to see a doctor and he didn't want to talk about it. He had a terrific smoking habit and a beastly cough."

A few days after the Cinegrill gigs, Kai returned to Mendocino. "The last day I saw my father, which is really kind of a sweet memory for me, he was completely sober and getting on his feet and doing good the last day I was saying good-bye to him. To me, that was very important. I didn't see him all messed up or anything. I didn't know, of course, that that was going to be the last time that I would ever see him."

Gene had been estranged from Terri since before the Cinegrill engagement, but the week before he died, Terri called Gene. "I was conscious that Terri was trying to be a part of his life again," confirms Karen. "She called him and he went to visit her. That was the only time he had contact with her and he didn't see her before or after that during the 46 days I knew Gene. They were broken up largely because they were both drug addicts and they knew that they would encourage each other to go out and use. He did have great remorse for the turbulence of their relationship. He was not without love for her, but they were clearly broken up. They were not physically together."

Karen witnessed Gene's tendency to compartmentalize his life and friends, creating separate groupings that seemed to be independent of each other, with Gene as the common axis. "That was true. Exactly right. A lot of that was ignorance and fear because he wasn't sure who wanted what. And he didn't understand the business of music enough to know who was really going to help him. So he kept those separate because he couldn't really explain from one group to the other who these people were." These circles included Garth, Hillary, and Jason; Pat, Shannon, and John; the Byrds tribute players; and Saul, Carla, and Tom and his retinue.

Karen harbors suspicion over the motives of some who claimed to be Gene's best friend. "There were a group of people who provided drugs and alcohol, and a group of people who were sycophants, and the one in the business besides myself who was trying to do something to further his career was Saul Davis."

Despite his weakened condition, Gene remained true to his muse, composing new songs at the kitchen table and sharing them with visitors or fellow players. It was, after all, the one constant in his life that he could count on. "He started to do a few things artistically, like write a few new songs," Karen remembers. "He would sit and play the guitar and he played his new songs." With his porta-studio set up in the second bedroom, illuminated by a string of colored Christmas lights, Gene continued to make tapes of new songs, hoping for a follow-up album with Carla or a project with Shannon. As Carla recalls, "Gene had called me a couple of weeks before he died and said, 'Man, I'm on a roll. I'm writing all kinds of songs, I haven't had a drink in weeks.' He really sounded good. I talked to him on the phone for 15 minutes and he sounded great, he sounded really happy."

Those tapes would disappear after his death.

What transpired over the last three days of Gene's life remains clouded by controversy. What is clear, though, is that Gene fell off the wagon and began a binge that ultimately took his life. Who was there with him, what was consumed, what was and was not done about it, and the motivation behind his return to excess after weeks of sobriety are all subject to con-

The last known photograph of Gene, taken one month prior to his death, April 1991.

jecture by those closest to Gene. Each has some vested interest in perpetuating their own version of events. Conspiracy theories abound; accusations have been leveled. There are some constants, but the perceptions remain deeply divisive.

It is agreed that Gene began drinking again on the evening of Wednesday, May 22. What prompted this is speculative, though it is known that Gene was distraught over his last-minute decision not to attend his parents' fiftieth anniversary back home in Bonner Springs. "The second night before he died he was drinking, because that was the night he was supposed to meet with Scott," confirms Karen. "I know he was drinking, because he called me and left a message on my answering machine saying he wasn't going to make it [the meeting]. He sounded very troubled and said something about 'the whole business is screwed up' and he couldn't get there. 'Tell him I'm really sorry. I really want to talk to him and want to make another appointment, but everything is screwed up.' He just sounded drunk. He left that as a voice message."

Garth was with Gene on that Wednesday evening. "That week was his parents' fiftieth wedding anniversary and he felt so guilty for not going that he spent the week drinking wine. I saw him two nights before he died and he went on a bender, on a binge. He felt so guilty about missing his parents' anniversary, but he just didn't want to go. His exact, precise reason for not going home I don't know, but he just didn't. And he drank his way through that week to kind of get it past him, to get it behind him." Jason adds, "He was too fucked up to go. He couldn't face his parents and that's why he got drunk that night. He was depressed that he didn't go, but add a hundred other things to it." Whether Gene also indulged in drugs that evening is not clear. He did not have much money, certainly no money to score hard drugs.

"He and Mom had kind of a falling out, which made it worse," confirms sister Bonnie. "He wanted to come home and play 'Mr. Big Shot' and she wasn't having any of that. She knew he didn't have any money then and to quote her, she said to me, 'This isn't going to be the Gene Clark show.' I don't know whether she told him that, but she told me. So he felt unwelcome, I think, and Mom felt bad about that. This happened during the planning stages of the event. He felt he couldn't go home because he couldn't present himself the way he wanted to. He had gotten to the point where he knew people would feel sorry for him and he didn't want that. He knew that everyone would say, 'Oh, poor Gene.' I believe he was upset and troubled that he couldn't go to the anniversary. In fact, when he was talking to Mom about what he wanted to do, he did write a beautiful poem for them that was read at the ceremony. He was still Mom's favorite."

"Mom held out hopes to the very last minute that Gene was going to come," insists brother David. "In fact, even that morning I talked with her and she asked me if I had talked with Gene and I said, 'I talked with him a couple of days ago.' She said, 'Is he going to make it?' and I said, 'I don't know. He's thinking about it.' And she replied, 'Oh, I think he'll be here.'"

The next day, Thursday, Karen came by to check on Gene. "The day before he died, I went to his house and he was sitting on the couch with his waist all the way bent forward and his head hanging down. I walked up and I got within a few feet of him and I felt this boundary of something saying, 'Move away from me.' I just talked to him tenderly and said, 'Gene, I want to help. Let me know what I can do to help you.' And he didn't say anything. He was passed out. He was clearly alive, though. I went outside and talked to the [property] manager in the back, Ray Berry. I passed the rose bush where Gene used to pick me the yellow roses from that bush. I went to Ray and said, 'Will you please watch him tonight?' and he said he would. I went back into the house and Gene was in the bathroom. I heard him vomiting in the toilet and it was an odd kind of vomiting. It sounded like he was really retching."

Jon Faurot visited Gene that evening, ostensibly to work on some songs and hang out together. He also wanted to urge Gene to make good on a postdated check Gene had given drummer Rick Schlosser for the bandmembers of the Cinegrill shows. But Gene was drinking vodka
when Jon arrived. He left Gene alone around midnight and returned the next morning.

"I was up really early and was in the Valley and just went over to his house about seven or
seven-thirty to check on him because I could see he was not in good shape the night before
and he had been drinking vodka a lot," Jon confirms. "With beer he knew where he was, but
liquor went straight to his head. He had been drinking vodka, I remember that, and he had a
lot of it around. But he didn't have any drugs. There were no drugs around. I went over early
and he was there and was up and wanted me to go with him to get some more vodka. I got the
sense he was up all night because he was really trashed and looked in bad shape. I wouldn't go
with him, but I waited for him to return and I hung out with him for a while. I wanted to see if
he was okay.

"He came back and made another drink and went over and sat on the couch. He was kind
of sitting up on the couch and I had a guitar and we were kind of playing. Then he just got really tired and just slumped over. That was the last time I saw him alive or awake. I tried to wake
him up to try and get him to bed, but I couldn't move him. He was a big guy. I just didn't think
much about it. He was breathing, so I thought he was okay. I just figured I would let him sleep
it off. So I went home."

Jon insists that Gene was expected that morning at a recording session for folksinger John
Prine, produced by Tom Petty and the Heartbreakers' bass player, Howie Epstein. Jon and Howie
were longtime friends. The session was to take place at Howie's home studio. In recent interviews, neither John Prine nor his manager, Al Bunetta, recall Gene being invited to participate
in the sessions. Howie died in 2003.

"So it was like twelve noon and Howie called me at my house in Silverlake and he was
kind of pissed off," Jon continues. "'Where's Gene?' He was mad at me. I said, 'I don't know,'
so I figured I would go check. I hung up and went over there and let myself into the kitchen.
The house was unlocked. I walked into the kitchen and looked into the living room and there
he was on the floor, face down, sort of in the same fetal position I had left him in. Same
clothes. I don't know whether he went into a coma right after I left or three hours after I left,
but I think that's what happened and he had thrown up. He had vomited quite a bit and
choked. There was still some vomit on his face. I turned him over. I remember the first thing
I noticed was that when someone is dead they don't look asleep. I knew right away he was
gone. His eyes were closed but there was something about his face that I knew. Still, I wiped
his face off carefully and tried giving him mouth-to-mouth. I tried to do something to get
him going again. I actually took that stuff when I was a kid, a lifesaving course, so I kind of
knew what I was doing. It didn't work, so I got up right away and called 911. They showed
up right away, in about three minutes, the fire department. So the fire department came in

with all their gear and tried to resuscitate him in a number of ways and checked all his vital signs."

It was Friday, May 24, 1991, and Gene Clark was dead at age 46.

After calling the paramedics, Jon called Jason, who was living with Garth and Hillary in the Hollywood Hills. "I didn't know who to call and I couldn't find Gene's phone book. I knew he was dead. They hadn't actually told me that yet, but I knew he was gone, that was pretty clear to me, and Jason was the only one I knew who could help me at that particular moment. I didn't know where to turn."

"I was the first one he called, not his brother, not Terri," confirms Jason. "It was early afternoon. And he says, 'Jason, I think Gene's dead.' I went, 'Nah, nah. I've seen this a hundred times. Just bang him on the back, turn him over, and he'll be all right. I'll be over in a minute.' So I get in my car and I'm taking my time about going there. Jon had just got there when he called me. He already cleaned him up, turned him over, and cleaned up the puke. I'm about 15 minutes away. As I pull up I see the ambulance driver in the front smoking a cigarette and I knew it was over. Because if he were in bad shape that guy would be in the ambulance and they'd be gone. I've done enough TV shows playing the bad guy to know that if the ambulance driver is smoking a cigarette out in front, he's waiting for the coroner. I pull up my old Caddie in front and Jon comes out with his arms spread apart and he says, 'Hey, man, he's gone.' I just broke up. Then I took over right away."

Jason called Hillary's nanny and housekeeper, Helen Margaret. "She knew all the phone numbers. She was there in like 15 minutes." Helen and Jason began making calls. One of the first calls was to Terri, who arrived within 20 minutes accompanied by her mother and brother. Tom Slocum arrived soon after. "I was trying to hold it in and keep it together," Jason recalls. "You gotta remember I was broke up real bad. I couldn't even look at Gene. He was on the floor in the living room and I told everyone to gather around and we all held hands, Helen Margaret, Jon Faurot, myself, and Terri, even Slocum, and we said the Lord's Prayer and I never even looked at Gene. I didn't want to see him dead." Saul arrived around the same time, followed closely by Shannon, who had been informed by Tom.

What happened next depends entirely on who is telling the story. Jason claims he searched the house looking for drugs and did not find any—contrary to claims by others that drugs and drug paraphernalia were present in the house. "I already went through the house looking all over for drugs when we were waiting for the coroner. There was nothing there. There was the usual bottle of Smirnoff in the freezer and a gallon of fresh orange juice. That's what killed him, all that sugar. He puked and choked on his puke." That is consistent with Jon's adamant account that no drugs were found anywhere in the house or near Gene's body. "I know there were no drugs around the night before and I don't think that's what killed him," Jon affirms. "He just died from too many cigarettes and too much vodka. He had no money before he died. He had a credit card, that's how he was buying stuff. So if there was money, there were drugs, and if there was no money, there were no drugs. But I'm 99.9 percent sure there were no drugs in the end." Saul agrees, "There were no drugs that I saw."

Still, there are those conspiracy theorists who continue to insinuate that drugs and certain characters were, indeed, present that night, and that Gene's death was the result of misadventure, necessitating a panicked clean-up campaign that morning. Carlie, for one, remains skeptical. "It was heroin and alcohol. All the newspapers were saying heart attack, but do I believe that?" The overdose story continues to make the rounds to this day.

"If you're going to label him, he was an alcoholic that used drugs," Pat Robinson states simply. "He wasn't a drug addict, but it was his solution whenever he got depressed. Alcohol was probably his main thing, though. He used drugs, he was a user, for comforting himself when he would get depressed. Not a drug addict, but an alcoholic, that was one of the consistent things about him, but he tried to fight that." In his later years, Gene had begun to reach out to his mother. "He used to get depressed and he would call his mom. I remember him calling her a lot at four or five in the morning and it was six in the morning back there. Oh, yeah, all the time. Here he would be drinking beer and calling his mom."

Jason's hasty search of the house revealed no drugs. "I was looking for his guns," he clarifies. "I didn't want his kids to pick up his guns when they came. I looked around to see if I could find his .357 and I couldn't find that. And I knew that him and I both had .38s and I looked for his .38 and I couldn't find that either. I'm sure Terri did most of the looting."

After giving his report to the police but before leaving Gene's house, Jon made one more call—to Rick Schlosser. "I got a call from Jon saying, 'Hey, did you ever get that money?' and I said, 'No. Why?' And Jon said, 'Well, I'm here at Gene's apartment and he's on the floor, dead. I suggest you see if you can cash that check.' It was a Friday afternoon and traffic here in L.A. to go over to the Valley from where I lived was horrendous, but I figured they would freeze his account by Monday and I would never get that money, so I jumped in my car and I went to the bank and I cashed that check. The money was there. I felt terrible. Here was this guy lying dead in his living room and I'm racing to the bank to try and cash his check before they close his accounts."

Arriving on the scene at the house, Saul took it upon himself to contact the media with the news, another bone of contention with some, given that Saul was not serving as Gene's manager at the time. "I called a friend at the *Los Angeles Times* because I figured that by the time Gene gets to where they're going to take him, these ambulance drivers are going to know who he is and it's going to end up being some OD story because they're going to pick up a few bucks leaking it. I tried to get the story out to someone who other people will call to get it right."

Terri intervened and a confrontation ensued. "Saul was calling up all the radio stations and newspapers and telling them right from our telephone in our house. He was calling them all and giving the news to everybody and playing himself out as the big shot. 'I'm Gene Clark's manager and blah, blah, blah,' just to get his name in the newspaper. It was a total lie—he was telling everyone that he was Gene's manager. At one point I told him to get out of the house. I asked him to leave."

"This is a moment of contention between Terri and I," counters Saul. "Gene is lying on the floor in the living room. People are there—the police are there as well as the ambulance. They were out there and I was in the bedroom going through drawers and I did pull out some stuff and flush it down the toilet. But they were like blue pills, probably not illegal pills, but I just figured why take a chance. They were probably painkillers. Then I made a couple of phone calls. As I was leaving to go get Carla, Terri Messina wanted to search me to make sure I wasn't taking anything." In a scene of utter humiliation, Saul was forced to empty his pockets and open his briefcase in front of those assembled before he was allowed to leave. "After I left, her brother or her father took everything—recordings, the Rock & Roll Hall of Fame award, tapes. None of this has been returned to Kelly and Kai, Gene's children. So she was worried about me or other people taking stuff when, in fact, her plan all along was to take as much stuff as early as possible before the house had been locked, or before his kids showed up, or whoever was going to show up to protect the goods."

According to Tom, "What happened was that Saul said he wanted to take the guitars to keep for Gene's kids. Meantime, Terri Messina's brother, Joe, shows up, who's a sweet guy but a guy you don't want to fuck with, period. He's muscular; he's got a construction business. He's there to support his sister. Then the mother shows up and is there to look after her daughter. They're decent people, the father is a prominent L.A. physician. So I'm just observing people. But there were things that went down there. Saul Davis got on the phone to the press, which was nuts. Very crazy, in my opinion. I don't believe he did it to keep the ambulance drivers from telling the story. It wasn't his place to do that. Here was a death scene and you just don't do this.

"So [property manager] Ray Berry enters the scene and Ray was in World War II in Special Ops. The Messinas are over here, I'm over there, and Ray's behind me, and I say to Ray, 'Ray, I'm trying to keep the peace.' It was that intense. I was trying to figure out a way to ameliorate the situation between these two factions and it's intense. There's one guy on the phone, and Terri, who's only about five foot two, and she's going after Saul. 'You fucker!' There's this whole drama going on. Terri got some journals and some tapes, maybe some photographs. Then they came and took Gene away. And Ray Berry says, 'Look, this is my property.' In the meantime, her brother and her mother had been taking stuff out. 'Nothing is to be taken out. Nothing. Get out of here.' He threw everybody out except Shannon and me. It was pretty intense."

"What I took out of the house was the most valuable stuff," admits Terri, "and that was Gene's music. I wasn't going to leave it for other people to fuck around with. If they wanted to deal with it, they were going to have to go through me over that stuff. I have Gene's award for being inducted into the Rock & Roll Hall of Fame. That's the only statue I have. I took the most valuable things like his award because it meant a lot to me. You know why? Because when he got up to say his thank you, he thanked me. Not one of the other guys in the band said thanks to their old lady, not even their wives. That meant a lot to me. And I took all the music that I knew he wrote all the songs for me. What I didn't take out of the house were all my personal belongings, which I never got to see again. They were all stolen from me."

While this bizarre brouhaha played out in the kitchen, Gene's body continued to lie on the living room floor, face up. "The weirdest thing was that I had never seen Gene looking as peaceful and happy as he looked lying there dead," notes Shannon about the rather ghoulish spectacle of Gene's friends arguing over the spoils while the body was barely cold. "He was kind of on his side on the floor next to the couch. There was your friend, dead on the floor. It was surrealistic." Adds Tom: "Gene had an odd smile on his face. There were two guys in black undertaker jackets looking like the Blues Brothers, I kid you not, just looking at everybody."

Karen had taken to calling Gene each day to check up on him. That morning she called and someone else answered. "I was having a meeting with Jennifer Warnes and you never leave a meeting with an artist while they're in the middle of talking about what they want done on their album cover. But I said I had to go make an important call. So I went to my office and called and someone very rudely said, 'He's gone. He's dead.' I was told that there was an empty bottle of Vodka on the floor and he was lying next to it. My reaction was, I don't know why, but I started crawling. I crawled to one of my fellow workers, Janey, and said, 'He's gone! He's gone!' I went into shock immediately."

Someone—whether Jon, Jason, or Helen Margaret, no one is quite certain anymore—called Carlie up in Mendocino. Carlie claims it was Jon. "On the day that Jon called me from Gene's house, he said he'd gone over there to pick Gene up to rehearse and he was dead and he didn't know what to do. I said 'You should call 911.' And he said, 'But there's drugs everywhere.' [Jon categorically denies ever saying this.] I said, 'Well, it's not going to matter now.' Then he called me and told me CNN was there and that I better tell the boys before they saw it on TV. Well, TV isn't really a reality in Mendocino. So I went out to find Kelly and Kai and, as old as they were, they were still into skateboarding and they would go out into the forest with all their friends and build these ramps and go flying through the air. I went out there in the middle of nowhere and told them their dad's dead."

Kelly immediately made plans to fly down to Los Angeles. "I was the first family member at his house. I got in my truck and drove home alone, took a shower and cried through the shower, then I got in the car and drove to the airport. Annalise [Lindal, a family friend] picked me up at the airport and took me straight to my dad's house. I was there alone for 24 or 48 hours. Everyone was gone because they knew I was coming. I was angry with my father when he actually died. I hated him. I was really fed up with him. He was really a mess and I had gotten sober and I was really hoping we could do that together. It took a little while for his death to sink in."

Terri had called the Clark family back in Kansas from Gene's house. Preparations were underway in earnest for the gala anniversary party the following day. Bonnie was at her parents' house, helping her mother with the arrangements. "I was ironing some tablecloths, standing in my mother's living room. The renewing of vows was at the church, but we were planning this big family gathering at the Eagles Hall. It was a big to-do. I was standing there doing this when all of a sudden I got this horrible feeling and I just couldn't be there anymore. It was like, 'I've got to get out of here.' I said, 'Mom, I'm going to have to go and take a break. I'll be back to help you later.' And I went home and sat down and felt that something just felt so wrong. And before I got back over there she called me and told me he was gone. I just thought, 'Oh, my god!'"

In spite of their grief, Kelly and Jeanne Clark determined to soldier on with their anniversary celebration. "When I got back to Mom and Dad's, she said, 'I am just not going to let him ruin this for me. We're going to go through with it.' And we did and it was a nightmare. Everybody was walking around in a state of shock. You can see it in the pictures taken and I never want to see them again. And Mom was so angry that she couldn't even mourn. She was just so livid with him. He had ruined her fiftieth wedding anniversary. It was just another one of a whole sequence of things. She was angry that he was dead, she was in shock that he was dead, and she said later, 'I walked through that thing totally numb.' But we had people coming in from out of town, all of Dad's brothers were in for it, all of her brothers and sisters were in for it, and it was just an utterly horrendous situation. At the ceremony everybody was just walking through it stunned. I can remember Rick, who is very sensitive, was just coming totally unglued. So not only did we have Mom and Dad in shock but we had Rick, who doesn't come unglued quietly."

Rick and David had learned of their brother's death from their father. As David recalls, "We were back at my place, fishing in the pond, and Nanci, Rick's wife, came out and said, 'David, come here.' I said to her, 'What's up?' She said again, 'Come here.' She was trying to keep Rick from noticing and I could tell something was wrong. So I went up to her and she said, 'You better come and talk with your dad. And don't say anything to Rick right now. I don't even want to tell you.' I just thought, 'My god, somebody's had an accident trying to get here.' I ran the quarter of an acre to get to the house and called Dad. He said, 'You got a hold of yourself?' It was one of the few times that I heard Dad's voice tremble, so I knew it was bad. 'Gene's dead.' And I said, 'What?!' 'Gene's dead. We just got a call about 20 minutes ago from Terri and apparently Gene's died.' I told him I was going to hang up and call and find out what was going on and I would get back to him. And so I called Gene's house and that's when this whole conversation started with Terri. I told her that everything better be left intact because I didn't trust those people. And there was so much commotion going on in the background, you could hear it over the phone. I asked the coroner, 'How many people are in that house?' and he said there were about a dozen people there. So I got her on the phone and told her to get those people out of that house and to leave things alone. 'If I find anything different there's going to be hell to pay!' That was the end of the conversation with her.

"Between the time we got the news and the ceremony the next day, I made travel plans for Rick, Nanci, and I to get back out there to California. It was Memorial Day weekend and the earliest flight we could get out of Kansas City was midnight on Sunday. Everything was booked up. So we left that Sunday night and it was one of the worst plane rides I ever experienced in my life. I had talked with Kelly three times over that period of time. He had finally got to the house and he was almost incoherent to me, he was so upset. I told him that no matter what was going on to stay at the house until I got there. 'Don't talk to reporters, don't do anything.' He was all over the spectrum with this thing.

"We got there and Terri and her mother picked us up at the airport. It had already been a four-day ordeal for me and I had hardly three or four hours of sleep by then and this woman started in talking to me about how Gene did this and that and how Terri was the rightful bene-factor to everything. This kept up all the way to the house. First of all, Kelly would not let Terri or her mother into the house. So I told them that under the existing circumstances I would ap-preciate it if they would leave until I sorted it all out. 'Something isn't right and I'll get to the bot-tom of it. But until I call you I would appreciate it if you would leave.' And this woman starts in on me again and Annalise, who was a friend of Carlie's and was kind of a surrogate mother to the boys, told her to get the hell out of here or she would rip their heads off. And they left."

What David found was a house cleaned out of much of Gene's personal belongings. Clothes, boots, his favorite jacket, tapes, recording equipment, speakers, guitars, his journals and books of lyrics, Hall of Fame statue—all missing. "Gene did have a little studio in his house on Otsego, but the day he died it was gone," notes Tom Slocum. "He had an old Tascam or Soundcraft board and two 4-track TEACs. The day I was there he had a rack of cassettes. It was all gone before Gene was cold." To his astonishment, David also discovered that Terri had already requested that the coroner's office release Gene's body to a funeral home for embalming.

"Tuesday afternoon I called the coroner to ask him about the disposition of the body at that point," David recalls, "and they said they had already sent it to the funeral home for preparation. 'Under whose orders?!' I demanded. And that's when they filled me in that Terri had done that. 'Terri has nothing to do with Gene,' I told him. 'She is not his wife. In fact, she is an estranged girlfriend and has been for some time. She has no say in this whatsoever. The only person who is even remotely legal to have a say in this is either Kelly or myself.' I found out where the body was and what had been done to him. The funeral home had already gone through the em-balming procedure. I told the coroner to go ahead and perform an autopsy and then Terri later avowed that she was Gene's wife and wouldn't allow it. I made the coroner go get the body and do an autopsy at that time, but we had lost so much of what could have been the stomach con-tents and blood content that could shed any light on what he might have ingested. From then on it was an uphill battle. We were stonewalled. We couldn't get anywhere."

On arriving at the house, one of David's immediate concerns had been comforting Kelly and Kai. "I got together with the boys, who had no idea how to deal with all this. They were griev-ing, they were angry, the whole gamut of emotions at the same time because of all of what was happening. I just sat them down and told them that it's here and we have to deal with it. I told them that we weren't going to do anything that night, that we all needed some sleep, and the next day we would deal with it. So I stayed in the house that night with the boys."

"My brother and my Uncle Rick cried the whole time," recalls Kelly. "David and I were on the phone dealing with everything—where all that money went, how are we going to pay the bills, what kind of casket are we going to get, what will we dress him in? I dealt with my demons on it later."

The coroner's office ultimately ruled the cause of death as heart failure. Drugs were not a factor, however the ingesting of considerable quantities of alcohol and a heavy smoking habit most likely contributed to his death. "My father got shocked too much," Kelly suggests. "He was going for ten days straight, then ten days loaded, ten days straight, then ten days loaded, and I think he had just come off a four- or five-day trip being straight. They found no drugs in his system and the doctor said death due to cardiac arrest due to shock. They said he probably would have lived if he had stayed drunk or sober, but going through the detox every time was hard on his system. That's why he died. And I think the throat cancer thing freaked him out."

As if the circus surrounding Gene's death was not enough, the aftermath was equally tragic and contentious. Karen arranged for Gene's memorial service at Praiswater Meyer-Mitchell Mortuary on Van Nuys Boulevard near his home. At the well-attended service, actor David Carradine, one of Gene's running buddies in his darkest drug period, caused a scene over the open casket. "When Carradine came up," Pat Robinson notes, "he wasn't as much drunk as he was on acid, I think, and his girlfriend and business manager at the time was there with him. And we're standing there and Carradine says, 'You cocksucker . . .' and grabs Gene by the lapels. When you pull somebody up from a coffin and they have nothing inside for guts they bend higher up. It really was shocking to me to see that. And Carradine goes, 'You pissed on my daughter when she was 13.' And he said it pretty loud and then he says, 'I saw him snicker, boys, heh heh.' Oh, man, that was weird."

Carradine was alluding to an alleged incident in the early '80s when, following an argument with Bob Dylan at David's house, Gene unintentionally wandered into Calista Carradine's bedroom and urinated. Many attending Gene's funeral believed David had shouted, "You fucked my daughter," but that was not the case. "Gene never fucked her," insists Jason. "I did. Gene never had anything to do with his daughter. They never had anything going on. Zero.

"If you ever saw the movie *Missouri Breaks*," Jason explains, "there's a scene where Brando walks in and grabs the guy in the casket and says, 'You sonofabitch! Why did you do this?! Why did you die!' And then he lets him go and he walks out of the chapel. I think that's what Carradine was trying to do. He's such an asshole."

Joanelle Romero came in from Santa Fe to attend the service and remembers Carradine being more subdued. "David and I were sitting next to each other and all these people were there. And I just had this urge to start singing this traditional song. I didn't care what anyone else was doing. Everybody was there and at the end of the thing I just started singing this traditional song. And then David started singing it with me and all of us started singing it. It was very moving."

Gene's history with the Byrds dogged him to the very end. Virtually every newspaper story, television report, and obituary notice tagged him as "ex-Byrd Gene Clark." He never managed to escape the long shadow of that group. John York has pondered that shadow: "Even with the lesser Byrds, the secondary Byrds like me, you go through a thing where you realize that when you die and something is written in the papers, it's going to say, 'Ex-Byrd John York died today.'

We've all gone through this thing where we've thought, 'Why does it have to be that way?' But it's just something that you have to accept. You have to say, 'That's how everybody sees you.' It doesn't matter if tomorrow I found a cure for cancer, they would still say, 'Ex-Byrd finds cure for cancer.' You know what I mean? So I think Gene struggled with that a great deal."

None of Gene's Byrds mates attended the service.

Roger McGuinn recalls his last encounter with Gene: "He showed up at a thing I was doing for Arista Records in 1991 at the Whisky. I said hi to him, but I was doing a band thing and I didn't invite him up. I guess I should have. That's the last time I saw him. I remember that I had hugged Gene that night and told him that I'd always loved him as a friend. So the last time I saw him alive was a positive experience."

Gene had visited David Crosby shortly before dying. "I hadn't seen him in a while. He was looking for something, I don't remember exactly how it went, but I know that he was calling out for help and I didn't give it to him. I tried to tell him that he needed some help, but I can't re-member if he listened to me or not. I just remember there was a sense of need about him see-ing me. But I can't remember being able to do anything for him other than tell him what I had done to get myself out of the hole. That's when he told me he had a piece of stomach taken out and they told him that if he drank anymore it would kill him. But he kept drinking. I wish we had all gotten back together again. I think if we had been able to work together, I don't think he would have died. That's just my opinion.

"I do think about him, yeah," Crosby admits. "He was my compadre. Whether we were best buddies or not, he was my comrade in arms, someone I went through a lot with. I felt he was a valuable guy. I'm sure I didn't always treat him that way because I didn't always treat *anybody* that way. But I sure miss him in hindsight. He was a nice guy."

Chris Hillman was the one Byrd who understood Gene best. "I always said that Gene should have packed up in 1967 and gone back to Bonner Springs, married some beautiful girl back there, and raised a family. It wasn't supposed to be for him, this lifestyle. It killed him; it really killed him. The fight just got taken out of him. Of all the people I know, a sweet soul was just stomped on. It's a brutal place for many people, Hollywood. It really sees them coming."

In accordance with Gene's wishes, his body was interred in the Sommerhauser family plot in St. Andrew's cemetery outside Tipton, Missouri. A service was held in Bonner Springs, Kansas, attended by family members. According to brother David, Gene had cut himself off from the community and friends decades ago, so few were in attendance. Terri and her mother flew in, as did Karen. The latter was welcomed; the former were not. "I met Terri Messina at Gene's funeral," Bonnie states ruefully. "She was with her mother. And that was one woman who I turned around and shot her down on the spot. We were bringing her from the airport and she was trying to tell me what a bastard my brother was. I turned around and said, 'Lady, I know what my brother was like.' She was going on about how he mistreated her daughter and what he owed her daughter."

Terri doesn't mince words in her contempt for Karen, viewing her as an unwelcome inter-loper. "The next thing I know, she flies back to Missouri for the funeral and she's got her arms

HAROLD EUGENE
CLARK
NOV. 17   MAY 24
1944   1991
NO
OTHER

around Kelly and Kai like she's the best friend they ever had in the world. Talk about humiliating. I was so humiliated by this. I couldn't believe this girl would show up to my old man's funeral at his family's home, being the little fairy godmother to Kelly and Kai now."

By this point, Karen had proven to be a pillar of strength and support for Kelly and Kai. She even helped the Clark family pay for Gene's headstone. Along with his date of birth and date of death, there's a simple inscription framed inside a heart: "No Other."

"The boys invited me to go to Missouri," Karen stresses. "The spiritual connection I had with Gene moved me to go, and the children invited me to go. That's where we really sat down and got to know each other better. That was the beginning of our relationship. I stood behind everyone and tried to be respectful of the family. I wasn't involved in trying to gain anything from Gene's estate. This was a time for the family. His parents were clearly grieving in the deepest sense. I sensed that the father seemed to act as if he felt some guilt and the mother said she knew Gene was tender and vulnerable. And they both said over and over again that he shouldn't have died at 46. There were pictures of him all over the house. There was a clear, strong bond between Gene and his mother. I think Gene had had difficulty with his father, but he was grieving and crying and seemed to feel guilty, I thought."

"Karen Johnson is an amazing person," declares Kelly, who acknowledges that his mother was in no condition to travel with her sons, dealing as she was with her own spiraling drug addiction. "Karen helped my brother and I through this whole thing. She was the only person who I felt I could trust. Karen really loved my father. I think he told her more about his family than anyone else, even my mother, because she had an insight into his childhood that none of us had and she helped me understand that. Karen was probably the only person who was around my father who had her head on straight in the last month of his life."

Epitaph

Here Without You

Gene had neglected to leave behind a last will and testament. In the absence of any formal documentation for the dispersal of his assets, the most significant being his songs and royalties (which continued to generate a sizeable income), Terri formally challenged Gene's estate. His rightful, legal heirs were Kelly and Kai, but Terri battled the two sons for several years. She claimed it was Gene's wish that she be the beneficiary because they had lived together for many years and that at the time of death she remained his girlfriend. Both assertions were fallacious. Terri and Gene were not cohabiting when he passed away nor was she his girlfriend at the time of death. Nonetheless, Terri staked her claim.

"I definitely thought that I was due things," protests Terri, "because, number one, as God is my witness and may he strike me dead if I'm lying, Gene totally wanted me to inherit everything if anything happened and to be the executor of the estate and to take care of his sons for him, put something aside and make sure that they got what they needed. He trusted me, he knew he could rely on me for that, and that I would never cheat them and that I would make sure that I had money put away for them."

Initially, Gene's brother David took the lead in asserting Kelly and Kai's claims to Gene's estate but, operating from a distance in Kansas City, he soon found the going difficult. Gene's business affairs were in utter disarray and navigating through the labyrinthine maze of copyrights, publishing rights, and royalties proved a Herculean task beyond his limited expertise. As the eldest son, Kelly was way over his head, too. The boys clearly needed to engage an expert who was experienced in the music business.

"I went to the probate lawyer and she showed us what she had, the paperwork and contracts and all that stuff," recounts David. "Kelly asked me if I thought it looked all right and I said that as far as this part it was okay, but this wasn't all of it. This was only the probate side. Originally Kelly and I agreed to be co-administrators. He wanted me to be helping him as a co-administrator." However, in the months following Gene's death, Kelly supplanted David in that role. David bore no ill will toward Kelly or Kai, but recognized that the young men were overwhelmed. "Kelly had a real hard time with it because he wasn't a very good reader and his whole background did not prepare him for this thing. He had a terrible time accepting this situation as it was, without getting all this dumped on him. His mom was in trouble, he had a younger brother and a half sister, all this going on and the poor guy had no help. And I couldn't give him any. I was shut out."

"I had to grow up fast," admits Kelly. "I'm not as big as my little brother, but I'm intense, and I think everyone wanted to get out of my way. I had a bad reputation as a kid being violent—my father had the same problem. When you're 19 years old and your father dies and you have to figure out where over $200,000 went over the last year and the rent's not paid for two months and you have no paper work because Terri took it all, that's really kind of stressful. She took everything that was worth anything."

As she had done with Gene before his death, Karen suggested her ex-husband, Scott, step in to assist Kelly and Kai. It would prove to be wise advice. "It was just one thing after another," sighs Kai. "We were assigned a probate attorney and it took her some eight years to assess the value of the property. This is right when Scott got involved. He had actually been talking to us during this whole time and said this was ridiculous. He actually went in and said, 'We can go on for ten more years or we can take care of this now.' And we did, and he was really smart about things. It was kind of a bad time, really hectic. People were coming out of the woodwork saying, 'Your dad owed me this.' That'll happen when people have some fame and they pass on."

After a frustrating, seesaw battle that lasted eight years, Scott was finally able to bring closure to the situation. He established Gene Clark Music with Gene's two sons as co-managers, administered by Scott in Baltimore, Maryland. "The boys really came to me because they felt overwhelmed," acknowledges Scott. "They didn't trust a lot of people. I think they trusted Karen, my ex-wife, and I think they trusted me. They wanted me also involved to oversee the music part of it because the probate attorney didn't have experience in the music field. Some of the things she really needed help on, how some of these contracts are interpreted in the music field, and royalty issues. They can be very complex and confusing, the difference between types of royalties related to the same product, trying to figure out what's the difference between an artist royalty and mechanical royalty. So there was a lot of ongoing participation between me, Kelly and Kai, and their probate attorney, up through the time the estate wrapped up—at which point we incorporated Gene Clark Music to just take all the rights, whatever they were that the boys had, put them together, and let those be administered from their corporation, which they each own half of."

"Scott took care of Kelly and Kai because it was all about them," offers Carlie, who entered a rehab program after the shock of Gene's death and is now clean and sober. "It's their legacy. I signed a paper that I had no claim to it, no right to it, and didn't want it. That's all Kelly and Kai have and thank god they have it. I worry about them, except that they have that income no matter what. It's still earning money. It'll see them through. Scott has it all invested and they get so much a month, which is like the interest. He's like their father. If they want to spend any money they have to call and ask him. I'm just grateful that they have him. He is their voice, for sure. He has their best interests at heart. He's steady-as-she-goes."

Terri remains bitter towards Karen. "Gene had nothing to do with her first husband, Scott, and he is handling the Gene Clark estate! You want to talk about why I detest this girl? To me she's nothing but a snake. A total snake. She knew that I wasn't living with Gene at the time because of his using, obviously, although I'd made sacrifice after sacrifice in my life for that man, many sacrifices including my own careers. I had my own careers. I gave them up to be with him. He didn't force me to do it, that was my decision, but there were sacrifices that I made and this person walks in and takes over at a time when I'm very fragile."

Rather than continue to pursue her claim to the estate, Terri eventually withdrew her case. "Little did I know that I put myself in a position that I had to go through all this hassle with the estate and then end up getting nothing out of it anyway," she complains. "In the end, I gave up. I couldn't take it anymore. My parents stepped in. They saw what it was doing to me and they said, 'Is this really worth it, to put yourself through this? Why do you need to do this?' So I had to let go of this because it was too emotionally hard for me. I gave it up. In the end, I don't have any financial problems. I just rebuilt a house down in Malibu that's worth a million dollars and it's my house. I did it on my own, but those are the kinds of things I would have liked to have done with Gene."

She insists that Gene did, in fact, prepare a will, but never followed through on it. "We drew up a will, I wrote it out and he wrote parts of it out, it was all written out, but he never signed it because in the end—me, I'm the one, it's all my fault again and I have no one to blame but myself and don't think I haven't cried a million times—after we made up this will I said to Gene, 'This is like really hokey. We need to have this written up properly where it is designated that such and such money should be in a trust for the boys,' because I knew how irresponsible they were and I knew they had no experience with money, either one of them. And then we never finished it. We started working on it in Mammoth before he started drinking, before that episode happened. And the only reason we never got married legally was me. Gene always wanted to get married. I'm the one who didn't get married because I was so worried if the thing didn't work out I didn't want to go through all that hassle with a messy divorce."

"That was never brought up or raised," Scott responds to Terri's assertion of a will. "Nobody was aware of anything like that." He does indicate, however, that there was a time when the possibility for détente existed. "I think there was a period of time when people would have been very receptive to some kind of a rapprochement. Certainly I'm one of these guys that I'm always encouraging people to try and get along and find common ground. I don't think there was ever a sense that anyone was itching for a fight or to hurt her."

"We loved Terri Messina," professes Kai, always the more conciliatory of the two brothers. "We knew her for a long time, but there is bitterness because some people can't let go. Sometimes you cling to things that are superficial. It's hard to explain how people could put that over being a friend. But it does happen and it's unfortunate. But we still have feelings for those people. Terri did some awful things. She took a lot of our dad's stuff and tried to take a lot more, too. After going through it with my mom being a heroin addict, there's nothing you can do. People have to help themselves. Basically that's all you can do. So I forgive these people. There's no sense in these people holding these grudges. And it's still going on. The lady spent years and years with my dad, probably longer than my mom. But it was a love/hate relationship, very volatile.

"Terri feels like, 'I gave him all that love for so many years, but he never gave me that payback.' She was looking for a payback for all this effort that she put into my father. If she had just taken it as being a part of the family she would have been much more accepted and probably gotten a lot more out of it than what she has. To forgive and forget causes a lot less trouble and pain than to fight. I have no hate towards Terri. I'm obviously upset that we couldn't work together to make something happen with all that new music he had in his house. That's sad. Maybe someday she'll forget about all the bad things and remember the good stuff."

Like yin and yang, Kelly is less magnanimous toward Terri. "I'm really thankful how things have come about and thankful that we got to shut down the Terri Messinas and all the other people who were milling around. She cost us probably two or three years. And she took his Rock & Roll Hall of Fame award and everything that my brother and I should have. Why did she take that?"

In his 1991 interview with Ken Viola, Tommy Kaye revealed that he and Terri were considering collaborating with writer David Dalton on a package that would reproduce many of the items in Terri's possession. "I want to put together, with Terri Messina and David Dalton, a songbook, a book of poetry, and a storybook—a three-book thing. Gene had this unbelievable penmanship and everything he ever wrote he kept, he saved it on all different kinds of paper. To see his handwriting is a whole other thing. We have a couple of thousand things written down." Nothing ever came of it, and Tommy died in 1994. (Tommy also revealed in the Viola interview that he and Gene were planning an acoustic album together, just days before Gene passed away.)

Early on, while still acting in his capacity as co-administrator with Kelly, David Clark met with Len Freedman, then owner of the Byrds catalog (Tickson Music). David's overriding concern was that his brother's musical legacy not be denigrated by a series of low-budget, cash-in releases. "He told me that the Byrds catalog *is* Gene Clark," confirms David. "Without Gene Clark's music, the Byrds catalog is just so much toilet paper. I told him I did not want to see Gene's music perverted. Anybody that does anything with his music, I want it done professionally and with care, the way Gene would have done it because he was a consummate professional and very particular about his records. I did not want his catalog or his music to become a barroom buddies and pals situation."

Scott and the boys have ensured that this will not happen. Any releases bearing Gene's name and music must first be vetted through Gene Clark Music. Because of the ongoing battle over the estate, few Gene Clark songs were released between 1991 and 1998. Sony Music, who purchased CBS, was in the process of compiling a retrospective CD titled *Echoes* when Gene died. It was released later that same year. Saul Davis, with the cooperation of Kelly, Kai, and Scott, spearheaded the release of Gene and Carla's *Silhouetted in Light* live album the following year. With the estate finally settled, A&M Records in the UK issued a two-CD compilation titled *Flying High* that included some of Gene's best-known tracks and several unreleased gems. Other releases have gradually appeared, including reissues of several of Gene's solo albums, *So Rebellious a Lover* with Carla Olson, and a collection of later demos titled *Gypsy Angel,* again shepherded through by Saul.

The latter release, however, was perceived by some to be scraping the bottom of the barrel. Ever articulate, John York worries about the artistic merit of such collections: "There's a joke among a lot of us. 'Well, when I'm dead they'll take my music seriously.' Gram Parsons had that kind of thing around him. I don't know if Gene had that, but the danger is that everything you've ever done becomes public. Outtakes, songs you were working on. Sometimes I get this stuff sent to me, CDs of Gene Clark's stuff from fans, and I think, 'Gene wouldn't have wanted all of these songs out.' Sometimes you have to write 50 songs to get ten really good ones. And the other ones are kind of on the way to the good ones. It would be like being some master chef but people want to taste the stuff that you burned. 'I want you to eat this meal, I made this meal and it's really wonderful,' and people replying, 'Oh no, no. We want to see what's in the garbage can. We want the asparagus that fell off the plate when you were preparing it.' It's a bit obsessive. It's the cult of personality."

That cult of personality certainly has grown around Gene's name. But beyond that, there is genuine respect for his art as well. "I'm really happy that people are interested in Gene's music," John continues. "Unfortunately, the whole demon side of his personality is also fascinating to people. But I think it's worth it if they get into his music. People love to hear all that stuff, but if you examine the music he wrote. . . ."

In 2000, the independent label Not Lame Records issued a critically acclaimed tribute CD, *Full Circle: A Tribute to Gene Clark,* boasting covers of Gene's songs by a crop of fresh young talents. And an Australian-only CD titled *You Can't Hide Your Love Forever: A Tribute to Gene Clark* was released in 2002. Tribute shows have been organized in several cities, some with brother Rick performing. In recent years there has been renewed interest in Gene's music from young fans who have come to appreciate his gifts. Scottish band Teenage Fanclub wrote and recorded their own tribute, titled simply "Gene Clark," while contemporary folk artist Pam Richardson did the same with her moving song "Tipton's Vein of Silver."

An artist with as rich a recording legacy as Gene Clark is most deserving of a multi-CD box set retrospective. A wealth of unreleased studio tracks dating as far back as 1964 remains locked up, either in studio vaults or in the hands of private collectors. Perhaps someday it will all be released. Meanwhile, fans in recent years have compiled their own seven-CD Gene Clark bootleg box set that is in circulation among dedicated collectors.

G ene's parents died within months of each other in 2000: Kelly in March and Jeanne in May. Sister Bonnie avers that Jeanne never fully recovered from Gene's death. "After he had been dead for a while and she was still angry and couldn't mourn him, I suggested she go to some grief counseling. So we went together. And to the counselor she referred to Gene as her beloved son and I said to the counselor, 'That's right. Her beloved son, her favorite.' And she said, 'None of my children were favorite.' I said, 'Mom!' and she finally owned up and it helped her. She told Rick later that getting her into that counseling probably saved her life because she was in severe depression."

Bonnie, too, took time to come to terms with Gene's life and death. "I can't remember whether it was months or years later, I got in an argument with my husband and I got in my car and drove out to Wyandotte County Lake, which is one of the gathering spots for people around here. I sat down on a bench and realized I wasn't upset with my husband, I was upset with Gene, still upset with him. So I said to myself, 'Okay, what do we do now?' and his voice came to me, saying, 'Make peace.' And that was the resolution for me. I had been mad at him for throwing his life away, throwing that tremendous talent away, and for stealing a moment from my parents that should have been a happy event for them."

Rick, like Gene, has battled his own demons and suffers from health problems. He and Nanci currently live on the Northern California coast. "Rick still grieves the loss of Gene," says Bonnie. For Rick it is about missed opportunities and living under his famous brother's shadow. "After Gene's death I went into hiding," Rick admits. "I quit associating with a lot of the people who were around at the time. One of my main regrets is that Gene and I never got to make the album that we wanted to do together. That's just something I have to live with, knowing that it would have been a really great piece of work."

David still lives in Kansas City and operates a machine shop. He is preparing his own book of childhood reminiscences about his famous brother. Bonnie also lives in Kansas City, as do many of Gene's brothers and sisters. Carlie has turned her life around and now lives near Sacramento, California, where she coordinates a string of homes for women with drug and alcohol problems. She is proud of her two sons and the way they have turned out. She also sees their father in each of them.

"Kelly *is* Gene," Carlie smiles. "Sometimes I get goose bumps because he is so much like his dad. Kai, when he was a little boy, he would be sitting on the couch with his guitar and he would be writing songs and I would think, 'How can this child write this? He has no life experience whatsoever.' And the writing was totally amazing. It's got to be like his dad.

"I don't know anybody I respect more as far as values, ethics, and morals than my two boys," she beams. "They are, actually, the best people on the earth, coming from Gene and I, not that we were thieves or anything, but it was a little erratic childhood they had. They weren't raised in a normal mold so it's very difficult for them to fit in, but I'm very proud of them."

"I think I'm a little more jaded than my father," Kelly confesses, "a little more savvy about what people are up to. I think my brother and my father shared the eternal want to trust people." His rebellious youth long behind him, Kelly has learned to become a businessman, a skill his father never accomplished. But there is an artistic side to him as well. "I like books and I like literature. I don't want to write music." After years in real estate and other business ventures, he recently enrolled in college with the goal of one day becoming an English professor. The money from his father's estate provides him the financial cushion to pursue his dream. "I realized at one point that it wasn't going to go on forever. It's been rolling for ten years and it's been doing very well. We're not rich by any means, but we do have a comfort zone that is really nice and I'm very appreciative of that. And I'm also appreciative of the fact that my dad didn't have his shit together when he died and it wasn't just handed to us either. I wasn't ready to handle it when he died and the only way I became ready to handle it was that I had to be patient and piece it all together and deal with the Terri Messina issue and the probate attorney issue and all that stuff. And that's how I learned my crash course in business."

The lessons learned from the excesses of his parents left an indelible imprint on Kelly. "I was a pretty drunken, rowdy mess when I was younger. I ran away from home pretty young. I was in a lot of trouble and my mom was not being a very good parent. So Kai got stuck with the brunt of raising my half sister while my mom was out to lunch. I had just lost my father and my mom was on her way out too, and I could not handle it. So I split. Shortly thereafter my mom pulled herself together, which is good, and I'm glad she's doing what she's doing now. I quit drinking and my mom did too. I've been sober for almost 11 years now. My dad showed me that we're genetically programmed to not deal with alcohol very well. I watched my dad make a lot of bad decisions behind drinking. My own personal experiences with alcohol were not that good. At times, now being a man, I've wanted my father to be here because I think he would be pretty proud of my brother and I."

Kai has pursued a career in music as a songwriter and bandleader since his late teens (although he has worked at several day jobs). He has recorded a number of demos of his own songs and is shopping for a recording contract. "People would say to me when I was young, 'You need to learn how to play guitar. You know who your father was,'" says Kai, whose income from the Gene Clark estate allows him to follow his muse. "There was a little bit of that kind of pressure from people who were around that were very influenced by my dad and saw the potential of putting something into my hands that could further his legacy. At around 14 I started carrying a guitar around all the time, an acoustic guitar, along the Headlands of Mendocino. We would ditch school and I would be with all my friends and I had my guitar and even though I wasn't very good I was the only entertainment for them. So it was good for me. I think I was influenced by pretty much everything around me. It wasn't until my father's death that I knew the potential of his music and what he really put into it. After he died I definitely went through all of his music and listened to all of his songs. The words he put in his songs and the chord changes he used are still amazing to me. I think I'm influenced by my father more now than ever and I started learning his songs and doing them my own way. They are special to me, so if I'm going to perform or record his songs I really want them to be kind of my own way, something from my heart. I'm really an original songwriter. In my eyes it would be special in his memory, and also in my own eyes, to do something my own way.

"I don't really put it out there that Gene Clark is my dad," Kai continues. "I want people to hear my music first. Once they hear it, and if they like it, I'll tell them who I'm influenced by and my history. I really don't tell many people unless they pry into it. But my friends often will tell people, 'Do you know who he is?! He's Gene Clark's son!' I don't mind it. It's fine. It's really kind of nice to see that people are excited by it and that my father still touches people in some way. Not Lame Records did a tribute album to my dad and they let me do a song ["In My Heart"]. If you hear it, it's great bands from all over the world doing Gene Clark songs, young artists not so mass publicized. I really love that album, it's very good."

Carlie is apprehensive, though, about Kai following in his father's footsteps. "I hadn't seen Kai perform in eight or ten years, so I flew to San Diego because he had a gig and I went to this performance in this seedy nightclub and it was packed. I'm telling you, Kai came out onstage and started singing and I broke into tears. For one thing he holds his guitar with these arms that are just like Gene's, like they work out every day. They can be totally unhealthy, but they don't look it. It blew me out of the water it was so good. But can I support him doing what he does? I could probably give his name to a couple of people in L.A., but would I want him to live his dad's life? No. Is he determined to do it? Yes. He doesn't see all the pitfalls. I tried to tell him if you play the music for your heart and do something else for the pennies in your pocket, you'll be okay."

Brother Kelly, too, worries about Kai's chosen path. "The rock 'n' roll scene killed my dad early," he laments.

"But," he pauses, "it's his deal and I'm going to let him do it."

Perhaps that's what Jeanne and Kelly Clark thought to themselves as their oldest son, Harold Eugene, set off in pursuit of his own dreams.

Tipton's Vein of Silver

Waking the birds
With a song so sweet and thrilling
Should've made a killing
But the cards were all wrong
It's all said and done
Your story reads like fiction
A walking contradiction afire

Handsome and tall
Standing out amongst the others
Your sisters and your brothers
Wish you'd never left home
A gift and a prayer
And a voice like running water
Don't you think you ought to slow down

Angel of words
Gone unheard for so many years
So this song's for you
And I sing it very softly
This song for Harold Eugene

Illumination
A pure and inner brilliance
Affable resilience
When you hit their brick walls
Try this, try that
But the muse needs constant feeding
She's getting what you're needing tonight

Train whistle blow
Off you go to some mise-en-scene
So pour me a strong one
How I wish it made a difference,
This song for Harold Eugene

Hollywood burning
Till you learn it's not so starry
Fade to sad and sorry
It's the country in you
Just when you thought
You had it all, you got it coming
Hit the ground running away

Who could've seen
That the end was fast in coming
The song that you were strumming
Was it all just a dream
Now you're a genius, oh the eulogies they give you
I guess that would give you a laugh

Somebody knows
So don't suppose it was wasted
And I catch your tears
In the inkwell as I'm writing
This song for Harold Eugene

Blow, cold winds, blow
Don't you know how we miss you
So rest your sweet soul
And I'll try to sing it pretty
This song for Harold Eugene

Blow, cold winds, blow
I hope you know how we miss you
So rest your sweet soul
And I'll try to do justice
To this song for Harold Eugene

Acknowledgments

I would like to extend my sincerest thanks to the following people who were instrumental in getting this book up and running and ultimately completed. First, thank you to Scott Johnson for giving me the green light to proceed and to Kelly Clark and Kai Clark for their endorsement of the project from the outset. Special thanks to my dear friend Nurit Wilde for so many things, but especially for being so supportive and encouraging (as well as facilitating contacts with many people). I tip my hat to Gene Clark fan par excellence Cheryl "Pinkie" Jennings for her support, insights, materials, and contacts. An extra special thank you to Bonnie Clark Laible, David Clark, and Rick Clark for opening their homes to me and sharing the family history and their private and personal reflections on their brother (and thank you to Christine Clark Davis for the family photos and details). Kudos to Dennis Kelley, Paul Birch, Domenic Priore, Tom Slocum, Barry Ballard, and Jim Prichard for their ongoing dialogue with me at various times during the process of writing this book. To my country-rock compadre Buddy Woodward (check out Buddy Woodward & the Nitro Express) who does, indeed, make a damn fine potato salad: thank you for the insightful critique of the manuscript and for your continued support and encouragement. Thanks to Richard Johnston at Backbeat Books for believing in this project.

Nearly 100 firsthand interviews were conducted for this book. Those who so freely gave of their time to share their remembrances of Gene Clark are cited throughout and I extend my sincere appreciation to them all. In addition, thank you to the following people, who, in ways large and small, went above and beyond the call of duty on my behalf in providing support, encouragement, contacts, and/or materials for the preparation of this book:

Chip Douglas for the contacts; David Clark for his ongoing support and personal insights; UK Gene Clark expert Barry Ballard for being a wonderful source of information and materials; Byrds fan extraordinaire Whin Oppice for all the archival material; Philip O'Leno for his ongoing support and insights; Pat Robinson for his contacts (and for the marvelous Byrds of a Feather show); Tom Slocom for the contacts, stories, speculations, and clarifications (Go Blue Bombers!); Chris Hillman for a great lunch together and for his continued support (someday we'll do the Chris Hillman story); David Crosby for the backstage interview and CSN concert tickets; Holger Peterson (Stony Plain Records, Edmonton, Alberta, Canada) for the interview tape, contacts, and continued support and encouragement, as well as those great Stony Plain CDs; Shannon O'Neill for the many contacts and the CDs; Saul Davis, who, from the get-go, offered unwavering encouragement, support, materials, and contacts; Carla Olson for the wonderful music and memories; Bernie Leadon for being so supportive and for connecting me with Larry Marks; Eric Sorensen for pointing me to Scott Johnson early on; my good friend Morgan Cavett for all the contacts and the exclusive Hollywood tour (really, $36 for two drinks at the Chateau Marmont bar?!—too bad we couldn't make it a triple play for that Troub photo); Bob Irwin at Sundazed Records for Columbia session information; "Petite Powerhouse" Dawn Eden for clarification on Curt Boettcher's role; Andrew Sandoval for the session details; musicologist Alec Palao at Ace/Big Beat Records for details on the Fugitives and the Gosdins; James Lawrence for recording information; David Jackson for being a valuable and supportive contact; my friend Paul Nicholas in Wales for the Byrds book and for picking up those UK-only CDs; Bill Elander, Charlie Wade, Jim McCombe, and Marco Zanzi in Italy for the various CDs; writer and friend Matthew Greenwald for contacts and encouragement; Brian Burnes at the *Kansas City Star* for all the local contacts and location details; my fellow writer and friend Richie Unterberger—the first writer to document the evolution of folk-rock in his marvelous books *Turn! Turn! Turn!* and *Eight Miles High* (Backbeat Books)—for his contacts and support; Tom Pickles for his wonderfully detailed information and insights on the New Christy Minstrels; Chris Hollow in "the land down under" for his terrific Gene Clark article; David Godden for the contact information and photograph; my friend and CSNY expert Dave Zimmer for always being in my corner and for being my sounding board (look for Dave's books *Crosby, Stills & Nash: The Biography* and *Four Way Street: The Crosby, Stills, Nash & Young Reader* from Da Capo Press); Rob Hughes at *Uncut* for the insightful August 2003 Byrds cover story; Peter North (CKUA Radio Network, Edmonton, Alberta, Canada) for his personal reflections; Karen Bate for raising Gene's name to Mark Lindsay; Deb Johnson for her personal insights; Pam Richardson for "Tipton's Vein of Silver" and details on the box set; my Poco friend Steve Casto for all the detective work on that video tape; Jeff Watt at Old Goat for all the archival articles and clippings; my good friends John and Jutta Kay for their contacts; St. John's-Ravenscourt School nurse Kathleen MacRae for medical terminology; Jim McCummings in Mendocino for passing along my message to Carlie and Philip; Paul Kerr for scanning the articles; Gordon Anderson at Collector's Choice Music for *No Other;* Harvey Kubernik for his many contacts; Denise Waldrep for the lyrics and letter; Neal Skok for the tapes; and Kathie Allen for the live recordings.

A special thank you to writer and music archivist Domenic Priore for the 1985 videotaped interview with Gene Clark at his Sherman Oaks home; Jon Butcher for his 1987 unpublished Gene Clark interview; Holger Peterson for his 1984 unpublished interview with Gene Clark and Michael Clarke; and Mike Griffiths in Victoria, British Columbia (thanks, John Cody), for his unpublished 1983 Gene Clark interview. The Ken Viola quotes from Tommy Kaye are from an exclusive, unpublished 1991 interview copyrighted to Ken in 2004 (thank you, Ken).

As always, I would like to extend my thanks to my family—my wife, Harriett, son, Matthew, and daughter, Lynsey—for their continued support and encouragement of my writing. I couldn't do it without you.

About the Author

John Einarson is a respected Canadian rock-music historian and writer based in Winnipeg. He has written feature articles and reviews for *Mojo*, *Goldmine*, *Discoveries*, *Record Collector*, *Rock Express*, and *Western Report* among others, and is a frequent contributor to the *Winnipeg Free Press* as features writer, editorialist, and book reviewer. In addition, John has written for television, hosted his own CBC radio series entitled *This Time Long Ago* chronicling the Winnipeg music scene, and contributed to several television specials on Canadian rock-music history including a CBC tribute to the Guess Who and their Hall of Fame induction ceremony, *Burton Cummings: Wheatfield Soul* for CBC Winnipeg, and *Randy Bachman: Life and Times*. He has also written liner notes to several CDs for artists such as the Guess Who and Steppenwolf. John served as the driving force and inspiration for the Manitoba Museum's acclaimed exhibit *Get Back: A Celebration of Winnipeg Rock 'n' Roll* and was guest curator for the museum's successful *Linda McCartney's Sixties* photo exhibit. John hosted a 28-week CBC radio series on Saturday mornings entitled *The 45s Cupboard* featuring local music of historical interest, and is currently hosting a new CBC radio series entitled *Made in Manitoba*. He is also a contributor to the national CBC radio series *50 Tracks*.

In addition to publishing a number of music history books on Neil Young, Randy Bachman, Buffalo Springfield, Steppenwolf, and the Guess Who, John has written a TV documentary on Canadian singer/songwriting legend Buffy Sainte-Marie. He recently assisted with production of an A&E *Biography* of Neil Young, and is also spearheading the creation of a Canadian Rock 'n' Roll Center to be located in Winnipeg.

Photo Credits

page ix, 250, and 271: Gary Nichamin

pages 6, 10, 13, and 20: Courtesy of Christine Clark Davis

page 22: Courtesy of Jack Godden

page 35: Courtesy of Tom Pickles

pages 46, 62, and 77: Michael Ochs Archives.com

page 73: Courtesy of David Zimmer

page 103, 105, 181, and 261 : Henry Diltz

page 123: Courtesy of Alex del Zoppo

pages 129, 138, 153, and 228: Jim McCrary

pages 144 and 146: Nurit Wilde

pages 173 and 191: Courtesy of Philip O'Leno

page 220: Arnie "Tokyo" Rosenthal

page 245: Courtesy of Michael Hardwick

page 265: Courtesy of Pat Robinson

page 299 and 305: Harold Sherrick

page 316: Courtesy of John Einarson

Index